17th International Conference Mobile Learning (ML 2021) and 8th Educational Technologies (ICEduTech 2021)

AA005000

Online
3 - 5 March 2021

ISBN: 978-1-7138-3073-3

Printed from e-media with permission by:

Curran Associates, Inc.
57 Morehouse Lane
Red Hook, NY 12571

Some format issues inherent in the e-media version may also appear in this print version.

International Association for Development of the Information Society (IADIS)
Rua Sao Sebastiao Da Pedreira
No. 100, 30, 1050-209
Lisbon, Portugal

Phone: 351 21 3151373
Fax: 351 21 3151244

secretariat@iadis.org

Additional copies of this publication are available from:

Curran Associates, Inc.
57 Morehouse Lane
Red Hook, NY 12571 USA
Phone: 845-758-0400
Fax: 845-758-2633
Email: curran@proceedings.com
Web: www.proceedings.com

8th International Conference on Educational Technologies 2021
17th International Conference on Mobile Learning 2021

CONFERENCE PROGRAM

IMPORTANT NOTICE: listed times are in GMT+0 (Lisbon Time), you can check your timezone at https://greenwichmeantime.com/time-zone/gmt-plus-0/ (you can use the provided URL to insert your location and see your time in relation to GMT+0).

Wednesday 3rd, March 2021

09:15-09:30 Session O – Opening Session
OPENING SESSION
Profs. Pedro Isaías and Inmaculada Arnedillo Sánchez

09:30-10:30 Session KL1 – Keynote Presentation
"MLEARNING: WHERE TO NEXT? COVID-19 AND THE 'NEW NORMAL' POINT THE WAY"...N/A
Professor John Traxler, Professor of Digital Learning, University of Wolverhampton, UK

10:30-10:45 Break

10:45-12:15 Session FSPP 3.1
Critical Thinking Skills // Creativity Skills // Learning Citizenship
Chair: Peter Ilic

12:15-14:00 Lunch Break

14:00-16:00 Session FSRP 3.2
Innovative mLearning approaches // Tools, technologies and platforms for mLearning
Chair: Lúcia Pombo

16:00-16:15 Break

16:15-17:15 Session KL2 – Keynote Presentation
"HOW WHATSAPP BROUGHT US TOGETHER AT A TIME OF ISOLATION"...N/A
Professor Johannes Cronjé, Dean of Informatics and Design, Cape Peninsula University of Technology, South Africa

17:15-18:45 Session FP 3.3
International Higher Education // Enculturation and International Teacher Accreditation
Chair: Maura Pilotti

Thursday 4th, March 2021

08:30-09:30 Session KL3 – Keynote Presentation
"VARTEL EDUCATION INNOVATION"...N/A
Professor Yiyu Cai, Nanyang Technological University (NTU), Singapore

09:40-10:30 Session FSP 4.1
Learning analytics and mobile learning
Chair: Lúcia Pombo

10:30-10:45 Break

10:45-12:35 Session FSP 4.2
Integrating Educational Technologies
Chair: Lourdes Guardia

12:35-14:00 Lunch Break

A TRAINING DESIGN FOR PUBLIC SPEAKING ANXIETY

Charito G. Ong and K Marie D. Zambas
University of Science and Technology of Southern Philippines
CM Recto Avenue, Lapasan Highway, Cagayan De Oro City, Philippines

ABSTRACT

This study developed a training design for Senior High School students and teachers. The design was composed of four learning packets which were revised and finalized after an on-line try out. The researcher used five stages in the model to undertake the study. Seels and Glasgow's (2018) ADDIE model was modified by the researcher into Needs Analysis, Plan, Create, Try Out and Assess (NAPCTA) and was followed in the duration of the entire research process. The results of the needs analysis served as basis for the topics in the learning packets. Specifically, the study determined: (1) the anxiety level of the senior high school respondents, (2) the needs to be addressed in speech anxiety and (3) the contents of the learning packets as the research product. The paper employed the Research and Develop (R&D) design.

KEYWORDS

Training Design, Anxiety, Public Speaking

1. INTRODUCTION

Communication is a primary need of humanity. This dates back since the origin of man. People strive to satisfy this need in various ways throughout the ages, yet the most effective way has constantly been speaking. The primary goal of all languages is to aid humans to communicate with each other so they can convey their thoughts.

According to Arnold (2000), speaking in a foreign language is an integral aspect of regarding language learning in that, when individuals refer to speaking, sometimes they mean knowing a language. Hence, many researchers have pointed out that speaking is the greatest anxiety producing skill (Conway, 2017). Communicative apprehension (CA) was then found to have a connection with speaking skills and is defined by Horwitz et al. (2006) as a type of shyness characterized by fear or anxiety about communicating with people. It is also regarded as an individual's level of fear or anxiety associated with either oral or anticipated communication with another person or people. Self-confidence and self-esteem are also important parts of communication. Kitano (2001) argues that speaking skill is usually the first thing that learners compare with that of peers, teachers, and native speakers. Hence, learners' low self perception of speaking ability is a cause and source of anxiety in second language learning.

What attracts attention in language classes or in any free conversation areas is that when students talk to someone in English, they apologize for how much English they speak, thinking their level is poor. Most of these students who apologize for their level of English feel like they should speak better than they do. As pointed by Russell (2017), achieving fluency in any language is a process that takes time. Students cannot be expected to become fluent instantaneously. Within social contexts, language anxiety may be experienced due to extrinsic motivators (Schwartz, 2002; cited in Scovel (2008:16), such as different social and cultural environments, particularly the environments where L1 and L2/FL learning takes place. The researcher stresses that the respondents of this study came from different social environment.

To be able to understand the affective factors that may aggravate foreign language speaking anxiety, it is important to understand the nature of speaking as a separate skill in language learning. Carter and Nunan (2002) explain speech production in terms of steps such as conceptualization, formulation, articulation and self-monitoring. First, the speaker plans the speech, considering the speech situation, necessary ideas and patterns of discourse. Secondly, the speaker formulates correct sentences and sound patterns. Next, the sentence is uttered with the help of articulatory organs, and finally, the speaker establishes an inner mind, a kind of self-monitoring to check and correct any mistakes while speaking. These processes require automaticity on the part of the speaker and each stage must be accomplished in a limited time. Since the ultimate aim of the speaker is to convey the meaning successfully, it can be said that the demanding nature of speaking can be a source of anxiety. Young (2002) suggests that recognizing learner manifestations of anxieties related to speaking, negative evaluation, and foreign language learning-generated anxieties are important first steps in coping with language anxiety.

In the Philippine context, Azagra (2017) posits that the utmost concern of schools and educational managers for many decades is the deteriorating performance of the students in all subject areas particularly English, Mathematics, and Science where the English language is used. The Philippine academe then innovated a milestone through the implementation of the K to 12 curriculum. This responded to the demand of the 21st century education. Moreover, it answered the problem of decreasing performance of Filipinos academically. Generally, the ultimate goal was to produce holistically developed students with 21st century skills equipped with operative communication skills thus focusing on using English in the area of communication.

It has been known that a skilled oral communicator is demanded globally. The careers offered by the global village such as banking, commerce, business, tourism, education, engineering and medicine among others use the English language as a means of communication. This is supported by Kachru (2006), as he cites that English is the international language of business and banking, aviation, tourism, negotiation, scientific research, and intellectual exchange. Hence, Filipino learners should respond to this demand of the global world; that is to learn and use the English language. Consequently, this paper placed emphasis for learners to develop their speaking skills. Among senior high school classes in this country, students usually encounter varied speech problems. These evidently hinder their ability to communicate and eventually negatively affect their general proficiency and academic performance. Therefore, resolving their problems in communication and finding out the finest solutions is deemed vital to help these learners in their oral language development.

English proficiency, specifically in speaking is a major concern not only in the academe but also in economics. With the ASEAN Integration there are two areas that should be dealt with; first is for Filipino graduates to keep their edge over their Asian counterparts in the English language. English used to be the Filipinos' competitive advantage in the job market. Second, there is a rise in business process outsourcing and influx of foreigners who want to learn English as a second language, therefore there is a greater demand of English Proficiency in speaking. However, the Filipinos' mastery is fast being eroded by rising competition from other countries coupled with declining mastery of the English language by most college students. If Filipino graduates cannot regain this edge, it would mean lesser, rewarding job opportunities and lesser income.

Nonetheless, it is the desire of the researcher to find out why speech anxiety still commonly occurs in the Philippine classrooms despite the early exposure to English as a second language. The researcher intends to discover the perspectives of the English teachers regarding speaking anxiety in the classrooms and how they handle these situations, the students' perspectives on the causes of these anxieties and address these needs by developing a speech module that can be implemented to create a low speech anxiety classroom especially to senior high school students. The training design will equip these students with the necessary skills and techniques, strengthen their confidence for them to become engaging audience and contribute in ensuring to maintain the Filipino's edge in the spoken English language.

Generally, this research aimed to identify and investigate the causes of anxiety among Senior High School students in public speaking. Thereafter, it recommended steps to overcome their anxiety level by developing a training design. This is supported by Tanveer (2007) as he posits that an apt utilization of strategies by language teachers can help reduce second/foreign language anxiety and can potentially increase students' confidence to learn and speak the target language. Teachers really need to structure classroom activities so that the amount of learner talk is increased at the expense of teacher talk. This will motivate students to communicate since they will do actual practice in the target language. By providing a rich classroom interaction, an avenue that this research designed, a communicative classroom mode was achieved among the English classes.

This study developed a training design for students to manage public speaking anxiety. It determined: 1.) the individual anxiety level of Senior High School students in Kong Hua School, 2.) the needs addressed among the respondents related to speech anxiety, and 3.) the contents of the training design for speech anxiety.

2. THE THEORETICAL FRAMEWORK

This research utilized concepts from the theory of Johns (2007), which is the Eight Steps to Planning an Effective Training Event and the Systematic Approach to Training (SAT) which is similar to Seels and Glasgow's (2013) Instructional System Design Model (ISD). These models begin with Analysis. As the first phase, it rationalizes the necessity for the training. This phase can be likened to steps 1 and 2 of John's model. Next is the Design phase referred to as the decision-making phase. Also similar to steps 3 and 4 of John's model, this phase will complete three important activities: (1) deciding what participants will learn, (2) what will be taught and (3) the instructional methods to be used and what competency will be required from the participants. In the Development phase, the training concept is made into a material in the form of the training design with different parts. This is step 5 of John's model, of developing instructional activities. Both models refer the Implementation phase as the "actual training". This is where the developed training design will be placed into a realistic context. Step 6 of John's model also refers to this as the training scheme preparation and implementation. Evaluation is listed last in these models. It ensures that processes work well and improvements are identified right away. Step 8 of Johns model, preparing evaluation forms and determining follow-up activities discusses this also. By combining the different concepts of the three theorists cited above, the researcher came up with her theoretical framework. Although some concepts were modified, these were adopted from the key concepts gleaned from the three models as subsequently shown in figure1.

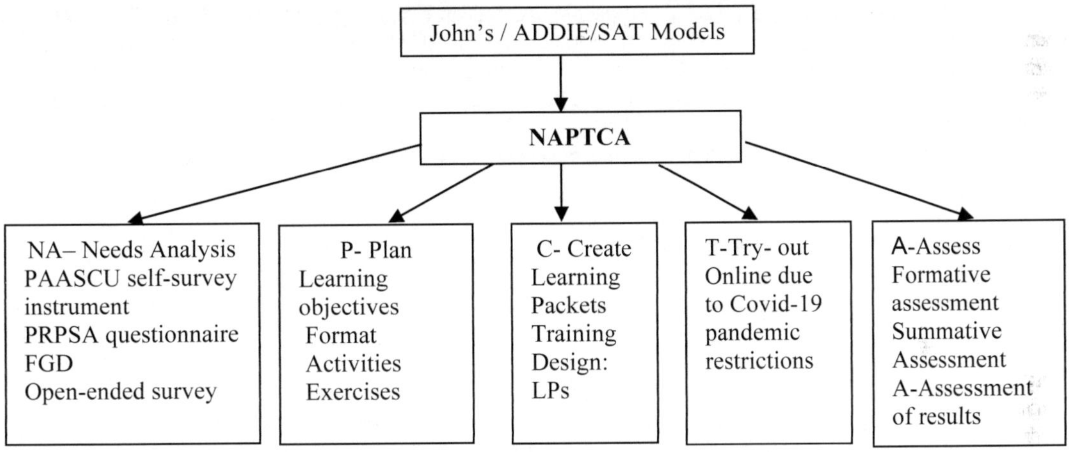

Figure 1. The Theoretical Framework of the Study

3. METHODOLOGY

The specific procedures in the preparation of the speech module and the try out stage to validate this research are discussed as follows. The research locale and respondents are likewise explained.

This research was conducted in Kong Hua School, a Filipino-Chinese Basic Education Institution located in Kauswagan Road, Barangay Kauswagan Cagayan de Oro City. It has a population of more than a thousand from Early Childhood Education Department to Senior High School Department. The respondents conducted the needs analysis among the Senior High Classes. This was done in the second semester of academic year 2019-2020. The try-out and assessment phases were conducted in the respective homes of evaluators as an online evaluation was undertaken due to community quarantine brought about by the Corona virus pandemic.

The researcher began the analysis stage of her research by conducting the Personal Report on Public Speaking Anxiety (PRPSA) questionnaire, Focus Group Discussion (FGD), open-ended survey, and used the Philippine Accrediting Association of Schools Colleges and Universities (PAASCU) self-survey instrument. The Personal Report on Public Speaking Anxiety (PRPSA) questionnaire, Mc Croskey's (2015) PRPSA questionnaires were distributed to 78 Grade 11 students. The researcher used the questionnaire developed by McCroskey to collect information from students regarding their level of anxiety. This is a commonly used method in both ethnographic and quantitative research. The grade 11 students rated statements numerically as to the level of how they feel in speaking situation. Moreover, the researcher distributed an 8-item open-ended survey questionnaire to all 78 students. Questions were modified from Dr. Nick Morgan, one of America's top communication theorist and coach. The questions included public speaking related questions on past experiences, physical effects, emotional effects, exposure, and need.

The results of these needs analysis showed that the respondents belong to the high anxiety level. This led the researcher to the design of topics and activities addressing the anxiety. After the design topics were identified, the next step was taken, the development stage. With the design phase already done in the form of the training design, it was further simplified in the form of the learning packets.

The first learning packet brings the trainees to a self-journey bringing them back to past experiences that might have contributed to all the negative feelings you have towards public speaking. Activities are provided for them to unlock the causes of public speaking fear, recognize the need to overcome public speaking, clean off negative experiences in public speaking, uncover one's strengths and weakness in public speaking, and recognize opportunities and threats in public speaking anxiety.

The effectiveness and efficiency of the learning packets were measured afterwards. The evaluation occurred throughout the entire instructional design process – within phases, between phases, and after implementation. This appeared in dual form, the formative and summative evaluation. The formative evaluation was done before and during the implementation of the training design. These were made possible through the consolidated effort of the panel members, and the research adviser. The panel examined the needs analysis results during the thesis proposal of the researcher. The research adviser corrected and made the refinement of the packets. The implementation, which was in the form of online assessment focused on content, training objectives, organization, and methodologies. The summative evaluation occurred after the final version of the training scheme was tried out. This assessed the overall effectiveness of the learning segments. Both teachers and student evaluators did this. A training evaluation form developed by Ong (2009) was modified by the researcher. This was used by the students and teacher evaluators in evaluating the learning packets.

4. RESULTS AND DISCUSSION

The score range in the PRPSA was between 34 and 170. It is described as High = > 131, Low = < 98 and Moderate = 98-131. After getting the scores, the researcher categorized the anxiety results as Low, Moderately Low, Moderately High, and High. The results of the aforesaid PRPSA showed that 54%, which is 42 out of the 78 respondents from grade 11 experienced moderately high and high anxiety level.

Twenty-five (25) out of forty-six (46) female respondents commented during the written survey that they felt conscious and scared to make mistakes. These reasons made them avoid speaking in front. If forced, for grades purposes, they tend not to give their all, for apprehensions that they may be laughed at. This result is affirmed by Yamna & Rahma (2018) stating that female students get more anxious than males while giving speech publicly. The same responses are mentioned in the study of Wicks-Nelson & Israel (2006), who postulate that female students feel more anxious when it comes to oral activities in class. Accordingly, this is due to the fact that female students need to feel secure in class, thus trying to avoid any kind of activities that might expose their mistakes. Also, some of them are more concerned about 'maintaining their faces' in front of others especially from the male students. In addition, five female respondents wrote that they feel conscious when all eyes are on them on stage.

Female students naturally do not like to appear less proficient and less confident (Bruce et al, 2005), therefore escalating their anxiety whenever they are asked to get involved with activities like speaking and listening. This is perceived as a demonstration of weakness in front of others especially while presenting in front of the opposite gender (Tom et. al, 2013). Some male students on the other hand, do have more self-control and the ability to detach themselves from unpleasant feeling. In short, some of them might adopt the 'shutting down' technique where they appear to be more laid back and careless exteriorly. Additionally, according to the results of the quantitative research of Öztürk & Gürbüz (2013), female students demonstrate a higher level of foreign language learning motivation than male students. The results also showed that the female students get more anxious than the male students while speaking in English in the classroom. The results of the qualitative data showed parallelism with the quantitative results which occurred in this study. This is found in the needs assessment stage when 21% among males or 8 out of 32 experience low anxiety compared to 13% among the females or 6 out of 46 only. Apart from this, struggling in understanding instruction is too major a problem for female students compared to the male ones. Agitation and apprehension are projected when they could not execute the task according to the instructions, thus making them more vulnerable in front of the class. This is consistent with Mclean & Anderson's paper (2009) which found out that females develop greater risk of anxiety according to their social factor and surrounding. This lowers down their confidence level thus making them feel more insecure in class. In this paper, it showed that 10 out of 32 female respondents mentioned "scared" to make mistakes as one of their feelings towards public speaking.

The open-ended survey conducted among the Senior High School respondents on December 10, 2019 generated similar results. The students manifested public speaking anxiety through stuttering and stammering, often leading to mental block. These manifestations directly affect spontaneity and clear expression of ideas. The students' reported experience in public speaking is coherent with the committee's self-survey ratings. This result was also agreed by the body during the plenary session.

The areas examined comprised of feelings towards public speaking, manifestations of their anxiety, past experiences, and the needs they have. The highly repeated answers in the open-ended survey when asked about their feelings towards public speaking is on *nervousness and anxiety*. This matched the results in the Personal Report on Public Speaking Anxiety (PRPSA). Thirty percent (30%) of the students further shared, their anxiety and nervousness would depend on the audience and topic.

When asked about their past experiences in public speaking, negative experiences such as mental block, being laughed at, being conscious on how people perceive him/her and were repeatedly mentioned. Based on their classroom exposure, they claimed they need help in public speaking which were categorized into encouragement before, during and after delivery; provision of more speaking opportunities and mentoring. These were the common answers.

Kankam (2017) postulates that the anxiety that usually comes with a speaking performance is said to be both personal and situational. Researchers have over the years sought to understand how the combined effects of personal traits of an individual and situational conditions such as the nature of the speaking environment, the size of the audience and negative perception over the outcome of a speech, affects a person's ability to effectively communicate. While studies on speech-related anxiety in the academic environment is not new (Basic, 2011; Behnke et al., 2006), the attention of many of these studies has focused on students rather than lectures/instructors. This study found that out of fear of being negatively evaluated, students became highly apprehensive when asked to perform a speech-related task in the classroom. This, the study found, can potentially have adverse effects on the academic and professional performance of students. Most importantly, the study established the significant role of teachers in managing a friendly and pleasant environment that facilitate speaking and positive learning outcomes. As Varron (2011) asserts, the teacher is the one that facilitates the whole process of learning and creates a favorable environment, where there is a smooth flow of communication. The study of Varron (2011) proves to be in consistency with this research because the needs raised by the students can be addressed through motivation for encouragement, guidance and feed backing for mentoring, and integration of communicative approach in the Language classroom to provide more exposure. The teachers also, can avoid situations that could cause embarrassment to the student speaking by proper orientation on the responsibility and decorum of the audience.

A study conducted by Wu (2010) entitled The Relationship between Language Learners' Anxiety and Learning Strategy in the CLT Classrooms indicated in the results that most of the participants express a favorable attitude toward the Communicative Language Teaching (CLT) approach; however, they also reveal their high level of anxiety in the language classroom. Accordingly, language anxiety is usually reported to have adverse effects on the learning of a second language. It is the language instructors' mission to accelerate the language learning of their students. One way is to teach students how to learn more effectively and efficiently. Language learning strategies (LLS) are procedures that learners can use to facilitate learning. Wu's (2010) research results have some bearing to this study as revealed in the needs assessment. The Senior High School respondents experience anxiety in public speaking but they also identified in their needs to have more exposure. This shows they want to be helped and they have a favorable attitude towards Communicative Language Teaching (CLT).

Sapuya (2018) conducted an analysis of students' speaking anxiety towards their speaking skills. According to the results of speaking test, using Communicative Language Teaching (CLT) had positive meaningful effect on improving students' speaking skill viewed from different speaking anxiety. In the needs analysis administered by the researcher through an open ended survey, the Grade 11 students have identified that there is less talk time in their classes. If there are speaking activities, the same students repeatedly do the talking. 50% said, they get anxious but never refuse whenever asked to speak in front.

In summary, the needs assessment results showed that 100% of the teachers observe students with public speaking anxiety in their classes. They observed the apprehension through the students' verbal and non-verbal language. Students did shy away, refuse to speak, and requested to code-switch. While speaking, the students stuttered, stammered, had difficulty maintaining an eye contact and exhibited incorrect posture. According to four teachers, they observed that students intentionally spoke in a low voice so that they were not heard. When the teachers were asked what the perceived causes of anxiety are, majority of them reiterated that the student is probably just shy, lacks vocabulary and fluency. These identified reasons served as basis for the researcher in designing and developing the learning packets.

5. CONCLUSIONS

Taking the findings as strong points for evaluating this research, the following conclusions were drawn: (1) various opportunities for student-talk should be provided in senior high school classes, this calls for teachers' creativity in designing meaningful and communicative tasks; (2) the activities provided in class did not encourage enough class interaction, students therefore need exposure to communicative teaching to reduce speech anxiety level; and (3) to place high regard for class mentoring to widen the spectrum of language learning areas. These were the baseline data used in the production of the training design's final form, classified into learning packets.

6. RECOMMENDATIONS

The researcher recommends to physically implement the Training Design when the situation affected by COVID19 pandemic improves. After the training, it is suggested to have a follow through on the trainees after 6 months to a year to see the impact on the level of their public speaking anxiety.

For teachers, who are curriculum designers and mentors, it is further recommended that they will undergo more trainings across levels with the integration of Communicative Language Teaching (CLT) Approach through professional learning communities. Further researches on addressing public speaking anxiety starting in the primary grades is also recommended.

REFERENCES

Arnold, N., 2007. *Reducing foreign language communication apprehension with computer-mediated communication: A preliminary study*. System, 35(4), pp.469-486.

Azagra, M., 2017. *Speech Anxiety and Academic Performance in Oral Communication in Context*. Retrieved from https://www.academia.edu/33514065/speech_anxiety_and_academic_performance_in_oral_communication_in_conte xt

Basic, L., 2011. Speaking anxiety: an obstacle to second language learning?.

Behnke, R.R. and Sawyer, C.R., 2001. Patterns of psychological state anxiety in public speaking as a function of anxiety sensitivity. *Communication Quarterly*, 49(1), pp.84-94.

Bruce et. al, 2005. Influence of psychiatric comorbidity on recovery and recurrence in generalized anxiety disorder, social phobia, and panic disorder: A 12-year prospective study. *American Journal of psychiatry* 126 (6), pp.1179-1187.

Conway, C. C., Zbozinek, T., &Vervliet, B., 2017. *Maximizing exposure therapy: An inhibitory learning approach. Behaviour research and therapy*, 58, 10-23.

Horwitz, E., 2006. Language Anxiety and Achievement. *Annual Review of Applied Linguistics*. 21. 112 - 126. 10.1017/S0267190501000071.

Johns, J., 2007. Instructional design: The ADDIE Model. portal: *Libraries and the Academy*, 16(3), pp.477-489.

Kachru, Y., 2006. Kachru revisits contrasts. *English Today*, 12(1), 41-44.

Kankam, P. K., & Boateng, S. O., 2017. Addressing the problem of speech anxiety among students. *International Journal of Public Leadership.*

Kitano, K., 2001. Anxiety in the college Japanese language classroom. *The Modern Language Journal*, 85(4), 549-566.

McCroskey, J. C., 2015. Personal Report of Public Speaking Anxiety (PRPSA). Measurement *Instrument Database for the Social Science. Retrieved from www.midss.ie*

McLean C. P. & Anderson E. R., 2009. *Brave men and timid women? A review of the gender differences in fear and anxiety.* Clinical Psychological Review 29 (6), pp. 496-505.

Nunan, D., 2012. *Learner-centered English language education: The selected works of David Nunan.* Routledge.

Ong, C.G., 2009. A Training Scheme for College Communicative Teaching. *JPAIR Multidisciplinary Research.* 2. 10.7719/jpair.v2i1.67.

Öztürk, G., & Gürbüz, N., 2013. *The impact of gender on foreign language speaking anxiety and motivation.* Procedia-Social and Behavioral Sciences, 70, 654-665

Russell, J. A., 2017. *Comments on articles by Frijda and by Conway and Bekerian. Cognition and Emotion*, 1(2), 193-197.

Saputra, J. B., 2018. An analysis of students' speaking anxiety toward their speaking skill. Premise: *Journal of English Education*, 7(1), 111-123.

Scovel, T., 2008. *A time to speak: a psycholinguistic inquiry into the critical period for human speech.* New York: Newbury House.

Seels, B. and Glasgow, Z., 2018. Survey of Instructional Design Needs and Competencies.

Tanveer, M., 2007. *Investigation of the factors that cause language anxiety for ESL/EFL learners in learning speaking skills and the influence it casts on communication in the target language.* University of Glasgow, Scotland.

Tom, A.A. et al., 2013. Factor Contributing to Communication Apprehension among Pre-University Students. *Academic Journal of Interdisciplinary Studies* 2(8). Pp. 665-669

Wicks-Nelson, R. & Israel, A. C (2006). *Behavior Disorders of Childhood* 6th Edition. New Jersey: Person Education, Inc.

Wu, K. H., 2010. The Relationship between Language Learners' Anxiety and Learning Strategy in the CLT Classrooms. *International Education Studies*, 3(1), 174-191.

Young, D. J., 2002. *Language anxiety from the foreign language specialist's perspective: Interviews with Krashen, Omaggio Hadley, Terrell, and Rardin.* Foreign Language Annals, 25(2), 157-172.

THE MICRO:BIT AND COMPUTATIONAL THINKING. EVALUATION RESULTS OF A COMPUTATIONAL PROJECT

Gerhard Brandhofer
University College of Teacher Education Lower Austria
Mühlgasse 67, 2500 Baden, Austria

ABSTRACT

The overall project *Denken lernen - Probleme lösen* has been expanded in recent years after an initial sub-project in elementary school to include one for the lower secondary level. Schools throughout Austria were provided with the micro:bit and related materials. A training initiative for teachers was rolled out. In this article I would like to present a part of the evaluation results of this project. The investigation covers two aspects: the students' ability to solve problems and the students' opinions and views on working with the micro:bit.

KEYWORDS

Computational Thinking, Computer Science, Creativity

1. INTRODUCTION

The project *Denken lernen - Probleme lösen* (Learning to think - solving problems, in short DLPL) was coordinated by the University College of Teacher Education of Styria and the Private University College of Teacher Education of the Diocese Linz and was carried out from September 2018 to April 2020. The aim of the project was to implement coding and robotics with the help of the microboard micro:bit in secondary level I schools. Computational Thinking is a term coined by Jeanette Wing (see section 2). The OER textbook for micro:bit was developed by people from six University Colleges of Teacher Education and the Graz University of Technology. This textbook does not contain instructions for reproduction, but ideas and approaches on how to use BBC micro:bits in a comprehensive way. This approach was intended to promote the activation of the learners and to raise their creative potential.

On the part of the project management, a multi-level concept of information events and training courses was developed. Meetings and training sessions were held with the state coordinators and the Education Innovation Studio contact persons at the universities of teacher education. Passing on information about the project and training the teachers in the schools was then the responsibility of the state coordinators of the project *Denken lernen - Probleme lösen*. The training courses were organized according to local conditions and were partly held on site in the schools.

The content concept of the project is designed for interdisciplinary use. The main focus is on working with micro:bit in the subject *Digitaler Grundbildung* (Digital Basic Education), but objects such as works of art, visual education, geometric drawing or physics are also suitable.

2. PROJECT DESCRIPTION

2.1 BBC Micro:Bit

The hardware used in the project consists mainly of the BBC micro:bit and a small motor in combination with Matador components, which is also reflected in the project title "Computational Thinking, Coding and Robotics". This was accompanied by rolling cases with convertible laptops/tablets - depending on the wishes and availability for the participating schools.

As the name "BBC micro:bit" suggests, the British Broadcasting Corporation (BBC) is also behind this initiative - an allusion to the home computer "BBC Micro", which was used by the BBC in the 1980s for teaching and learning purposes on television. In October 2016, the project was transferred by its founders, including names such as ARM, Microsoft, Lancaster University, British Council, and others, into a non-profit foundation (Micro:bit Educational Foundation, 2016). Since then, this foundation has been responsible for the further distribution and support of the single-board computer, which is also available to private individuals through electronics retailers - currently priced between 16 and 28 EUR (as of December 14, 2020).

2.2 Scope of Functions

As can be seen in the schematic diagram (see Figure 1), the micro:bit has a size of four by five centimeters and is based on an ARM Cortex processor, similar to that used in today's low-cost smartphone. It has all the sensors usually associated with it, such as Bluetooth, temperature, compass, acceleration, brightness, and can be expanded via pins for external measurement and control and can be connected to a motor, e.g. with crocodile clips.

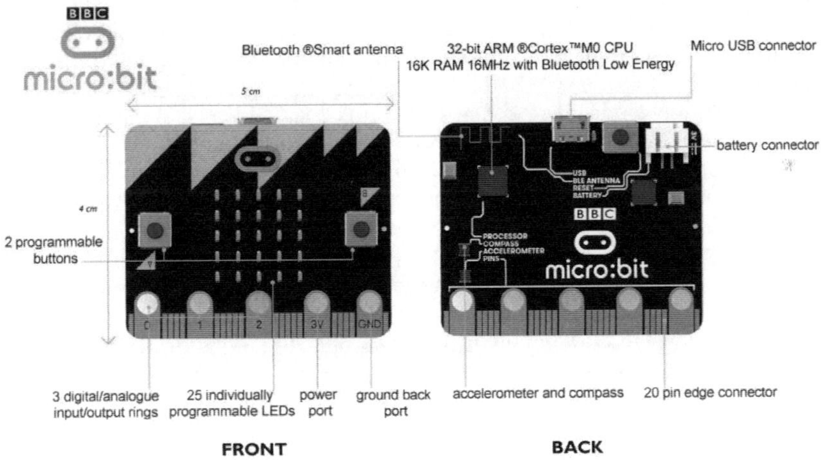

Figure 1. Front and back of the micro:bit, Gereth Halfacree, CC BY-SA 2.0, https://www.flickr.com/photos/120586634@N05/

To power the device, either the battery connector located on the top rear panel with a standard battery pack (2 AAA batteries) or the Micro-USB connector is used. This also serves to transfer the finished program to the micro:bit.

The 25 LEDs or the two programmable buttons on the front panel are used for input and output. On the back side between the Micro-USB connector and the battery connector is the reset button to reset the device and restart the current program.

The micro:bit is programmed with very little effort using MakeCode (Microsoft MakeCode, 2020). This visual, block-based programming interface, similar to Scratch (Scratch Foundation, 2020), runs without any installation in the browser and, in addition to the blocks, allows for advanced display in JavaScript - since the latest update even in Python. You can switch between the different views of the programming environment with a simple mouse click. Furthermore there are several other ways to program the micro:bit, which are not officially supported by the Micro:bit Educational Foundation. Worth mentioning are an offline Python editor with Intellisense for text input and the possibility to program directly in C/C+. For the work in the project the view in blocks was used throughout, suitable for the age level of the secondary school from 5th to 8th grade.

3. THE STUDENTS' ABILITY TO SOLVE PROBLEMS

The project *Denken lernen - Probleme lösen (DLPL)* pursued, among other things, the goal of promoting the students' problem-solving abilities. Computational Thinking as a concept was to be improved by the micro:bits as well as the materials created and made available. It is obvious to investigate whether this goal was achieved within the project. The research question for this part of the evaluation is therefore: To what extent was the problem-solving ability of the students promoted within the DLPL project?

3.1 Research Design

In order to answer the hypothesis, testing is preferable to observation or content analysis due to its construction (Schnell, Hill & Esser, 2011, p. 314). From the point of view of research design, the quantitative research method of a written survey using an online questionnaire was therefore chosen.

Computational Thinking is a concept of teaching and learning that consciously focuses on (digital) problem solving and thinking strategies of general relevance. The term refers "to the individual ability of a person to identify and abstractly model a problem, to break it down into sub-problems or steps, to design and elaborate solution strategies and to present them in a formalized way so that they can be understood and executed by a person or even a computer" (Eickelmann, 2018, p. 20). Learning is not primarily the digitalization of processes, but rather an individual problem-solving competence for action and decision-making - also independent of technical devices - which implies an own, very specific approach to the world and the environment. This is characterized by the following didactic design elements: (1) Decomposition - to logically structure complex problems into smaller parts, (2) Pattern Recognition - to recognize and describe patterns, (3) Algorithm Design - logical-analytical instructions and the design of solution structures, (4) Abstraction - the abstract development of concepts and (5) Generalize (Patterns and Models) as a recognition and understanding of generalized patterns and models in order to make them usable for different contexts of action (Himpsl-Gutermann, Brandhofer, Bachinger & Steiner, 2017; Brandhofer & Wiesner, 2018).

It had to be clarified how the construct problem solving capability can best be operationalized (Brandhofer, 2017; Brandhofer & Wiesner, 2018). A pragmatic approach was chosen: According to the Beaver Contest on Computer Science, task collections on computational thinking are available for secondary schools according to self-definition. The Bebras Initiative was founded in Lithuania in 2004. In the meantime numerous countries participate in the beaver competitions (Bebras, 2020). The tasks of the Bebras Initiative are described as follows: "Computational thinking involves using a set of problem-solving skills and techniques that software engineers use to write programs and apps. The *Bebras* challenge promotes problem solving skills and informatics concepts including the ability to break down complex tasks into simpler components, algorithm design, pattern recognition, pattern generalisation and abstraction" (Bebras, 2020). According to their own description, the authors of the Bebras materials aim to use the materials to quantify the students' problem solving ability. It was obvious to use these questionnaires to measure problem-solving ability. For the survey, the existing materials were used to create online test sheets. Each of the four questionnaires contained five tasks.

The goal of this evaluation was to explore the effect of a particular setting. Therefore, a longitudinal study was conducted with pre-testing, a treatment and a post-intervention test. To increase the quality of the results, the sheets were additionally presented to a control group that had not worked with the micro:bit and associated materials. Since the research question aims at a detectable clear change through an intervention, alternatives to the chosen method would have been less appropriate for answering the research question.

3.2 Pre-Test and Test Execution

To check the clarity and comprehensibility of the questions, to optimize the design and to estimate how much time should be available for the review, a pre-test was conducted with two school classes. The pre-test was also used to fine-tune the four questionnaires and to adjust their level of difficulty.

The survey was carried out by means of online questionnaires in the classroom. The teachers received the necessary instructions. The survey was carried out partially anonymously, student names were replaced by codes. Demographic data was collected on the type of school, grade level, date of birth, state and mother tongue. In addition, there were questions about the number of micro:bit teaching units, the subject in which the work with the micro:bit was carried out, and the use of the OER textbook. A total of 1341 students took at least one test, of which 778 students took both the pre-test and the post-test, 553 of which were students from the DLPL project classes. 129 students took the post-test but not the pre-test. Of the participating students, 79 stated that they were in the fifth grade, 84 in the sixth, 254 in the seventh and 181 in the eighth grade, with the rest not specified. The survey was conducted between March 2019 and April 2020.

3.3 Descriptive Evaluation

Most of the students who took part in the online survey came from Lower Austria, Styria and Salzburg. Vorarlberg and Burgenland were not represented. The majority of the students who took part in the online survey attended a general secondary school (AHS). In 80.5 % of the cases the BBC micro:bits were used in computer science. In addition, the BBC micro:bit was also used in math, physics, works, music, Education in arts and crafts, movement and sport, religion, descriptive geometry as well as in project teaching (e.g. MINT) or in social learning.

The students needed on average 10 min 43 s for the Pre-test. The maximum was 31 min 41 s, the minimum 2 min 22 s. For the Post-test, the average duration of work was slightly longer at 12 min 54 s (min = 2 min 28 s, max = 36 min 51 s). A closer look at the results shows that the student with the shortest working time achieved a slightly below average but good result in the Pre-test with 24 points. The student who took the least time to complete the post-test achieved a score of 40 points, well above the average.

3.4 Evaluation of Problem Solving Ability

The mean value of the achieved performances increased slightly in the DLPL Group 5/6 ($M = 30.59$ / $M = 31.37$). The post-test showed a slightly lower standard deviation ($SD = 14.85$ / $SD = 12.79$). The control group 5/6 fell slightly behind in the post-test ($M = 35.14$ / $M = 33.43$). The standard deviation remained almost constant ($SD = 14.79$ / $SD = 14.93$).

In the Pre-test, the mean value of the services performed was significantly higher in the control group. The difference in post-test performance between the DLPL group 5/6 and the control group 5/6 is not significant ($p = 0.957$), nor is it significant in the pre-test ($p = 0.233$).

The mean value of the achieved performances slightly decreased in the DLPL group 7/8 ($M = 33.65$ / $M = 33.41$). The post-test showed a slightly lower standard deviation ($SD = 13.52$ / $SD = 16.64$). The control group 7/8 achieved slightly lower values in the post-test ($M = 26.89$ / $M = 25.91$). The standard deviation was slightly higher in the post-test ($SD = 13.93$ / $SD = 14.34$).

The difference in post-test performance between DLPL group 7/8 and the control group 7/8 is significant ($p = 0.032$), while it is not significant in pre-test ($p = 0.867$).

The online survey also asked for the number of teaching units in which the micro:bit was used. The analysis of these results clarifies the picture very clearly: Within the DLPL group, micro:bits were used with varying intensity. There were also students in the DLPL groups who did not work with micro:bit in any of the lessons and thus could be assigned to the control group. Therefore, the following analysis of the values was based on the number of teaching units worked with the micro:bit.

A correlation analysis of the number of teaching units with the micro:bit and the results obtained in the post-test yields a correlation of 0.87 between these two values. The correlation according to Pearson is significant ($p = 0.03$). This means that there is a significant correlation between the number of teaching units in which the micro:bit was used and the ability to solve problems.

More detailed analyses show that the scores achieved by the students who worked with the BBC micro:bit in the 5th and 6th grade were about 4 points higher than those of the boys, both in the pre-test and in the post-test. In the 7th and 8th grades, girls scored better on the Pre-test (M = 34.1) than on the Post-test (M = 31.44). While the scores of boys increased, those of girls decreased. When the Pre-test and Post-test results are added together, the girls' overall performance (M = 66.07) was significantly (p = 0.035) better than the boys' (M = 63.00).

Among the students participating in the survey were 120 students whose first language is not German. The evaluation showed that in the DLPL group 5/6, the results of students with a first language other than German were about 7% worse in both the pre-test and the post-test, and about 3% worse in the DLPL group 7/8. It is therefore reasonable to assume that the complexity of the respective task text has an influence on the results achieved. However, a text analysis with regard to the readability of the analysis tools LIX3 and Wortliga4 did not show a clear correlation between the difficulty of the text and the respective mean value of the achieved points for the corresponding question. The Pre-test showed that example 5 was the most difficult text to read for grades 5 and 6 (LIX: 40.8; Wortliga: 34), while example 3 was the most difficult text for grades 7 and 8 (LIX: 47.3; Wortliga: 33).

4. STUDENTS' OPINIONS AND VIEWS ON THE PROJECT *DENKEN LERNEN - PROBLEME LÖSEN*

In addition to the study of problem-solving ability, the opinions and views of the students were also of particular interest. The question that interested us: What are the opinions and views of the pupils on the project *Denken lernen - Probleme lösen* and its concrete implementation at the school location? This can be divided into the following sub-questions: What did the pupils like about the project, what did they like less? How did the concrete work with the micro:bit in class look like? How were different teaching materials used? What is the students' opinion about micro:bit, programming and computer science education? How was the social environment of the students involved in the project?

To answer the research question and the sub-questions, the guideline interview with open questions was chosen as the survey instrument. The guide for the interviews comprised 14 questions. The interview partners were students from the secondary school of the University College of Teacher Education Lower Austria. The aim was to reconstruct the subjective view of the interview partners. The guideline provided orientation within the topic and was intended to make the individual interviews comparable with each other.

For data backup purposes, the interviews were recorded with the consent of the respondents. All data was anonymized. The data preparation was done by transcription. Subsequently, the transcripts were evaluated using the qualitative content analysis according to Mayring (2003). For this purpose, the answers were first paraphrased, then generalized and reduced so that a categorization was possible. The categorization was deductive and was based on the content areas of the questionnaire (Mayring, 2015, pp. 97-114).

4.1 Presentation of the Results

In January 2020, seven interviews were conducted and the subjects were chosen at random. The sample consisted of students in grades 4D and 4F of the Practical Secondary School of the University College of Teacher Education Lower Austria. According to the timetable, the students of this school have one hour of computer science lessons per week from the 2nd to the 4th grade. Further interviews at two project schools were planned for spring 2020. Due to the pandemic-related changeover of teaching to distance learning, the interviews could not be conducted.

4.2 The Lessons with the Micro:Bit

One result of the categorization is that the topic of teaching design was the most frequently represented, accounting for about 20% of the responses. The students were very satisfied with the use of this topic in class. A total of ten teaching units were used for the micro:bit. After a theoretical introduction, the students were able to learn how to use and program the micro:bit using concrete examples. Subsequently, more open tasks were set, which could then be solved individually or in a team. Some students were unfamiliar with this type of task. Student A said: "And when I made the Blackjack, I was only given the assignment, I was not given precise instructions." Again, student A: "Then you had to try and experiment and do it yourself."

In case of questions, the teaching materials, the classmates or the teacher could be consulted. Pupil A: "If you were stuck, then Mr. N. helped a little." The handbook as well as the wiki were used as framing. The students also had to answer the questions about the beaver contest on computer science (Bebras, 2020). The difficulty of these questions was judged very differently by the pupils. Schoolgirl S.: "Some questions were difficult. In contrast, student E.: "They were about logic and actually not very difficult." These different points of view are important and must be taken into account in the further roll-out of the project.

4.3 Tasks and Examples for Micro:Bit

In 11% of the statements of the students, concrete tasks and examples were programmed in class or at home (materials: Bachinger & Teufel, 2018a, 2018b; Micro:bit Educational Foundation, 2016). They mainly reported on the development of the tasks 'Scissors, Rock, Paper', 'Blackjack', 'Ping' and their own creations. They also remembered more difficult tasks, such as the communication between two micro:bits. The examples were well received. Student A: "You could enter many commands, you could be creative." In summary, the tasks corresponded to the students' level of knowledge and were well graded. Step-by-step examples were followed by more open tasks.

4.4 Technical Challenges

Technical peculiarities and problems when working with the micro:bits were also addressed. However, the problems described were obviously not based on bugs of the micro:bits, but rather on misjudgements in the handling. One student reported that his created program was not saved, a student told that her mico:bit crashed and the program was lost. In the interviews, however, the shortcomings described were very minor, rather the technical possibilities of the micro:bit were mentioned. Mentioned was the stand-alone version with the battery pack and the possibility to continue programming on the platform at home.

4.5 Learning with the Micro:Bit, Challenge Reading

According to the categorization, 9.4% of the students' statements could be assigned to the area "Learning with the micro:bit". Initial ambiguities (student D: "At the beginning I did not understand anything because it sounded like computer language to me.") were quickly followed by feelings of success (student A: "Yes, that actually explains itself with the micro:bit"). The pupils recognized that one had to work already exactly, precisely (pupil D) and bring along an understanding for variables (pupil S).

Due to the numerous mentions, a separate category was created for the topic "reading", 5.1 % of the statements referred to it. The students found it particularly challenging to read, analyze and implement the tasks. Student D: "Only my weakness is reading. I hate to read. And you always had to read. "Student E's statement summarizes this very well: "If you can read, you have an advantage."

4.6 The Social Environment

The students were also asked with whom they had talked about the project from their family and circle of friends. What is striking about the answers is that they were not asked by their parents, but some of them reported back home. The parents were informed in advance by the project. Pupil D: "Nobody at home asked about it now and then I just told them. Similarly, student T: "I told my dad, but he doesn't understand all this. More frequent were discussions about the project with older and younger siblings. Some of them also worked together on a project at home. Pupil A finally got two micro:bits as a Christmas present from her brother, and they experimented with them afterwards.

4.7 The Micro:Bit, Opinions about the Project and the Professional Future

The personal opinions on the work with the micro:bit comprise 10.6% of the answers. The result is a heterogeneous picture: While some were enthusiastic about the board, others saw it in a more differentiated way and two initially stated that they did not like the project that much. Schoolgirl K: "It was once a change and was pretty cool."

A noteworthy development occurred with student D during the interview. When asked at the beginning what he liked about the project, he said: "Should I be honest? Not at all. I hate working with these things." In the course of the interview, however, he expressed his satisfaction with the introduction of the micro:bit in class: "Yes, I also think Mr. N. explained it well." He then reported in detail about the individual examples and that he enthusiastically told his brother about the project. It finally turned out that his initial reluctance was more related to the fact that he had to read through assignments. Student D: "You had to read through the assignments. Then I just read through them. I also checked it, but you had to read through it several times. You also have to understand it. In retrospect, I understood it anyway."

A homogeneous picture can be drawn by the statements of the students about the meaning of the work with the micro:bits for the vocational future. The unanimous opinion is that if one wants to become a programmer later, the experience with the micro:bit is valuable. If one does not intend to do so, it is interesting, but not necessary. As an example for this, the statement of student K can be used: "For someone who wants to become a programmer later on, it is fine because it is an experience, but for me, for example, it is not really useful". And student S: "Only, I know that I don't need this for the rest of my life, because I won't be programming or something." Similarly student E: "I liked the fact that you could program games together with others." Student C states: "This is a kind of programming for beginners. If someone wants to be a programmer, I would say, yes, that's very good and important. Two students stated that they want to become programmers later.

5. SUMMARY

The evaluation of the data confirms the hypothesis that working with the micro:bit has an effect on the students' problem-solving ability. The longer the students worked with the micro:bits in class, the better the results of the post-test with the beaver tasks. Within the DLPL group, the school classes worked with the micro:bits with very different intensity.

Overall, the girls scored better on the assignments. The understanding of the text is probably a relevant factor in the processing of the tasks, this thesis is confirmed by the interviews with the pupils.

The design of the lessons with the micro:bit, the increasing difficulty of the tasks and the accompanying materials were perceived positively by the students. The problem-oriented, open learning setting was unusual for some. The technical problems were limited and were not necessarily micro:bit-specific. The reading of tasks turned out to be the biggest hurdle, which was also recognized by the students themselves. The class teacher also noticed that some students had little stamina for certain tasks. The parents asked the children very little about the project, but with their siblings the students partly had an intensive exchange about the possibilities of micro:bit. In summary, it can be said that the project was well planned and implemented in a goal-oriented manner from the perspective of the students at the respective school. Some aspects that emerge from the answers are not limited to the micro:bit project, but must be seen more comprehensively (text comprehension, ability to concentrate, communication, professional expectations).

In summary, the results of the evaluation of the project Denken lernen - Probleme lösen, Secondary Level I are consistent with the findings of the project Denken lernen - Probleme lösen, Primary Level (Himpsl-Gutermann et al., 2018, see also Antonitsch & Hanisch, 2014 and Repenig, 2016). As other studies have also shown (Denning & Tedre, 2019; Eickelmann et al., 2019, p. 382), it has been shown that computational thinking as a metacognitive ability is in itself difficult to teach or promote and must always be embedded in contexts - in this case, the system micro:bit. The project was conceived on the basis of the discourse on computational thinking and the orientation of computer science in schools (Gesellschaft für Informatik, 2016; Bollin, 2016, p. 23, Bollin & Micheuz, 2018), so the results are also relevant for the further development of computer science in Austria.

REFERENCES

Antonitsch, P. & Hanisch, L. (2014). *Computational Thinking im Unterricht der Primarstufe*. IMST.

Bachinger, A. & Teufel, M. (2018a). micro:bit - Das Schulbuch. *Wiki*. Access on 14.12.2020. Available at: https://micro:bit.eeducation.at/wiki/Hauptseite

Bachinger, A. & Teufel, M. (Hrsg.). (2018b). *Digitale Bildung in der Sekundarstufe – Computational Thinking mit BBC micro:bit*. Grieskirchen: Austro.Tec.

Bebras. (2020). What is Bebras | www.bebras.org. *Bebras: International Challenge on Informatics and Computational Thinking*. Access on 14.12.2020. Available at: https://www.bebras.org/?q=about

Bollin, A. (2016). Didaktik der Informatik: Herausforderungen und Blick in die Zukunft. *OCG Journal*, Jg. 41(02), 22–23.

Bollin, A. & Micheuz, P. (2018). Computational Thinking on the Way to a Cultural Technique. *Empowering Learners for Life in the Digital Age*. OCCE 2018, Linz.

Bortz, J. & Döring, N. (2006). *Forschungsmethoden und Evaluation: für Human- und Sozialwissenschaftler* (Auflage: 4., überarb. Aufl. 2006.). Heidelberg: Springer.

Bortz, J. & Lienert, G. A. (2003). Kurzgefaßte Statistik für die klinische Forschung: Leitfaden für die verteilungsfreie Analyse kleiner Stichproben; mit 91 Tabellen. Heidelberg: Springer.

Brandhofer, G. & Wiesner, C. (2018). Medienbildung im Kontext der Digitalisierung: Ein integratives Modell für digitale Kompetenzen. *R&E-SOURCE. Open Online Journal for Research and Education*, 10.

Brandhofer, G. (2017). Coding und Robotik im Unterricht. *Erziehung und Unterricht*, 7–8, 51–58.

Denning, P.J. & Tedre, M. (2019). *Computational thinking*. Cambridge, Massachusetts: The MIT Press.

Eickelmann, B., Bos, W., Gerick, J., Goldhammer, F., Schaumburg, H., Schwippert, K. et al. (2019). *ICILS 2018 #Deutschland computer- und informationsbezogene Kompetenzen von Schülerinnen und Schülern im zweiten internationalen Vergleich und Kompetenzen im Bereich Computational Thinking*.

Eickelmann, B. (2018). Digitalisierung in der schulischen Bildung. Entwicklung, Befunde und Perspektiven für die Schulentwicklung und die Bildungsforschung. In: McElvany, N., Schwabe, F., Bos, W. & Holtapples, H. G. (Hrsg.): *Digitalisierung in der Schulischen Bildung. Chancen und Herausforderungen*. Münster: Waxmann, S. 11-26.

Gesellschaft für Informatik. (2016). *Dagstuhl-Erklärung: Bildung in der digitalen vernetzten Welt*. Access on 14.12.2020. Available at: https://www.gi.de/aktuelles/meldungen/detailansicht/article/dagstuhl-erklaerung-bildung-in-der-digitalen-vernetzten-welt.html

Himpsl-Gutermann, K., Brandhofer, G., Bachinger, A., Steiner, M. & Gawin, A. (2017). Das Projekt, Denken lernen – Probleme lösen (DLPL)". *Medienimpulse*, 2, 1–12.

Himpsl-Gutermann, K., Brandhofer, G., Frick, K., Fikisz, W., Steiner, M., Bachinger, A. et al. (Hrsg.). (2018). *Abschlussbericht im Projekt „Denken lernen – Probleme lösen (DLPL) Primarstufe*". Wien, Baden. Verfügbar unter: https://bildung.bmbwf.gv.at/schulen/schule40/dgb/dlpl.html

Mayring, Philipp (2003). *Qualitative Inhaltsanalyse. Grundlagen und Techniken*. Beltz.

Mayring, Philipp (2015). *Qualitative Inhaltsanalyse: Grundlagen und Techniken* (12., überarbeitete Auflage). Weinheim: Beltz.

Micro:bit Educational Foundation. (2016). micro:bit. Access on 14.12.2020. Available at:: https://microbit.org/

Microsoft MakeCode (2020), MakeCode, Access on 14.12.2020. Available at: https://makecode.microbit.org/

Repenig, A. (2016). Computational Thinking für alle! *OCG Journal*, Jg. 41(02), 30.

Schnell, R., Hill, P. B. & Esser, E. (2011). *Methoden der empirischen Sozialforschung*. München: Oldenbourg Verlag.

Scratch Foundation (2020), Scratch, *Scratch Foundation und Lifelong Kindergarten Group am MIT Media Lab*, Access on 14.12.2020. Available at: https://scratch.mit.edu

A GLOBALIZED CURRICULUM: THE NEXT EVOLUTION OF EDUCATION

Micah Shippee
PhD, Syracuse University, Syracuse, NY, USA

ABSTRACT

Curriculum is a dynamic, iterative cultural artifact. Historically, educational curricular shifts have gone from Socratic dialogue, to master-apprentice programs, to humanities enrichment, to STEM focus, each with varying degrees of equitable access. Gaps in equity have led to economic-driven curricular designs. In recent years, access to learning has increased dramatically, not just the privilege of the elite. We can now focus our curricular priorities to address the needs of our global society. With this in mind we need a curriculum that is culturally responsive and iterative in nature. This paper addresses curricular evolution at a global level with insights for the future of learning.

KEYWORDS

Curriculum, Globalization, Sustainable Development Goals

1. INTRODUCTION

Curriculum design is an iterative, cultural process. Culture is defined as the shared beliefs, social forms, and material traits of a social group. There are five key tenets of culture (Haviland, Prins, Walrath, and McBride, 2005): Culture is learned, shared, based on symbols, integrated, and dynamic. Curriculum design is linked to culture by the way we define who we are and where we want to be from our collective shared experience. Shaping a globally-responsive curriculum takes purposeful, diligent effort in observing, selecting, and presenting experiences (Shippee, 2019).

Curriculum design requires we are cognizant of, and responsive to, the context in which we have been working. Historically, cultural forces have pressured an educational perspective that embraces newer, trending technology, specifically in regard to film, radio, television, and eventually computers (Shippee, 2016; Cuban, 1986). This is reinforced by the concept of the *technological sublime,* a theoretical context for interpreting underlying motivations of decision makers advocating for the pursuit of greatness (Frick, 2017). To move forward in our continued iteration of curriculum, we must first look back through a historical perspective on curriculum to examine throughlines and outliers that can serve to inform our discussion (Popkewitz, 1984).

2. A BRIEF HISTORY OF CURRICULUM

For the Hellenistic period, Greek education was largely esoteric having focused on the humanities and the curation of educated people. Here students were taught to be "critical" in all or almost all branches of knowledge. The scope and sequence for instruction was based on the trivium: grammar, rhetoric, and logic and the quadrivium: arithmetic, geometry, astronomy, and music. While the names are antique, the seven "subjects" were comparable to a modern liberal curriculum of languages, philosophy, mathematics, history, and science. The education of the Roman Empire consisted of a focus on Politics and Law, influenced by aspects of Greek education that focused on philosophy and language yet, reflecting on Roman-cultural priorities, centering on oratory (speech giving) due to its political significance. (Van Doren, 1992). Formalized medieval education yielded a culturally-specific, religious focus with a temporary reprieve from Greek influence. The Renaissance, or "Rebirth," yielded renewed interest in Greek and Roman systems that began transcending the geographic spheres of antiquity. In response, Renaissance education began a lasting shift back to curriculum guided by ancient wisdom.

Throughout the 1700s and 1800s education continued to be the luxury of the elite. Efforts were made in various pockets of the globe to increase and equity in regard to educational opportunity, yet education was elusive to many.

Contemporary education grew out of the Industrial Revolution as a form of mass production, a mass education, the product of the Industrial Age (Lahav, 1973). "The whole idea of assembling masses of students (raw material) to be produced by teachers (workers) in a centrally located school (factory) was a stroke of industrial genius" (Toffler, 1970). In this system, content was broken apart into distinct units of study, veritable silos of learning. In the Twentieth Century, even universities felt the impact of the silo-ing of content. The "uni" in university became pointless, as universities' separate worlds ceased to talk to one another. Each college, department, etc. began possessing more and more autonomous power as government funding for research turned them into a loose confederation of disconnected mini-states, instead of a uni-fied organization devoted to the joint search for knowledge and truth. (Van Doren, 1992). Curriculum, teaching standards, and learning objectives all became uniquely tailored to each content category. The silo-ing of education has remained in K12 classrooms systematically validating the existing Industrial Aged model where work stations (courses) were separated and meaningful curriculum-driven collaboration is lacking.

Conversations about curriculum design were deeply impacted in the United States in the Cold War and the Soviet launch of Sputnik. The Space Age became a cultural phenomenon yielding a hyper-focused approach that lauded math and science as the keys to a successful future, a technological sublime, that is, the pursuit of nationalistic greatness. From this thinking was born STEM education.

3. STEM EDUCATION

A STEM education focuses on Science, Technology, Engineering, and Math with the belief that these will help prepare learners to compete in their future economy. STEM remains a curricular priority in our global education systems today (Freeman, Marginson, & Tytler, 2019). Many policymakers, economists, and futurists believe a solid foundation in STEM will make students more marketable and successful, particularly in an increasingly globalized economy with the spread of products, technology, information, and jobs across national borders and cultures.

For decades, in the United States, multiple national policy documents have asserted that global competitiveness is contingent on students being actively engaged in science, technology, engineering, and mathematics (STEM) at all levels of education (National Academy of Sciences, National Academy of Engineering, & Institute of Medicine of the National Academies, 2007). In response to growing concerns about the future workforce "STEM" was introduced in 2001 by the National Science Foundation (NSF) who stated: "*A well-prepared, innovative science, technology, engineering, and mathematics (STEM) workforce is crucial to the Nation's prosperity and security. Future generations of STEM professionals are a key sector of this workforce, especially in the critical scientific areas...To accelerate progress in these areas, the next generation of STEM professionals will need to master new knowledge and skills, collaborate across disciplines, and shape the future of the human-technology interface in the workplace.*" (Carpenter, Regassa, and Watson, 2020). Critics argue STEM itself is a socially constructed label developed in response to economic and global pressure (Akerson, Burgess, Gerber, Guo, Khan, & Newman, 2018), yet one would ask: Is that not part of the role of education? To respond to changing times? After all, education is changing because the world is changing.

The truth of the matter is that the actual educational meaning and practice of STEM is not clear. Do we approach all four as siloed curricular areas with distinct course objectives to be mastered? Or, do we instead break down the silos and leverage each of these areas around a central goal or project? I would argue the latter is where the most powerful learning potential is found. Rather than focus on the individual contents of Science, Technology, Engineering, and Mathematics learners will make the most meaning by leveraging them all together with a STEM-approach to solving real world problems. Perhaps a more realistic goal is to continue the mantra of over a millenia of education, what some call "the hidden curriculum," (The Glossary of Education Reform, 2013) that is, to motivate learners to care about the future, an empathy-driven focus to cause positive change in our world.

4. CURRICULAR EVOLUTION

The world is rapidly changing as a result of both wanted and unwanted disruption. The COVID19 pandemic has forced an increase in remote/distance and hybrid learning which has caused us to question our best practices for teaching and learning. While emergent technologies have afforded us the opportunity to teach and learn in new and exciting ways. Both of these disruptions will have lasting impacts on our culture and on our curriculum. One example of changes in technology is Artificial Intelligence (AI). AI is an area of computing science focused on the creation of intelligent machines that work and react like humans. The product of impressive STEM-based work, AI learns through the data we generate in our real-time efforts and many AI products impact and improve our daily lives through automation (Shippee, 2020). But then automation means "machines will become very good at being machines...so we need to be extremely good at being humans again...to dig into individual abilities, allowing people to do their best & live out their potential." says innovator and futurist Liselotte Lyngsø (Lindzon, 2018). Herein is the need to evolve our curricular focus, one that responds to a change in our global culture as seen through our understanding of the future of work. In 2018, former LinkedIN CEO Jeff Weiner stated "Not surprisingly, there continues to be an imbalance with regards to software engineering. But somewhat surprisingly, interpersonal skills is where we're seeing the biggest imbalance. Communication is the No. 1 skill gap." (Mautz, 2018).

Our planning and strategizing in education has often been a means to an ends approach rather than understanding that the ends would shape the means. Our focus must be on the world that our students will face. To plan without having a clear idea of what one is planning for is seemingly futile as setting out on a journey without a map, future thinking "can serve the same role for the educational planners as did the geographers for the explorers of the Renaissance!" (Lahav, 1973).

5. REAL-WORLD FOCUSED CURRICULUM

Setting aside agenda-driven, esoteric rhetoric, about curriculum. From a purely teaching and learning perspective we find direction from the field of instructional design where many powerful principles help us prescribe effective teaching and learning practices. Among them are the work of Dr. M. David Merrill (2002) who describes 5 principles of instruction: Learning is promoted when: 1) learners are engaged in solving real-world problems, 2) existing knowledge is activated as a foundation for new knowledge, 3) new knowledge is demonstrated to the learner, 4) new knowledge is applied by the learner, and 5) new knowledge is integrated into the learner's world. These 5 principles explain the power of hands-on learning where each individual learner makes real meaning of the process. We must incorporate these principles into our curriculum design. Our future must have a problem-based approach which employs STEM-*thinking*, over siloed content understanding, to prepare our learners for their globally conscious future. Like any innovation, curriculum change involves some overlap in practice. Changes that look and feel similar to what we know are easier to adopt. The choice to adopt begins with an initial decision about fit as it gives way to actual implementation (Shippee, 2016; Shippee 2019; Lubinsky & Shippee 2021).

STEM-thinking is a familiar set of skills that we can employ to identify important questions for important problems, in real-life situations. STEM-thinking supports our explanation of both the natural and designed world through evidence-based conclusions, as a cognitive process of inquiry and an attitude that exhibits a willingness to engage in issues as a reflective citizen.

Meaningful adoption of a problem-based teaching with STEM-thinking serving as a lens to approach concepts can positively impact learners when it is translated into policies, education programs, and practically applied in classrooms. This adoption will lead to a prepared workforce with 21st-century competencies, an advanced research agenda, and a focus on innovation. Those of us seeking to understand the future of work in an increasingly globalized world have increased discussions about the relevance of STEM in education addressing how a STEM education leads learners to better understanding the interconnectedness of concepts and ideas.

6. THE UNITED NATIONS SUSTAINABLE DEVELOPMENT GOALS

The free-trade economics of globalization aside: does STEM have potential to have a positive impact on our world? From a problem-based learning global, cultural-perspective… absolutely. How then do we decide, on a global level, on what problems to prepare our learners to solve?

The United Nations (UN) Sustainable Development Goals (SDGs), are 17 specific areas which serve as an urgent call for action by all countries, developed and developing, to employ a global partnerships that recognize "ending poverty and other deprivations must go hand-in-hand with strategies that improve health and education, reduce inequality, and spur economic growth, all while tackling climate change and working to preserve our oceans and forests." (United Nations, 2020).

Figure 1. Sustainable Development Goals (United Nations, 2020)

The SDGs provide guidance for helping cultivate focus areas for our future citizens who will understand and be ready to address them with a STEM-thinking skill set.

7. A GLOBALIZED CURRICULUM

The global challenges we face now, and in the future, are clearly significant and will require more than an academic solution, but STEM-thinking must be part of our strategic response and be more than simply tinkering with current policies and programs, or just updating science curriculums (Bybee, 2013). From a humanities perspective STEM coursework appears to tell only part of the story. Should we simply keep adding letters to the acronym like "A" for "Arts" giving us STEAM or "R" for "Reading" and/or "Research" and thus STREAM? I would suggest that we instead accept "STEM" as a guided thought process and propose that we understand the humanities (reading, writing, fine arts, history, social studies, etc…) as the *glue* that links the components of STEM together through context driven accounts, and stories, which both explain and illustrate the meaningful application of STEM. As an illustration of this, let us reflect on how science, technology, engineering, and math are employed to explain an Archimedean Screw. We understand that the explanation is better illustrated by both the historical accounts of its development and the stories of modern use which illustrate how it works. Further, the humanities also serve as a civic compass to help us understand the global impact of our actions through a culturally-focused perspective, a critical component when trying to help others adopt meaningful change.

Dr. Christopher Charles' "Lucky Iron Fish" account embodies a Globalized Curriculum focusing on a real-world problem that only became effective solved when culture was understood:

In 2008, Christopher Charles, then a Masters, student travelled to Cambodia for a research project. While there, he was shocked at the high rates of iron deficiency anemia and anemia in the region. He decided to dedicate his future research to developing a safe, and affordable solution. Now Dr. Charles, he was inspired by previous research which showed that cooking in a cast iron pot increased the iron content in food. He developed an iron ingot that could be boiled in soups or drinking water. But not everyone was ready to throw a block of iron into their drinking water. It was clear that Dr. Charles had to better understand the culture in which he was working.

After doing more research on the culture, he realized what he needed to do in order to persuade people to use the ingot, Dr. Charles cast the ingot into the shape of a fish that was considered to be lucky in Cambodian folklore. As explained in his thesis the concept of a lucky iron fish design did not pander to superstition, but created a cultural relevance for a solution based on science. To make the fish more attractive to the users, he gave the fish a smile. He called this prototype the "Happy Fish". He went on to show that almost everyone used the fish and results from his research showed that regular use of the Happy Fish decreased anemia by 46%. (Roxby, 2015)

The Lucky Iron Fish story illustrates multiple SDGs, with a solution developed through a STEM-thinking lens that would have failed to make an impact if it was not for the humanities-directed understanding of culture.

8. CONCLUSION

Education is changing because the world is changing. Curriculum design is, and should be, in a constant state of dynamic iteration that responds to these changing times. As equitable access to education increases, so to should our desire to increase global awareness through a globalized curriculum. We have an opportunity to help plan a bright future for all humankind that transcends geography and economic status and highlights the creative abilities we have to solve our shared problems.

REFERENCES

Akerson, V. L., Burgess, A., Gerber, A., Guo, M., Khan, T.A., and Newman, S. (2018) Disentangling the Meaning of STEM: Implications for Science Education and Science Teacher Education, *Journal of Science Teacher Education*, 29:1, 1-8, DOI: 10.1080/1046560X.2018.1435063

Bybee, R. W. *The Case for STEM Education: Challenges and Opportunities*. Arlington, Virginia: National Science Teachers Association, 2013.

Carpenter, E., Regassa, L.B. and Watson, C.L. "*Accelerating Discovery: Educating the Future STEM Workforce | NSF - National Science Foundation*." Nsf.gov. 24 Jan. 2020. Web. 14 Dec. 2020 https://www.nsf.gov/funding/pgm_summ.jsp?pims_id=505552

Cuban, L. (1986). *Teachers and Machines: The classroom use of technology since 1920*. New York: Teachers College Press.

Freeman, B., Marginson, S., and Tytler, R. (2019). *An international view of STEM education*. 10.1163/9789004405400_019.

Frick, K. T. (2017). *The Cost of the Technological Sublime: Daring Ingenuity and the new San Francisco-Oakland Bay Bridge*. Escholarship.org Web. 4 Jan. 2021. https://escholarship.org/uc/item/2d00f48t

Haviland, W.A., Prins, H.E.L., Walrath, D, and McBride, B.. *Cultural Anthropology*: The Human Challenge., 2005. Print.

Lahav, R. (1973). Futurology and Education: Four Futurologists and Their Theories of Education. *The Journal of Educational Thought (JET) / Revue De La Pensée Éducative,* 7(1), 48-64. Web. 17 Dec. 2020. https://www.jstor.org/stable/pdf/23768782.pdf.

Lindzon, J. (2018, July 18). This is what work will look like in 2100. *Fast Company*. Web. 4 Jan. 2020. https://www.fastcompany.com/90180181/this-is-what-work-will-look-like-in-2100

Lubinsky, J. and Shippee, M (2021) *Esports and strategic organizational adoption of innovation*. (Andrews, S. and Crawford C. eds.). Chapter in Pathways and Opportunities into the Business of Esports. IGI Global (in press)

Mautz, S. "What Job Skill Is Most Lacking in the U.S.? LinkedIn CEO Jeff Weiner Has a Surprising Answer." *Inc.com*. 23 Apr. 2018. Web. 4 Jan. 2021. https://www.inc.com/scott-mautz/linkedin-ceo-jeff-weiner-just-revealed-employees-lack-this-1-surprising-job-skill-more-than-any-other.html

Merrill, D.M. "First principles of instruction." *Educational Technology Research and Development*. 1 Sept. 2002. Web. 28 Oct. 2020. https://link.springer.com/article/10.1007/BF02505024

National Academy of Sciences, National Academy of Engineering, & Institute of Medicine of the National Academies. (2007). *Rising above the gathering storm: Energizing and employing America for a brighter economic future*. Washington, DC: National Academies Press.

Popkewitz, T. (1984). *Paradigm and ideology in educational research: the social functions of the intellectual*. London New York: Falmer Press.

Roxby, P. "Why an iron fish can make you stronger." *BBC News*. 17 May 2015. Web. 14 Dec. 2020. https://www.bbc.com/news/health-32749629

Shippee, M. (2016). *mLearning in the organizational innovation process.* Dissertation. Syracuse University. Syracuse, NY

Shippee, M. (2019) *WanderlustEDU: An Educator's Guide to Innovation, Change, and Adventure*. San Diego: Dave Burgess Consulting, Inc.

Shippee, M. (2020) No brainer AI in the classroom. *Teach Magazine*. September/October 2020.

Stohlman, M., Moore, T. J., and Roehrig, G. H. (2012). Considerations for teaching integrated STEM education. *Journal of Pre-College Engineering Education Research*, 2(1), 28–34.

Toffler, A. (1970). *Future shock*. New York: Random House.

The Glossary of Education Reform. "Hidden Curriculum Definition." The Glossary of Education Reform. 3 Dec. 2013. Web. 14 Dec. 2020. https://www.edglossary.org/hidden-curriculum/

United Nations. "THE 17 GOALS | Sustainable Development." *Sdgs.un.org*. 11 Dec. 2020. Web. 14 Dec. 2020. https://sdgs.un.org/goals

Van Doren, C. (1992). *A history of knowledge: past, present, and future*. New York, N.Y: Ballantine Books.

A FRAMEWORK TO ANALYZE LOGS OF CODERUNNDER FOR IMPROVING PROGRAMMING EDUCATION

Kohei Hatano
Kyushu University, Japan

ABSTRACT

We propose a framework to analyze logs of CodeRunner, a moodle plugin for automatic evaluation of students' programming assignments. Our framework can accumulate students' programming attempts for each specific problem, which enables teachers to observe how students fail to solve and to design better problems by analyzing the logs.

KEYWORDS

Programming Skills, CodeRunner, Automatic Evaluation, Learning Analytics

1. INTRODUCTION

Education of programming skills becomes more important than ever due to the development and popularity of data science or machine learning in various disciplines and applications. For example, Python programming language is quite popular, because they are simple, easy to use/teach and contains many tools or libraries for data science (e.g., numpy, scikitlearn and etc.). On the other hand, teaching loads on programming skills are increasing, as there are more classes or students. In particular, evaluation of programming assignments is a time-consuming task for teachers when there are many students. Also, delays of evaluation of assignments imply delays or lack of feedbacks to students, which is not desirable in education of programming skills.

CodeRunner (Lobb and Harlow, 2016)(*CodeRunner*) is a plugin of the moodle LMS (*Moodle*) which automatically evaluates programs submitted by students. It supports various languages such as C, C++, Python, matlab and so on. CodeRunner is used at more than 1700 sites (*Question types: CodeRunner*). With appropriate setting of problems and answers, teacher can reduce evaluation loads significantly. Also, CodeRunner gives feedbacks instantly to students when they submit answers, which promotes students' learning of programming skills. Another potential benefit of CodeRunner lies in its logs of student answers accumulated in the moodle database. The database contains attempts of students to CodeRunner questions. Administrators of the moodle site can access the logs via the database, but it requires the knowledge of SQL languages and the related schema of the database to obtain the logs.

In the poster, we will report our ongoing project of constructing a framework to analyze logs of CodeRunner for observing students' attempts and improving problems and course designs. There are other approaches using Jupyter notebook which enables teachers or administrators to accumulate logs of students's programming attempts. For example, Data 8 (*Data 8*), Szygy (*Syzygy*), and Courseware hub (*Courseware hub*) are cloud-based programming infrastructures based on Jupyter Hub (*Jupyter Hub*). Compared to these cloud-based notebook systems, our framework focuses on logs specific to program assignments, thus it can contribute directly to improving assignment and course designs. Also, analyzing problem-specific logs can clarify students's bottlenecks to solve the problems easier.

ACKNOWLEDEMENTS

This study was supported by JST AIP grant number JPMJCR19U1.

REFERENCES

CodeRunner. Available at: https://coderunner.org.nz (Accessed: 22 February 2021).
Courseware hub. Available at: https://github.com/NII-cloud-operation (Accessed: 22 February 2021).
Data 8. Available at: http://data8.org/ (Accessed: 22 February 2021).
Jupyter Hub. Available at: https://jupyter.org/hub (Accessed: 22 February 2021).
Lobb, R. and Harlow, J. (2016) 'Coderunner: a tool for assessing computer programming skills', *ACM Inloads*, 7(1).
Moodle. Available at: https://moodle.org/ (Accessed: 22 February 2021).
Question types: CodeRunner. Available at: https://moodle.org/plugins/qtype_coderunner (Accessed: 22 February 2021).
Syzygy. Available at: https://syzygy.ca/ (Accessed: 22 February 2021).

M-LEARNING IN HIGHER EDUCATION: TECHNOLOGY OWNERSHIP AND COMMON ATTRIBUTES AMONG MILLENNIALS IN SOUTH AFRICA

Chama Devi Ramchurn, Sumarie Roodt[1] and Sarah Mulaji
[1]*Dr.*
University of Cape Town
Leslie Commerce Building, University of Cape Town, Rondebosch, Cape Town, South Africa

ABSTRACT

This research investigates the mobile technology ownership concerning M-learning and identifies Tapscott's (2009) common traits of Millennials in a South African context. Technology growth and adoption is impacting the education sector by changing teaching and learning through an innovative form of learning commonly known as M-learning. Along with the growth in adoption of technology, students learning profiles have also changed over time, evolving toward another generation of learners referred to as Millennials. A total of 103 Millennial student respondents in a higher education institution in South Africa were surveyed to collect primary data and descriptive statistics were used to summarize the results according to which the entire sample population owned at least one type of mobile devices. The findings also indicated that technology acquaintance and innovation are the most relatable attributes shared among Millennials.

KEYWORDS

M-Learning, Millennials, Technology Ownership, Higher Education

1. INTRODUCTION

Mobile technologies, principally smartphones, have spread rapidly in both developed and developing countries. According to the International Telecommunication Union (ITU), global mobile cellular subscriptions increased from 2205 million in 2005 to 8152 million in 2020, of which 6441 million relates to developing countries (Statistics, 2021). ITU's latest figures also show that around 50-59% of the South African population owns a mobile phone (Measuring digital development: Facts and figures 2020, 2020). This phenomenon has brought new opportunities which enabled more people to have access to education through M-learning. (Kaliisa et al., 2019).

In the education sector, the introduction of mobile technology such as personal computers, provides learners and teachers with a flexible platform to engage in learning and use of technological tools dynamically and asymmetrically. Mobile devices have gained immense prominence since its launch in the 1980s (Mwapwele & Roodt, 2016). In 2014, approximately 86% of undergraduates were reported to be smartphone owners (Chen, Seilhamer, Bennett & Bauer, 2018). Consequently, the increasing application of M-learning and the rapid development in the mobile landscape have given rise to incredible opportunities in higher education (Alhassan, 2016).

Higher education is constantly evolving with the advent of new technologies (Serrano et al., 2019). Current university or college students who are part of the Net Generation, also known as Millennials, have grown up with technology. Consequently, it is perceived that conventional learning practices are inadequate or irrelevant for the Millennials (Barnes, Marateo & Ferris, 2018). Hence, there is an increasing need for higher education organizations to modify their teaching practices to accommodate the evolving demand of the Millennial student. However, to address Millennials needs for the improvement of current learning practices, it is necessary to investigate their mobile technology ownership pattern first (Talan, 2020).

The aim of this research is to investigate mobile technology ownership in higher education and to identify which of the common traits of Millennials outlined by Tapscott (2009) are relevant in a South African context. By doing so, this study sets a tone for further research in understanding the perception of M-learning by Millennials as well as the implementation and adoption of M-learning in higher education. This research study might contribute to the educational sector by providing the legislators and other stakeholders, insights into the need of students regarding the provision of M-learning. This study might also prove to be of significant value to the academic sector by providing bodies of knowledge a better understanding around the adoption of M-learning in a developing economy.

Before diving into the findings, the following section discusses the fundamental concept of the research topic, namely mobile learning and trait of Millennials.

1.1 Mobile-Learning (M-Learning)

Different researchers have attempted to define Mobile learning. According to Mcconatha, Praul and Lynch (2018), M-learning consists of learning using small computing portable devices including smartphones. Talan (2020) defines mobile learning as "the ability of learners to access information independently of time and space through mobile devices" while customizing their learning processes depending on their preferences and needs. M-learning is a subject that has evolved from distance learning and is now a subset of e-learning which incorporates the adoption of mobile technology (Alzaza and Yaakub 2012). Before studying this phenomenon or designing M-learning solution, it is recommended to know the benefit and constraints involved in other for the study result to be more efficient and useful for learners (Talan, 2020).

As its name suggests, one of the main features of mobile learning is mobility. Mobility in the context of M-learning can be analysed from three different angles namely: learners, learning and technology (Sinen, 2015). M-learning improves the mobility of learners because it eliminates physical barriers such that the learning process can occur anywhere. Portable devices enable learners to gain access to information and engage in forum discussions at their comfort irrespective of location (Latchem, 2018). With M-learning, "a student can learn whatever, wherever and any- time" through teaching applications installed on a portable device, such as a smartphone, iPods, tablet, notebook and so on (Khan et al., 2019). These devices are equipped with advanced attributes such as Wireless Fidelity (Wi-Fi) and Wireless Application Protocol (Hao et al., 2017). Hence, technology allows learners to be "always-on" through improved connectivity and internet access.

As a result, information is readily available at a click or a touch away, at arguably lower costs and the portability of devices offers the opportunity for a customized learning process (Talan, 2020). Students can tailor their learning tools and the environment as per their preferences. In a mobile learning environment, authenticity can be improved through contextualized learning exercises. Collaboration between learners is facilitated through the sharing of resources and improved networking connections. According to Al-Emran & Shaalan (2015), M-learning assists the interaction and sharing of knowledge between stakeholders.

M-learning comprises of certain limitations including "hardware and software problems caused by technologies, internet and infrastructure problems, screen, keyboard, battery problems of mobile devices" (Talan, 2020, p81). Since the elementary resources required for M-learning systems to work include electricity and good network connectivity (Ameen et al., 2019), "internet bandwidth and power failures" appear to be the most challenging issue of mobile learning (Khan et al., 2019). Moreover, a suitable mobile device is necessary to fully optimize the use of M-learning. These mobile devices are usually very expensive and might not fit a student's budget (Sabah, 2016). Additionally, Ryu (2009) highlights that the size of mobile devices also gives rise to input type challenges, followed by the issue of battery life of mobile devices used for M-learning. The size of the screens of mobile devices is relatively small and is inconvenient for learning purposes (Sabah, 2016). If used excessively, students might even face vision problems in the long run. Furthermore, mobile devices are limited in storage and hence hindering the sharing of information and resources (Sabah, 2016). Besides, Churchill & Hedberg (2008) think that bringing learning to mobile devices creates some form of dependence on the use of the battery life of devices.

Another major constraint to M-Learning is that of inconsistency in mobile devices platforms. Huang, Kuo, Lin, & Cheng, S. C. (2008) states that variability in devices very often led developers in designing mobile learning apps that are cross-platform, however lacking in certain functionalities due to the need to accomplish cross-platform operability. Looking at the constraint of M-learning from the perspective of learners' attention, it was found that M-learning seems to bring into factor multi-tasking which is not always a productive way to learn. Dolittle, Lusk, Byrd & Marianob (2009) in a study investigating the level of attention among groups of students who were sitting and working at a desktop as compared to those using mobile learning. It was found that the group of those students who happen to work on desktop computers scored higher test score as compared to those receiving content through m-leaning platforms. Subsequently, M-learning entails a form of considerable exposure to distraction through the use of mobile devices.

1.2 Traits of Millennials

Conventionally, the education system constituted of mass production and standard dissemination of knowledge (Rossing, Miller, Cecil & Stamper, 2012). However, in the current scenario, traditional learning and teaching approaches have become obsolete because students have changed drastically over the last years (Barnes, C Marateo & Ferris, 2018). Presently, a large proportion of students pertain to a group commonly referred to as Millennials. Millennials or the Net Generation is defined as a group of people who got exposed to technology since childhood and who have differing expectations from bodies of knowledge as compared to the preceding generations (Monaco & Martin, 2018). As described in Table 1 below, Millennials have distinctive traits that differentiate them from their predecessor generations.

Table 1. Traits of Millennials

Trait	Description
Freedom	Millennials feel entitled to freedom of choice in all aspects of life. They demand variety in consumption, and they do not compromise on their preferences.
Customization	Homogeneous goods and services do not appeal to Millennials. The Net Generation values personalization of various activities to gain maximum satisfaction.
Scrutiny	Net Geners have gained exposure to various media platforms and hence, information overload. Consequently, they analyze the validity and accuracy of data before acknowledging or accepting a statement, product or service.
Integrity	Millennials value Integrity such that they expect openness and honesty from businesses. They are very understanding of genuine mistakes.
Collaboration	Millennials can adapt easily to group work such that they are very efficient when working in teams. They are open to collaboration and sharing of ideas.
Entertainment	The Net Generation gives significant importance to their hobbies and relaxation time. They expect a good quality of entertainment in their routine to exploit their productivity
Speed	Millennials are confident users of technology. Activities are expected to be speedy and efficient. They expect good internet access so that they can acquire information promptly. Net Geners demand quick decision-making.
Innovation	Millennials adjust easily to changes and they constantly anticipate novelty, improvement and creativity. Goods must be innovative to match the demand of Net Genres.

Due to their incessant exposure to technology since birth, it is perceived that Millennials demands from academic institutions differ from that of their predecessors because of their distinct preferences and social interaction patterns (Prensky, 2001). Studies have inferred that the brain of a Millennial has developed differently as compared to other generations such that Millennials have a more acute vision and increased spatial awareness (Mthembu & Roodt, 2017). Tapscott (2009) identified 8 unique traits of the Millennials described in Table 1 above. This study is taking into consideration the above-mentioned traits to determine the attributes of Millennials in the research.

2. MATERIALS AND METHODS

This section explains the research methodology that is being followed throughout this empirical research. The following segment elaborates on various aspects of research such as approach, purpose and time frame, population, sampling method, data collection method, data collection instrument, method of analysis, and ethical considerations.

2.1 Research Approach and Time Frame

This research was conducted using an inductive approach. After data collection, a summary of the results was produced to describe the data. The description then brought knowledge of the technological ownership patterns as well as the most common traits of Millennials in higher education with regards to M-learning in South Africa.

A quantitative research approach was used by collecting data from online questionnaires which Millennials had to complete to describe their technological ownership about M-learning. A quantitative research method is best suited to assist the positivist research paradigm because it comprises the use of scientific methods to conclude.

A cross-sectional research study evaluates a sample at a point in time (Maree, 2016). The study was cross-sectional because the research investigated data collected from a population at a specific time. In other words, the study analysed the technology ownership and common trait of Millennials specifically during less than one year whereby the time spent on data collection did not affect changes in the data gathered.

2.2 Data Collection and Analysis

The research population involved students who are considered as Millennials studying at universities in South Africa. The accessible population consisted mainly of students at the University of Cape Town. The purposive sampling method was used because the study had to analyse data from a population. Homogenous purposive sampling also known as judgmental sampling is a non-probability sampling technique (Maree, 2016). In other words, a sample was chosen by taking into consideration the common traits of Millennials, year of birth and the country of study. The sample comprised mostly of students studying at the University of Cape Town who have been categorized as Millennials based on common traits and year of birth as specified by the sampling method. The common traits were established by a series of questions. The study received a total number of 120 responses. However, an initial clean-up of data was carried out to discard invalid responses. Eventually, the sample size consisted of 103 respondents.

Since new data had to be generated, for this research, a primary source of data was required. Hence, the data collection method consisted of a survey and the data collection instrument involved online questionnaires. The questionnaire had two sections: the demographics profile of the sample population section (which includes mobile ownership) and the Millennials classification section. The questions in the demographics profile section were related to age, year of study, place of study and mobile technology ownership. The questions in the Millennials classification section were set to determine if the sample population fit some of the characteristics identified by Tapscott (2009), as outlined in Table 1. The questions are related to the Year of Birth and the following traits: Technology Acquaintance, Innovation, Collaboration and Customization. This is to fit the sample population into a Millennial profile based on some of the common traits of Millennials as discussed by Tapscott (2009) and the year of birth.

The data analysis method selected for the study is descriptive statistics. The reason for this choice is simply to align with the nature of the study which is descriptive and not correlational. This study aims to summaries trends rather than compare relationship among variables. The descriptive analysis helped to describe patterns of technology ownerships as well as common traits of Millennials regarding M-learning in high school, mainly by using the percentage. Graphical representations of data helped to better visualize some of the findings.

2.3 Ethical Considerations

The study did not necessitate any confidential information and the respondent remained anonymous. A cover letter was attached to the questionnaire stating that participation in the survey was entirely voluntary and no personal details were published. Furthermore, the cover letter included a clear explanation of the purpose of the research and the contact details of the researcher were stated. Additionally, participants were given the option to withdraw from the survey at any point in time. Information collected was used for academic purposes only. Questioners were sent only after the approval from the Research Ethics committee of the University of Cape Town.

3. RESULTS AND DISCUSSION

This section consists of the analysis and representation of data collected for the study. The data analysis was carried out based on 103 participants as stated previously. Eventually, the section will proceed by describing the demographic profile of the sample and then the analysis of common attributes of Millennials based on data collected to show how the sample fits the desired profile. Eventually, an analysis will be given on the perceptions of Millennials in South Africa towards M-learning in higher education. The section will also include the statistical representation of data accompanied by narratives and interpretations. The findings of this study will be discussed thoroughly to answer the research questions.

3.1 Demographic Profile

This section will give an overview of the demographics of the sample population. The different elements that will be looked at consist of Age, Place of study/Location, and Year of study/level of education.

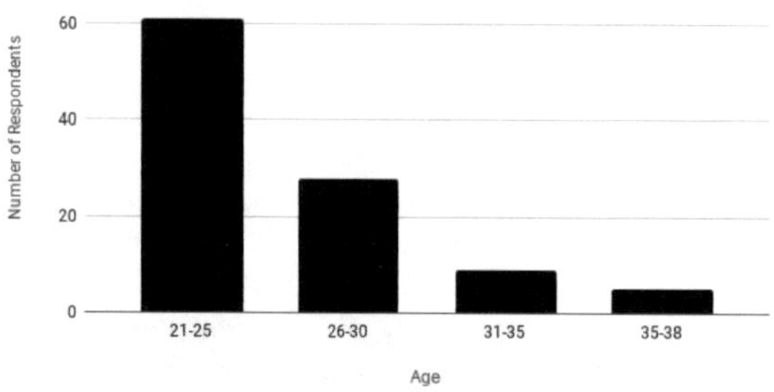

Figure 1. Age group of respondents

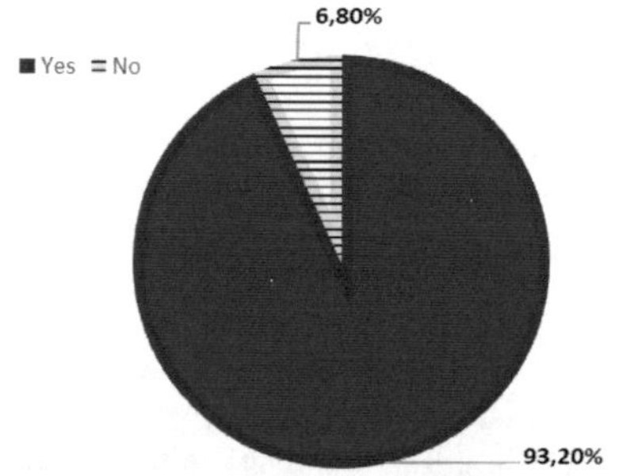

Figure 2. Respondents studying at a tertiary institution in a developing country

Figure 1 above gives a visual representation of the different age groups from which respondents were asked to choose. The age of the entire sample population lies between the range of 21 and 38 years old. As per the data collected, most of the respondents (approximately 60%) were in the age group of 21-25 years old. This is explained by the fact that the survey was carried out among university students. University students consist of mostly young people who enter tertiary education institutions immediately after secondary school. Having a high percentage of young respondents is significant and relevant in this study because it is believed that the younger generation is the most active users of mobile technology (Srivastava, 2005).

In the online survey carried out, participants were asked whether they study at a university or a tertiary institution in a developing country. As shown by Figure 2 above, a large proportion (93.2%) of the sample population replied "Yes" to the question asked while only around 6.8% of the respondents are not registered at a university in a developing country. For this study, the data gathered is relevant because this research is specifically investigating Millennials in the context of a developing country, in this case, South Africa.

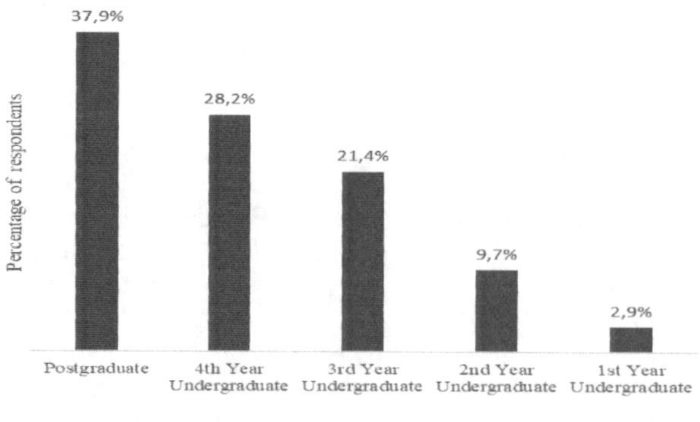

Figure 3. Year of study of respondents

To get an insight into the level of qualification of the sample population, the respondents were asked to choose their year of study. As shown by Figure 3 above, most of the respondents (37.9%) are doing their postgraduate studies while 28% of the sample population is in the fourth year of study at university. These percentages correspond to the age groups of the respondents.

3.2 Mobile Technology Ownership Pattern

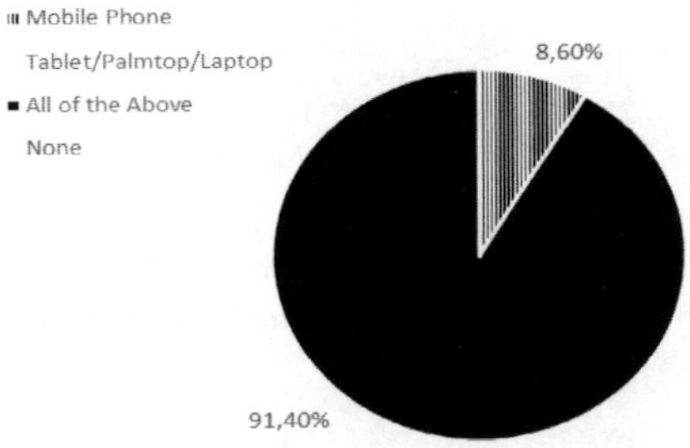

Figure 4. Mobile technology ownership pattern

Mobile phones, tablets, palmtops and laptops are popular examples of mobile technology devices. As per data collected, all the respondents owned a mobile phone. Figure 4 above shows that around 91.4% of the respondents owned either a tablet or a palmtop or a laptop in addition to a mobile phone. Since the sample data was collected in South Africa, it can be deduced that Graph 4 represents the mobile technology ownership pattern in a developing country. Furthermore, this attribute is vital and acts as a prerequisite given the subject of this study which is M-learning.

3.3 Millennials Classification – Common Traits

The key attributes driving the survey's questions includes Year of Birth, Technology Acquaintance, Innovation, Collaboration and Customization. For every attribute, respondents were asked to answer a question by "Yes" or "No", and the findings are summarized in Table 2 below. For the attributes, the results of the survey confirm the literature review such that it can be visually seen that Millennials, in general, do share some of the common traits which were identified by Tapscott (2009). It can also be observed that Technology Acquaintance and Innovation are the most relatable attributes of Millennials according to the sample population. Respondents were also asked if they consider themselves to be Millennials. 94.2% of the participants replied positively while 5.8% replied otherwise. The results discussed in this section confirms that overall, the sample population does consist of Millennials hence, validating the relevance of the research.

Table 2. Millennials classification

Response	Were you born between 1981 and 1996?	Have you been acquainted with technology since at least 10 years?	Do you get used to new technology relatively fast?	Do you adapt easily to group work?	Do you like customizing your belongings?
Attribute	Year of Birth	Technology Acquaintance	Innovation	Collaboration	Customization
Yes	99%	95.1%	85.4%	79.6%	78.6%
No	1%	4.9%	14.6%	20.4	21.4%

3.3.1 Year of Birth

For analytical purposes, the Millennial generation is born between 1981 and 1996 inclusive (Dimock, 2018). Participants of the survey were asked if their year of birth lies in the desired range. As shown in Table 2, a large majority of respondents positively responded to this question. 99% of the sample population stated that they were born between 1981 and 1996. Hence, based on year of birth, it can be deduced that the sample population consists of Millennials.

3.3.2 Technology Acquaintance

According to Tapscott (2009), Millennials have been familiar with technology since birth or at a very early stage of their life. The sample population has been asked if they are familiar with technology for at least 10 years. The results indicate in Table 2 that, out of the 103 respondents, 98 (95.1%) participants responded positively. Consequently, it can be deduced that the sample population is well acquainted with technology and hence, is relevant to the nature of the study while also meeting another key criterion of Millennials.

3.3.3 Innovation

As mentioned in the introduction section, innovation is a key attribute of Millennials. Millennials adjust to new technology relatively faster than the preceding generations and they are in a constant quest for innovation (Tapscott, 2009). Participants of the survey were asked if they adapt quickly to new technology. The descriptive statistics of the results are shown in Table 2. A large majority (85.4%) of the sample population meet this particular trait of Millennials.

3.3.4 Collaboration

Another trait of Millennials consists of collaboration. Millennials are very efficient and comfortable when working in a team (Tapscott, 2009). In this survey, as shown by Table 2, around 82 respondents gave a positive reply when asked if they can adapt easily to group work. Given the significant proportion of 79.6%, it can be inferred that the sample population meets the collaboration trait of Millennials.

3.3.5 Customization

The survey has also explored the customization trait of Millennials. According to Tapscott (2009), Millennials prefer customizing their assets. In Table 2, the frequency of people who admitted to preferring customization is high with 81 respondents. Subsequently, it can be established that the sample population tends to fit this characteristic of Millennials.

4. CONCLUSION

4.1 Summary of Findings

This study was primarily investigating technology ownership among Millennials in South Africa with regards to M-learning in higher education. The study has given an insight into the mobile technology ownership pattern amongst the participants of the survey. It has been found that the entire sample population owned at least one type of mobile devices, notably a mobile phone. Taking into account Sabah‘s claim of mobile devices being possibly very expensive for students (Sabah, 2016), it could be inferred that students surveyed have the financial means to purchase such a device given that they can afford the tuition fees of a university. Furthermore, it was found that Millennials, in general, do share some of the common traits which were identified by Tapscott (2009). It was also observed that Technology Acquaintance and Innovation are the most relatable attributes of Millennials according to the sample population. Conclusively, the data collected, and the data analysis method were relevant in reaching the research aim of this study.

4.2 Research Limitations

This section will briefly outline the limitations of this research. Firstly, time constraint proved to be a major issue. The Ethics application process and the approval from the Student Affairs had exceeded the time expected and as a result, there have been delays in the data collection process. Furthermore, the researcher had a lack of experience with regards to conducting research and analyzing data. However, a lot of support and guidance was received from the supervisor and the UCT Department of Information Systems which led to the successful completion of this study.

REFERENCES

Al-Emran, M., & Shaalan, K. (2015). Learners and educators attitudes towards mobile learning in higher education: State of the art. *2015 International Conference on Advances in Computing, Communications and Informatics (ICACCI)*, 907–913. https://doi.org/10.1109/ICACCI.2015.7275726

Alzaza, N. S., & Yaakub, A. R. (2012). [JOURNAL BI] Proposed Research Model for Students ' Acceptance of M-learning Services among Malaysian Higher Education. *UUM, July*, 4–6.

Ameen, N., Willis, R., Abdullah, M. N., & Shah, M. (2019). Towards the successful integration of e-learning systems in higher education in Iraq: A student perspective. *British Journal of Educational Technology*, *50*(3), 1434–1446. https://doi.org/10.1111/bjet.12651

Hao, S., Cui, M., Dennen, V. P., Türel, Y. K., & Mei, L. (2017). Analysis of mobile learning as an innovation in higher education: a comparative study of three countries. *International Journal of Mobile Learning and Organisation*, *11*(4), 314. https://doi.org/10.1504/IJMLO.2017.087080

Itu.int. 2021. *Statistics*. [online] Available at: <https://www.itu.int/en/ITU-D/Statistics/Pages/default.aspx> [Accessed 17 February 2021].

Kaliisa, R., Palmer, E., & Miller, J. (2019). Mobile learning in higher education: A comparative analysis of developed and developing country contexts. *British Journal of Educational Technology*, *50*(2), 546–561. https://doi.org/10.1111/bjet.12583

Khan, S., Hwang, G. J., Azeem Abbas, M., & Rehman, A. (2019). Mitigating the urban–rural educational gap in developing countries through mobile technology-supported learning. *British Journal of Educational Technology*, *50*(2), 735–749. https://doi.org/10.1111/bjet.12692

Latchem, C. (2018). *Mobile Learning* (pp. 29–35). Springer, Singapore. https://doi.org/10.1007/978-981-10-6741-9_4

Mwapwele, S. D., & Roodt, S. (2016). The extent of usage of mobile devices for learning outside the classroom in a secondary school in Tanzania. *International Conference on Information Resources Management 2016*, *Paper 15*, 1–11.

Serrano, D. R., Dea-Ayuela, M. A., Gonzalez-Burgos, E., Serrano-Gil, A., & Lalatsa, A. (2019). Technology-enhanced learning in higher education: How to enhance student engagement through blended learning. *European Journal of Education*, *54*(2), 273–286. https://doi.org/10.1111/ejed.12330

Sinen, H. Bin. (2015). A literature review on mobile learning. *Int. J. Social Media and Interactive Learning Environments*, *3*(3), 219–229. https://doi.org/doi:10.1504/IJSMILE.2015.072266

Talan, T. (2020). The effect of mobile learning on learning performance: A meta-analysis study. *Educational Sciences: Theory and Practice*, *20*(1), 79–103. https://doi.org/10.12738/jestp.2020.1.006

2020. *Measuring digital development: Facts and figures 2020*. [ebook] Geneva: International Telecommunication Union. Available at: <https://www.itu.int/en/ITU-D/Statistics/Documents/facts/FactsFigures2020.pdf> [Accessed 18 February 2021].

MOBILE LEARNING WITH THE DISK-ONLINE APPROACH

Marc Beutner[1] and Rasmus Pechuel[2]
[1]*Prof. Dr., Chair of business and human resources education II*
University of Paderborn, Warburger Str. 100, 33098 Paderborn, Germany
[2]*CEO Ingenious Knowledge, Friedrich-Karl-Str. 200, 50735 Cologne, Germany*

ABSTRACT

Mobile learning has become extremely important. In the challenging times of COVID-19 it is crucial to provide mobile solutions for learners which are easy to access and which provide solutions for direct feedback and interactive learning. The DISK-online approach describes settings that use tablets / laptops on the side of teachers and offers the chance to use any mobile device for the learners. This interaction setting reviewed by learners in a qualitative study in October 2020.

KEYWORDS

DISK-Online, m-Learning, Hybrid-Learning, COVID-19, Streaming

1. MOBILE LEARNING AS AN OPPORTUNITY TO COPE WITH THE CHALLENGES OF COVID-19

With regard to COVID-19 pandemic the situation is a tremendous challenge the world over. The pandemic affects economy, education, political decision making and daily life in many states and countries. When social distancing became crucial (Beutner & Pechuel 2020a, 2020b, 2020c) education was impacted directly. The situation has changed how we teach, learn and work together at schools, companies and education providers. In education we can see different ways of dealing with the challenges. Some countries focus on schooling at home and digital approaches, some on small groups and keeping distance at school. But, for such education providers digitisation has become more important. A large number of people come together in schools. So, the pandemic protocols must be carefully implemented. Countries developed diverse methods; some completely closed all schools and provide education entirely online, some use a mixture of online and onsite learning, while a few continue to use face-to-face learning with safety restrictions. Regardless, many decision makers in education across the globe recognise the importance of digital learning (cf. Beutner & Pechuel 2020c). 2015, O'Byrne and Pytas found that most schools lack technical equipment as well as lacking specific pedagogic or didactic concepts designed for this new method of learning.(cf. O'Byrne & Pytash 2015). Despite seeing a willingness to invest in technology, we see little pedagogical guidance for schools during the crisis. In additon, the technological boom period in which we are living, affects nearly all sectors (see eThink 2020) but despite having the technology readily available we are still struggling to use it efficiently. MLearning can be done with different devices. In 2009 Sharples et. al. found that over years the focus on mLearning changed from a minor research interest to "projects in schools, workplaces, museums, cities and rural areas around the world" (Sharples / et al. 2009). Meanwhile it has grown to a significant pillar of elearning in Europe, offering solutions for the COVID-19 situation. "Mobile learning is the use of portable devices, like mobile phones, tablets and laptops in pedagogical formal, non-formal and informal settings with an emphasis on supporting the learning process and the necessary feedback processes. It combines information exchange, acquisition of knowledge, collaboration and competence development and often offers the use of the internet as well." (Beutner, Pechuel 2020, 22 or 2012). Moreover, Mossavar-Rahmani & Larson-Daugherty stated in 2007 that "the hybrid format applies to any instruction where content is delivered both online and in onsite facilities." (Mossavar-Rahmani & Larson-Daugherty 2007, 67). In 2011 Movahedzadeh found that "integrating technology into the classroom in small steps is part of a natural evolution of teaching and learning" (Movahedzadeh 2011, 15). With regard to the research of Garrison & Vaughan 2008, Mayers et al. 2006 and Bonk & Graham she concluded that "a blended learning system includes a committed, sustained, and well thought-out implementation plan, combining appropriate technology with traditional classroom interaction, so that it leads to better outcomes for students." (Movahedzadeh 2011, 16). Taking this into account a step-by-step approach of hybrid learning is the basis for mobile learning activities in today's education and the basis of our DISK-Online approach.

2. DISK-ONLINE - MOBILE HYBRID LEARNING WITH STREAMING OF EDUCATION

This means that today mobile learning can also be provided in a hybrid way, which combines learning in the classroom with online learning like in a blended learning approach with a specific pedagogical and organisational design. The DISK-Online model offers a perspective to integrate mobile learning in combination with hybrid or online learning in educational scenarios. In 2011 Horn & Staker developed six models of blended learning, (a) the face-to-face driver model, (b) the rotation model, (c) the flex model, (d) online lab model, (e) the self-blend model and (f) the online driver model (cf. Horn & Staker 2011, p. 4-6 and see as well Beutner & Pechuel 2020c). All these different types of blended learning can be combined with our DISK-Online approach. The social ecological mobile learning integration framework of Crompton 2017 was considered when creating the DISK-Online approach. Crompton´s approach highlights several systems as well as practices involved in technology integration (Crompton 2017). It also illustrates that teachers' beliefs are influenced by the training they received concerning different ways of integrating mobile learning and the necessary devices in their teaching. Today, the use of mobile devices in education is also crucial for school because in 2020 Bernacki, Green & Crompton were able to underscore the importance of mobile technologies and different ways they can be used to enhance learning processes. DISK-Online stands for Didactic Interactive Streaming Know-how and this approach is designed for providing a quick solution to tackle the problems schools have when forced to implement distance learning in times of a pandemic. The DISK-online approach has four interaction levels and inexperienced teachers can start at the basic level on which interaction is quite low and focused on the teacher. In general DISK describes how teachers can connect with groups of learners through live streaming class content. Within the DISK-Online approach many schools or education providers are connected to a streaming platform. Teachers are using tablets or laptops to get connected and to stream educational processes. They just need the integrated camera and a streaming software like Streamlabs OBS (Beutner & Pechuel 2020a). Moreover, the learners can use their mobile devices at home (smart phones, tablets, laptops etc.), but also their computers to get easy access to the streaming platform just using a browser. This helps to provide hybrid learning in the classroom and via the internet without the need of too many technical resources. With DISK-online, teachers or trainers can decide to which degree of interaction the online part of learning should be enhanced. Beginning with DISK1, a level of eLearning where teacher centred interaction is in focus and only some interaction happens up to DISK4, a level of interaction where learner-oriented teaching and learning processes are in the centre and therefore, a much higher degree of interaction is needed. At each school several teachers can be in contact with the streaming platform and stream their individual class. Every teacher can decide on his or her own which interaction level is best for the class and the current IT competencies of teachers and learners. Therefore, one class may work on interaction level DISK1 while another is already on a higher level like DISK3. The stream of a teacher could also be used in another class or when the teacher is not available. This is helpful if the teacher is at home due to corona restrictions, when a teacher is in quarantine or if teachers implement team teaching in a second class:

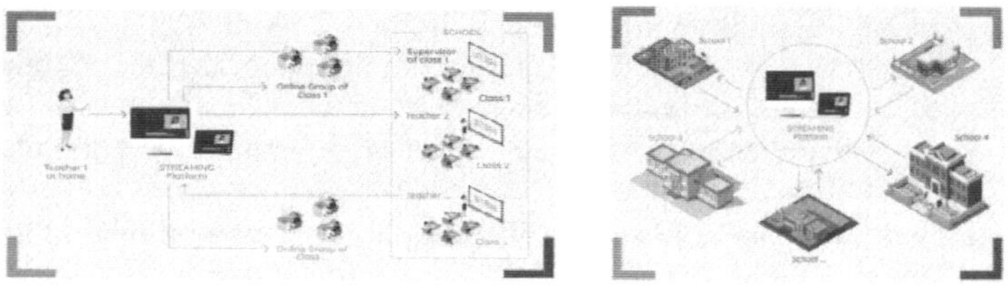

Figure 1. Streaming of a teacher from home and team teaching opportunities within the DISK-Online approach and streaming from different schools

The streaming platform can be connected with different schools and not only with one, which brings economies of scale into the learning process. At schools, different teachers / trainers may work on different DISK levels and can provide schooling at home as well as hybrid learning with different learning subgroups in their class. Different learning groups could switch between face-to-face learning in the classroom and online learning in a specific period of time which offers the opportunity that the numbers within each group are smaller and that every learner has the opportunity to see the teacher face-to-face within this period and can get direct feedback and has the possibility to clarify questions and take part in direct classroom interaction:

Table 1. Groups and subgroups within the DISK-Online approach (cf. Beutner & Pechuel 2020a)

	Subgroup of the class present in the classroom	**Subgroups of the class participating in the class online**
First day of teaching	Group A	Group B and Group C
Second day of teaching	Group B	Group A and Group C
Third day of teaching 3	Group C	Group A and Group B

After such organizational issues we focus on different levels of interaction that we call DISKs. Our idea is flexible and offers a model for basic learning arrangements. It can be enhanced by additional levels where interaction can be more intensified. In this article we focus on the basic levels from DISK1 up to DISK4 which can be used as a step-by-step approach to improve the degree of interaction. "The four implementation stages also show a transition from relatively teacher-centred teaching (in DISK1) to strongly learner-centred teaching (in DISK4). While in DISK1 a frontal teaching character for the online learners is paired with a teacher-dependent teaching character (from frontal, via activating to experience- oriented designing or moderating) for the face-to-face learners, DISK4 has a clearly group-oriented and target group-related orientation with a clear moderation role of the teachers." (cf. Beutner & Pechuel 2020c).

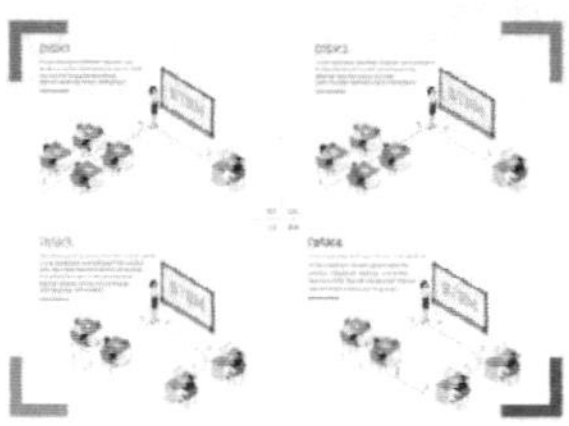

Figure 2. DISK-Online and the different DISK levels of interaction

Implementation Stage of Interaction level 1: DISK1

DISK1 is the easiest implementation level which offers simple teaching situations online in which the teacher shares the screen of a tablet and his or her voice in a live stream. It is one-way communication from a teacher to students. The tablet can be used like a whiteboard. Only small changes compared with traditional teaching can be found. DISK1 is suitable for classes with online students and students who are in the classroom.

Implementation Stage of Interaction level 2: DISK2

DISK2 adds interaction with the online group to DISK1. The teacher streams the lesson via a streaming platform but implements a way to communicate with the online students as well (e.g. text chat, for instance).

Implementation Stage of Interaction level 3: DISK3

DISK3 expands DISK2; adding interaction between online learners. It shifts the idea from a teacher-centred concept to one that focuses on the learners. Interaction between learners happens via text, voice or video chat.

Implementation Stage of Interaction level 4: DISK4

DISK4 adds the communication between online students and students in the classroom to DISK3. This means that there is a focus on the learners and the approach is better suited for group work of the learners.

3. SOME ISSUES ABOUT TECHNICAL REQUIREMENTS

From a technical point of view, it is possible to provide a system in which everything is preconfigured in such a way that teachers only have to start the devices and switch them off after their lessons. Especially at the DISK1 level the necessary technical knowledge of teachers is reduced to a minimum. This means that existing devices can be integrated without any problems. Technical components needed are:

WiFi Router and fast Internet Access: For schools it is important to access fast internet in order to stream videos. Streaming requires at least 5 Mbps. Having several streams simultaneously means that you share the available Mbps (megabits per second). A good wireless network is needed. This will make it easy for teachers to connect their tablets to the internet and ideally it also allows them to connect to a projector in the classroom without dealing with any cables. We highly recommend not to open the WiFi network that is used for streaming to students. WiFi routers are standard and there is a huge variety such routers available. It is crucial that teachers get good signal when streaming and a speed higher than the speed of the internet connection.

Projector and projection screen: Ideally classrooms have projectors that are mounted to the ceiling and have a wireless connection. Projection screens can be as simple as a white wall. There are many modern projectors that support wireless connections. So, a quick connection is offered to teachers who start sharing the screen with the projector so that the students who are present own the classroom can follow the class. However, it is of course possible to connect projectors with cables to tablets, in most cases you will just need adapters.

Tablet and Digital Pen: We recommend using a tablet to replace the blackboard. It is important to get a good digital pen to write and draw on the tablet. There are huge differences in quality when it comes to drawing with a digital pen on a tablet and teachers should be comfortable with. Compared to a blackboard a tablet offers a lot of advantages such as functions to draw straight lines or circles, different colours and thickness options, the option of including pre-made clipart pictures and the option of saving each screen for later use. There are many tablet choices, from small and cheap Android tablets to large touchscreen devices powered by Windows.

Microphone: A good microphone is essential. Many tablets are good at picking up sound with their internal microphones but viewers can feel a difference between internal microphones and external microphones that are connected. For teachers the easiest solution is a simple microphone that clips to the shirt and has a wire that plugs into the microphone port on the tablet. Sometimes an adapter is needed. For teachers who move around a lot there are wireless microphone solutions available that usually connect to the tablet via Bluetooth.

4. SOME STUDY RESULTS ABOUT THE USE OF MOBILE LEARNING IN THE DISK APPROACH

The hybrid mobile learning approach of the DISK-Online model was discussed with teachers and learners at VET schools in Germany in interviews and short questionnaires in September / October 2020. The interviews were analysed according to qualitative standards. In these cases, we used content analysis with regard to basic structures of Mayring 2000 and Strauss / Corbin 1998. We added interview tables and used MaxQDA for labelling and text analysis as well as paraphrasing. With both target groups (teachers and learners) the feedback on the DISK-Online approach was excellent. We conducted a total of 50 in person and telephone interviews with teachers and 35 telephone interviews with learners from VET and general schools. Moreover, we addressed 104 teachers at VET schools and 126 learners at VET schools with the quantitative survey. 31,7% of the teachers came from North-Rhine-Westphalia, 24% from Rhineland Palatinate, 23,1% from Hesse, 17,3% from Brandenburg and 3,8% from Bavaria. All addressed learners came from North-Rhine-Westphalia. The number of male (about 52%) and female (about 48%) was in both cases nearly equal. German learners stated that they enjoyed learning via the mobile opportunity at home. 94% stated that they had no problems getting a device and every learner said that they were able to get online after getting a device. 98% of the learners stressed that they had no problem connecting the streaming portal with mobile devices. Our learners mentioned that they would be happy to get direct explanations (33 of 35 learners) and would like to have more interaction. Learners who get accustomed to the DISK-Online idea would appreciate to use it more often at school (87%). First tests of the DISK-Online approach also took place with 15 teaching students in Germany providing brilliant results (Beutner & Pechuel 2020a) of this step-by-step approach. This highlights the importance of dealing with different interaction structures. 93,33% of the teacher students were ´very happy´ and one teacher stated that she was ´happy with the results´ (6,66% - 1 person). 93,33% found it very easy to use streaming for schooling at home and the other teacher answered that it was easy to use streaming. In the interviews the teachers stated that DISK-Online is perfect support in times of COVID-19. The teachers think that the concept enhances mobile learning and interactive activities at school. Many teachers described DISK-Online as a smooth path into hybrid learning and an opportunity to establish mobile approaches at school. 77,8% of the teachers had no contact with mobile learning before, these were 81 people. From those teachers who had no contact, 88,8% (72 teachers) would like to integrate DISK-Online in their teaching. Currently, the teachers are using different streaming platforms like Twitch but 86% of the teachers who provided feedback stated that they would appreciate a common streaming platform provided by the government.

5. CONCLUSION

The DISK-Online approach is a model to be tested on a broad scale. The current results are excellent. However, the approach currently just focuses on DISK1 to DISK4 and the interaction could be enhanced. Here other formats have to be discussed and tested to be integrated in the DISK-Online approach. The use of mobile learning in education can help cope with the challenges of COVID-19 and also offers the chance to implement hybrid learning after the COVID-19 pandemic. A crucial aspect is the need to get a common streaming platform which is safe for schools to use. If this were provided to schools by ministries or government agencies schools wouldn't have to find their own solutions and sort out difficult issues such as data security.

REFERENCES

Bernacki, M.L., Green, J.A. & Crompton, H. (2020). Mobile technology, learning, and achievement: Advances in understanding and measuring the role of mobile technology in education. *In Contemporary Educational Psychology*. Vol. 60, January 2020, pp 1-8. https://doi.org/10.1016/j.cedpsych.2019.101827.

Beutner, M. & Pechuel, R. (2012). *mLearning. Akzeptanz von Mobile Learning. Chancen und Probleme in der betrieblichen Bildung.* In Siepmann, F., Müller, P. (Eds.): Jahrbuch eLearning und Wissensmanagement 2013. Die Zukunft der Bildung und die Rolle der digitalen Medien. Albstedt 2012, pp. 30-34.

Beutner, M. & Pechuel, R. (2018). *Mobile Learning for Teachers. A Journey Through A World of new Opportunities!* Köln: Ingenious Knowledge. Retrieved form: http://www.eduproject.eu/mobile/downloads/GoMobile-Book-V4.pdf, access date: 18.10.2020.

Beutner, M. & Pechuel, R. (2020a). The use of streaming for online lessons – A basic implementation option in the context of the COVID-19 situation. *Proceedings of SITE Interactive Online 2020*. Currently in Print.

Beutner, M. & Pechuel, R. (2020b). *DISK-ONLINE - Basiskonzept für die Gestaltung von Online-Unterricht mit neuen Medien durch Lehrkräfte an Schulen - Einfache Umsetzungsmöglichkeiten im Rahmen von COVID-19.* Köln / Paderborn: Ingenious Knowledge.

Beutner, M. & Pechuel, R. (2020c). DISK Online Streaming Concept for hybrid learning – Dealing with the challenges of COVID-19 in learning settings. *Proceedings of Innovate Learning Summit 2020 Online. USA 2020.* Currently in Print.

Bonk, C.J. & Graham, C.R. (eds.) (2006). *The Handbook of Blended Learn-ing: Global Perspectives, Local Designs.* San Francisco: Pfeiffer.

Crompton, H. (2017). Moving toward a mobile learning landscape: Presenting a mlearning integration framework. *In Interactive Technology and Smart Education Journal*, Vol. 18, No. 2, pp. 97-109.

eThink (2020): *What is Hybrid Learning? How to Implement a Hybrid eLearning Strategy. 30th of March 2020.* Retrieved from: https://ethinkeducation.com/blog/what-is-hybrid-learning-how-to-implement-a-hybrid-learning-strategy/, Access Date: 01.10.2020.

Garrison, D.R. & N.D. Vaughan (2008). *Blended Learning in Higher Education: Framework, Principles, and Guideline.* San Francisco, CA: John Wiley and Son.

Mayers, P., S. Gialamas, S., Cherif, A., Stefurak, L., Graver, B. & Murkar, K. 2006. *DeVry University's iOptimize Integrated Learning System (Optimizing the Power of Onsite and Online Teaching and Learning).* Paper presentation. Academic Affairs Department, DeVry University, Oakbrook Terrace, IL. Retrieved from http://www.abourcherif.com/pdfs/iOptimizeIntegrating%20Learning%20System.pdf, July 9, 2011, Access Date: 01.10.2020.

Mayring, P. (2000). *Qualitative Inhaltsanalyse.* Forum Qualitative Sozialforschung / Forum: Qualitative Social Research. Online Journal,1(2). Retrieved from http://qualitative-research.net/fqs/fqs-d/2-00inhalt-d.htm, Access Date: 01.10.2020.

Mossavar-Rahmani, F. & Larson-Daugherty, C. (2007). Supporting the Hybrid Learning Model: A New Proposition. *In MERLOT Journal of Online Learning and Teaching*. Vol. 3, No.1, March 2007, pp. 67–77.

Movahedzadeh, F. (2011). Improving Students' Attitude Toward Science Through Blended Learning. *In Science education and civic engagement Journal.* Vol.3, No. 2, Summer 2011, pp. 13-19.

O'Byrne, W. I. & Pytash, K. E. (2015): Hybrid and Blended Learning. Modifying Pedagogy Across Path, Pace, Time, and Place. *In Journal of Adolescent & Adult Literacy.* Vol. 59, No. 2, September/October 2015, pp .137-140.

Sharples M., Arnedillo-Sánchez I., Milrad M. & Vavoula G. (2009). *Mobile Learning.* In Balacheff N., Ludvigsen S., de Jong T., Lazonder A., Barnes S. (eds). Technology-Enhanced Learning. Dordrecht: Springer, https://doi.org/10.1007/978-1-4020-9827-7_14

Strauss, A. & Corbin, J. (1998): *Basics of Qualitative Research. Techniques and Procedures for Developing Grounded Theory.* 2nd Ed., London 1998.

MOBILE ARTEFACTS AND LANGUAGE TEACHING, THE EXAMPLE OF THE SPOC+ PLATFORM

Hamed Asgari and Georges Antoniadis
Université Grenoble Alpes, Laboratoire LIDILEM, France

ABSTRACT

Devices which are used for mobile learning may be different and change over time, but the notion of mobility in all definitions is the only thing that does not change. With the progress in technologies and tools, teaching methods have to be updated too. In this article, the pedagogical and technological aspects of SPOC+ is investigated as a new mlearning platform. In this way, the platform is based on the SPOC, NLP tools and MIRTO project.

KEYWORDS

SPOC, NLP, MIRTO, mLearning, SPOC+, FLE

1. INTRODUCTION

Mobile devices such as smartphones and tablets that are the most widely used digital technology in the world (Bernacki et al., 2020), lead to reshaping learning and teaching by supporting, developing and enhancing course content, learning activities and student interactions with instructor, peers and learning content (Wu, 2014). Mobile learning is a growing area of academic interest by the rise and reach of mobile technologies. Mobile technologies are also more convenient for students as it corresponds to their daily use of mobile in everyday life (Sulisworo & Santyasa, 2018). A complete system of learning must combine technological advances and the facilitation of the teacher's tasks (who is not always an expert in the computer field) while at the same time bringing the possibilities of new technologies such as the use of Natural Language Processing (NLP) to enable continuous learning anytime, anywhere (Liu & Chen, 2015). Technologies break down many of the limitations and barriers of traditional teaching and promote individualized learning, feedback and interaction with the learner (Ahn & Lee, 2016). Small Private Online Course (SPOC), also known as the "post-MOOC[1] era" (Chen, 2019) has been created by professor Armando Fox (Fox, 2013) in 2013. It is an online course with a clear pedagogical objective, which suggests a form of formal registration (Kaplan & Haenlein, 2016) with a limited number of learners that allows for a personalized follow-up by the teacher, and learners, learn better in SPOC rather than MOOC environments (Fox et al., 2014).

As SPOC stimulates learners' interest in learning and encourages their participation, it is more attractive than traditional classrooms (Chen, 2019). Up to now, many of the educational theories and practices of SPOC have been implemented (Fox & Patterson, 2013), nevertheless, SPOC pedagogical case studies are used in renowned universities (Li et al., 2019).

As presented in our article (Asgari & Antoniadis, 2020), SPOC+ integrates SPOC and NLP tools for language learning, in this article we will examine the structure and functionality of our platform in more details. The main purpose of this study is to present a complete system for French language learning in the pursuit of the MIRTO[2] (Georges Antoniadis & Ponton, 2004) platform on mobile devices with modular tools.

---

[1] Massive Open Online Course

[2] Muti-Learning Interactive through Text and Oral Research (in French Multi-apprentissages Interactifs par des Recherches sur des Textes et l'Oral)

2. MOBILE LANGUAGE LEARNING

Nowadays language learning with mobile artefacts is so important because on one hand, second language brings considerable advantage for intellectual development (Diaz, 1984), and on the other hand education in the mobile age offers a way to extend the support of learning (Sharples et al., 2010). It was shown by Moura and Carvalho (Moura & Carvalho, 2009) that learners' attitudes and perceptions towards the effectiveness of mlearning in French language skills such as writing and reading are improved through the use of mobile phones and an increase in student motivation and satisfaction in individual and collaborative learning was seen. In the same line, SPOC+ proposes a new approach to learning the French language on mobile artefacts, a concept that did not exist before.

3. SPOC+

Our platform, SPOC+, with the base of SPOC, is in the continuity of the MIRTO project which was developed by Antoniadis.

The three key aims of MIRTO are:

- The set of NLP software resulting from scientific research and laboratories.
- The diversity and richness of textual and oral corpora.
- A set of NLP functions (NLP function is obtained from NLP software) (G. Antoniadis, 2008).

SPOC+ is designed with the same aims as MIRTO, a reliable and automated tool which is also easy to use by teachers who do not necessarily have computer skills. As MIRTO, our platform is modular and can accept new functionalities and updates according to advances in the NLP domain. Apart from our presentation site, SPOC+ consists of a web interface developed in the C# language with the ASP.net framework and SQL databases, intended only for the teacher and the administrative body and a mobile application developed on the React Native platform to be used on smartphones with Android or IOS operating system. The mobile application uses different APIs to communicate with the server.

We integrated the open-source and Windows compatible morphosyntax analyzer TreeTagger[3] with a reliability rate of 95.7% (Mars, 2016) which automatically provides texts with holes or multiple-choice exercises for 33 different labels such as adjectives, adverbs, determinants, interjections, nouns, numbers, interjections, prepositions, pronouns and verbs. According to these items and its pedagogical purpose, teacher can automatically create exercises and generates activities for learning the French language with any type of text he wants to use or refers to our text database. Even if it was necessary, teachers can take advantage of previous texts which have been updated by other teachers. Exercises that are generated automatically can be corrected automatically. We have designed our platform as simple as possible to allow the teachers who are not computer specialists to use the NLP and Computer-assisted Language Learning (CALL) tools and focus on the purely pedagogical aspects. If teachers are interested, they can use and propose exercises and activities that require manual correction.

A chat module is integrated into our platform to be used between each learner and his teacher; this tool allows a personalized follow-up. The Forum module is intended for collaborative work between learners of the same course and their teacher who is the forum moderator. The Forum module can be used to promote project-based learning.

We have added Google Analytics4 allows gathering usage data from each screen and buttons of SPOC+ mobile application, and Google's Firebase5 tools such as In-App Messaging and Cloud Messaging which will allow us to send targeted notifications which are easy to use for teachers or administrative members. The use of tracks will allow the teacher to adapt and improve their teaching strategy. The complete architecture is shown in figure 1.

[3] http://www.cis.uni-muenchen.de/~schmid/tools/TreeTagger/
[4] https://analytics.google.com/
[5] https://firebase.google.com/

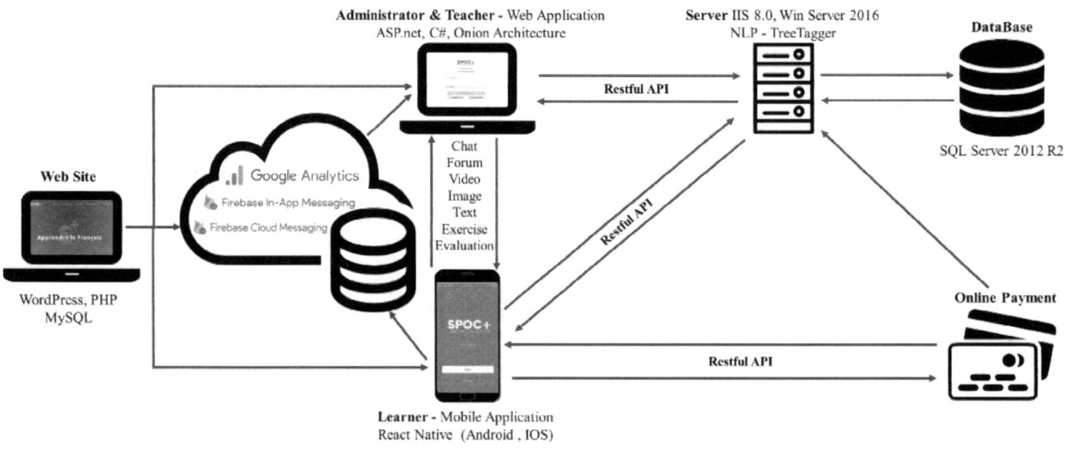

Figure 1. SPOC+ complete architecture

4. SPOC+ PEDAGOGY

Our project-based pedagogical approach is based on John Dewey (Dewey, 1986) work. According to Stephanie Bell (Bell, 2010) "Project-Based Learning (PBL) is a student-driven, teacher-facilitated approach to learning". The strategy of project-based pedagogy allows students to face a real situation (Biasutti & EL-Deghaidy, 2015) and promotes self-regulated learning in online mode (Bagheri et al., 2013). SPOC+ learners will be selected on pedagogical criteria beforehand to form a homogeneous group of learners of the same level. In our platform each course is divided into several lessons which includes a detailed pedagogical sheet made available by the teacher for the learners to view before the beginning of each lesson. For his pedagogical strategy each teacher could add videos, PDF and JPG files, soundtracks and texts for each lesson of his course. The videos made by the teacher, with a maximum duration of 15 minutes for each video, can be uploaded via the web interface dedicated to teachers. To allow learners to concentrate on the pedagogical content and avoid destabilization by the change of software (application) to perform the tasks required in their pedagogical processes; all videos, images, PDF documents, soundtracks and texts are presented directly in the SPOC+ mobile application, without the need of any third-party software. For the same purpose, the use of the chat and forum module is done directly in the SPOC+ mobile application. With the integrated chat and forum modules in our platform, the teacher not only transmits information, but also acts as a mentor, facilitator, tutor and mediator throughout the teaching process (Frank et al., 2003) to promote project-based learning. We have prepared a 4-week program to teach the French language to a pre-selected adult audience who decided to start B2 level based on the criteria set out by the CEFRL[6] in a non-French speaking country. At the end of the course, all data will be collected by two questionnaires on a mixed methodology (quantitative and qualitative) on learners' attitudes towards and perceptions of the use of SPOC+. A System Usability Scale (SUS) questionnaire defined by Brooke (Brooke, 1986), to gather users feedbacks on the ease of the use of our platform, and a second questionnaire to evaluate the pedagogical perception of our mobile learning system.

[6] Common European Framework of Reference for Languages

5. CONCLUSION

As it is described, our platform, SPOC+ is modular and enables the incorporation of new functionalities from scientific advances in the field of NLP as well as technological innovations, such as virtual reality and augmented reality. We have developed the SPOC+ learner interface only on smartphones, to allow learning anytime, anywhere. SPOC+ covers all four skills of learning language; listening, reading, speaking and writing. We plan to test our platform, collect data, analyze the results and evaluate the possibility of offering courses for other levels of French language learners.

REFERENCES

Ahn, T. youn, & Lee, S.-M. (2016). User experience of a mobile speaking application with automatic speech recognition for EFL learning : Speaking app with ASR. *British Journal of Educational Technology*, *47*(4), 778‑786. https://doi.org/10.1111/bjet.12354

Antoniadis, G. (2008). Du TAL et son apport aux systèmes d'apprentissage des langues. *Contributions. Habilitation à Diriger des Recherches, Université Stendhal Grenoble*, *3*.

Antoniadis, Georges, & Ponton, C. (2004). *Mirto : Un système au service de l'enseignement des langues*.

Asgari, H., & Antoniadis, G. (2020). SPOC, Future of M-Learning and Language Learning? *16th International Conference Mobile Learning 2020*, 128‑133.

Bagheri, M., Ali, W. Z. W., Abdullah, M. C. B., & Daud, S. M. (2013). Effects of project-based learning strategy on self-directed learning skills of educational technology students. *Contemporary educational technology*, *4*(1), 15‑29.

Bell, S. (2010). Project-Based Learning for the 21st Century : Skills for the Future. *The Clearing House: A Journal of Educational Strategies, Issues and Ideas*, *83*(2), 39‑43. https://doi.org/10.1080/00098650903505415

Bernacki, M. L., Greene, J. A., & Crompton, H. (2020). Mobile technology, learning, and achievement : Advances in understanding and measuring the role of mobile technology in education. *Contemporary Educational Psychology*, *60*, 101827. https://doi.org/10.1016/j.cedpsych.2019.101827

Biasutti, M., & EL-Deghaidy, H. (2015). Interdisciplinary project-based learning : An online wiki experience in teacher education. *Technology, Pedagogy and Education*, *24*(3), 339‑355.

Brooke, J. (1986). System usability scale (SUS) : A quick-and-dirty method of system evaluation user information. *Reading, UK: Digital Equipment Co Ltd*, *43*.

Chen, J. (2019). Exploration and Application of SPOC-based Belended Teaching Mode in Comprehensive English Course. *Journal of Physics: Conference Series*, *1237*, 022115. https://doi.org/10.1088/1742-6596/1237/2/022115

Dewey, J. (1986). Experience and education. *The Educational Forum*, *50*, 241‑252.

Diaz, R. M. (1984). *The intellectual power of bilingualism*.

Fox, A. (2013). From MOOCs to SPOCs. *Communications of the ACM*, *56*(12), 38‑40. https://doi.org/10.1145/2535918

Fox, A., & Patterson, D. (2013). *Software Engineering Curriculum Technology Transfer:* 9.

Fox, A., Patterson, D. A., Ilson, R., Joseph, S., Walcott-Justice, K., & Williams, R. (2014). Software engineering curriculum technology transfer : Lessons learned from MOOCs and SPOCs. *UC Berkeley EECS Technical Report*.

Frank, M., Lavy, I., & Elata, D. (2003). Implementing the project-based learning approach in an academic engineering course. *International Journal of Technology and Design Education*, *13*(3), 273‑288.

Kaplan, A. M., & Haenlein, M. (2016). Higher education and the digital revolution : About MOOCs, SPOCs, social media, and the Cookie Monster. *Business Horizons*, *59*(4), 441‑450. https://doi.org/10.1016/j.bushor.2016.03.008

Li, M., Qi, X., Song, M., & Li, Y. (2019). *The Feasibility Study of Blended English Teaching Based on SPOC*. *329*, 4.

Liu, P.-L., & Chen, C.-J. (2015). Learning English through actions : A study of mobile-assisted language learning. *Interactive Learning Environments*, *23*(2), 158‑171. https://doi.org/10.1080/10494820.2014.959976

Mars, A. (2016). *Le TAL au service desenseignants des langues : Mise en oeuvre d'une plate-forme pour l'enseignement du français et de l'arabe, langues étrangères.* [PhD Thesis, Grenoble Alpes]. http://www.theses.fr/2016GREAL031/document

Moura, A., & Carvalho, A. A. A. (2009). *Mobile phone appropriation and pedagogical mediation by students in educational contexts*.

Sharples, M., Taylor, J., & Vavoula, G. (2010). *A theory of learning for the mobile age : Learning through conversation and exploration across contexts*.

Ulisworo, D., & Santyasa, I. W. (2018). Maximize the mobile learning interaction through project-based learning activities. *Educational Research and Reviews*, *13*(5), 144‑149.

Wu, T.-T. (2014). The Use of a Mobile Assistant Learning System for Health Education Based on Project-Based Learning: *CIN: Computers, Informatics, Nursing*, *32*(10), 497‑503. https://doi.org/10.1097/CIN.0000000000000089

AI-ENABLED GAMIFICATION FOR LEARNING AND ASSESSMENT

Stephen Bezzina, Alexander Pfeiffer[1] and Alexiei Dingli[2]
[1]*Dr*
[2]*Professor*
Department of Artificial Intelligence, Faculty of ICT, University of Malta, Malta

ABSTRACT

Games and gamification can potentially inform and transform learning by providing meaningful and engaging learning environments. The application of Artificial Intelligence (AI) algorithms and systems in education is envisaged as an opportunity to provide students with adaptive and personalized learning, especially in the context of mobile learning and assessment. However, such endeavors highly contrast with the provision of standardized test-driven curricula, which continue to force assessment practices to endure a meagreness of pedagogical innovation and transformation (Perrotta and Whitelock 2017) and which remain the fixation of formal educational institutions (Hazelkorn 2014). This short paper comprises of the initial theoretical framework for a proposed academic research, which seeks to critically analyze the traditional quantification of learning and the processes for measuring and certifying academic achievement, in view of a more adaptive, personalized and engaging learning and assessment experience, put forth and underpinned by gamification and AI. Consequently, the main research question that will be addressed is: What is the effect of AI-powered gamification on students' learning and assessment experience? A mixed-methods approach involving both qualitative and quantitative data at different stages of the research will be adopted. A number of distinct data sources will be targeted, including students, educators, game designers and AI scientists. The proposed research, has the potential to contribute new and original insights to the body of knowledge and practice in the fields of Gamification and Artificial Intelligence, whilst providing a solid foundation for future academic studies.

KEYWORDS

Learning, Assessment, Gamification, Artificial Intelligence

1. INTRODUCTION

Early influential scholars and academics in the field of psychology and education have closely linked play and games to cognitive development and learning (Bruner 1983, Dewey 1910, Piaget 1962, Vygotsky 1978). This has nourished the professional interest of educators in using games for educational purposes (Dingli et al 2013, Gee 2017, Steinkuehler 2016, Wernbacher et al 2020), as the native game environments, including gameplay and game mechanics, have begun to resemble and support prime learning contexts (Camilleri et al 2017, Franco & DeLuca 2019). Similarly, Artificial Intelligence (AI) has lately risen to the fore as an emerging technology underpinned by autonomous and adaptive functions, which are capable of providing personalized education in view of 'the persistent and unsolved challenges of learning in the 21st century' (Luckin et al 2016, p 51), especially in the context of mobile learning and assessment (Liu et al 2010).

This short paper comprises of the initial theoretical framework for a proposed academic research, which seeks to critically analyze the traditional quantification of learning and the processes for measuring and certifying academic achievement, in view of the adaptive and personalized learning and assessment, underpinned and put forth by gamification and AI, in a truly anytime anywhere context. Such endeavors highly contrast with the provision of standardized test-driven curricula, which continue to force assessment practices to endure a meagreness of pedagogical innovation and transformation (Perrotta and Whitelock 2017) and which remain the fixation of formal educational institutions (Hazelkorn 2014).

2. GAMIFICATION AND ARTIFICIAL INTELLIGENCE

The broad use of games in teaching and learning, defined as and exemplified in game-based learning (Homer et al 2020), has resulted in the design and development (Dingli and Seychell 2015) and actual deployment of games in education (Panoutsopoulos and Sampson 2012, Sykes 2018). Research suggests that, potentially, digital games and other game-based methods can support and allow for higher cognitive gains and improved attitudes towards learning than traditional didactic methods (Posso 2016). In recent years, games have also seen their adoption in education materialize on a novel conceptual dimension. The theoretical basis underpinning the term gamification or the 'use of game design elements in non-gaming contexts' (Deterding et al 2011, p 1), moves away from the deployment of actual games in learning contexts but instead focusses on the use of specific design elements, including game mechanics and thinking to engage and solve problems (Pfeiffer et al 2020). Initial empirical research on the utilization of gamification in education suggests positive effects on students' engagement and motivation (Kingsley and Grabner-Hagen 2015, Leaning 2015). On the other hand, critics argue that gamification largely relies on basic reward systems like points, badges and leaderboards which simplify and exploit game design elements, resulting in a false sense of achievement (Woodcock and Johnson 2018). The relationship between gamification and cognitive development and learning remains largely unexamined as the limited empirical evidence existing with respect to gamification in education is mostly related to students' motivation and engagement (Alsawaier 2018, Jayalath and Esichaikul 2020).

As an interdisciplinary field, AI has been adopted to diverse contexts, ranging from healthcare, criminology to linguistics and education (Canbek and Mutlu 2016). Over the last twenty years, the field of AI in Education (AIEd) has undergone important developments in areas such as grading automation, adaptation to students' needs, predictive analysis of students' learning, differentiation and personalization of learning activities, real-time learning analytics, anytime-anywhere support from AI tutors and targeted individualized feedback (Dingli and Montaldo 2019, Montebello 2018, Roll and Wylie 2016). The application of AI algorithms and systems in education continues to gain momentum. As such, as a prominent emerging technology that is pushing new boundaries in the educational sector, AI has the potential to improve the overall quality of teaching and learning (Chen et al 2020). However, notwithstanding that various AIEd systems have been developed over the years, limited scientific evidence of the impact on the quality of learning is available (Canbek and Mutlu 2016).

In the context of mobile learning and assessment, continued access to a motivating and engaging educational environment, which provides students with personalized and adaptive learning is even more crucial for the holistic learning and assessment experience. As such, the proposed research will investigate the use of machine learning and behavioral analytics to improve the overall gamification experience of students learning and assessment. Through the build of intrinsic motivation, this will be aimed at improving the students' cognitive learning, whilst gaining insights and anticipating risks, by allowing for dynamic learning objectives, feedback and rewards (amongst others), underpinned by AI.

3. AIM AND RESERCH QUESTION

The aforementioned conceptual and pragmatic novelties in education contrast with the paucity of pedagogical and technological innovation that traditional assessment modes and practices have continued to suffer along the years (Perrotta and Whitelock 2017). The ability of games to resemble active and constructivist learning environments (Homer et al 2020) and the potential of AI in education to power teaching and learning (Luckin et al 2016) can possibly transform assessment tasks into a more authentic, situated and experiential form of assessment for learning (Bezzina 2019, Mohamed and Lebar 2017). However, due to the fairly novel pedagogical models underpinned by gamification and AI, specifically in the field of learning and assessment, extremely limited empirical evidence exists regarding the effectiveness, especially in terms of pre-defined learning outcomes (Attali and Arieli-Attali 2015). As such, the aim of the proposed research is to constructively align gamification and AI to digital assessment, in order to provide a more personalized and adaptive assessment experience for students.

Consequently, the main research question that will be addressed is: What is the effect of AI-powered gamification on students' learning and assessment experience? In order to investigate how gamification and AI can potentially inform the learning and assessment practices and effectively improve the overall students' assessment experience, this overarching question will be further broken down into four research questions. More specifically, the research project will seek to answer the following:
(Q1) How are educators conducting learning and assessment?
(Q2) How are educators using gamification and AI for learning and possibly assessment practices?
(Q3) What are the principles of learning and assessment found in gamification and AI, which could potentially inform assessment practices?
(Q4) Does an AI-powered gamification approach to learning and assessment improve students' satisfaction, engagement and cognitive learning?

4. METHODS

A mixed-methods approach involving both qualitative and quantitative data at different stages of the research will be adopted. A number of distinct data sources will be targeted, including students, educators, game designers and AI scientists. Initial data in the first part of the research, will involve preliminary interviews with a small, purposive sample of educators on the themes of learning and assessment, gamification and AI. Data elicited from these interviews will be used to create a survey aimed at a wider audience of educators. This will investigate the different ways in which educators are conducting learning and assessment in their own contexts (Q1) and more importantly, will examine the use of gamification and AI for learning and possibly assessment practices (Q2). In the second phase of the first part of the research, another round of interviews, again with a small, purposive sample of educators and the inclusion of a sample of game-designers and AI scientists will be held. These will examine the views of the interviewees on the principles of learning and assessment found in gamification and AI and how these could potentially inform assessment practices. This will serve as the basis for another survey, again aimed at educators (Q3).

In the second part of the research, the resulting data from Q1, Q2 and Q3 will be quantitatively evaluated through the capacity of AI-powered gamification approach to act as a catalyst for improvement in the students' learning and assessment experience, in terms of satisfaction, engagement and cognitive learning (Q4). The latter will be operationally defined as the score or grade obtained on standardized tests measuring the different levels of the cognitive domain set by Bloom's taxonomy of educational objectives (Bloom 1956). This will be achieved through a switching replications quasi-experimental design (Trochim 2001). This type of non-equivalent group design allows for the lack of random assignment of the two intervention groups and is built on two phases and 3 stages of measurement. Both groups of students start with a pre-test on the constructs of interest. As such, a survey attesting students' satisfaction and engagement in digital assessment practices, together with a standardised test measuring students' cognitive learning will be administered to all participants. One group will then act as the control for the experimental group. At the end of the AI-powered gamification intervention, both groups will be post-tested on the respective constructs. In the second phase of the design, the groups switch their functions (the control group becomes experimental and vice-versa) and again, both groups are post-tested on the same constructs. This research design is very strong with respect to internal validity and may enhance external validity and reliability, while being one of the most ethically just and unbiased quasi-experiments since all participants receive the educational intervention (Trochim 2001). Thematic analysis will be used to analyse the data resulting from the interviews, while the surveys' data will be analysed in SPSS (IBM 2010) using frequency and crosstabs analysis, while a reliability-corrected analysis of covariance (ANCOVA) (Trochim 2001) will determine whether there are any statistically significant differences, including effect size, between the means of the scores for the constructs of interest (satisfaction, engagement and cognitive learning), between the two groups, attributed to the educational intervention.

5. CONCLUSION

The proposed research, based on the author's personal and professional development interests, has the potential to contribute new and original insights to the body of knowledge and practice in the fields of Gamification and Artificial Intelligence. The critical evaluation of the innovative application of AI-powered gamification to learning and assessment is aimed to inform and influence future thinking and practice in the respective scholarly areas. Although not immediately generalizable, the theoretical and empirical stances of the proposed research are aimed at a paradigm shift in formative assessment conceptualizations and practice, while providing a solid foundation for future academic studies.

REFERENCES

Alsawaier, R. S., 2018. The effect of gamification on motivation and engagement. *The International Journal of Information and Learning Technology*.

Attali, Y. and Arieli-Attali, M., 2015. Gamification in assessment: Do points affect test performance? *Computers & Education,* Vol 83, pp 57-63.

Bezzina, S., 2019. Games, Design and Assessment: How Game Designers are Doing it Right. *European Conference on Games Based Learning* Odense, Denmark, pp 67-73.

Bloom, B. S., 1956. *Taxonomy of Educational Objectives, Handbook I: The Cognitive Domain*. David McKay Co Inc, New York, USA.

Bruner, J., 1983. Play, thought, and language. *Peabody Journal of Education* Vol. 60, No. 3, pp 60-69.

Camilleri, V. et al, 2017. Games and Citizen Engagement: Towards Democracy 3.0. In *World of Games 360° - Anthology of the Center for Applied Games Research*. Danube University Krems.

Canbek, N.G. and Mutlu, M.E., 2016. On the track of artificial intelligence: Learning with intelligent personal assistants. *Journal of Human Sciences* Vol. 13, No. 1, pp 592-601.

Chen, L. et al, 2020. Artificial Intelligence in Education: A Review. *IEEE Access* Vol 8, pp 75264-75278.

Deterding, S. et al, 2011. Gamification. using game-design elements in non-gaming contexts. In *CHI '11 Extended Abstracts on Human Factors in Computing Systems*. New York, USA, pp 2425-2428.

Dewey, J., 1910. *How We Think*. MA: D.C. Heath & Co, Boston, USA.

Dingli, A. et al, 2013. Games in the classroom. *ICERI2013 Proceedings*, pp 2846-2852.

Dingli, A., Montaldo, L., C., 2019. Aspects of an Artificial Intelligence Assisted Learning (AIAL) System, In *Embracing Digital Learners in an Age of Global Educational Change and Rapid Technological Advancements* (IGI Global): pp 317-338.

Dingli, A., Seychell, D., 2015. *The New Digital Natives: Cutting the chord.* Springer, Berlin, Germany.

Franco, P. F. and DeLuca, D. A., 2019. Learning through action: Creating and implementing a strategy game to foster innovative thinking in higher education. *Simulation & Gaming* Vol 50, No 1, pp 23-43.

Gee, J.P., 2017. Affinity spaces and 21st century learning. *Educational Technology* pp 27-31.

Hazelkorn, E., 2014. Reflections on a Decade of G lobal Rankings: what we've learned and outstanding issues. *European Journal of Education* Vol 49, No 1, pp 12-28.

Homer, B. D. et al, 2020. Games as Playful Learning: Implications of Developmental Theory for Game-Based Learning. In *Handbook of Game-Based Learning*. J. L. Plass, R. E. Mayer and B. D. Homer (Eds.) MIT Press, Cambridge, USA, pp 25-52.

Jayalath, J. and Esichaikul, V., 2020. Gamification to Enhance Motivation and Engagement in Blended eLearning for Technical and Vocational Education and Training. *Technology, Knowledge and Learning* pp 1-28.

Kingsley, T. L. and Grabner-Hagen M. M., 2015. Gamification: questing to integrate content, knowledge, literacy, and 21st-century learning. *Journal of Adolescent & Adult Literacy* Vol 59, No 1, pp 51-61.

Leaning, M., 2015. A study of the use of games and gamification to enhance student engagement, experience, and achievement on a theory-based course of an undergraduate media degree. *Journal of Media Practice* Vol 16, No 2, pp 155-170.

Liu, Q., Diao, L. and Tu, G., 2010. The application of artificial intelligence in mobile learning. In *2010 International Conference on System Science, Engineering Design and Manufacturing Informatization* Vol 1, pp 80-83.

Luckin, R. et al, (2016). *Intelligence unleashed: An argument for AI in education*. Pearson, London, UK.

Mohamed, R. and Lebar, O., 2017. Authentic assessment in assessing higher order thinking skills. *International Journal of Academic Research in Business and Social Sciences* Vol 7, No 2, pp 466-476.

Montebello, M., 2018. *AI Injected e-Learning*. Springer, Switzerland.

Panoutsopoulos, H. and Sampson, D, 2012. A study on exploiting commercial digital games into school context. *Educational Technology and Society* Vol 15, No 1, pp 15-27.

Perrotta, C. and Whitelock, D., 2017. Assessment for learning. In *Technology Enhanced Learning*. Springer, Cham, Switzerland, pp 127-135.

Pfeiffer, A. et al, 2020. Beyond Classical Gamification: In-and Around-Game Gamification for Education. In *Proceedings of the 19th European Conference on E-Learning*. C. Busch, M. Steinicke and T. Wendler (Eds). University of Applied Sciences HTW, Berlin, Germany, pp 415-420.

Piaget, J., 1962. *Play, Dreams and Imitation in Childhood*. Norton, New York, USA.

Posso, A., 2016. Internet usage and educational outcomes among 15-year old Australian students. *International Journal of Communication* Vol 10, p 26.

Roll, I. and Wylie, R., 2016. Evolution and revolution in artificial intelligence in education. *International Journal of Artificial Intelligence in Education* Vol 26, No 2, pp 582-599.

Steinkuehler, C., 2016. Videogames as a serious medium. *On the Horizon* Vol 24, No 2, pp 175-178.

Sykes, J.M., 2018. Digital games and language teaching and learning. *Foreign LanguageAnnals* Vol 51, No 1, pp 219-224.

Trochim, W. M. K., 2001. (2nd ed.) *Research Methods Knowledge Base*. Atomic Dog Publishing, Ohio, USA.

Vygotsky, L. S., 1978. *Mind in Society*. Harvard University Press, Cambridge, USA.

Wernbacher, T. et al, 2020. Create Digital Games for Education: Game Design as a teaching Methodology. In *Proceedings of ICERI2020 Conference* Vol 9, pp 10-16.

Woodcock, J. and Johnson, M. R., 2018. Gamification: What it is, and how to fight it. *The Sociological Review* Vol 66, No 3, pp 542-558.

SCRATCH JUNIOR APP IN PRESCHOOL EDUCATION

Tatiana Havlaskova, Tomas Javorcik and Katerina Kostolanyova
University of Ostrava
Frani Sramka 3, Ostrava, Czech Republic

ABSTRACT

In a world where new technologies appear all the time, offering a vast amount of information, entertainment and games, it is children who are one of the most attractive target groups. However, since they cannot distinguish between right and wrong, they are also the most vulnerable one. Therefore, it is vital that children start to learn about digital technology at the preschool age. And if teachers intend to use digital technology in preschool education, they need to educate themselves in this area. The first part of the paper focuses on the changes in Czech preschool education that digital technology will bring about. The second part of the paper centers on how future kindergarten teachers are being prepared for those changes at the Pedagogical Faculty of the University of Ostrava – work with a touch device, work with the Scratch application and its implementation in the teaching of preschoolers.

KEYWORDS

Digital Technology, Preschool Education, Scratch Junior, Activities

1. INTRODUCTION

Even though a large number of Czech teachers are not happy about it, technological development cannot be stopped. Digital technology is everywhere – one encounters it in their working life, spare time, it is used for entertainment, and is gradually becoming an integral part of (modern) education. Almost everyone is familiar with smartphones, tablets, fitness trackers, smartwatches, etc.

When incorporating digital technology into instruction, it is important how and for what purpose it is used. On the one hand, it can help modernize instruction and make it more attractive for pupils. On the other hand, it can easily be used for non-educational purposes. The teacher needs to establish a set of ground rules for working with digital technology, and pupils need to adhere to those rules. Digital technology also requires changes in the organization of instruction and didactic and assessment methods.

Since games are the most important part of preschool education, all digital technology-based education activities should be games. Digital technology can help children develop their critical and logical thinking, as well as the key competencies. According to Kalaš and Moravčík (2012), digital technology is *"a wide set of resources, processes and knowledge used to process and communicate information. In education, those are computational and communication resources, processes and information sources that, in one way or another, enhance the education process".*

Using different criteria, digital technology can be divided into different categories. Kalaš (2011) argues that in preschool education digital technology is divided into two large groups:

- Standard division – hardware and software
- By purpose – research and discovery tools, construction tools, recording tools, communication tools, role-playing tools, tools for those with special educational needs

Digital technology-based educational activities used in kindergarten are based on experimentation, discovering and children's personalities. If preschool teachers are to use digital technology to help their pupils develop digital literacy and digital competencies, they need to continually educate themselves in this area.

2. DIGITALIZATION IN PRESCHOOL EDUCATION

The Ministry of Education, Youth and Sports of the Czech Republic created the so-called digital strategy, which focuses on the integration of digital technology into education. Speaking of the so-called awakening of digital education, Švancar (2016) argues that "the Digital Education Strategy is more than just a school document as it also covers non-formal education in an extracurricular environment. Schools need to make sure their teachers know how to use digital technology and effectively incorporate it into instruction".

2.1 Strategy for Education Policy of the Czech Republic until 2030

A document titled Strategy for Education Policy of the Czech Republic until 2030+ was published at the end of June 2020. It is a set of guidelines that should help solve the problems of the Czech education system, taking into account the changes that are happening in society. The goal of the Strategy 2030+ is to modernize the education process in order to help children be successful in this dynamic 21st-century world.

The Strategy 2030+ has two main goals (Fryč et al, 2020):

1. Transform educational content and methods,
2. Reduce educational inequality and develop potential of all children.

The Strategy is divided into three implementation stages. The following issues will be addressed during the first stage (MEYS, 2020):

- Preschool education support.
- Revision of the primary education curriculum document; methodological support.
- School management and teacher support.
- Subject system upgrade.
- Improving quality of education in structurally challenged regions.

2.1.1 Preschool Education Support

The main goal is to continuously improve the quality of preschool education and include more children in it. In order to achieve this goal, educational content needs to be transformed, focusing on the key competencies, teacher support and individualized approach. Four measures with related key activities were created. This paper focuses on two of the measures and activities, respectively (Fryč et al, 2020):

- Revision of the preschool education curriculum document and improving the quality of preschool education
    - **Updating the curriculum document** – mastering the key competencies, development of motor skills, initiative, **independence, problem-solving, creativity, team collaboration**, age appropriate **use of technology**.
- School management and teacher support
    - **Improving the quality of preparatory education** – analyze the quality of secondary and university education with respect to practice requirements, and accordingly update **educational content and methods at all educational levels.**

If the current generation of students are to become teachers who are not only unafraid to use digital technology, but are aware of its pros and cons, the changes specified in the Strategy 2030+ need to be implemented, i.e. updating the curriculum of existing courses, designing new courses that would teach future teachers how to use digital technology to help pupils develop their logical thinking, pre-mathematical skills, creativity and, last but not least, communication and collaboration.

3. PREPARATION OF FUTURE PRESCHOOL TEACHERS

In the study program Kindergarten Teacher Training at the Pedagogical faculty of the University of Ostrava, future teachers learn how to incorporate digital technology into instruction in the course **Kindergarten Informatics**. In the course future teachers learn how to effectively use digital technology in preschool activities. Students learn (among other things):

- To choose and implement appropriate digital learning resources (based on various criteria),
- How to use digital learning resources to help develop literacy, mathematical concepts, problem-solving skills and computational thinking,
- To create their own digital technology-based educational activities to help their pupils develop the aforementioned skills.

Students are able to practice the aforementioned skills; they are assigned tasks designed to make them think about the pedagogical-psychological aspect of the solution.

In the course students become acquainted with a number of digital learning resources, from tablets to robotic toys to all kinds of applications and open source software, that can be used in preschool education. The application Scratch Junior have been extremely popular with students as it can be used for developing imagination, creativity, spatial awareness and computational thinking.

3.1 Proposal of Educational Activities in Scratch Junior App

The Scratch Junior app is ideal for teaching algorithmization and programming. Suitable for little children, this app has a simple user interface, making it perfect for kindergarten. The app includes commands for movement (step, turn), output commands (conversation, sounds), cycle commands (repetition) and simplified conditions. There can be several figures on the screen at the same time that can communicate with each other.

The Scratch Junior app supports visual programming. Using intuitive commands represented by well-known symbols that fit together like puzzle pieces, it allows users to program in an easy, creative and enjoyable manner. As a result, children can create everything from simple animations to stories with interesting plotlines. Scratch Junior is a free app available for smart devices as well as desktop computers.

In the Kindergarten Informatics course, students tried programming in the Scratch Junior app on all types of devices. Their task was to design an activity for children between the ages of 4 and 6. Some of the activities are described below.

Activity 1

Activity title: Astronaut returning to Earth from the Moon

Activity goal: Combination of movements, programming creativity, being aware of the sequence of steps.

Instructions: Choose an astronaut and a rocket from the menu and change the background setting to Space. Position the rocket on the left and the astronaut on the right. Program the astronaut to come closer to the rocket, so the rocket could take off and return back to Earth. Figures 1 and 2 show the possible sequences of steps.

Figure 1. Astronaut character and its program

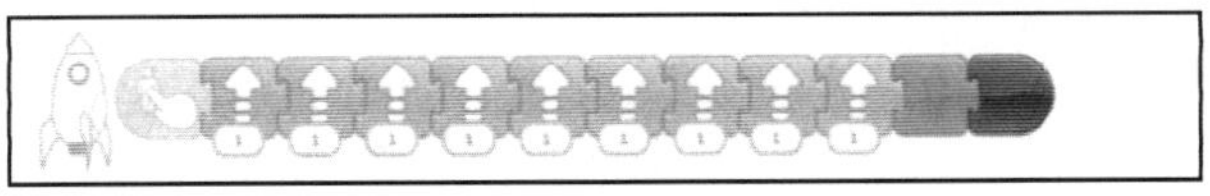

Figure 2. Rocket character and its program

Activity 2

Activity title: Fun Park

Activity goal: Developing creativity, becoming familiar with basic geometric shapes, connecting characters and their movements.

Instructions: Create a fun park. The Sun is shining and there is a dog running around, with the Sun turning around, looking like a ring, and the dog running around, creating a square with his movement. Figures 3 and 4 show the possible sequences of steps.

Figure 3. Sun character and its program

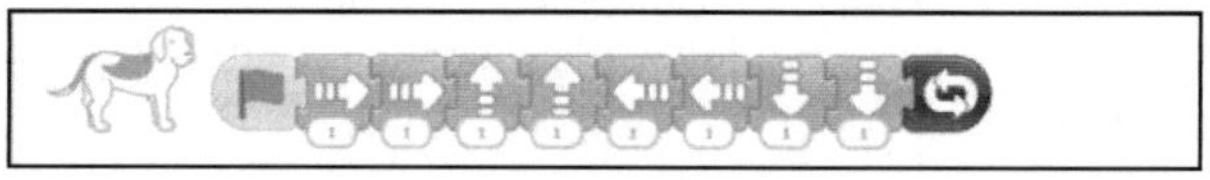

Figure 4. Dog character and its program

3.2 Implementation of Activities

Students had the opportunity to apply these activities created within the course to teaching in kindergartens. The activities were included in the educational area "Child and his psyche" and "Child and the world". What was the goal of the activities? Focusing on the development of cognitive abilities, imagination and fantasy, thought operations, creativity and fine motor skills. At the same time, the goal was to build awareness of one's own relationship with the world, with animate and inanimate nature, the planet Earth. An iPad with the Scratch Junior app was used as an aid – one iPad for a group of 2 to 3 children. A time of 30 minutes was set aside for one activity. The age structure of the children ranged from 4-6 years. Number of children: 15.

The children sat in a circle and before the start of the activity, the motivational part took place: *Have you ever played with a tablet? What games do you like? Today I brought you iPads and we will play with them together. What do you think about it? Want to play with iPads?*

First, it was necessary to gen up the children with the environment of the application – how the application is launched, description of individual parts, how we connect the blocks, adding a new character, etc. The children very quickly understood the principle of control – finger control is simple for them, the meaning of blocks in the application is very intuitive.

At the beginning of each activity, we asked the children questions related to the activity and guided them to the topic they will be working on – questions related to the environment in which they live, space, planet Earth, technical progress… animate and inanimate nature, seasons, the relationship between humans and animals, etc. Then each group started working on the activity.

What we noticed. The children helped each other, not only within their own group, but also across. We evaluate it positively, because it strengthens mutual relations, cooperation and collaboration. There were also more active groups, which inserted other objects into the story (beyond the assignment) and thus expanded the story. It was interesting to watch how the children "lived" very quickly with the application, with the controls, even though some children never held an iPad (or other touch device) in their hands. Among the problematic parts in some groups was the orientation in the plane - place the character on the right, on the left, move the character up, down. What surprised us was that there were only two groups that had problems with realizing a stepping sequence – for example, what block I have to start for the character to move, what order of blocks I have to choose for the character to draw a geometric shape (square, circle), how to achieve repetition, etc.

4. CONCLUSION

Digital technology brings a number of benefits to education, improving the learning experience and work organization. Moreover, digital technology is extremely popular with children. However, one must not forget that in order to be able to effectively use digital technology in instruction, teachers need the support from school administration, proper training, methodology, etc. It is essential that the students and current as well as future teachers keep their knowledge up to date with the latest developments in the digital technology field.

The paper presents the direction in which preschool education is heading: the focus will be on updating educational content, implementing digital technology (age and skill appropriate), teacher training and development and changing the way in which future kindergarten teachers are taught at the secondary and university education levels.

The paper also outlines how future kindergarten teachers could incorporate digital learning resources such as touch devices into instruction and use them to create simple activities in the Scratch Junior app that would help children develop their creativity, logical thinking and programming skills.

REFERENCES

Fryč, J., Matušková, Z., Katzová, P., Kovář, K., Beran, J., Valachová, I., Seifert, L., Běťáková, M., Hrdlička F. et al, 2020. *Strategie vzdělávací politiky České republiky do roku 2030+.* Ministerstvo školství, mládeže a tělovýchovy, Praha.

Kalaš, I., 2011. *Spoznávame potenciál digitálnich technológií v predprimárnom vzdelávaní.* Ústav informácií a prognóz školství, Bratislava.

Kalaš, I., Moravčík, M., 2012. *Digitálne technologie v materskej škole 1. Práca s obrázkami, Práca s textom.* Metodicko-pedagogické centrum, Bratislava.

MEYS, 2020. *Strategie vzdělávací politiky ČR do roku 2030+.* Qtd. 11. 1. 2021, available at: https://www.msmt.cz/vzdelavani/skolstvi-v-cr/strategie-2030

Švancar, R., 2016. Probuzení projektu digitálního vzdělávání: podle experta nabralo MŠMT na jaře konečně potřebné tempo. *Učitelské noviny: týdeník pro učitele a přátele školy*, Vol. 119, No. 29, pp. 20-22.

ALTERNATIVE LEARNING APPROACHES IN A PANDEMIC CONTEXT: FROM THE COLLABORATIVE OUTDOOR EDUPARK GAME TO A VIRTUAL VISIT

Lúcia Pombo and Margarida M. Marques
Research Centre on Didactics and Technology in the Education of Trainers (CIDTFF)
Department of Education and Psychology, University of Aveiro, 3810-193 Aveiro, Portugal

ABSTRACT

Over the last years, there has been much interest in mobile technologies for teaching and learning. Despite the focus on these emerging and innovative tools, mobile learning (mLearning) is facing many challenges. In response to the spread of the COVID-19 pandemic, many schools implemented eLearning or mLearning during school closures. However, mobile activities that involve collaboration of students in outdoor environments need to be rethought, as social distance is advised. This paper provides a pragmatic example of how to respond in the uncertain present, and plan systematically for an unpredictable, post-pandemic future. It presents an alternative learning approach in a pandemic context, as the EduPARK can be explored in a virtual visit, reinforcing the connection between physical and virtual learning spaces. This way learning can happen without face-to-face interactions for those who are avoiding physical contact, for those who are far away from the location, or even for students with motor difficulties. As a reflection, the authors examine major educational changes that have recently been imposed upon teachers and educational researchers, as well as key aspects of the current emergency response in education, and resultant implications for educational technology and mLearning.

KEYWORDS

Real-World Learning, Virtual Visit, Smart Education, Mobile Games, Augmented Reality

1. INTRODUCTION

Game-based and mobile learning (mLearning) are growing fields of research with positive empirical results in learning (Zydney & Warner, 2016; Pombo & Marques, 2019). The competition created by games may increase students' engagement in challenging learning situations and improve their overall sense of enjoyment (Huang, Chang & Wu, 2017). The challenge is how to create better learning experiences and develop game-based learning, supported by the users' experience *in situ* and their performance while playing (Groff et al., 2015; Zhonggen, 2019). Real-world learning opportunities provide students with competencies that cannot be taught in a classroom, because real-world situations include different kinds of challenges, communication styles, politics, and so forth. So, what we need is a system that recognizes and rewards interdisciplinary excellence, and real-world achievements. With the use of Augmented Reality (AR), real-world environment can be augmented by providing users with accurate digital overlays. AR is a promising technology that has the potential to encourage learners to explore learning materials from a totally new perspective (Sungkur et al., 2016; Pombo & Marques, 2020).

Smart Education concept integrates the potential of the adoption of mobile technologies to generate and collect data for situated games outside the classroom (Gianni & Divitini, 2015), fostering authentic and situated learning, but also personal and collaborative learning within a lifelong perspective (Schreiber-Barsch, 2017). Additionally, Smart Education can be used to create new learning ecosystems, where technologies enhance the multidimensional well-being of all learning players. Mobile devices, and apps, are pervasive and can be used to promote contextualized and interdisciplinary learning (Zydney & Warner, 2016; Laine, 2018; Pombo & Marques, 2020). Under these principles, emerged the EduPARK project, funded by FEDER and FCT, that seeks to promote outdoor learning strategies under geocaching principles, by means of an interactive mobile AR app that supports educational guides, in formal, non-formal and informal contexts, in the Aveiro green park, in Portugal (Pombo et al., 2019). The EduPARK allows learning to move from traditional classroom environments to natural spaces, through an outdoor game with educational guides, in a treasure hunt format specific to certain school levels, and by adding AR to an everyday technology - the smartphone (Pombo et al., 2019). The fact that the educational guides were designed to be explored in the Park provides an example of a truly authentic context for situated learning, where the location is essential for learning. The app can be explored either individually or in a group, although working in groups may support the users' construction of meaning, being this influenced by the interaction of the learners' prior knowledge with the new experiences, as well as by their interactions with others (Pombo & Marques, 2020). However, since the 2020 quarantine period, social distancing is recommendable across universities and schools, and the selection of collaborative outdoor games might not be the most convenient solution to pursue educational aims. Many authors claim that the emergence of COVID-19 has shaped a new type of learning, the "digital learning", which can be approached through eLearning and mLearning technologies (Al-Emran, 2020; Naciri et al., 2020). They also reinforce the preparation for mLearning infrastructure as this would be the key to handle future global risks (Al-Emran, 2020). But specificities among mLearning and games should be considered, as well as different types of context, among which the learner's needs, location, and time. In the EduPARK context, during pandemic times, the virtual visit might be a good alternative, as it reinforces the connection between physical and virtual learning spaces without face-to-face interactions.

This paper is based on the emergency changes we had to apply in the mobile game educational approach, avoiding physical contact, but allowing virtual education outside the classroom, also with interdisciplinary and contextualized AR resources. The purpose is to demonstrate how a collaborative outdoor game can be explored through a virtual visit, without leaving home, to access the learning materials. The paper starts by briefly presenting the EduPARK app game, created for exploration in a park. Follows the alternative learning approach, integrating a virtual visit, which is suitable for pandemic situations. The paper ends with some final considerations and future needs. The main contribution of this paper is to demonstrate the advantages of taking virtual visits as alternative learning environments to the *in situ* locations, such as green parks. This encompasses elements of formal and informal learning, in activities that happen in distributed settings (indoors and outdoors), across physical and virtual spaces, also allowing learning anytime, anyplace, and anywhere.

2. THE EDUPARK APP GAME

The EduPARK app is an example of a successful mobile AR game for learning. The app was developed for Androids and can be installed from the project website (http://edupark.web.ua.pt/app), requiring guides (games) update after download. It was developed to foster collaboration, authentic and situated learning outside the classroom, under the umbrella of constructivist learning, as the learner assumes an active role by constructing new knowledge within the articulation between the learning experience, previous knowledge and interaction with others (Pombo & Marques, 2020). With the EduPARK app, learning takes place in a green park, where students interact with the setting to gain an experiential connection to the ideas, concepts, and subjects. For educational relevance of the app and game approach, it was important to carefully analyse the National Curriculum to identify multidisciplinary issues (e.g., integrating Biology, History, Maths, among others), so that students may correlate the experiences promoted by the app with the aimed curriculum learning. The app can be explored in two different ways: free mode or game mode. The free mode gives access to content in AR, without having to follow a predetermined path, allowing total liberty in the exploration of the Park. In the game mode, the app gives access to excellent educational guides, with cross subjects' educational materials specific to different school levels, from primary to higher Education. A specific guide for the public, with local culture and curiosities, is available in Portuguese and in English. In each guide users are welcomed by the EduPARK mascot, a female monkey, created to foster student engagement, who explains the game rules to the players. The objective is to correctly answer the largest number of questions, gathering points, while stablishing connections between the real world and the school contents (Pombo et al., 2019). Afterwards, the mascot guides the players through the game's four stages, each one corresponding to a specific area of the Park, in which the user is challenged to search for points of interest, collect information, answer multiple choice questions and receive immediate and adapted feedback, whether they answer the question correctly or not. In the EduPARK game, the dynamics of a multiple-choice question are associated to several types of multimedia resources, such as audio, photography, illustration, video, or 3D objects in AR. This is not suitable for just a particular type of education, it could be any type, formal, informal or non-formal education. The ability to understand ecosystems is enhanced by experiences in real environments, so this justifies teacher's effort to take students outside the four walls of the classroom for effective learning. It comprises a very useful tool for Portuguese teachers and students to explore scientific knowledge by accessing contextualised and appealing information on biological and historical references that augment the experience of exploring a local urban green park. mLearning game-based strategies are very appreciated by the students (Huang, Y.-L. et al., 2017), as they are familiar to mobile phones, but normally they are not allowed to use them for learning in the classroom. Therefore, this approach creates opportunities to use those day-to-day technologies to learn. In addition, the use of interactive educational resources reaches students with difficulties in understanding abstract concepts, enhancing their spirit of observation, as e.g. AR allows 3D visualisation of phenomena, which might not be clear in traditional textbooks. Outdoor activities become a form of community contact instructional strategy adopted in the formal school system for the purpose of education (Obadiora, 2016) to create conditions to promote students' enjoyment, motivation and involvement in learning with hands-on activities. The EduPARK capitalises the education value of urban spaces, as green parks can act as a natural laboratory to learn. This type of innovative educational resource is not common in Portuguese speaking countries, hence, adding to the relevance of the EduPARK app (Pombo et al., 2019).

3. EDUPARK VIRTUAL VISIT

Although the EduPARK app has been designed to be explored in a specific green park, as the idea was to provide other learning environments outside the traditional classroom, the project also created a virtual visit to the park with some AR elements that can be explored indoors. This 360º visit, with access through the project's website (http://edupark.web.ua.pt/visit), is advantageous for those who are far away from the park, who have motor difficulties or are avoiding social contact in a pandemic situation, in which distance learning and confinement are advised. This last situation was not foreseen at all when this virtual visit was created, but its importance became evident in this critical period, since learners can explore the park virtually. Through the virtual visit, it is not possible to play the game, because its aim was to enhance the user will of going to the park to live the experience *in loco*. However, it is possible to search and find 23 hotspots with multimedia information that are scattered throughout the park. These points of interest contain informational text, images, and videos with real experiences. For example, the *Torreão* (historical water deposit) is usually closed to the public, but it can be explored inside with this virtual tour. When winding up the *Torreão* stairs it is possible to have access to several informative posters about the city and park. Those posters can be used as educational resources in History classes, promoting students' knowledge of local culture and historical facts, allowing students to know and analyze the importance of the water deposit in the city's history. Additionally, from its four upper windows, it is possible to sight magnificent landscapes over the city. These privileged views can reach the vast green spot of the park, its vegetation, the interesting geometry of its gardens, as well as its biodiversity of plant species, which can be used to explore real-world issues and interdisciplinary problems to enhance integrated and contextualized learning.

4. FINAL CONSIDERATIONS

Learning can take place everywhere, not only in the classroom or in the school environment (Obadiora, 2016). It could happen on the street, in the market place, in the park, etc. mLearning is finding an increasing adoption in education, as it encompasses elements of formal and informal learning, in activities that happen in distributed settings (indoors and outdoors), across physical and virtual spaces. Game-based and mLearning enable students to develop their conversational and technical skills, find answers to their queries, facilitate knowledge sharing and collaboration, and enhance their learning outcomes (Al-Emran, 2020). The collaborative outdoor EduPARK game was created to support the users' construction of meaning through experiences in an urban green park. In this experience, meaning construction is influenced by the interaction of the learners' prior knowledge with the new experiences, as well as by their interactions with others

(Pombo & Marques, 2020). However, the physical distance imposed by the emergence of COVID-19 has shaped the "digital learning" that can be approached through eLearning and mLearning technologies (Al-Emran, 2020). Educators can personalize their teaching strategies through mLearning and enable learners to self-regulate their learning without any restrictions to time and location. The proposed approach acts as an example for educators, systems developers, policymakers, researchers and stakeholders interested in implementing mLearning programs. The virtual visit strategy may become an adequate alternative to the traditional field trip strategy which involves, in the EduPARK context, a collaborative game. However, on the 360 visit, the park can be visited and explored virtually, although it is not possible to play the game, as its primary aim was to increase the user's will to go to the park to experience the game *in locus* (Pombo et al., 2019). However, the authors recognize that the virtual game experience can be explored in a near future project. As limitations, it is worthy to point out that some schools do not have enough resources to provide mLearning opportunities for students, and not all children have internet access at home (Naciri, 2020). However, given its benefits (Al-Emran, 2020), within and beyond the era of COVID-19, educational institutions might consider the mLearning and games as an effective approach for digital learning during the current and future crises.

ACKNOWLEDGEMENT

This work is financially supported by National Funds through FCT/Fundação para a Ciência e a Tecnologia, I.P. under the project UIDB/00194/2020. The second author's work is funded by national funds, through FCT/Fundação para a Ciência e a Tecnologia, I.P., in the scope of the framework contract foreseen in the numbers 4, 5, 6 of the article 23 of the Decree-Law 57/2016 of August 29, changed by Law 57/2017 of July19.

REFERENCES

Al-Emran, M., 2020. Mobile learning during the era of COVID-19. *Revista Virtual Universidad Católica del Norte*, No. 61, pp. 1-2.

Gianni, F. and Divitini, M., 2015. Technology-enhanced smart city learning: a systematic mapping of the literature. *Interaction Design and Architecture(s) Journal - IxD&A*, No. 27, pp. 28–43.

Groff, J. et al, 2015. *Better Learning in Games: A Balanced Design Lens for a New Generation of Learning Games*, Learning Games Network & MIT Education Arcade, Massachusetts, USA.

Huang, Y.-L. et al, 2017. Mobile Game-Based Learning with a Mobile App: Motivational Effects and Learning Performance. *Journal of Advanced Computational Intelligence and Intelligent Informatics*, Vol. 21, No. 6, pp. 963–970.

Laine, T., 2018. Mobile Educational Augmented Reality Games: A Systematic Literature Review and Two Case Studies, *Computers*, Vol. 7, No. 1, Article No. 19.

Naciri, A., et al, 2020. Mobile Learning in Higher Education: Unavoidable Alternative during COVID-19. *Aquademia*, Vol. 4, No. 1, Article No. ep20016.

Obadiora, A.J., 2016. Comparative Effectiveness of Virtual Field Trip and Real Field Trip on Students' Academic Performance in Social Studies in Osun State Secondary Schools. *Mediterranean Journal of Social Sciences*, Vol. 7, No. 1, pp. 467–474.

Pombo, L. and Marques, M.M., 2019. Learning with the augmented reality EduPARK game-like app: its usability and educational value for primary education. *Computing Conference*, London, U.K., pp. 113–125.

Pombo, L. and Marques, M.M., 2020. The potential Educational Value of Mobile Augmented Reality Games: the case of EduPARK app. *Education Sciences*, Vol. 10, No. 10, Article No. 287.

Pombo, L., et al, 2019. Evaluation of a Mobile Augmented Reality Game Application as an Outdoor Learning Tool. *International Journal of Mobile and Blended Learning*, Vol. 11, No. 4, pp. 59-79.

Schreiber-Barsch, S., 2017. Space is more than place: the urban context as contested terrain of inclusive learning settings for adults and arena of political subjectivation. *Learning the City*. Cham, Switzerland, pp. 67–81.

Sungkur, R.K., et al, 2016. Augmented Reality, the Future of Contextual Mobile Learning. *Interactive Technology and Smart Education*, Vol. 13, No. 2, pp. 123–146.

Zydney, J.M. and Warner, Z., 2016. Mobile apps for science learning: Review of research. *Computers & Education*, Vol. 94, pp. 1–17.

FOUR CORNERS OF THE WORLD: PROJECT-BASED LEARNING IN A MULTICULTURAL VIRTUAL ENVIRONMENT

Michael Stoica, Dmitri Nizovtsev and Russell E. Smith
Washburn University, USA

ABSTRACT

The paper details a course offering that centers on student transformational experience and self-efficacy growth in an international environment by merging business, entrepreneurship and cultural experiences. Self-efficacy is achieved through both a mastery experience, mastering a task and controlling the environment, and vicarious experience through observation of people and activities. An inexpensive but very effective combination of multi-cultural virtual and *in situ* team work with a strong cultural component provides the transformational experience. Originally involving only two universities, one in China and one in the United Sates, the course has expanded over the years of its existence to four participating universities, each representing a different continent. The virtual pre-travel component, which was always an important part of the course design, became especially prominent during the COVID-19 pandemic. The advantages and challenges associated with the course design and implementation are discussed.

KEYWORDS

Project-Based Learning, Multi-Cultural Environment, Virtual Team Work, Vicarious Learning, Networking Ties, Transformational Experience, Self-Efficacy

1. INTRODUCTION

The increasing importance of international virtual teams in organizations has an impact in the academic community. The adoption of real-time cross-cultural interactions has increased noticeably (Gonzalez-Perez et al., 2014). More consideration is given to experiential learning opportunities that prepare students to work in virtual organizations (Gavidia et al., 2004). The importance of settings that favor multi-cultural interactions and virtual work in course design has been pointed out in several studies (Gilson et al., 2015; Oertig and Buergi, 2006; Shea et al., 2011; Taras et al., 2013). The COVID-19 pandemic made the topic even more relevant. The course design process involves challenges in designing the goals and outcomes as well as the intricacies in defining assignments and course requirements (Alexandra, 2018; Gonzalez-Perez et al., 2014; Shea et al., 2011).

The innovative international business and entrepreneurship experience course presented in this paper was developed to offer students an opportunity for transformational experience. It is exposing them to multi-cultural interactions, virtual and *in situ* work opportunities, and cultural experiences, all in a structured framework that enables self-efficacy growth (Bandura, 1969) and vicarious learning (Myers, 2018). The course merges business project work with entrepreneurship and cultural experiences. The design substantiates a hands-on approach whereby students have the opportunity to perform consulting work on projects proposed by and negotiated with local business clients.

The course draws from the literature and achieves transformational experience at the intersection of project-based learning (Hu, 2009, Nakayama et al., 2012), virtual team work (Hubbard, 2013; Shea et al., 2011) and multicultural environment settings (Taras et al., 2013) in which it takes place. Figure 1 presents the conceptual model that will be detailed further in the paper. The project-based learning coupled with client and instructors' mentoring sets the grounds for vicarious learning experience and positions students for self-efficacy growth. The course experience of over thirteen years gives an indication of long-term model viability.

The next section introduces the major dimensions of the course structure and strategy as reflected in the literature. The third section presents the details of the course organization. The concluding section discusses advantages and challenges this model can pose to students, faculty, and businesses involved and elaborates on the generalizability of the model and the prospect of its adoption by other institutions, either independently or via the expansion of the existing academic venture.

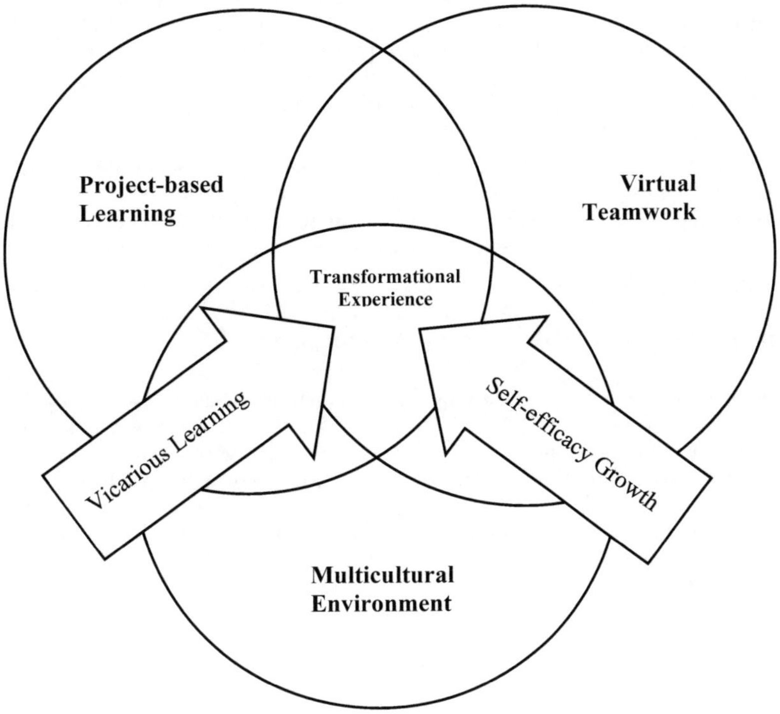

Figure 1. The Conceptual model for the offered course

2. BUILDING BLOCKS OF THE COURSE OFFERING: A REVIEW OF RELEVANT LITERATURE

2.1 Global Virtual Team Work

Global virtual teams were rare or had limited visibility a decade ago, but today they serve as important entities for acquiring knowledge and for decision making around the world (Hu, 2009; Malhotra et al., 2007; Maznevski and Chudoba, 2000; Swartz et al., 2020). Technological developments helped global virtual teams to become a more common method to work on complex projects within organizations. Technology also helped higher education to move from traditional learning into the world of real-time cross-cultural interactions (Gonzalez-Perez et al., 2014). There are, however, numerous challenges international business courses have to address when building virtual teams. Such challenges include language barriers, communications styles that differ across countries, unfamiliarity with the course content, cultural differences, and concepts that might be too abstract for students (Crittenden and Wilson, 2006a; Gavidia et al., 2005; Kardes, 2020).

Virtual team research has looked into ways to overcome these challenges. Gilson et al. (2015), in their comprehensive ten-year analysis of themes and opportunities, pointed out ways to enhance virtual team success. Settings, planning, training, member well-being, member mobility, adaptation are among the routes to success mentioned in their analysis. Years before to the above analysis, Hu (2009) developed an international virtual team-based project that anticipated some of the directions pointed out by Gilson et al. (2015). Pre- and post-training, group supervision, and within-group communication were several of the activities integrated into the project design and implementation.

Kardes (2020) addressed classroom engagement in international business courses and proposed tools to help educators enhance the learning experience of undergraduates. Since the new generations of students spend more time in a digital environment, they experience stronger connectedness. Connectedness shapes their expectations and their behavior both in the classroom and in a virtual setting. Thus, according to Kardes (2020), creating an active learning environment with a high level of student engagement through the incorporation of digital platforms in the classroom represents a necessary condition for highly connected students to engage in active learning. Swartz et al. (2020) also analyzed the way students are exposed to the challenge of cooperating in international settings but the focus of that study is on intercultural communication competency. The development of cultural intelligence and global identity in a virtual global context is critical for communication and connectedness (Erez et al., 2013). The findings point to difficulties encountered in intercultural interactions and, thus, to the need to teach intercultural competencies to reduce the impact of ethnocentrism and stereotyping in virtual team work.

2.2 Self-Efficacy Growth and Vicarious Learning

Vicarious learning is defined as individual learning that occurs through being exposed to and deriving meaning from somebody else's experience (Myers, 2018). The term "vicarious learning" was coined by Bandura (1969) to signify learning of behavior from watching videos of that behavior and originally had a negative connotation. Over time, however, learning from the experience of others was acknowledged to be significant for organizational, team, and individual success (Bresman, 2013). Vicarious learning is now an accepted training approach that involves observing or hearing about others' actions or experiences. At the present time, vicarious learning is considered an important component of experiential learning (Hoover et al., 2012; Jimenez and De La Fuente, 2016; Lee et al., 2020; Reynolds et al., 2018; Wang and Lee, 2017). Vicarious learning is a key element of Bandura's social learning theory (Bandura, 1994), which underscores the role of observational learning and social experience in the development of a persona (student or employee). The main concept in social cognitive theory is that an individual's actions and reactions, in almost every setting, are influenced by the actions that person has observed in others (Zimmerman, 2000). Any form of observing and modeling behavior (thus vicarious learning) involves four components: attention, retention, reproduction, and motivation (Bandura, 1994).

Srinivasan et al. (2007) studied the vicarious learning associated with launching new products and presented evidence of the vicarious learning process in an innovation context while Choi et al. (2020) compared experiential learning with vicarious learning in the context of performance measure noise, pointing out that vicarious learners showed more learning than experiential learners as the noise increases. Thus, indirect sources, such as observation or hearing, are at least as important as direct instruction. Indeed, Ivanova et al. (2016) established a positive association between vicarious learning and firm performance. This result is confirmed by Ali et al. (2020) in the context of international SMEs, where vicarious learning is an important way of improving performance. Jimenez and De La Fuente (2016) found that vicarious learning moderates the relationship between psychic distance and foreign direct investment while Hoover et al. (2012) saw vicarious learning as an enhancement of direct experience. The course offering presented in this paper follows the last-mentioned philosophy.

Self-efficacy is a personal judgment of how well one can execute courses of action required to deal with prospective situations (Bandura, 1969). It is another element at the focal point of Bandura's social cognitive theory. Because self-efficacy is developed from external experiences and self-perception and is influential in determining the outcome of many events, it is an important aspect of learning (DeRue and Morgeson, 2007; Sherer et al., 1982). Self-efficacy represents the personal perception of external social features. According to Bandura's theory (Bandura, 1994), people with high self-efficacy—that is, those who believe they can perform well—are more likely to view difficult tasks as something to be mastered rather than something to be avoided. Pajares (1996) investigated self-efficacy beliefs in academic settings and concluded that schools should develop and cultivate self-efficacy beliefs that enhance students' performance. Self-efficacy at the individual and collective levels (Byars-Winston et al., 2017; Pajares, 1996) was considered when the assignments and structure of the course were elaborated.

2.3 Project-Based Learning

Project-based learning represents a type of active scholarship and inquiry used by both organizations and academic communities (Hu, 2009; Nakayama et al., 2012). Commonly, if used in the classroom, it represents a student-centered learning method that involves a dynamic studying approach. Students acquire knowledge through active exploration of real-world challenges and problems by identifying the problem, investigating the industry and the markets, and offering a solution. They learn about a subject by working for an extended period of time to investigate and respond to a complex question, challenge, or problem (Knoll, 1997). Along these lines, it represents a style of active learning and inquiry-based learning.

Freeman et al. (2011) applied the project-based approach in international settings by using an interactive platform allowing students working in teams to explore the marketing of brands across three countries. Hu (2009) developed an international virtual team-based project involving Chinese and American students. The assessment demonstrated that participating students showed increased understanding of concepts as well as theoretical models. Further, Larson and Baburaj (2020) considered a similar model of collaboration by developing multiple international learning projects. Project-based learning represents the cornerstone of the present study. This thesis will be developed further in the next section.

3. COURSE DESIGN AND SCHEDULING

The above discussion helps placing the scope and goals of the present paper in context. An innovative international business and entrepreneurship experience course was developed more than a decade ago to offer students an opportunity for transformational experience and self-efficacy growth in a global environment by integration of three central experiences: business, entrepreneurship and cultural. The first version of the course was offered in 2007 when two founding schools from Asia (China) and North America (USA) joined their efforts and determination to design a project-based course that combines virtual and in situ team work in a multicultural environment. Later, they were joined by institutions from Europe (Belgium) and Latin America (Brazil), resulting in the current status quo of four universities offering a common field case course. The core idea of the course consists in students from each university with at least three semesters of business course work working in mixed teams to solve a problem for a client a company in China or Brazil. The *in situ* portion of the course invariably takes place in one of these two countries.

Figure 2 below details the main events and the timeline of the activities. The course does not follow the standard academic calendar - it starts in early March and ends in late May with the travel to China or Brazil where students finalize their project while working *in situ* for their clients and acquire cultural experience. In the fall semester preceding the course, faculty of the participating universities meet regularly to discuss the assignments, and establish the set of businesses that will serve as clients in the following spring semester. A pool of companies willing to participate as clients is formed by the future host universities and consequently vetted and finalized by the faculty of all the participating universities. Student recruitment also takes place during the fall semester, with enrollment ending by February.

In the first course meeting in early March, which is done virtually via social media, students introduce each other, self-select their teams, and select their client companies from the list presented to them. At the same time, the teams learn the projects of interest to the client firms and the scope of the projects. Historically, the majority of projects relate to the marketing strategy of the businesses. Each team includes students from all participating universities.

The initial phases of work on the projects in March through early May are also conducted in a virtual environment with the teams interviewing their clients, discussing and negotiating the scope and objectives of their project. Teams analyze the industry and the client's markets, refine the problem and the goals, divide the tasks, and start developing an action plan that details the solution or recommendations. The lecture component of the course is very limited. The role of faculty is primarily that of mentoring.

Prior to year 2020, this was followed by travel in May to the host university location (in China), where the work on refining the action plan continued *in situ*. Student teams aggregated their findings into a final project that was defended in a workshop where they had to substantiate their action plans. In the workshop, organized by the host university, students, faculty and businesses interact and feedback was provided to each team by clients and course mentors. The full version of the course concluded with students traveling to major historic and touristic sites and experiencing the culture of the host country.

In the year 2020 version of the course, the COVID-19 pandemic made travel impossible. Therefore, the last two phases of the course were also conducted virtually. Travel to historic and artistic objectives was unattainable, however the virtual work and the virtual workshop were successful and the Brazilian clients expressed their satisfaction with the results presented by the students.

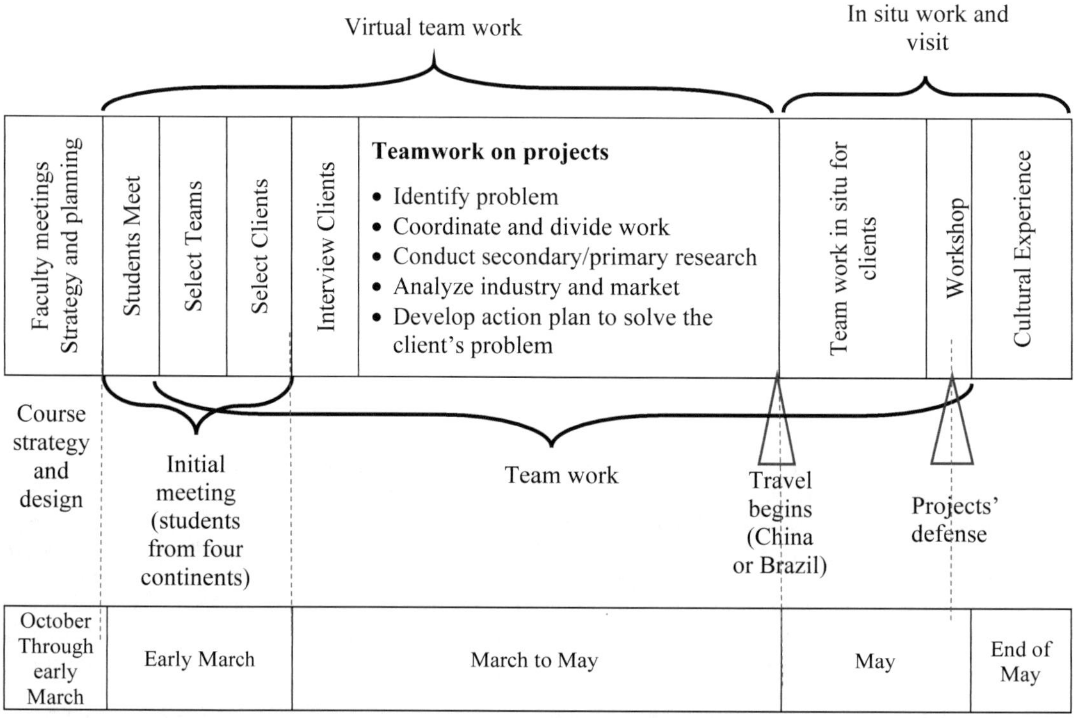

Figure 2. Timeline of the semester work on clients' projects

This approach brings multiple benefits to the participating students. They learn to conduct research in an international business environment, to investigate international business opportunities, to work on a complex project and defend their results, and to think and act both globally and locally due to the pressure from global integration and the need for local responsiveness. Learning and working on projects is student driven, therefore the vicarious and self-efficacy components of learning are abundantly present. Students get to know and work with colleagues from different continents and for companies from different countries. For the faculty, opportunities are available for fruitful networking with colleagues and instructors from other universities, as well as with managers and employees from a multitude of companies. As previously mentioned, the lecture component is reduced to a minimum. As a result, students learn primarily from each other and from their clients. This aspect of the course, typical of project-based learning, proves especially effective in multicultural teams, the members of which were exposed to different instructional styles and contents at their universities, and their life experience. The post-course travel experience also adds value to the program, by exposing students to foreign cultural values as well as creating an added opportunity for networking and developing long-lasting relationships.

Self-efficacy is increased through understanding and becoming proficient at the assigned tasks, grasping the multicultural environment and the vicarious experience. Team work encourages students to develop a collective mind, share information and knowledge and develop networking ties (Crittenden and Wilson, 2006b; Morrison, 2002; Rasmussen et al., 2015). That helps them build team cohesiveness and deliver good quality projects. Overall, virtual team work, less expensive but very effective combined with a strong cultural component, provides the transformational experience needed to thrive in a multicultural environment (Lee et al., 2020). From then on, the course was constantly evolving based on feedback from students, participating companies and involved faculty. Those improvements and refinements made the approach appealing to other institutions. In 2015, a Belgian university joined the program, transforming it into a three-university venture. In 2019 the course expanded further with an addition of a Brazilian university. The timeline of the course growth is shown in Figure 3. The combination/sequencing/balance between the virtual and *in situ* work also varied over the years and across different versions of the course.

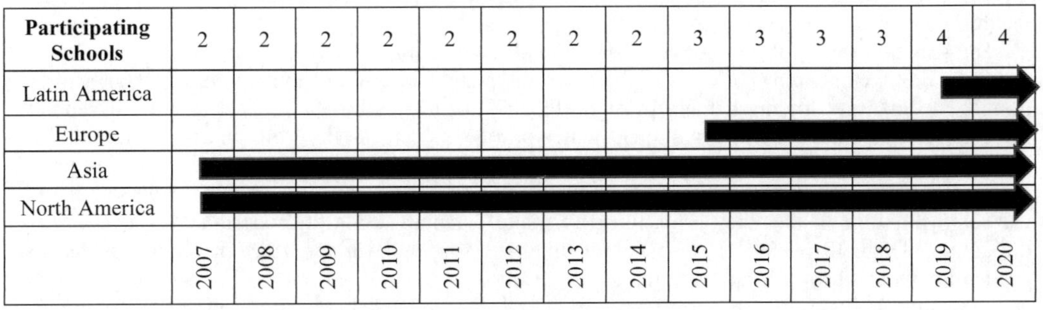

Figure 3. Timeline of the course evolution

4. CONCLUSIONS

This course has been offered successfully every year for fourteen years, beginning with two partner institutions (USA and China) and growing to three (adding Belgium) in 2015 and four (adding Brazil) in 2019. Initially, the project site was in China. Because of the global pandemic, the on-site project planned for Brazil in 2020 pivoted to online with a mix of Brazilian and Chinese companies. At the time of this writing, a Brazilian site is anticipated for 2021, health conditions permitting, with a backup in China. Each year the course was improved based on the findings about the technology used, the international settings experienced, and student and faculty feedback from the previous year. The course became more robust and more versatile and is better reflecting the needs of the companies that participate as clients. The multi-year learning experience has helped the faculty better understand the requirements of the specific multicultural settings, the way students interact with each other, with their clients (local businesses), and with the faculty from all the participating universities.

In addition, faculty benefit from network ties, research opportunities, co-teaching opportunities, examples for the classroom, cultural experience and enrichment and opportunities for exchange of notes on teaching, consulting and research. Students have the opportunities for the elements of a transformational experience, including cultural experiences, networking ties, long-term relations with other students, faculty, and businesses, as well as friendships and opportunities to build self-efficacy, including a better CV and ease in travel and communication. Businesses can acquire new perspectives and fresh eyes for looking into their problems, implementation of novel ideas, refreshing work, and cooperation from hosting the international teams of students. For universities, the benefit might be better programs, visibility, and an additional recruitment tool. The course/program presented is easy to adopt by other institutions. Another option could be to join the already existent program, expanding it to more schools and therefore adding more value to the ongoing cooperation between schools.

Apart from the challenges to international travel and high-density living brought by the current, COVID-19 pandemic in 2020 and 2021, this model of project-based learning in a virtual multi-cultural environment has other, perhaps less dramatic challenges. For example, coordination takes a lot of time and effort. The course has to be prepared ahead of time, multiple faculty meetings happen in the fall semester prior to the start of the project. That involves multiple meetings with the interested companies. The pool of potential companies has to be always extended and new companies have to be vetted for compatibility with the student work, availability in mentoring students, etc. While each partner participates in the coordination in a different way, there is much to be done by the host institution and professorial leaders of the course. As this is primarily an experiential and project-based course, there are few lectures. The faculty-team guidance effort is significant and the coordination of this guidance with the other faculty requires permanent contact and multiple virtual faculty meetings as well as additional travel, conditions permitting. However, significant preparatory work and even class meetings can take place virtually. With staff continuity, the program leaders and support personnel can learn from each cycle and add improvements. Finally, although COVID-19 transformed the course to virtual-only learning experience for the spring of 2020, it should be noted that broadly about half of the course work from the students' perspective is done prior to travel to the host site for project completion. The 2020 experience has demonstrated that the entire course can be delivered remotely by virtual, but very real teams. The uncertainty is not whether or not the company-based projects can be completed, but rather when and how the decision is made to travel or not.

The generalizability of the model is based on all or most of the participating institutions already having some or all of the operating elements of the partnership and curriculum although not necessarily already fully mobilized. First and foremost, there must be faculty members who are at least interested in international projects, curriculum experience in student teams and consultancy-style projects, and institutional processes supporting student and faculty travel and institutional partnerships in all participating institutions. Not all elements must be equally present at institutions. Second, there must be active faculty leadership in most of the partner institutions in that they are willing to make communication and coordination a primary personal obligation. Third, there must be substantial understanding and support (buy-in) from key leaders in the academic unit and central administration at all participating institutions and willingness to show that support at key junctures. In our case, there is a basic bi-lateral partnership between the Chinese and American partners that operates at the levels of faculty development, student exchange including a coordinated degree program, and presidential-level delegation visits. Third partner institution is also student exchange partner through a multi-country undergraduate exchange consortium, while we met the fourth partner through an introduction by an alumnus.

REFERENCES

Alexandra, V. 2018. Predicting CQ Development in the Context of Experiential Cross-Cultural Training: The Role of Social Dominance Orientation and the Propensity of Change Stereotypes. *Academy of Management Learning & Education*, Vol. 17, No. 1, pp. 62-78.

Ali, I. et al. 2020. How International SME's Vicarious Learning May Improve Their Performance? The Role of Absorptive Capacity, Strength of Ties with Local SMEs, and Their Prior Success Experiences. *Industrial Marketing Management*, Vol. 88, pp. 87-100.

Bandura, A. 1969. *Principles of Behavior Modifications*. New York: Holt, Rinehart and Winston.

Bandura, A. 1994. Self-Efficacy. *Encyclopedia of Human Behavior*, V. S. Ramachaudran (Ed), Vol. 4, pp. 71-81.

Bresman, H. 2013. Changing Routines: A Process Model of Vicarious Group Learning in Pharmaceutical R&D. *Academy of Management Journal,* Vol. 56, No. 1, pp. 35-61.

Byars-Winston, A. et al. 2017. Unique Effects and Moderators of Effects of Sources on Self-Efficacy: A Model-Based Meta Analysis. *Journal of Counseling Psychology*, Vol. 64, No. 6, pp. 645-658.

Choi, J. et al. 2020. Bring the Noise, But Not the Fun: Does the Effect of Performance Measure Noise on Learning Depend on Whether the Learning is Experiential or Vicarious? *The Accounting Review*, Vol. 95, No. 4, pp. 153-172.

Crittenden, V. L. and Wilson, E., J. 2006a. Content, Pedagogy, and Learning Outcomes in the International Marketing Course .*Journal of Teaching in International Business*, Vol. 17, No. 1-2, pp. 81-101.

Crittenden, V. L. and Wilson, E., J. 2006b. An Exploratory Study of Cross-Functional Education in the Undergraduate Marketing Curriculum. *Journal of Marketing Education*, Vol. 28, N. 1, pp. 81-86.

DeRue, D. S. and Morgeson, F. P. 2007. Stability and Change in Person-Team and Person-Role Fit Over Time: The Effects of Growth Satisfaction, Performance, and General Self-Efficacy. *Journal of Applied Psychology*, Vol. 92, No. 5, pp. 1242-1253.

Erez, M. et al. 2013. Going Global: Developing Management Students' Cultural Intelligence and Global Identity in Cultural Diverse Virtual Teams. *Academy of Management Learning & Education*, Vol. 12, No. 3, pp. 330-355.

Freeman, I. et al. 2011. A Tri-Country Marketing Project – Preparing Students for Realities of a Global Marketplace. *Journal of Teaching in International Business*, Vol. 22, No. 4, pp. 277-299.

Gavidia, J. V. et al. 2004. Using International Virtual Teams in the Business Classroom. *Journal of Teaching in International Business*, Vol. 16, No. 2, pp. 51-74.

Gilson, L. L. et al. 2015. Virtual Teams Research: 10 Years, 10 Themes and 10 Opportunities. *Journal of Management*, Vol. 41, No. 5, pp. 1313-1337.

Gonzalez-Perez, M. A. et al. 2014. Virtual Teams and International Business Teaching and Learning: The Case of the Global Enterprise Experience (GEE). *Journal of Teaching in International Business*, Vol. 25 No. 3, pp. 200-213.

Hoover, J. D. et al. 2012. Eyes On, Hands On: Vicarious Observational Learning as an Enhancement of Direct Expereince. *Academy of Management Learning & Education*, Vol. 11, No. 4, pp. 591-608.

Hu, H. 2009. An International Virtual Team Based Project at Undergraduate Level: Design and Assessment. *Marketing Education Review*, Vol. 19, No. 1, pp. 17-22.

Hubbard, R. S. 2013. How to Improve Global Virtual Teams. *Global Business and International Management Conference Journal*, Vol. 6, No. 3, pp. 49-58.

Ivanova, A. et al. 2016. Direct and Vicarious Learning and Firm Performance. *Journal of Behavioral & Applied Management*, Vol. 17, No. 2, pp. 134-151.

Jimenez, A. and De la Fuente, D. 2016. Learning from Others: The Impact of Vicarious Expereince in the Psychic Distance and FDI Relationship. *Management International Review*, Vol. 56, pp. 633-664.

Kardes, I. 2020. Increasing Classroom Engagement in International Business Courses via Digital Technology. *Journal of Teaching in International Business*, Vol. 31, No. 1, pp. 51-74.

Knoll, M. 1997. The Project Method: Its Origin and International Development. *Journal of Industrial Teacher Education*, Vol. 34, No. 3, pp. 59-80.

Larson, B. V. and Baburaj, Y. 2020. Alternative Multi-Mode International Learning: A Model Establishing Collaboration. *Journal of International Business Disciplines*, Vol. 15, No. 1, pp. 13-28.

Lee, J. Y. et al. 2020. Learning SME Inetrnationalization: A New Perspective on Learning From Success versus Failure. *Management International Review*, Vol. 60, pp. 485-513.

Malhotra, A. et al. 2007. Leading Virtual Teams. *Academy of Management Perspectives*, Vol. 21, No. 1, pp. 60-70.

Maznevski, M. L. and Chudoba, K. M. 2000. Bridging Space Over Time: Global Virtual Team Dynamics and Effectiveness. *Organization Science*, Vol. 11, No. 5, pp. 473-492.

Morrison, E. W. 2002. Newcomers' Relationships: The Role of Social Network Ties During Socialization. *Academy of Management Journal*, Vol. 45, No. 6, pp. 1149-1160.

Myers, C. G. 2018. Coactive Vicarious Learning: Toward a Relational Theory of Vicarious Learning in Organizations. *Academy of Management Review*, Vol. 43, No. 4, pp. 610-634.

Nakayama, M. et al. 2012. A Human Resource Development Program for Information Technology Engineers Using Project-Based Learning. *Journal of Advanced Corporate Learning*, Vol. 5, No. 4, pp. 9-15.

Oertig, M. and Buergi, T. 2006. The Challenges of Managing Cross-Cultural Virtual Project Teams. *Team Performance Management*, Vol. 12, No. 1/2, pp. 23-30.

Pajares, F. 1996. Self-Efficacy Beliefs in Academic Settings. *Review of Educational Research*, Vol. 66, No. 4, pp. 543-578.

Rasmussen, E. et al. 2015. The Transformation of Network Ties to Develop Entrepreneurial Competencies for University Spin-offs. *Entrepeneurship and Regional Development*, Vol. 25, No. 7-8, pp. 430-457.

Reynolds, G. et al. 2018. A Comparison of Positive Vicarious and Verbal Information for Reducing Vicarious Learned Fear. *Cognition and Emotion*, Vol. 32, No. 6, pp. 1166-1177.

Shea, T. P. et al. 2011. Managing Global Virtual Teams Across Classrooms, Students and Faculty. *Journal of Teaching in International Business*, Vol. 22, No. 4, pp. 300-313.

Sherer, M. et al. 1982. The Self-Efficacy Scale: Construction and Validation. *Psychological Reports*, Vol. 51, pp. 663-671.

Srinivasan, R. et al. 2007. Vicarious Learning in New Product Introductions in the Early Years of Convergent Market. *Management Science*, Vol. 53, No. 1, pp. 16-28.

Swartz, S. et al. 2020. Building Intercultural Competence Through Virtual Team Collaboration Across Global Classrooms. *Business & Professional Communication Quarterly*, Vol. 83, No. 1, pp. 57-79.

Taras, V. et al. 2013. A Global Classroom? Evaluating the Effectiveness of Global Virtual Collaboration as a Teaching Tool in Management Education. *Academy of Management Learning & Education,* Vol. 15, No. 3, pp. 414-435.

Wang, Y-C. and Lee, Y-M. 2017. The Effectiveness of Two Positive Career Counseling Modules for Working Parents in Taiwan, *Journal of Employment Counseling*, Vol. 54, pp. 23-37.

Zimmerman, B., J. 2000. Self-Efficacy: An Essential Motive to Learn. *Contemporary Educational Psychology*, Vol. 25, pp. 82-91.

ONLINE STUDIES IN HIGHER EDUCATION DURING THE COVID-19 PANDEMIC: STUDENTS' PERSPECTIVE

Edita Butrime[1] and Vaiva Zuzeviciute[2]
[1]*Lithuanian University of Health Sciences, A. Mickeviciaus g. 9, LT 44307 Kaunas, Lithuania*
[2]*Mykolas Romeris University, Maironio g. 27, Kaunas; Ateities g. 20, Vilnius, Lithuania*

ABSTRACT

Globally universities today almost universally employ online (distance, remote) teaching and learning due to COVID-19 coronavirus pandemic. Fully online studies were not universally offered by all higher education institutions before the pandemic both globally and in Lithuania. Therefore, it can be argued that before 2020, studies, which analysed distance teaching and learning were to a major degree intended to discuss experiences and attitudes of technology enthusiasts and visionaries. The aim of this paper is to discuss a swift and forced innovation in terms of universal expansion in online learning models and to reveal the perspective of students towards online studies, because the lessons learnt in 2020 may serve for enhancement of higher education didactics even after the quarantine is over.

KEYWORDS

Online Studies, Forced Innovation, Virtual Learning Environments, Online Studies during the COVID-19 Pandemic

1. INTRODUCTION

If history serves as judge, we may recall historical incidents when crises prompted innovations, which seemed unrealistic, at times unnecessary, and even undesirable before crises emerged. In 2020 situation universities globally shifted to full online studies: either online teaching and learning during the COVID-19 coronavirus pandemic was implemented, or universities curtailed activities. The rapid spread of new COVID-19 coronavirus throughout China and the world in 2020 has had a grave impact on world economic and social development. The pandemic has radically changed people's lives and activities. Though at first it seemed a temporary emergency, however, experts in various fields are already predicting significant changes in various areas of people's lives. Before the pandemic both on-site and off-site (online) modes were carried out by different universities: at some universities these two modes were complementing each other, when other universities focused largely on on-site activities, however, there were many, which also focused on off-site educational services. Twelve months ago, almost all teachers knew how to teach and understood how their students learn, but to a major degree they applied traditional teaching methods. Now university teachers have changed the nature of their work and they have learnt new skills themselves, for example, while using web-camera for teaching, because even maintaining proper eye contact and monitoring facial expressions require skill and will. It is imperative already now to perform inventory about the experiences in 2020, because the lessons learnt may serve the enhancement of didactics in higher education after quarantine is over. While the pandemic resulted in unsurmountable loss and tragedy, at the same time, the reflection of experiences, including in education, may produce insights for filtering the productive practices, and those that should be reconstructed. According to Davidson and Waddington (2010), Jonson (2009), universities – at least before the pandemic – used to be - 'technology resistant institutions'. One of the key obstacles related to a successful implementation of ICT in some universities was the fact that the management sometimes did not support or determine relevant priorities for ICT. Such a situation might have been caused – presumably - by historical traditions; university management did not emphasise ICT and e-learning issues, as that was not considered being the basic field of activities (Rutkauskiene et al., 2006; Stacey and Gerbic, 2009), however, pandemic changed the situation dramatically.

The aim of this paper is to discuss forced innovation (swift implementation of universal online study models) on higher education and to reveal the perspectives of students towards online studies, which may serve as advice for enhancement of higher education didactics.

The research question addressed in the study: In what way do students reflect on using virtual learning environment (VLE) for their online studies? What is the perspective of students, who have studied in a VLE in extreme conditions, to online studies?

The study involved students who shared their learning experiences at least in Autumn 2019 and then - in the Spring and the Autumn semester of 2020 (i.e., when they had to learn under the conditions of forced innovation).

In this paper e-learning is analyzed as a socio-cultural system, as 'a multi-dimensional' concept. (Mamardasvili, 1958, Butrime and Zuzeviciute, 2014). The analysis of e-learning as a socio-cultural system enabled the formulation of interdisciplinary problem, for the solutions of which it is necessary to invoke theories and outcomes of computer science, also culture and education.

2. ONLINE STUDIES: YESTERDAY AND TODAY

University studies, under the influence by contemporary information and communication technologies (ICT) were already changing from the teaching paradigm to the learning paradigm even before the pandemic for at least the last twenty years. What are the characteristics of e-learning (and teaching) in university academic community, and what comprises the phenomenon of e-learning as socio-cultural system?

Socio-cultural system of e-learning is a system. ICT have been artificially designed by a human being; however, ICT, as a consequence, now influence the development and structure of this system (Butrime and Zuzeviciute, 2014). Key elements of each and any e-learning episode are: participants (teachers, students, IT professionals); technologies (ICT); processes; relationship/connections/interaction; material/contents (information).

Modern ICT are identified as one of the factors in this system. An individual is identified as a key element of socio-cultural system – he or she is the creator of knowledge seeking to respond to the needs of knowledge society. The socio-cultural system of e - learning is disclosed as a contemporary phenomenon, as earlier classic pedagogical systems (Butrime and Zuzeviciute, 2014) did not identify ICT as the element of the system. Universities operate now in the society, which changes faster than ever before (Zuzeviciute, 2011). The so called "knowledge society" is only a symbol which denotes the fact that the structure of the society that we used to know has collapsed. Society under our very eye is becoming a multi – dimensional/bubble society in which different models of a society operate at the same time, starting from the agrarian, industrial, information and ending, of course, with knowledge and many other models. Shiva (2005) notes that a function of science is to investigate and to find out, whereas a function of technologies is to act on what has been found out. Today these processes are inseparable.

In several publications authors of this paper conceptualize ICT in higher education, as a system, emphasizing the importance of all comprising elements involved (e.g.: Butrime and Zuzeviciute, 2014). Traditional education system (primary, secondary, higher education, vocational training and informal education) remains essentially unchanged in its structure, management and the concept despite the changing conditions of life and is basically not adjusted to new social needs (Augustinaitis, 2004). The breakthrough of Web 2.0 sometimes brought confusion to the already well-established life of university (and other organizations), to its activities, communication, information movement and processing. Tools and means based on Web 2.0 in many instances are spontaneous, informal, horizontal, heterogeneous, volatile and unstable, which might result in a contradiction between the quickly spreading Web 2.0 and institutions (or, rather, their community members), which sometimes refused (or were afraid) to use these technologies (Davidson and Waddington, 2010; Stacey and Gerbic, 2009). Over the past 20 years, various scholars had studied distance teaching/learning in detail and highlighted its advantages (for example, flexibility in learning, opportunity to study at a convenient time and place). The authors identify nine dimensions, each of which has numerous options, highlighting the complexity of the design and decision-making process. The nine dimensions are: modality, pacing, student-instructor ratio, pedagogy, instructor role online, student role online, online communication synchrony, role of online assessments, and source of feedback (Means et. al., 2014). However, online studies/distance teaching and learning was not a mass phenomenon before 2020.

The results of survey, conducted in 2017 by European Digital Learning Network showed moderate level of employment of online studies mode at that time. The most popular forms were found: blended learning approaches (42 %); e-assessment (40 %); website development (40 %); learner engagement (38 %). It was also identified that 50,43 % of respondents while predicting the level of employment in 2020 thought the level to be moderate (What do you think about the future of digital Education and Training in EU? 2017). Little did they know...!

During the COVID-19 pandemic, educational institutions have been forced to employ more VLE, i. e. changed traditional teaching to distance teaching/learning. Many researchers have been analyzing this extreme situation (Truskauskaite-Kuneviciene et al., 2020; Kaunas University of Technology, 2020; Vytautas Magnus University, 2020; Lithuanian University of Health Sciences. 2020; World Health Organization, 2020). It can be argued that the studies, which analysed distance teaching and learning before 2020 in most instances were intended to discuss the experiences and attitudes of technology enthusiasts and visionaries (according to qualitative diffusion model of G. A. Moore (2002). Their diffusion model describes experiences of technology enthusiasts, early adopters, early majority, late majority and laggards.

The sudden shift from face-to-face to online studies triggered many challenges for teachers in university (and all other levels of education): "For many universities, these methods considered as new platform and the ability of using such tools for online teaching created many challenges among the teachers in higher education. The familiarity with new digital platforms and tools in short period of time as well as the pedagogical demands of online learning that they never had to think of in conventional delivery become one of the challenging factor among lecturers in higher education. Furthermore, they need to ensure to retain the program and module-learning objective even after adjustment of the teaching style" (Ramayah and Kumar, 2020).

Change has not been easy: there are both positive (Burgess and Sievertsen, 2020; Ramayah and Kumar, 2020; Rizk, 2020; Kucharczyk-Brus and Mielcarski, 2020) and negative experiences (Burgess and Sievertsen, 2020; Souleles and Laghos, 2020; Kucharczyk-Brus and Mielcarski, 2020).

3. ONLINE LEARNING DURING THE COVID-19 PANDEMIC

For the past two decades' universities were introducing opportunities presented by information communication technologies (further on – ICT) to a varied degree. Any organisation is an entity with structural parts and people, also teams, who have to work in systemic collaboration in order to ensure the systemic functioning of an organisation itself. Though certain principles are the same, e.g., the information is being produced and shared, each organisation is a unique entity, however. Though each organisation has its own structure, also the traditions will be different, as will be the style of management, at the same time, in each organisation we will find people, structures, technologies (Abarius and Liubinas, 2014; Kacinskaite and Motiejune, 2011).

University, as an organisation, employs ICT for its functioning, the same way any other contemporary organisation does. Communication is mostly ensured due to internet, intranet and extranet. Universities use the same technology, however, choice of software depends on financial situations, the experience of teachers, and on support personnel, including the IT professionals and the administrations. Online operation during the pandemic was essentially different from the gradual incorporation of online services into universities, therefore, it is legitimate to identify the conditions as extreme conditions. „Moving instruction online can enable the flexibility of teaching and learning anywhere, anytime, but the speed with which this move to online instruction is expected to happen is unprecedented and staggering" (Hodges et al., 2020). Even before the pandemic universities had necessary infrustructure and support personnel, who could have been relied on for supporting teachers for online work. However, before the pandemic, only a part of teachers were seeking advice from support personnel, those in most cases were the teachers, enthusiastic about online studes. Hence we all experenced extreme conditions when during the extremely short time, having limited resources and not that many support personnel, we still had to teach teachers to transform from traditional teaching to online work. Hodges et al. (2020) argue that 2020 online work deserves a special event status and suggests the term for denoting it: emergency remote teaching. Authors argue, that teachers had to cope with the heaviest workload, because it was critical during an extremely short time to ensure the access to both synchronous and a-synchronous process and contents for studies. Moreover, the necessary changes for the regulation of online studies had to be introduced, which meant an additional workload for administration in order to legitimise "emergency remote teaching", a huge workload was on the IT professionals who suddenly had to re-arrange access opportunities within the capacities, which had not been designed for the scope needed. The support personnel suddenly had to consult also teachers who had never even tried online teaching tools. Thus it is useful to analyse the "emergency remote teaching", because lessons learnt during the time may be used for the future.

Contemporary global situation in universities is (distance) teaching and learning/online studies during the COVID-19 pandemic. COVID-19 has urged universities around the globe to relocate traditional classes to online classes. The COVID-19 health crisis has resulted in school and university closures affecting over 90% of the world's students (Protecting and Transforming Education for Shared Futures and Common Humanity, 2020). From the beginning of COVID-19 pandemic the International Association of Universities (IAU), has been closely monitoring the impacts on higher education around the world. IAU with partners from around the world has developed two Global surveys, one has been held in the beginning of pandemic, the second global survey will be held in the fall 2020. Based on the first survey the major challenges have been already listed and possible solutions provided (COVID-19: Higher Education challenges and responses, 2020). Although ICT was used by universities around the world as part of study process, the traditional paper-based learning approaches were still the most commonly utilized, as opposed to web-based and electronic learning methods. COVID -19 urged the university to adopt distance learning as a necessary option to keep education going on.

3.1 Online Learning during the Covid-19 Pandemic: Lithuania

Today most higher education institutions in Lithuania employ different academic information systems, some of them use intranet and content management systems. For online studies Lithuanian universities (and colleges) use learning management system Moodle. In Spring, 2020 Lithuanian Ministry of Education, Research and Sports purchased platform Microsoft Teams for Education. The majority of higher education organisations use Microsoft 365 family products. For synchronous communication teachesr use those tools, which are recommended by their respective organisations, or the most user-friendly (BigBlueButton, MS Teams, Google Meet, Zoom, etc.).

Lithuanian academia, starting 16th March, 2020, had two weeks to fully re-organise activities and introduce universal online studies. The universities and colleges charged of planning and setting the following guidelines surrounding distance learning:

- The course must be ensured even in the case of technical difficulties.
- The process and methodology of distance learning can be openly chosen in the light of the above recommendations. Technological and logistical support was provided using the tools, which universities and colleges owned at a time (Moodle, BigBlueButton, MS Office 365, MS Teams, Google Meet, Zoom, etc.) The universities and colleges provided an opportunity for teachers to prepare for work online. Teachers had 2 weeks to upload the study content into a virtual learning environment.

At least in Lithuanian the first wave of quarantine was curtailed on 17th June, 2020, the second quarantine (in Lithuania) was announced on 9th October, 2020. Surely, in other countries the specific dates were a bit different, but the principle remains: after the first quarantine, after a short respite during summer, almost globally, in Autumn, quarantines were re-instated, which meant return to full online study mode for higher education in Lithuania during October. At least in Lithuania starting 16th December, 2020, restrictions of commutation between municipalities were introduced (and they remain in place during the time this paper is being developed, well into the third month). Interestingly, based on the assumption that students knew how to use ICT for studies, rarely they were provided with training how to use ICT for learning. Therefore, it is worth examining what were the experiences of students while studying fully online during the challenging 2020. Therefore, a pilot study was designed and carried out in late Autumn 2020, where students were invited to share their perspective.

4. STUDENTS' PERSPECTIVE ON ONLINE STUDIES IN AN EMERGENCY SITUATION

4.1 Methodology

Students were asked to assess their participation in online studies in Spring semester, 2020, and in Autumn semester 2020. Students were asked to provide a quantitative assessment. A scale of 1-5 was used: 1 meant 'did not like at all' to 5 'my competencies increased significantly'. Also a qualitative approach was used, where students were asked to provide an explanation for a grade given by formulating 3 explanatory statements. Due to limitations for the scope of the paper, only findings from this part of qualitative data are analyzed and discussed further in this paper. An online survey platform apklausa.lt was used to collect data in late Autumn, 2020.

Sampling and procedure. Though totally 72 students participated, however, the responses of 37 students are analyzed in this paper; these particular students had a totality of experiences as students at least in Autumn 2019 and then - in Spring and Autumn, 2020. Thus these particular students could compare their on-site and online study experiences (other participants were still in high school in Spring 2020). Students from three universities in Lithuania (in Klaipeda (1), Vilnius (1), Kaunas (1)) shared their perspective anonymously. 33 (20 in 4th year of studies; 6 in 3rd and 7 in 2nd year of studies) of students were undergraduates, 4 graduates. 24 women, 13 men shared perspective. One university represented technology studies; another social sciences, and the third - specifically studies in education.

Limitations. Due to the dominance of qualitative approach to study, and the number of participants, generalisations will not be provided, however, certain insights and implications for higher education will be formulated.

4.2 Results

As it was identified above, students were invited to provide explanations to the grade they gave for their experiences in studies in Spring 2020, when the first wave of Covid-19 struck, the quarantine was announced, and higher education in Lithuania (and globally) was swiftly re-organised to a fully online mode. Later, in Autumn semester after a brief respite in September (in some university-also early October), again a fully online mode was started, therefore in second part of November, 2020, students already had extensive experience on online studies in Autumn semester. It is important to note that N is fluid, it does not represent the number of students (37), because they were asked to provide three explanatory statements for each grade. However, some of them provided none, some of them provided more than three, therefore, the analyses finally resulted in 85 explanatory statements, 54 while evaluating experiences in studies in Spring semester and 31 while evaluating experiences in Autumn semester.

Firstly, we will note that the positive explanatory statements in Spring and in Autumn exceeded negative explanatory statements: 29 versus 21 (4 undetermined/other) and 22 versus 9 respectively. In Spring negative statements accounted for 38.8% of statements, in Autumn Semester the percentage is 29 %. Obviously, due to limitations of the study, generalisations should be avoided, however, certain positive perspective tendency towards online studies is evident.

Secondly, none of the statements, provided by undergraduate and even graduate (37 in total) students in any way was related to Covid-19. This finding, according to our opinion, is one of the most significant findings in relation to both the online study process and the educational realities at large, which deserves an in-depth further analysis. None of the students noted that the difficulties posed by online studies should have been overcome due to the circumstances of quarantine, or that this was a safer mode for studies, or a necessary choice. The only two statements, related to health were grouped into the group of 'negative' statements. The statements were provided by the same participant: "Due to online studies my back and eyes ache" and "Online studies lead to inactivity and that is detrimental to health". As professionals in education, we find the data worth further analysis, because, while global economy, policies, medicine, decision making processes were orientated towards managing the huge, at times almost insurmountable crises, however, the young people, students (at least those participating in the study) did not integrate the crises into interpretation of their immediate study experiences. While from educational point of view these are the most interesting questions: How is that possible? and then - What are the pillars/grounding rules for young person's interpretation of realities? – these questions are for the future however, because the direct focus in this paper is different.

Thirdly, some statements added to well established data on the reactions to online studies, however, some of the statements added new dimensions or nuances to subjective students' perspectives.

Among the statement that we had expected: positive ('saves time' (6 statements), 'saves money (for renting dormitory/flat and travel' (4 statements); 'flexibility and comfort' (5 statements). Also, among positive (1 statement), online being helpful for complementing work and studies was mentioned, which always, at least for 20 years, had been identified among the advantages of online studies.

Also, regarding teachers' competencies to provide educational online services, and the level of employment of opportunities and tools of VLP (predominantly, Moodle was identified, also students informed having used Zoom, BigBlueButton and MS Teams) a clear positive tendency was identified, Table 1.

Table 1. Students about their online study experiences

Spring semester (2020, first wave of Covid-19 triggered quarantine and thus swift shift to complete online studies)	Autumn semester (2020, second wave of Covid-19 triggered quarantine and thus shift to complete online studies)
Evaluation of teachers' competencies	
2 **positive** statements, e.g., Teachers did well, especially under the circumstances' 3 **negative** statements, e.g. ‚Not all teachers were competent in organising classes and seminars online'	5 **positive** statements, e.g, Teachers' competence clearly improved since last semester" 2 **negative** statements, e.g. ‚Still some teachers do not know how to use VLP'
Employment of various tools, opportunities, incorporated in VLP	
1 **positive** statement, e.g, ‚We used many methods and tools'	5 **positive** statements, e.g, ‚Teachers use more tools, such as breakout rooms' or ‚A variety of tools and methods are used, which are good for learning and keep up our motivation'.

Also, as expected, students shared concerns regarding the lower quality of studies, in particular, related to the laboratory work and practical assignments (4 statements in Spring, and 3 statements in Autumn semester).

The statements that add new dimension or at least nuance to the phenomena will be analysed further on.

1) Interestingly, students shared that online studies caused less stress. 10 statements were grouped into this group, when students described their experiences in Spring and 3 statements regarding experiences in Autumn. Interestingly, and we think, very importantly, 6 of the positive statements of less stress were on testing (in Spring: 'clear test – less stress'; 'tests for self-assessment reduce stress, very useful'; 'feedback on assignments - very useful'). In Autumn - 1 statement ('tests for assessment and for self-assessment- very useful', 'easy, I like tests, good for me'). One statement regarding lack of clear rules regarding assessment was provided in Spring and then again one in Autumn by the same participant.

2) Regarding methods used, students noted that online studies are well equipped for theory-orientated classes, and lectures. However, 1 statement in Spring and again 1 in Autumn, by different participants about the insufficiency of methods for group work and for project method were identified.

3) Also, unexpectedly, only 1 statement (out of total 85) was about having learnt a lot in Spring semester.

4) 2 statements in Spring semester seem interesting, they were not allocated to either group (Positive or Negative): 'On the one hand, very convenient, because I was multi-tasking, I could have coffee, and do other things during the class, but then, it was a bit difficult to follow the class, and thus the quality of my studies was not great". The statement is interesting, because at least one of 37 participants demonstrated quite a high level of self-reflection, and also, this is a good example, that nothing in social/educational realm is straightforward and one-dimensional. In this case, while the flexibility of online studies has been universally praised for decades, at the same time the flexibility and multi-tasking have their downturns too. Structure, clear time-table, clear genres (a class, a seminar, laboratory work, team work using project method) of activities contribute to effectiveness of studies, because flexibility will not at all times add to overall in-depth learning. As another participant (in Spring semester) shared: 'All in all, online classes, clear tasks, self-assessments gave the structure for my studies'.

The statements of general nature: 'More difficult'; 'Too much hassle', 'Difficult to concentrate", 'Lack of personal time management skills, 'It is always better to have actual face-to face consultations' were identified, however, they do not seem to add any significant new dimension to the general picture.

5. DISCUSSIONS AND CONCLUSIONS

The limitations of the study have to be taken into account, such as the relatively small number of participants. However, the fact that participants were asked to give the grade to their experiences in online studies in Spring and then in Autumn semester, and then provide explanatory statements for the grade. Therefore, they were encouraged for introspection in a structured, yet open way, which, we believe, compensated for some if the downturns.

Therefore, some of the results may generate interesting and productive insights for higher education didactics for online studies, because, we believe, even after the quarantine is over nationally and globally, universities will transfer a larger proportion of activities online as continuing practice. The 2020 may have prompted a major transformation in higher education.

While a significant portion of findings added to the existing body of findings or the educational practical experiences of authors, however, some findings potentially may add to the enhancement of didactics.

Firstly, the unexpected dimension regarding assessment. Our findings may be related to other findings on tests and testing. E.g., IAU completed a global survey on the impact of pandemic on higher education around the world; the survey was distributed in Spring 2020. It revealed that globally two thirds of institutions replaced classroom teaching and learning to an online studies (p. 11). More than a half of institutions planned (at the time of the Survey, in Spring 2020) to organise exams online, though the variation was identified, because as many as 80 % of European universities planned to organise online exams (The impact of covid-19 on higher education around the world IAU Global Survey Report, 2020). Evidently, back in Spring 2020, when the total swift shift to online studies had to be performed because of necessity, though institutions struggled with a task, some Lithuanian students (10 statements out of 85 totally comprise 11.8% of total number of statements) were positive about online testing, self-assessment tools. Lithuanian students noted the benefits of online feedback. While this particular finding remains to be further investigated, we, however, posit, that the positive reactions may be related to personal learning styles (Zuzeviciute, 2011). Here it is important to note that both summative assessment and formative evaluations, it seems, may be further integrated into post-quarantine higher education without detrimental effects to a significant proportion of students.

Secondly, the fact that 10.6% (9 statements: 7 statements about laboratory work and 2 statements about group work/project method) of all statements were about insufficiency of practice-related and even team activity methods, leads to formulating of at least two tasks for the immediate future.

1) There is a need to invest into teachers' competencies in the field, because there might be tools that will prompt students' more effective engagement in the group/project work. Though, evidently, some laboratory/practice work cannot - and must not –be transferred into online mode, however, there are many activities, which may be performed in teams. Teachers may not be aware of the assortment of tools already available;

2) There is need for further in-depth cooperation with the IT professionals, because it may be that in some cases the assortment is insufficient. It would seem that the IT and education professionals still need to invest into designing IT tools and IT based methods that will facilitate work in teams, support project method, may be even supplement to some degree laboratory work. Surely, again, not all laboratory/practice work can – and must - be transferred into the online mode. However, multi-way instead of two - way or one-way online communication needs to be strengthened both by developing teachers' IT- didactical competence, and the IT tools in this regard.

REFERENCES

Abarius, P. and Liubinas, V. 2010. Integration of electronic learning environment and academic information system, *Electronic learning, information and communication: theory and practice*, no. 1, pp. 22-52.

Augustinaitis A. 2004. Ziniu visuomenes rastingumas. *Information Sciences*. 2004 (31), p. 18-27.

Burgess S. and Sievertsen H. H. 2020 Schools, skills, and learning: The impact of COVID-19 on education. *VOX&CEPR. Research-based policy analysis and commentary from leading economists*. https://voxeu.org/article/impact-covid-19-education

Butrime, E. and Zuzeviciute, V. 2014. *E- Learning as a socio-cultural system: towards a balanced development*. Saarbrücken: LAP LAMBERT Academic Publishing.

COVID-19: Higher Education challenges and responses. *The Global Voice of Higher Education. International Association of Universities*. (2020). Retrieved from: https://www.iau-aiu.net/COVID-19-Higher-Education-challenges-and-responses#SURVEY%20REPORTS.

Davidson A., L. and Waddington, D. 2010. E-Learning in the university: When will it really happen? *eLearning Papers*. Nº 21 September 2010.

Hodges, C. et al. 2020. The Difference Between Emergency Remote Teaching and Online Learning. *EDUCAUSE Review*. Retrieved from: https://er.educause.edu/articles/2020/3/the-difference-between-emergency-remote-teaching-and-online-learning.

Jonson H. 2008. Why Higher Education Faculty Resist to Participate in Distance Education. *Proceedings of E-learning 2009*. M.B. Nunes, M.McPherson (ed.). IADIS Multi Conference on Computer Science and Information Systems (MCCSIS 2009). IADIS Press. p. 55-58.

Kacinskaite, J. and Motiejune, G. 2011. Information System Organizations in Internal Communication, *Mokslo taikomieji Tyrimai Lietuvos Kolegijose*, pp. 32-38.

Kaunas University of Technology. 2020. *Important information about COVID-19*. Kaunas University of Technology. 2020. Retrieved from: https://en.ktu.edu/covid-19/.

Kucharczyk-Brus, B. and Mielcarski M. 2020. Higher Education under Crisis Conditions – Experiences from the Remote Teaching of Artistic and Design Subjects. *ICERI2020 Proceedings. 13th annual International Conference of Education, Research and Innovation*, 2582-2589.

Lithuanian University of Health Sciences. 2020. Tyrėjai: naujienos apie COVID-19 studentams kelia nerimą. News. 2020-11-27. Lithuanian University of Health Sciences. Vytautas Magnus University. Retrieved from: https://lsmuni.lt/lt/naujienos/naujienos/tyrejai-naujienos-apie-covid-19-studentams-kelia-nerima-.html.

Mamardasvili M., K. 1958. Procesy analiza i sinteza. *Voprosy filosofii*, No 2. Moskva.

Means B. et al., 2014. *Learning Online: What Research Tells Us about Whether, When and How*. Routledge, New York.

Moore, G. A. 2002. *Crossing the Chasm: marketing and selling high-tech products to mainstream customers*. rev. ed., NY. HarperBusiness Publishers Inc.

Protecting and Transforming Education for Shared Futures and Common Humanity - *A Joint Statement on the COVID-19 Crisis. International Commission on the Futures of Education*. UNESCO. 17 Apr 2020. (2020). Retrieved from: https://reliefweb.int/report/world/protecting-and-transforming-education-shared-futures-and-common-humanity-joint.

Ramayah, B. and Kumar R. 2020. Challenges Towards Online Teaching During COVID 19 Pandemic in Malaysia: University Lecturers' Perspective. *ICERI2020 Proceedings. 13th annual International Conference of Education, Research and Innovation*, 425-432.

Rizk N. 2020. Grouping student by learning style and covid status. *ICERI2020 Proceedings. 13th annual International Conference of Education, Research and Innovation*, 2341-2346.

Rutkauskiene D. et al, 2006. *Lietuvos virtualus universitetas*. Kaunas.

Shiva V. 2005. Biotechnological Development and the Conservation of Biodiversity. *Internalising Cultural Studies. An Anthology*. (eds. Ackbar Abbas, John Nguyet Erni.) Blackwell Publishing.

Souleles, N. and Laghos, A. 2020. From Face-to-face to Online: Assessing the Effectiveness of the Rapid Transition of Higher Education Due to the Coronavirus Outbreak. *ICERI2020 Proceedings. 13th annual International Conference of Education, Research and Innovation*, 927-934.

Stacey, E. and Gerbic, P. 2009. Introduction to Blended Learning Practices. In E. Stacey and P.Gerbic (Ed.) *Effective Blended Learning Practices: Evidence-Based Perspectives in ICT-Facilitated Education*. Publisher: Information Science Reference. p. 382.

The impact of covid-19 on higher education around the world. *IAU Global Survey Report*. International Association of Universities. Retrieved from: iau_covid19_and_he_survey_report_final_may_2020.pdf (iau-aiu.net).

Truskauskaite-Kuneviciene, E. et al. 2020. Studiju pradzia COVID-19 pandemijos metu. Tyrimais gristos rekomendacijos universitetams ir studentams. *Psichotraumatologijos centras*. Vilnius University. (2020). Retrieved from: https://www.fsf.vu.lt/dokumentai/Dokumentainuorodos/Rekomendacijosuniversitetamsirstudentams.pdf.

Vytautas Magnus University. 2020. *Prevention Measures and Actions against Coronavirus at Vytautas Magnus University*. 9th November, 2020. Vytautas Magnus University, (2020). Retrieved from: https://zua.vdu.lt/en/prevention-measures-and-actions-against-coronavirus-at-vytautas-magnus-university/.

What do you think about the future of digital Education and Training in EU? Needs, issues, practices and possible improvements in education through digital transformation. European Digital Learning Network. 2017.

World Health Organization. 2020. Mental health and psychosocial considerations during the COVID-19 outbreak, 18 March 2020 (No.WHO/2019-nCoV/MentalHealth/2020.1). World Health Organization, (2020).

Zuzeviciute, V. 2011. *Learning at university: challenges, strategies, perspectives for lifelong learning*. Saarbrücken : Lambert academic publishing.

INTERNATIONAL TEACHER TRAINING COURSES - A NEW STEP TO GLOBALIZATION

Iliana Mirtschewa
Sofia University "St. Kliment Ohridski", Shipchenski Prohod 69A, Sofia 1574, Bulgaria

ABSTRACT

The paper presents the aims and the design of the international e-learning course for teacher training "International Project" / Internet and Competence to work on the Project"/IPC/, organized with students from the Sofia University "St. Kliment Ohridski" (Bulgaria) and universities from Germany, USA, Spain, Japan, Sweden and Poland (http://www.internationalproject-ipc.com/en/). The project has a long tradition and is developed in co-operation from university teachers by using different methods and approaches. The project is based on an inquiry-based learning. The topics of the student's investigations are connected with the school education and with the children's perspective on school, teaching and learning. Coached by university teachers and tutors the students work in many international groups using different research methods and web tools as wikis, chat forums or blogs. By working on topics selected from the teacher training curriculum the students improve their expertise related to the curriculum and develop awareness of cultural differences. At the end of the course the students from the different universities present the results of the comparative international research and do conclusions about the differences and similarities in the curriculum and the education in different countries and continents. The IPC project fosters the development of many competences for teacher students because of working and doing educational research in international team.

KEYWORDS

Teacher Training, Learning Process, International Research, e-Learning, International Project, Internet

1. INTRODUCTION

In the modern world without borders the formation of a variety of key competences acquires greater significance. Of great importance for the modern teacher is not only to know the theory of his specialty and pedagogical concept, but also to be able to communicate with their colleagues, to work in a team, to generate, share and justify ideas, to make valuable observations on the effectiveness of his work and the experience, the interests and the achievements of students he works with. The basis of various activities involving the modern pedagogue inevitably includes the modern technologies of the Internet as a global communications network.

Another contemporary trend that we cannot ignore is the global internationalization in education. Official international documents concerning generating line policies are approved and adapted. Various opportunities for communication and collaboration with colleagues from other countries are determined. Widespread is the participation of schools and other educational establishments in international /bilateral and multilateral/ projects in European and global programs. This implies the availability of information not only for the national traditions, but also knowledge of the educational systems of other countries. It also requires knowledge of English and skills to conduct a joint investigation.

2. BODY OF PAPER

2.1 History and Development

The e-course "Internet and competence to work on the project"/ "International Project" provides an answer to these challenges. The e-course was organized in 2006 by the Sofia University "St. Kliment Ohridski" during the training of the students in the pedagogical specialties. In the period between 2006 to 2021 it was attended by students enrolled in bachelor and master programs, of the specialties: Primary School Education and Foreign Language, Preschool and Primary Education, Primary school education and Preschool education and Foreign Language, Social Education and Pedagogy.

The concept of the course is the brainchild of Professor Jean-Paul Martin from Catholic University in Eichstätt-Ingolstadt, Germany (Martin, 2005). His idea was to connect students, future specialists, from different countries and continents, to work on joint projects through information and communication technologies.

During the first year of the course it was attended by students from different specialties (pedagogical, philosophic, economic), countries and universities. The experience has shown that the variety of subject areas, interests and competences of the students cover a wide range, making it difficult to work and also creates difficulties in the formulation of conclusions. That forced the full reconsideration of concept of the course. For effective implementation of the tasks of great importance was to find professors from foreign universities who work with students from pedagogical specialties and to enable the developed projects to overlap with the training programs of the students and thus to enrich their pedagogical experience (Mirtschewa, 2007, 480).

The original concept had been adapted to the teacher training curriculum in 2008 by Prof. Dr. Klaudia Schultheis (Catholic University Eichstätt-Ingolstadt) and was first tested with Prof. Dr. Iliana Mirtschewa (Sofia University St. Kliment Ohridski, Bulgaria) and in the following years evaluated with Prof. Dr. Leigh Ausband (University of North Carolina Charlotte, USA).

The current university training course was developed as innovative international project for training of teachers. Students and university professors from eight universities (Catholic University Eichstaett-Ingolstadt, Germany; Sofia University "St. Kl. Ohridski", Bulgaria; University of North Carolina Charlotte, USA; University of Granada, Spain; Catholik Junshin University Nagasaki, Japan; Yamaguchi University, Japan; California State University Fullerton, USA, Karlstad University, Sweden; Pedagogical University of Krakow and Adam Mickiewicz University in Poznan, Poland) take part in it.

During the period 2006-2021 more than 1000 students attended the course. In the beginning the basic work language was German, later German and English and in the last 11 years English. In the years of the implementation of the course different communication systems were used: Wikiwesity (during the first years), SNS mixxt (social communication net provided by mixxt GmbH), Haiku Learning and during the last year Schoology. To create a main web page, book with the participants in the course, forums, groups' pages, boxes of files, WIKI, chats, news and a calendar the Web 2.0 was applied.

In the process of training the students work in international groups and they make a scientific study of selected research topics related to their interests.

2.2 Competencies and Skills

The course has the following objectives:

- enrichment of pedagogical research experience of students /shaping the theoretical justification of the chosen topic, formulating of objectives and the working hypothesis, selection of an appropriate research methodology/;
- mastering the skills of the prospective teachers to monitor the characteristics of the learning process, to monitor students' behavior and to ascertain their concepts interests and preferences;
- formation of skills for analyzing, formation and presentation of the results of an implemented empirical study, formulation of scientific conclusions and conclusions;
- development of competence to work in international teams and projects;
- mastering of skills for communication with potential professional partners through Internet;
- mastering of skills to work with information and communication technologies;
- improvement of the skills for learning of foreign languages.

2.3 Phases

The common work passes through the following phases:

- Each student presents himself in a common forum and shares his interests and creates a personal profile on the Internet. This is the way to establish contacts with international partners.
- During the next phase, based on the topics, proposed by the students, international groups are formed to conduct research in a selected problem. Each group works in its own research and thematic forum. In this phase examining of scientific literature on the topic is also done. The aim and the hypotheses are also determined. The students select appropriate research methods. The suggestions of the individual students from each group are summarized by WIKI.
- In the third phase, students from different universities make theoretical and empirical researches in schools or other educational institutions. After the completion they summarize the results and analyze the results from the different countries. Then through a teamwork the students make a comparative analysis of the results and formulate conclusions.
- The last phase is related with the preparation of a common Poster or Power Point presentation or e-Book (using Book Creator) showing the research design and summarizing the results.
- On a special day organized for each research group the students present the phases and the results of their work. This is usually done at the national level, with each group presenting their results at their own university. During the last year (2020/2021), in a pandemic, the final presentations were held online, with the participation of all students from all countries and universities participating in the course. This enabled international groups to jointly present the results of their research. Thus, the team work in the group took place at all stages of the work, including the final one.

In all phases of their work the students were led and consulted by the university teachers participating in the teams of the different universities. Tutors are also included to help students. Each activity included in the different phases was discussed with the students from the different universities and the respective university classes. Successfully graduated students receive a certificate issued jointly by the Catholic University of Eichstätt-Ingolstadt University and the university in which they are trained.

2.4 Examples

In 2012/2013 the course "Internet and competence to work on a project" was attended by 111 students from six countries, who worked on nine topics. Discussions on individual projects were organized in thematic group forums. The number of participants varies among the groups. The comments in the group forums are numerous, well-grounded and testify to students' active participation in shaping the design of the pedagogical study developed by the respective team (see Table1).

Table 1. Participation of students in group forums

Group	**Number of participants**	**Number of comments**
Group 1	**18**	**230**
Group 2	**17**	**89**
Group 3	**17**	**162**
Group 4	**20**	**132**
Group 5	**22**	**123**
Group 6	**16**	**51**
Group 7	**16**	**94**
Group 8	**13**	**68**
Group 9	**18**	**127**

Within the academic year 2014/2015, the main theme, that the students research is "Homework". All 136 participants were divided into 10 groups. In each group there are students from different countries, they were all selected form classes of future primary school teachers, from six different universities and countries (Radeva/ Velkovski, 2015, 96).

The number of written comments was 1771, an average of 177 comments in group and 17.7 comments per participant. This statistic reveals that each participant had shared his thoughts on the subject around 18 times (Radeva/ Velkovski, 2015, 97).

Choosing the design of the study, is the step that caused the most serious discussions. Students were asked to give their own ideas and suggestions that can be used with children of primary school age. After a decision is made the group must decide which variables will they test and how, thus five tipes of disighn were formed (Radeva/ Velkovski, 2015, 97)

Seven of the groups have chosen to use telling a story to the students and to combine it with another method - writing a letter (three of the groups), completing the questionnaire has been used from three of the groups and drawing was used by one group (Radeva/ Velkovski, 2015, 97.

A total of 600 children took participation in the study from all countries involved in the project, an average of 60 children in ten groups. This allowed these three types of analysis:

- Qualitative analysis at group level;
- A comparative analysis between the groups used a uniform methodology;
- A common frequency analysis, allowing quantitative analysis of all respondents.

Results: The collected information was evaluated by the groups then the results were compared with the theoretical content and the data was analyzed according to the frequency of occurrence (Radeva/ Velkovski, 2015, 98).

Within the academic year 2020/2021, the main research topic is "Covid 19 Impact on Schools – Organizing Teaching and Learning in Difficult Times" because of the current pandemic situation in the world.

The objectives of the study were:

- to study the impact of the pandemic on people's lives;
- to establish how the epidemic situation changes the attitudes of adults and children;
- to monitor changes that occur in the field of education;
- to find out how the primary school students adapt to the situation;
- what impact does the current situation have on the health and well-being of students;
- what impact does the pandemic have on human communication;
- how the teacher's role changes;
- how the participants in the learning process feel when they are placed only in front of the screen and are deprived of direct contact with the other subjects involved in the process;
- how the role of the information and communication technologies in the learning process in a pandemic is changing.

About 100 students were divided into groups. They chose some of the following research topics (Table 2):

Table 2. Research topics (2020/2021)

Research topics
How Does Covid 19 Influence Learning and Teaching in the Future?
Impact of Covid 19 on Student's Mental Health and Well-being
How Covid 19 Affects the World? Challenges for Children
On the Other Side of the Screen
How Covid 19 Changes the World of the Children?
Navigating the New Normal in the Covid 19 Pandemic
Barriers for Learning Online and How to Deal with Them
The Differences in the Quality of Learning and Teaching Caused by Technical Devices Combination with Educational Disparities
Is Online Learning Effective Now?
Barriers for Learning Online and How to Deal with Them

The students used Padlet and Book Creator to summarize their ideas and the results from the research (theoretical and empirical). Replaced were the traditional ways to shape the ideas of working in groups and of presentation through Power Point and Poster. This made it possible to try new ways of designing and presenting a joint research product. The knowledge and skills of the students to use information and communication technologies were enriched.

In the conditions of a pandemic some changes in learning and communication between students from different universities were found. The desire of the students to discuss as often as possible the planning of the stages of their work and the results of the conducted research through online media/ platforms (Zoom, Skype, WhatsApp etc.) was strengthened. The organization of the final online meeting for all universities, concluding with a presentation of the results of the work, had a great influence on the motivation of the students to form their conclusions and e-Books for the presentation. The intensity of the meetings increased to 100%. The students also used often mobile phones to communicate and to study in groups. This allowed learning to take place outside the home and classrooms and to be held at a time convenient for students from different countries and time zones.

The increased desire for more intensive group learning can be explained in several ways. On the one hand, during the year of online training (Sommer semester 2019/2020 and Winter semester 2020/2021) in the conditions of a pandemic, the students got acquainted with various programs and means of online communication. This increased their competence in the field of information and communication technologies. On the other hand, artificially imposed social isolation causes the search for more opportunities to meet and exchange information with peers, including in the learning process. This significantly alleviates the problems associated with social distance. This also has a strong impact on training, leads to increased motivation and improved learning outcomes.

2.5 Survey

To evaluate the effectiveness of the ongoing course every year on-line polls are conducted. They ascertain the attitude of students to work in an international team and the attitude of the future teachers to work together. For example, the results of the survey conducted with students in 2008-2009 indicate positively that 95% of students believe that for the teacher of the 21st century is of great importance to know the teaching methods in other countries.

Respondents point to two aspects of this need (Ausband / Schultheis, 2010, 276):

- to know the pedagogical practice in other countries so that to assess the level of the educational system in their own country,
- to help the teachers who work with children from different cultures.

These responses highlight an important advantage of the ongoing international course, namely the preparation of the students for their future career as teachers in a globalized society.

A questionnaire created by the project leader, Prof. Dr. Klaudia Schultheis, was uploaded on the IPC project website enabling all the student participants worldwide to evaluate the project in its ending stage in early December 2013. The study takes into account the positive aspects of the participation in the course and also the difficulties that students encounter in the process of work (Suzuki, 2013, 3).

The questionnaire consisted of three parts about the respondents' background (Suzuki et.al., 2015, 75):

- Personal Data,
- International Experience,
- Internet Experience; as well as four parts about the IPC Project,
- Experience of Group Project,
- Learning Objectives,
- Problems,
- Conclusion.

Some of the results point the opinion of the students from the different universities and countries in a variety of areas:

Experience with IPC: Learning Objectives

The students reported their learning objectives could be achieved as demonstrated by the following results: i) improvement of international experiences (69.4%), ii) learned how to organize an online collaboration

(67.4%), iii) increase of knowledge on the group topic (61.7%), iv) broadened knowledge of education and schools in other countries (61.3%), v) familiarity with internet platforms (59.2%), and vi) benefit for future work as a teacher (59.2%).

Experience with IPC: Problems

Three problems rated at various degrees were reported by the respondents: i) knowing what to do (63.3% for 'partially', 12.2% for 'a lot', and 24.5% for 'no'); ii) time schedule (61.2% for 'partially', 14.3% for 'a lot', and 24.5% for 'no'); and iii) finding literature and information about the topic (57.1% for 'partially', 18.4% for 'a lot', and 32.7% for 'no'). On the other hand, the students reported the following to be mostly unproblematic: i) teachers (67.3% for 'no'); ii) other group members (55.1% for 'no'); and iii) group topic (51% for 'no'). (Suzuki et.al., 2015, 77-78)

Simultaneously with the international survey, discussions that aim to ascertain how students evaluate the course of training, are periodically carried out in each country. During the discussion, the students share their impressions of joint working. They share their previous experience in the field of e-learning and in the field in which they did the research. The students share the benefits, the new challenges in learning and communication, the issues and problems that have arisen.

Summary of the impressions of the prospective teachers from the Sofia University "St. Kliment Ohridski" the students highly evaluate the ongoing course activities, share the benefits of such training and communication (see Table 3).

Table 3. The impressions of the students from the Sofia University "St. Kliment Ohridski" for the university course "Internet and the competence to work on a project"/ "International project"

Impressions
We now have an idea of the way in which the educational process takes place in the other countries
We worked for the improvement of our communication skills
We learned how to work in a team
We found out that such projects require creativity and autonomy
Through such research we can understand a lot about kids on a certain topic by exploring
We established new contacts
We met with new perspectives on discussed issues
We established communication with people from different nationalities
We learned how to do a comparative study
We found out that working in team is of great importance for the equality of all group members

Students, who participated on the course in 2014/2015 at the Sofia university "St. Kliment Ohridski" did the following conclusions:

- The structure of the project allows participants to learn about specific steps and laws when engaging in a research.
- The IPC project allows active participation - exchange of experience and ideas for expanding horizons in the personal and professional aspect of its participants.
- Participation in international group requires good knowledge of the working language (English). Part of students experiencing difficulties with English and became passive participants. This creates some discomfort at all levels and makes difficult the completion of the task.
- Opportunity for discussion and exchange of different practices in different countries, allows comparison and exchange of knowledge towards different issues and allows the construction of a reasoned position of each participant.
- Group work, increases students' skills in organizing, good time management, tolerance and argumentation when participating in discussions.

- Knowledge of different cultures and educational systems and the creation of new professional contacts and research skills (Radeva/ Velkovski, 2015, 101).

2.6 Conclusions

The analysis of the international and national research shows that students positively identify their collaboration with foreign universities from different countries and continents and the joint work on the pedagogical project.

They appreciated the university course "Internet and Competence to Work on the Project"/ "International Project" and consider it of great importance for their future profession. In their opinion the future trends in education will require teamwork skills, communicative competences, skills for working with information and communication technologies and national and international collaboration with colleagues from different schools all over the world.

Obtaining information about foreign education systems, the comparison of pedagogical realities, learning about foreign cultures and traditions is perceived as a great advantage of the international online course.

In the conditions of a pandemic, the desire for online learning and communication between students working in international groups is intensifying because of a situation of social isolation, due to limited live contacts.

The variety of programs and means of online communication the students use during the pandemic is increasing. The competence of students to work with information and communication technologies is also growing.

The information and communication technologies are becoming a substitute for direct social contacts and communication in the conditions of a pandemic. They become a powerful means of communication and overcoming social isolation.

REFERENCES

Ausband, Leigh, Klaudia Schultheis, 2010, Utilizing Web 2.0. to Provide an International Experience for Pre-Service Elementary Education Teachers – The IPC Project. *Computers in the Schools,* 27: 3. 266-287.

Martin, Jean-Pol, 2005, Komplexitaet reduzieren: Europakompetenz im IPK erwerben. *Europa interdisziplinaer – Probleme und Perspektiven heutiger Europastudien.* Wuerzburg: Koenigshausen & Neumann, 61-74.

Mirtschewa, Iliana, 2007, Mezhdunaroden universitetski kurs na tema Ïnternet I kompetentnost za rabota po proekt. Rabota po pedagogicheski proekti chrez internet. *Priemstvenost I perspective v razvitieto na pedagogièskata teoriq I practica.* Sofia, "Veda Slovena – JG", 480-481.

Mirtschewa, Iliana, 2013, Mezhdunarodni studentski izsledovatelski proecti – globalizacia na podgotovkata na uchiteli chrez elektronno obuchenie. *Izsledvane I predstavjane na dobri practiki pri integrirane na informacionni I komunicacionni tehnologii v obrazovanieto.* Sofia, Avangard Prima, 45-51.

Radeva, Sn., D. Velkovsk, 2015, IPC International project. An innovative teaching project to provide international experience to teacher students. *Children's Perspective on School, Teaching and Learning.* Farrago: Sofia, p. 96-102.

Suzuki, Chizuko, Kenichi Ishida, Shota Yoshihara, Klaudia Schultheis, Barbara Riedhammer, 2013, An International Project Developed on an SNS mixxt System Making Use of Web 2.0. Technology to Increase the Students' Core Competence as Future Teachers. In: *WorldCALL*, Glasgow, UK, 2013.

Suzuki, Ch., Ishida, K., Yoshihara, Sh., Schultheis, K. & Riedhammer, B., 2015, A Report of IPC 2013: Analyses of student participants' response data to the project end-survey and the cultural awareness profiel survey in comparison with the preceding year. *Children's Perspective on School, Teaching and Learning.* Farrago: Sofia, 75-85.

A REFERENCE MODEL FOR MOBILE PLAYFUL LEARNING ENVIRONMENTS

Jan Maushagen and Olga De Troyer
WISE Research Group, Department of Computer Science, Vrije Universiteit Brussel
Pleinlaan 2, 1050 Brussel, Belgium

ABSTRACT

We propose a novel model for learning environments to target the characteristics of digital natives and to improve informal learning practices, i.e. the exploration, discovery and self-monitoring of learning content and the reflection on learning activities. The Mobile Playful Learning Environment (MPLE) model is defined as consisting of seven main features (mobile user context, data collection and analysis, learner visualization, self-monitoring, persuasion, playfulness, and micro-learning) intended to encourage continuous usage and self-reflection. As a case study we developed TICKLE, an application that implements the MPLE model to re-activate and re-motivate youngsters at risk for school dropout, for learning by stimulating curiosity and engagement through the recognition of non-formal learning opportunities.

KEYWORDS

Informal Learning, Mobile Learning, Playful Learning, Micro-Learning, Digital Natives, Reference Model

1. INTRODUCTION

In general, the traditional way of learning takes place in a classroom environment. In such an environment, the teacher can explicitly observe interaction and participation of the learners. The advantage is that the teacher can provide the appropriate interventions immediately. However, classic classroom teaching frequently faces difficulties. It might be difficult to gain attention from everyone in a large class due to the "one-size fits everybody" approach usually applied. Some teaching methods (e.g., flipped classroom or problem-based learning) can overcome this but may be challenging with a large class size. On the other hand, the ever-widening accumulation and access to information facilitated by modern communication technologies could lead to a situation of no boundaries to knowledge construction. Wherever we are, we can just take our smartphone and follow up the infinite trails of information. This can be considered as informal learning (Sharples et al., 2009) which is characterized as learning integrated with daily routines, triggered by an internal or external event, not highly conscious, and an inductive process of reflection and action. This way of learning could become an important part of lifelong learning (Sharples, 2000), which is the "ongoing, voluntary, and self-motivated" pursuit of knowledge for either personal or professional reasons.

However, in practice, most people are often overwhelmed by the sheer amount of information faced in the digital world. They may not possess the skills to make sense of all of it. Especially digital literacy skills (Ng, 2012), i.e. the ability to locate, filter, compare and judge digital information, and skills in data analysis, become increasingly important in this kind of learning (Gallardo-Echenique et al., 2015). With a steady stream of information and tools available, it is likely to miss out important information. Moreover, when information is scattered across different sources and in different tools, it is hard for users to create a complete mental model of the environment. Especially the so-called digital native learners (Thompson, 2013), born after the 1980s and grown up with digital technology, have an ambivalent relationship with this overabundance of information and tools. On the one hand they are used to a wide range of information technologies in their daily life: "They use search engines and social networks as a first port of call for knowledge unlike older generations who were used to printed press, radio and television" (Helsper & Eynon, 2010). Because information is received fast, they frequently switch activities. They prefer high visual content, animation and interactivity over static textual content (Dresang, 2005; Prensky, 2003). Digital natives expect information to give answers as well as to be engaging (Radford et al., 2007; Helsper & Eynon,

2010). However, the apparent familiarity and competence with computers disguises some worrying problems in information literacy (Pettenati et al., 2009). Fast switching between activities often results in a superficial view rather than an in-depth understanding of information. The speed of young people's information seeking suggests that little time is spent in evaluating information, neither for relevance, accuracy or authority. While independent learning is an admirable aspiration, many learners will continue to require guidance in their learning process. Leaving them entirely alone in learning activities can result in increased dropout rates and demotivation. Therefore, we argue that even for informal learning, a learning environment could provide added value. Such a learning environment should provide ways and guidance to explore interests freely and exploit them for future opportunities from a personal, professional or educational perspective.

In this paper, we introduce the Mobile Playful Learning Environment model that aims to provide a reference model for such type of learning environment. First, we motivate the main features of the model and present the learning pipeline to indicate how the main features interact with each other. Next, we explain how TICKLE, a mobile playful learning environment for youngsters at risk for school dropout was built based on this model. The paper ends with related work and conclusions.

2. MOBILE PLAYFUL LEARNING ENVIRONMENT

To fulfill the demands of digital natives and guide the future development of learning environments in the context of informal learning, we introduce the **Mobile Playful Learning Environment (MPLE) model** that uses the mobile platform to integrate micro-learning with journaling, persuasion, playfulness and visualization techniques to support self-reflection. The nature of the presented MPLE model is conceptual and architectural and should be considered as a reference model.

This section presents and motivates the main features of a MLPE, as well as its learning pipeline.

2.1 The Main features a MPLE

Mobile User Context. The learner's mobile context characterizes the situation of the learner. In e-learning, it is common to use a user profile containing information about the learner (such as personal information, goals, knowledge, interests, preferences, learning history, and possibly also the information about the user's context (such as location, time and device)) (Zhou & Rechert, 2008). We prefer to use the term Mobile User Context because in a MPLE, the mobile aspect is very important. With a mobile Internet-enabled device the user can connect to the MPLE from everywhere at any time. Information can be associated with locations and a wide field of topic areas such as history, culture, and sports to extend excursions or informal strolling through the neighborhood with up-to-date content. Therefore, the mobile user context includes information about the current position of the learner, as well as of relevant objects, like point of interests, in the public space. We distinguish the following dimensions for the mobile user context:

- The **personal context** contains personal information such as past learning behavior, current progress in learning activities, learning styles, cognitive abilities and learning goals.
- The **location context** includes learner's current location and previous location history.
- The **social context** includes information about peers in the learning communities.
- The **technology context** contains information about technology used or available (mobile, desktop or wearables) and their characteristics (e.g., GPS precision, touch input, screen size).

Data Collection and Analysis. To construct and keep the mobile user context up to date, but also to support the self-reflection, data needs to be collected and analyzed. Hence the need for data collection and analysis. Static user data can be collected in the traditional way (e.g., by questionnaires or from external sources), but the dynamic data needs to be collected by the MPLE. This data collection involves recording the interaction of the learner with the MPLE, stored as so-called learning traces. These are granular snapshots of student activity. The most basic kind is a "page-visit" trail in the environment (Clemens et al., 2018). Other learning traces include moving to a point of interest, performing a learning activity, or adding an interest to one's profile. These traces should be logged for later analysis, e.g. to create a historical log of the user's actions across time.

Learner Visualization. Information visualization has been proven to be a powerful means to present large amounts of information and give people insight and is thus a perfect choice to make various types of context information and learning traces visible to the learner, in order to provide structure, awareness and guidance. Visualizations can provide support for improving awareness on learning, for instance along a timeline. Moreover, they can aggregate data, such as participation rates in events and message reply delays, into a set of high-level indicators that can be displayed to learners (Govaerts et al., 2010).

Self-Monitoring. It is important that a MPLE offers resources for self-reflection on activities, learner context and peers to gain awareness of learning behavior. We propose to do this by providing journaling, which means automatically journal keeping by gathering learning traces and augmenting them with additional information. This can offer advice and guidance for future learning such as highlighting missed learning opportunities or recommending new learning material. In this process, also narration could be used as a mode of presenting events within a context. Many people perceive information as unrelated facts if they do not find personal value in them, but when it is placed in the context of a story, it is easier to find connections of personal interest and thereby improve recall, interpretation and synthesis of knowledge (Lambert & Hessler, 2018). These principles should be combined with an adaptive and personalized approach, meaning that what will be offered, how and when, should be adapted to the needs of the individual learner and be dynamically responsive to the learner's behavior.

Persuasion. To stimulate continuous use of the learning environment, persuasion strategies (Cialdini, 2001) are recommended. Mobile technologies create special opportunities for persuasive strategies, because they are closer to the human than any other device and used ubiquitous and pervasive throughout life; people have them with them all the time. Mobile platforms can more easily motivate people to achieve their own personal goals. According to (Fogg, 2002), it can layer information into our lives in a way that changes our behavior. This persuasion power has been shown in many domains, including marketing, healthcare education and environmental sustainability (Thieme et al., 2012). Mobile devices enable access to location, personal photos, movement acceleration or document access history. By exploiting these capabilities, they can use the personal data flows coming from mobile devices to persuade the user to change behavior positively.

Micro-Learning. We propose to use the concept of Micro-Learning which assumes that people can learn better and more effectively when the content is broken down into digestible parts (Kovachev et al., 2011). Learning in small steps better fits the way people consume information today on the Web, i.e. in terms of small text or status updates (Bruck et al., 2012). Following this approach, the role of the content creator is to create small learning activities that can be interwoven into the daily life of the learner. MPLE should deliver them in small self-contained context-related learning activities and provide users with instant feedback.

Playfulness. Next to the use of persuasion, the integration of game-based concepts familiar to youngsters, such as obtaining rewards, could be a way to motivate learners to use the environment. This is known as gamification. Game mechanics, such as points, badges, leaderboards, avatars or stories, can be integrated into the environment to scaffold playfulness. However, note that playfulness is not the same as gamification. Adding game elements can make a system more fun but it is by no means sufficient. It is not because one can earn points or badges with a learning activity that the activity will be perceived as fun. Moreover, some people may perceive some game elements such as points, badges and leaderboards, as annoying or childish. Play is an activity engaged in for enjoyment and is often a voluntary activity (Plass et al., 2015).

2.2 The Learning Pipeline of a MPLE

A pipeline (see Figure 1) is used to show how the user's mobile context and the micro learning can generate learning traces that can be visualized to turn awareness into insight. The figure shows how a MPLE's components, realizing the features mentioned above, interact and contribute to the final goal.

The Mobile User Context and Micro-Learning components contain all information needed for the extraction of learning traces, which happens in the Data Collection and Cleaning component. This data is further analyzed in the Data Analysis component. The Learner Visualization component is responsible to make the learning traces and analysis results visible. For instance, in this way, the learner can realize that (s)he crossed each week a famous monument with a long history in the city that can nurture her or his interest in that topic. These events are narrated with the help of Journaling Techniques to help generate awareness of the learning activities, which is needed to trigger the Self-Reflection, i.e. a cognitive process where insight is formed about learning problems and opportunities. The goal of this phase is to reinforce learning behavior by having the learner returning to the Micro-Learning component and perform more learning activities. For example, by revisiting all informal learning activities of the past week (which included several trips to museums of city planning) the learner can realize that (s)he has a deeper interest in the history of architecture and could decide to perform more learning activities related to this topic. The Persuasion component is used along the process to persuade the learner to keep using the MPLE. For this, persuasive techniques such as notifications, recommendations, rewarding, investments or tunneling can be used. For instance, recommendations can propose trips to related museums or monuments. To increase engagement of the MPLE, the Playfulness component is used to enrich the interaction with the system in a playful manner.

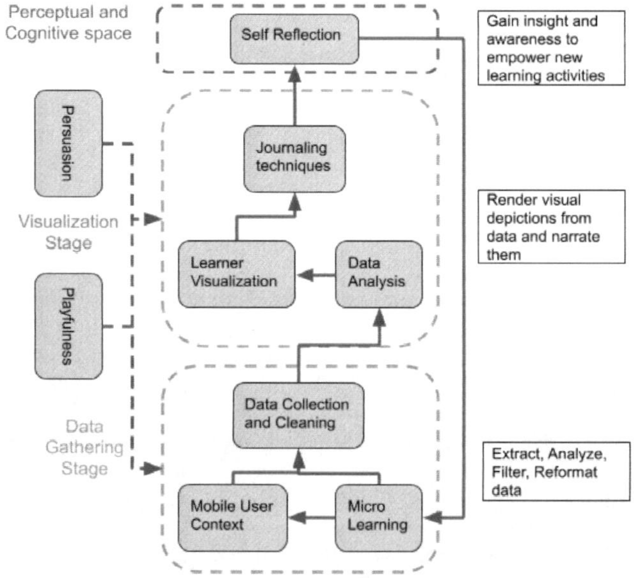

Figure 1. Learning Pipeline for the MPLE Model

3. AN EXAMPLE MOBILE PLAYFUL LEARNING ENVIRONMENT

TICKLE is a MPLE developed in the context of a project dealing with school burnout (https://wise.vub.ac.be/tickle/). School burnout refers to exhaustion at school, a cynical and detached attitude towards school, and feelings of inadequacy as a student. It often precedes school dropout, which has a great impact on further life (Walburg, 2014). The goal of TICKLE is to re-activate and re-motivate youngsters for learning through the recognition of non-formal learning opportunities. TICKLE, including its evaluations, is described in detail in (De Troyer et al., 2019) and (De Troyer et al., 2020). Here, we focus on how the main features of a MPLE are realized in TICKLE.

Micro-Learning & Mobile User Context. Micro Learning Activities (LAs) are the core unit of interaction to provide playful learning experiences. They are formed around new media (text, voice, music, graphics, photos, video) and situated in the personal context and interests of a youngster. The youngster's mobile context plays an important role, e.g. based on a youngster's personal interest in racing cars and current location, the platform could recommend a LA which can take place in a museum nearby. The LA could utilize augmented reality to exemplify the workings of an engine of a racing car. In principle, LAs can be located anywhere and performed anytime and they are explicitly not bound to a school context. LAs are embedded in cards, called ChallengeCards (see Figure 2a for an example). These cards provide an intuitive way to provide and access background information needed to successfully perform the challenge (i.e., the LA). ChallengeCards can be presented either purely digital (on a mobile device) or in mixed reality. For instance, the virtual card can be accessed by a youngster on his/her mobile device while standing relatively close to the physical location associated with the ChallengeCard. Or a real physical card (e.g., made from cardboard) can be placed on a physical location and the attached QR code can be scanned to reveal the corresponding ChallengeCard on the mobile device. Figure 2b shows the map view of the app providing the youngster an overview of ChallengeCards and their location in the environment.

Figure 2. a) Front side of a ChallengeCard; b) Map View of the TICKLE App: c) Photo Challenge d) Hangman

Playfulness. Playfulness is achieved by a combination of gamification and story elements. First, ChallengeCards can be collected, i.e. by succeeding in the challenge. Challenges can, for instance, include mini games, such as a Photo Challenge (i.e. the user must find a certain artifact and take a photo of it) (see Figure 2c) or a Hangman (i.e. the user must guess letters of a word. When too many mistakes are made a hangman is shown) (see Figure 2d). The architecture of TICKLE allows the integration of third-party LAs, such as the widgets from BookWidgets (BookWidgets, 2020), which range from timelines to 'fill the gaps' texts.

Moreover, each ChallengeCard is associated with some topics and a certain number of points (called Experience Points (XP)) (per topic) that can be collected by successfully performing the challenge. The XPs are saved in a wallet and can be used to buy rewards, such as badges, cinema tickets, or reduction coupons, or to unlock more content. Story elements are realized with the use of notifications and the Diary. The Diary keeps track of assessed and collected ChallengeCards and highlights special events, e.g. a streak of collected cards without failure; the completion of a card set; the exploring of a new neighborhood; etc.

Persuasion. Re-activating youngsters with school burnout implies a behavior change. To achieve this, we followed the Hook Model (Eyal, 2014). The principle of the Hook Model is to gradually replace external triggers to provoke a certain behavior, by an internal trigger, such as emotions of joy, fear or boredom. When the external trigger is not needed anymore to trigger the desired behavior, the new behavior has become a habit. We realized the Hook Model as follows. At the start, there are external triggers which prompt the user what to do next. In this phase, TICKLE takes the hand of the youngster by providing guided tours and notifications. To make it easy, the app also provides exact routing on how to find the physical location of these ChallengeCards. With more progress in terms of collected ChallengeCards and explored areas of interests, the app becomes more open and provides more freedom to the youngster, but notifications are still used to point the user to interesting opportunities. The notifications use persuasive messages tailored towards the personality of the youngster (currently using the Big Five taxonomy (Jia et al., 2016) and HeXad (Tondello et al., 2016)). The persuasive principles used in the notifications and feedback are derived from the literature, e.g. (Cialdini, 2001; Kaptein et al., 2011).

Learner Visualization & Self-Monitoring. As mentioned above, the Diary is keeping track of the youngster's activities. The diary is presented in a visual format to facilitate revisiting collected ChallengeCards, exploring related ChallengeCards, or perform the challenges not done yet. To create a coherent user story, the diary couples the presentation of the in-app events with personal data. For instance, GPS data is used to determine visited places or participation in social events such as concerts or museum visits. Figure 3 shows four important parts of the TICKLE Diary (from left to right):

A. Collected XPs are visualized in form of bar charts to give an overview of strengths and weaknesses.
B. Radial visualization showing nearby ChallengeCards by their distance to the youngster's location.
C. The topics associated with the ChallengeCards are visualized by Bubble Sets (Collins et al., 2009).
D. The timeline view shows ChallengeCards based on the point in time when they have been collected/accessed. By opening a context menu, the user can access related ChallengeCards.

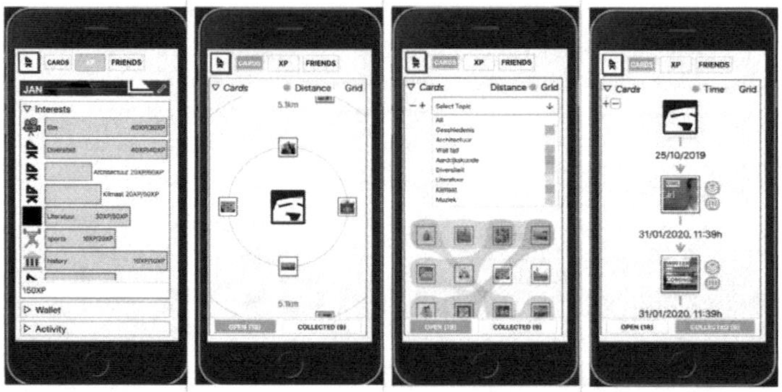

Figure 3. Screenshots of four important functionalities of the TICKLE Diary

Furthermore, when the user has collected a fair amount of ChallengeCards, (s)he also gains access to the card authoring system. From then on, the youngster is not a bare consumer of information anymore, (s)he is also encouraged to become a producer of ChallengeCards and to create new ChallengeCards for his/her peers. This card creation activity is an important part of the reactivation process because it demands creativity and imagination which are important skills for learning and for youngsters' self-esteem.

4. RELATED WORK

In this section, we provide an overview of related work, i.e. models and frameworks in the domain of technology enhanced learning.

In formal education, Learning Management Systems (LMS) are the main tools to provide structure and support for learning (Alias & Zainuddin, 2005). The LMS allows teachers to quickly distribute course content, assignments and announcements. Students can submit assignments through digital drop boxes and teachers can grade the work within the system. Traditional LMSs are teacher or institution centric, because the course structure and content are created by the teacher. Student initiated activities and interactions are mostly limited to content consumption. Whereas LMSs help to make teaching processes more efficient by streamlining content management, delivery, grading and analytics, they neglect informal learning activities.

Attwell (2007) and Vassileva (2008) acknowledge that modern learners have new patterns of information access, attention, and preferences which cannot be satisfied by LMSs. Therefore, they proposed the Personal Learning Environment (PLE) in which learners utilize a collection of resources and tools (e.g. search engines, blogging, social networks) to take control over their learning. PLEs are the opposite of LMSs.

Open Learning Networks (OLN) help to bridge the gap between PLE and LMS (Mott & Wiley, 2009). They consist of a series of modules that connect existing LMSs with web-based tools, applications, content stores, and a service layer that allow them to function together seamlessly. Until now, not many implementations of OLNs have been realized. (Wilson et al., 2009) described an extension of the Moodle LMS using the W3C Widget and the Google Wave technology which enabled to use informal learning functionality inside Moodle. Unfortunately, Google Wave was discontinued in 2012. García-Peñalvo et al. (2013) present a service-based framework to facilitate interoperability between a OLN and an LMS. However, OLN mainly remains a theoretical concept and has not been widely adopted by schools or universities.

As part of the Lifelong Learning initiative, Smart Learning integrates formal/informal learning and frees the learner from the space and time limitations of the traditional classroom (Temdee, 2020). Smart Learning focuses on the adaptability of learning content and presentation techniques based on the user's context which does not only include current location but also preferences, deficits and learning objectives to improve and accelerate learning. Learning environments that support this type of learning are called Smart Learning Environments (SLE) (Gros, 2016; Hwang, 2014; Spector, 2014). The 3Es meta-model (Jonathan Michael Spector, 2014) already highlighted the importance to promote engagement, i.e., the SLE must be capable of motivating and sustaining continuing interest and participation of a variety of learners. Besides providing learning activities to the learner, Koper (2014) argues that the key to engagement is the conditioning of the environment of the learner by providing positive and negative feedback, incentives, and contingencies. This means that there is an important overlap between the features of a SLE and a MPLE. The difference is in the emphasis on mobile and playfulness for MLPE, and a greater focus on the smart aspect in a SLE.

5. CONCLUSION

Even though modern communication technologies could lead to a situation of no boundaries to knowledge construction and thus independent learning, many learners require guidance in their learning process. Therefore, this paper proposes the Mobile Playful Learning Environment (MPLE) model that proposes a reference model for a new way of learning, mainly based on the concept of informal learning and taking into consideration characteristics of digital natives.

Our MPLE model combines seven features, among which persuasion and playful elements to encourage continuous usage and engagement. The other five features are Mobile User Context, Data Collection and Analysis, Learner Visualization, Self-Monitoring, and Micro-Learning. The aim is to support a learner in self-monitoring the progress of the learning activities for the purpose of self-reflection. The mobile context is crucial for a more informal learning approach. Learning progress should be collected, analyzed and presented to the learner with the help of playful, visualization techniques to facilitate self-reflection. Learning content is presented in small chunks, following the micro-learning approach. To exemplify the MPLE model we discussed TICKLE, an app to re-activate and motivate youngsters at risk for school dropout.

REFERENCES

Alias, N. A., & Zainuddin, A. M. (2005). Innovation for better teaching and learning: Adopting the learning management system. Malaysian Online Journal of Instructional Technology, 2(2), 27–40.

Attwell, G. (2007). Personal Learning Environments-the future of eLearning? Elearning Papers, 2(1), 1–8.

BookWidgets. (2020). Create Your Own Interactive Exercises and Automatically Graded Tests in Minutes! https://www.bookwidgets.com/

Bruck, P. A., Motiwalla, L., & Foerster, F. (2012). Mobile Learning with Micro-content: A Framework and Evaluation. Bled eConference. https://aisel.aisnet.org/cgi/viewcontent.cgi?article=1041&context=bled2012

Cialdini, R. (2001). 6 principles of persuasion. Arizona State University, eBrand Media Publication. https://www.pnahfoo.com/image/pnahfoo/image/data/images/learning/cialdini.pdf

Clemens, C., Kumar, V., Boulanger, D., Seanosky, J., & Kinshuk. (2018). Learning Traces, Competence Assessment, and Causal Inference for English Composition. In J. M. Spector, V. Kumar, A. Essa, Y.-M. Huang, R. Koper, R. A. W. Tortorella, T.-W. Chang, Y. Li, & Z. Zhang (Eds.), Frontiers of Cyberlearning: Emerging Technologies for Teaching and Learning (pp. 49–67). Springer Singapore.

Collins, C., Penn, G., & Carpendale, S. (2009). Bubble sets: revealing set relations with isocontours over existing visualizations. IEEE Transactions on Visualization and Computer Graphics, 15(6), 1009–1016.

De Troyer, O., Maushagen, J., Lindberg, R., & Breckx, D. (2020). Playful Learning with a Location-Based Digital Card Environment: A Promising Tool for Informal, Non-Formal, and Formal Learning. Information. An International Interdisciplinary Journal, 11(3), 157.

De Troyer, O., Maushagen, J., Lindberg, R., Muls, J., Signer, B., & Lombaerts, K. (2019). A Playful Mobile Digital Environment to Tackle School Burnout using Micro Learning, Persuasion Gamification. 2019 IEEE 19th International Conference on Advanced Learning Technologies (ICALT), 2161-377X, 81–83.

Dresang, E. T. (2005). Access: The Information-Seeking Behavior of Youth in the Digital Environment. Library Trends, 54(2), 178–196.

Eyal, N. (2014). Hooked: How to Build Habit-Forming Products. Penguin.

Fogg, B. J. (2002). Using Computers to Change What We Think and Do. Morgan Kaufmann Publishers Inc. San Francisco.

Gallardo-Echenique, E. E., Marqués-Molías, L., Bullen, M., & Strijbos, J.-W. (2015). Let's talk about digital learners in the digital era. The International Review of Research in Open and Distributed Learning, 16(3). http://www.irrodl.org/index.php/irrodl/article/view/2196/3337

García-Peñalvo, F. J., Conde, M. Á., & Del Pozo, A. (2013). A Mobile Personal Learning Environment Approach. Virtual, Augmented and Mixed Reality. Systems and Applications, 132–141.

Govaerts, S., Verbert, K., Klerkx, J., & Duval, E. (2010). Visualizing Activities for Self-reflection and Awareness. Advances in Web-Based Learning – ICWL 2010, 91–100.

Helsper, E., & Eynon, R. (2010). Digital natives: where is the evidence? British Educational Research Journal, 36(3), 503–520.

Jia, Y., Xu, B., Karanam, Y., & Voida, S. (2016). Personality-targeted Gamification: A Survey Study on Personality Traits and Motivational Affordances. Proceedings of the 2016 CHI Conference on Human Factors in Computing Systems, 2001–2013.

Kaptein, M., Duplinsky, S., & Markopoulos, P. (2011). Means based adaptive persuasive systems. In Proceedings of the 2011 annual conference on Human factors in computing systems - CHI '11. https://doi.org/10.1145/1978942.1978990

Koper, R. (2014). Conditions for effective smart learning environments. Smart Learning Environments, 1(1), 1–17.

Kovachev, D., Cao, Y., Klamma, R., & Jarke, M. (2011). Learn-as-you-go: New Ways of Cloud-Based Micro-learning for the Mobile Web. Advances in Web-Based Learning - ICWL 2011, 51–61.

Lambert, J., & Hessler, B. (2018). Digital Storytelling: Capturing Lives, Creating Community. Routledge.

Mott, J., & Wiley, D. (2009). Open for Learning: The CMS and the Open Learning Network. In Education, 15(2). https://ineducation.ca/ineducation/article/view/53

Ng, W. (2012). Can we teach digital natives digital literacy? Computers & Education, 59(3), 1065–1078.

Pettenati, M. C., Cigognini, M. E., M.C. Guerin, E., & Mangione, G. R. (2009). Personal Knowledge Management Skills for Lifelong-Learners 2.0. In Handbook of Research on Social Software and Developing Community Ontologies (pp. 298–315). IGI Global.

Plass, J. L., Homer, B. D., & Kinzer, C. K. (2015). Foundations of Game-Based Learning. Educational Psychologist, 50(4), 258–283.

Prensky, M. (2003). Digital game-based learning. Computers in Entertainment (CIE). https://dl.acm.org/doi/abs/10.1145/950566.950596

Radford, M. L., Connaway, L. S., Agosto, D. E., Cooper, L. Z., Reuter, K., & Zhou, N. (2007). Behaviors and preferences of digital natives: Informing a research agenda. Proceedings of the American Society for Information Science and Technology, 44(1), 1–15.

Sharples, M. (2000). The design of personal mobile technologies for lifelong learning. Computers & Education, 34, 177–193.

Sharples, M., Arnedillo-Sánchez, I., Milrad, M., & Vavoula, G. (2009). Mobile Learning. In N. Balacheff, S. Ludvigsen, T. de Jong, A. Lazonder, & S. Barnes (Eds.), Technology-Enhanced Learning: Principles and Products (pp. 233–249). Springer Netherlands.

Spector, J. M. (2014). Conceptualizing the emerging field of smart learning environments. In Smart Learning Environments (Vol. 1, Issue 1). https://doi.org/10.1186/s40561-014-0002-7

Thieme, A., Comber, R., Miebach, J., Weeden, J., Kraemer, N., Lawson, S., & Olivier, P. (2012). " We've bin watching you" designing for reflection and social persuasion to promote sustainable lifestyles. Proceedings of the SIGCHI Conference on Human Factors in Computing Systems, 2337–2346.

Thompson, P. (2013). The digital natives as learners: Technology use patterns and approaches to learning. Computers & Education, 65, 12–33.

Tondello, G. F., Wehbe, R. R., Diamond, L., Busch, M., Marczewski, A., & Nacke, L. E. (2016). The Gamification User Types Hexad Scale. Proceedings of the 2016 Annual Symposium on Computer-Human Interaction in Play, 229–243.

Vassileva, J. (2008). Toward Social Learning Environments. IEEE Transactions on Learning Technologies, 1(4), 199–214.

Walburg, V. (2014). Burnout among high school students: A literature review. Children and Youth Services Review, 42, 28–33.

Wilson, S., Sharples, P., Griffiths, D., & Popat, K. (2009). Moodle Wave: Reinventing the VLE using Widget technologies. In Proc. Mash-Up Personal Learning Environments - 2st Workshop MUPPLE'09, CEUR Proceedings, Conference, Nize France. http://citeseerx.ist.psu.edu/viewdoc/summary?doi=10.1.1.375.6460

Zhou, R., & Rechert, K. (2008). Personalization for Location-Based E-Learning. 2008 The Second International Conference on Next Generation Mobile Applications, Services, and Technologies, 247–253.

MOBILE LEARNING AND THE CREATION OF DIGITAL LITERACY IN A REAL PRACTICAL ENVIRONMENT

Valentina Milenkova and Vladislava Lendzhova
South-West University, 66 Iv.Mihailov str., Blagoevgrad, Bulgaria

ABSTRACT

The present article aims to examine the state of mobile learning in Bulgaria, presenting the policy framework in which the education processes themselves take place, and also to show the various platforms and software products that form the basis of mobile learning. A specific case is analyzed - the situation with Covid-19 and how the Bulgarian education system is being restructured in the direction of mobile learning under the influence of the new pandemic conditions. Methodology is based on qualitative methods, under the national project "*Digital Media Literacy in the context of "Knowledge Society": state and challenges", № КП–06–Н25/4, 2018,* funded by National Science Fund – Bulgaria.
The main conclusion is that Covid-19 puts Bulgarian education in a situation that requires comprehensive and universal mobile learning, which is in line with the modern knowledge society.

KEYWORDS

Mobile Learning, Covid-19, Digital Literacy, Online Platforms, Distance Education

1. INTRODUCTION

Mobile learning is a technologically created environment for learning and communication, in which users themselves publish lessons, data, and their experience as well as they communicate each other. The published information can be in different forms: text, images, audio and video recordings. Unlike traditional learning, learners of all ages are actively involved in a two-way process of posting and informing, because people can not only read, watch or listen, but also share, comment and discuss. Online platforms greatly facilitate and support mobile learning, as they connect individuals regardless of distances or situations that do not allow face-to-face learning, as is the case with Covid- 19.

This article aims to examine the state of mobile learning in Bulgaria, presenting the policy framework in which the education processes themselves take place, and also to show the various platforms and software products that are the basis of mobile learning. In addition, a specific case is analyzed - the situation with Covid-19 and how the Bulgarian education system is being restructured in the direction of mobile learning under the influence of the new pandemic conditions. The research questions are: is there a place for mobile learning in Bulgarian education? What are the specifics of mobile learning in the Covid-19 situation? What is the quality of mobile learning?

The article is focused on showing that Covid-19 put Bulgarian education in a situation requiring quick and adequate solutions and actions aimed at total and universal mobile learning, which, however, are not accepted and evaluated in the same way by the participating social actors.

2. BASIC CONSIDERATIONS

Mobile learning has been the subject of political efforts for a long time. There is a series of documents showing the commitment of the government on the need to digitalize social life. In 2014 A National Strategy for the Introduction of ICT in Bulgarian Schools has been developed (https://www.president.bg/docs/1352306506.pdf), which should identify ways to modernize the education system, improve access to quality education and increase the use of information technology in formal and non-formal education.

The strategy is aimed at creating a unified information environment serving school education, higher education and science. The expectations for the implementation of the Strategy are that the lessons become more interesting and attractive, to motivate students in order to attain higher achievements in learning the content, acquiring new useful skills - presentation skills, teamwork and more. Additional funds from the budget have been provided for ICT school infrastructure, e-learning platforms, wireless networks in schools, e-lessons, etc.

An evaluation of the state of digitalization is made in the EC report from 2020, the information about Bulgaria structured in five chapters (DESI report).

The 2020 report shows the importance of digitization and its integration in social life, because in a situation of health crisis, it is digital technologies that have contributed to the sustainability of the work process and especially to the maintenance of education and training activities. The EC evaluation report is that Bulgaria is the last 28th position in the EU for 2020. In 2018 the country was in the penultimate place, and in 2019 it is again last. The index shows that in Bulgaria there is the weakest development in most categories: general connectivity, basic digital skills of the population, low percentage of online trade, digital integration of public services and business. The overall result for Bulgaria for 2020 is 36.4 out of 100 compared to the EU average of 52.6. The results for 2019 were 33.8 for Bulgaria and 49.4 for the EU average, respectively. It should be emphasized that the country's overall score has risen to 36.4, but it ranks lower in the rankings because it lags behind other EU partners.

From the point of view of human capital, the report emphasizes that the level of skills in the field of digital technologies of Bulgarian citizens is among the lowest in the EU. Citizens with basic digital skills make up only 29% of the adult population in the country, compared to the EU average of 58%. Only about 11% have above average skills.

Use of Internet services is another major set of criteria assessed by the EC Index. The results there are not very encouraging either. Bulgaria continues to be in 27th place in terms of the use of Internet services, with the overall result well below the EU level. 67% of Bulgarians use the Internet (in the EU the average is 85%), and 24% have never used it. In terms of connectivity, according to the EC report, Bulgaria is doing relatively well, especially in terms of wide access to high-speed and mobile broadband networks. It has made significant improvements to the criterion of e-government, which has more and more users.

The results in the EC report show that efforts are being made in the country, there is progress on the criteria, but the EU average has not yet been reached. It can be summarized that the measures and actions contribute to creating conditions for the development of digital literacy of the Bulgarian population and mobile learning. Information technology has entered en masse and avalanche in the daily lives of children and young people, which reflects on the expectations of students in all forms of education. The information growth itself creates a favorable environment for learning and personal enrichment by applying specific practical actions for organized implementation of mobile learning in secondary education. They include:

- targeted investments for the purchase of computers and furnishing classrooms in secondary schools;
- organized training of teachers to work in an online environment and use different platforms;
- writing textbooks and manuals for both teachers and students and for general use;
- financing the creation of computer programs for educational purposes;
- organization of optional or regular classes in informatics, like "Fundamentals of Informatics", "Computer Science", "Computer Culture", etc.

The digitization and use of computers and information technologies covers the entire education system: from kindergartens, through secondary, higher education and postgraduate levels. The formation of basic digital skills begins at an early age, and for the acquisition of digital qualification, the most effective is the school age, when students have reached a certain level in which they easily acquire new skills and knowledge, open to innovation as thinking young people. In addition to accessible and diverse forms of knowledge dissemination, the network environment requires new skills such as: information retrieval, navigation, sorting, resource assessment and network and publication security (Milenkova, Peicheva, Marinov, 2018).

2.1 Practical Approaches for the Implementation of Digitization in Education

Mobile learning involves the use of new multimedia technologies and the Internet to improve the quality of teaching through access to resources and services. Mobile learning helps to adapt education systems to the new requirements of the European knowledge society and it is an opportunity for increased convenience, diversity and efficiency. In this context, it is important to take into account the serious work of the teacher in preparing lessons using technology. It is true that mobile learning involves the use of home or mobile devices by students in order to perform various tasks, but the preparation of the lesson itself requires reorganization of various activities and in general the successful implementation depends largely on the teacher. Pedagogical practices based on online platforms themselves require testing in the specific context and the decision to use them is the result of the teacher's assessment of how a tool or platform will be useful in online classes (https://teacher.bg/).

Along with the listed digital opportunities and software, the Bulgarian school also uses various platforms for conducting classes and sharing lessons in formal and non-formal education. These are Moodle, Zoom, Google classroom, Blackboard and others. The advantage of digital technologies is related to the reformatting of the entire educational environment. This applies both to teachers as a style of thinking, behaving, organizing teaching and testing, and to students, given the strengthening of individual work and responsibilities. Mobile learning has and other implications related to the criteria for teacher professionalism, such as new requirements for collecting, processing, illustrating information and giving feedback to students. In general, mobile learning stimulates the development of curricula that are applied to all ages; it is of great importance for the acquisition of skills to cope with the world around us, as well as for the development of digital education and culture (Milenkova, Manov, 2019: 96-102).

2.1.1 Mobile Learning in a Covid-19 Situation

Covid's situation has created a serious challenge - the need for secondary and higher education to move to an online environment. In these conditions, mobile learning in its various forms and variants has become a reality in the last year. During the COVID – 19 pandemic Bulgarian educational system meets the challenges posed by the need to restructure training and universal penetration of e-learning. The access to online training was the most discussed issue and is still so throughout the period of restrictions and quarantine. Without any doubt, first this started with the regulations/ normative regulations/orders. The forthcoming analysis focuses on the main dimensions of mobile learning in the Covid-19 situation in Bulgarian conditions.

In methodological aspect, the *qualitative method of document analysis* used. An analysis of the political documents related to the pandemic period in 2020 in the Bulgarian context, as well as the specific measures aimed at the education system and personal training has been made. The regulations for online learning and the platforms that are recommended to be used in the conditions of distance education have presented. The analysis also includes various opinions shared by parents, teachers and principals regarding the Covid-19 situation and the implementation of digital learning in a locked down environment.

2.1.2 Results and Policy Documents Analysis

In the Bulgarian case, this topic is related to the specific measures and rules for organizing educational activities. The policy documents have focused mainly on ensuring the safety conditions for children and educational materials in schools and kindergartens. At the beginning of March 2020 in the effort to contain the spread of COVID 19 pandemic, in line with broader social distancing and lockdown measures all universities, schools and kindergarten were closed in Bulgaria. The focus is on the ways in which national policy participants identified immediate and long term policy problems in e-learning and how they responded at different stages of the pandemic.

At the first phase of the pandemic outburst, with the wide spread closure of schools, Bulgarian policy makers were faced with two main challenges: *first ensuring the nutrition and e-learning needs of all students, but especially that of vulnerable students.* Ensuring access to education was made by flexible solutions at the Bulgarian schools and universities. Several measures were undertaking for supporting teachers, students and parents in distance learning process. An e-learning hotline was opened for receiving questions and recommendations related to e-learning.

The National Electronic Library for teachers was created to enable teachers to share educational resources, personal experience and innovative practices (https://www.mon.bg/bg/news/3893; https://e-learn.mon.bg/).

The second challenge that meet the Bulgarian policy makers in education was related to providing systemic responses for the long term educational, social and economic challenges generated by the pandemic. By looking at the first response to the crisis the analysis of the policy documents explores the first meaning-making attempts related to educational inequities and the struggles over proposed short and long-term solutions. In Bulgaria, following this first phase the Government tend to make use of crises by putting forward radical, controversial and social reforms. The extraordinary condition of the COVID 19 pandemic, most importantly the effects of social distancing and lockdown measures, offer ample opportunity to understand the dynamic relationships between the educational policy responses and the structural, systemic and historical inequities characterizing educational provision in Bulgaria.

The third challenge is concerning the shifting to emergency remote teaching that meant facing, almost overnight, the challenge of developing adequate infrastructure of educational technology and digital pedagogy which can be suitable for whichever chosen continuation strategy. This challenge impacted educational systems and organizations worldwide in the most diverse ways, ranging from expanding the use of well-articulated infrastructure already in place and use to having to invest into educational technologies suitable for remote teaching for the first time, facing cultural resistance to the widespread use of technologies for educational purposes, the luck of funding immediately available, and great socio-economic separates affecting the most students, parents and families living in the most marginalized communities.

In summary six are the main indicators followed in the policy documents research of the country. And these are:

1. Educational provision - In terms of policy making during the pandemic data indicate that the agenda-setting role was played by the government.
2. Access to education – the issue of access to education at the onset of COVID 19 pandemic resonated with conceptualizations and approaches to inequity issues in the policy discourse before the pandemic. It highlighted categories of vulnerable groups and manifestations of vulnerability nominated in the various political actors' positioning in reference to aspects in educational access.
3. Educational technology – the analyzed policy documents indicates that disadvantage communities are excluded from online teaching (due to the luck of stable internet connection, digital proficiency etc.) and that their professional disadvantage will likely to exacerbate as a result of the crisis.
4. Digital competence of teachers and professionals- digital competence was generally conceptualized as ability to use available digital technology for educational purpose (teaching, learning and assessment). It became visible in close proximity to discussing learning roles to teachers, students, and parents in the context of shifting to online education.
5. Curriculum- a focus on emergency were noticed on matters of curriculum, fragmentation and short term scope, unpacking specific curricular focus points polarizing a various political actors engaging with the topic: refugees, migrants and asylums-seekers on vocational education and on regulating upcoming national examinations in both procedural and learning contents aspects
6. Teachers learning and professional development - Crisis as opportunity for improvement and innovative solutions and for improving teachers' and students' digital competence and skills. In the communication of the government, this issue frame is completely independent from the issue of digital poverty.

2.1.3 Parents' Attitudes Towards Lockdown Situation

During the period from 30.10 to 4.11.2020 Parents Association together with the Institute for Research in Education conducted an online survey among parents about their attitudes towards the shifting of students to distance learning in an online environment in the conditions of emergency situation due to the COVID-19 crisis (https://roditeli.org/blog/distancionno-ili-prisastveno/). In general, the clear positions FOR and AGAINST distance learning are distribute as follows: 47.4% of all participating parents are entirely for face-to-face training, and for online distance learning of all students are 22.2% of the respondents. The idea of going online training for individual stages is supported by 14.2% of the parents, and 16.2% are for a mixed form of training (combining face-to-face and online training according to a specific scheme). The mixed form of education combining face - to - face and online learning in a specific scheme has the most supporters in the capital (17.6%), with a decrease in the size of the settlement decreases and their percentage - 16.8% in the regional centers, 12.6% in the small cities and 11.9% in the villages. The distribution of parents' preferences for online education is also influenced by the age of the child. The highest number of respondents supporting the present form is among the parents of children in the initial stage - 52.8%, and the least - among the parents of high school students: 43.6% of them want all students to stay in school..The biggest challenges for distance learning according to the parents are: "Difficulties of my child to master the learning material to the same extent as in the present learning" - 47.9%, process at a distance"- 38.5%, "Interaction between teachers and students"- 37%, "My child's ability to communicate with his classmates"- 34.6%, "The workload of parents with responsibility for children's learning"- 33.3%," Technical problems related to the electronic platforms used "- 29.9%, "Opportunities for teachers to organize an effective distance learning process "- 28.8%. The survey data shows that parents' attitudes towards the transition to distance learning in an online environment vary significantly depending on the age of the child, the place where the family lives (rural or urban area, small town or village, capital), the priorities of the parents and a number of additional factors, so it is impossible to deduce a single solution that is satisfactory to all parents. This necessitates a flexible approach based on local solutions, according to the specific situation of the different schools.

2.1.4 Teachers' and Directors' Attitudes Concerning e-Learning

In November 2020 over 70% of the Bulgarian parents want face to Face training. According to the Education trade union at the Podkrepa Labour Confederation (https://www.vesti.bg/bulgaria/658-ot-uchitelite-iskat-distancionno-obuchenie-ot-utre-6117079), by contrast with parents Bulgarian teachers and directors do not agree to continue face-to-face training. They were asked the question: "Do you think that in such a pandemic situation, educational institutions should work in a regular form or should move to e-learning at a distance?".

79.4% of the 4,270 teachers and directors answered that the entire education system should temporarily switch to e-learning at a distance, and 76.8% even said that the school environment was unsafe for work (https://offnews.bg/obshtestvo/79-4-ot-uchiteli-i-direktori-podkrepiali-onlajn-obuchenie-740116.html). Their main argument is that it is currently very difficult to create an organization for the learning process, given the fact that many teachers infected with COVID absent. Many teachers are worried and have taken a patient chart for a week or two. Their substitutes are overloaded.

We can conclude that there is a contrast in attitudes of the teachers and the directors in Bulgarian schools in the first wave of COVID-19 comparing with second wave COVID-19. In the beginning (march 2020) the most important issue was related with the access of education, educational technology and digital training of teachers, while after retuning in school the most discussed topic was this concerning the health of teachers and students.

3. CONCLUSION

In summary, it can be said that Internet and online platforms based on interactivity, individualization and new technological opportunities with free and easy access, are an excellent environment for learning and self-learning, for the increased potential of each person. The analysis shows that mobile learning has a place in Bulgarian education and its quality is at a relatively high level. Its specifics depend on and are related to the technological support, the technical and methodological training and qualification of the teachers, as well as the responsibility of the families. Information technology increases the scale and dynamics of data collection and management, allowing users to actively participate in the creation, sharing and combining of knowledge, to expand cooperation with each other in different websites through mobile learning. Bulgarian stakeholders realize that Information technology increases the scale and dynamics of management, allowing users to actively participate in the creation, sharing and combining of knowledge, to expand cooperation with each other in different websites through mobile learning. Equipped with the latest interactive platforms, learners have the advantage not only of being subjects of the learning process, receiving and storing information, but also of being active participants in the new digital environment to express their proactive, selective activities.

According to the teachers, thanks to the digitization of training, the possibilities for organizing the pedagogical interaction, regardless of time and space, as well as the number of the participants in it, the subject of pedagogical communication, etc., expanded. As a new information reality, the digital learning environment creates the conditions for using e-mail, newsgroups, forums for project-based learning, interdisciplinary work.

The COVID-19 pandemic demonstrated the undeniable importance of people's digital skills, the digitization of the education and the need for a reliable and fast internet connection. During the health crisis, networks faced a significant increase in demand. The COVID 19 pandemic necessitated a rapid and comprehensive reform of education and mobile learning.

ACKNOWLEDGEMENT

The article has been developed in the framework of the research project "Digital Media Literacy in the context of "Knowledge Society": state and challenges" № КП–06–Н25/4, funded by National Science Fund – Bulgaria.

REFERENCES

A survey conducted among teachers and directors- https://offnews.bg/obshtestvo/79-4-ot-uchiteli-i-direktori-podkrepiali-onlajn-obuchenie-740116.html

DESI report, the part for Bulgaria https://euractiv.bg/section/%D0%BD%D0%BE%D0%B2%D0%B8-%D1%82%D0%B5%D1%85%D0%BD%D0%BE%D0%BB%D0%BE%D0%B3%D0%B8%D0%B8/news/%D0%B1%D1%8A%D0%BB%D0%B3%D0%B0%D1%80%D0%B8%D1%8F-%D0%BF%D0%B0%D0%BA-%D0%B5-%D0%BF%D0%BE%D1%81%D0%BB%D0%B5%D0%B4%D0%BD%D0%B0-%D0%BF%D0%BE-%D0%B4%D0%B8%D0%B3%D0%B8%D1%82%D0%B0%D0%BB%D0%B8%D0%B7%D0%B0

Milenkova, V., Manov, B. (2019) Mobile learning and the formation of digital literacy in a knowledge society". *Proceedings of the 15th International Conference Mobile Learning*. pp.96-102 http://www.iadisportal.org/digital-library/mobile-learning-and-the-formation-of-digital-literacy-in-a-knowledge-society#,

Milenkova, V., Peicheva, D., Marinov, M. (2018) Towards defining media socialization as a basis for digital society. *International Journal of Cognitive Research in Science, Engineering and Education*, Vol.6 (2), pp.21-32. https://www.ijcrsee.com/index.php/ijcrsee/article/view/200

National online library - https://www.mon.bg/bg/news/3893; https://e-learn.mon.bg/

National Strategy for the Introduction of ICT in Bulgarian Schools has been developed https://www.president.bg/docs/1352306506.pdf

Parents Association and Institute for Research in Education online survey among parents to the COVID-19 crisis - https://roditeli.org/blog/distancionno-ili-prisastveno/

Students' digital skills https://teacher.bg/ %D0%B 4%D0%B8 %D0% B3% D0% B8%D1%82%D0%B0%D0%BB%D0%BD%D0%B8-%D0%B8%D0%BD%D1 %81%D 1%82 %D1 %80%D1%83%D0%BC%D0 % B 5%D0% BD%D1 %8 2%D0%B8-%D0%B8-%D0%BF%D0%BB %D0% B0%D 1% 82% D1% 84% D 0%B E% D 1% 80% D0%BC%D0%B8-%D0%B7%D0%B0/

Teacher's and parent's attitudes https://www.vesti.bg/bulgaria/658-ot-uchitelite-iskat-distancionno-obuchenie-ot-utre-6117079

DISTANCE LEARNING IN THE TIME OF COVID-19 LOCKDOWN: NEW OPPORTUNITIES FOR INFORMATION AND COMMUNICATION TECHNOLOGIES IN EDUCATION?

Marion Utéza and Christophe Reffay
ELLIADD, FR-EDUC, University Bourgogne Franche-Comté, France

ABSTRACT

This research aims to study the changing perceptions of primary and secondary school teachers towards information and communication technologies (ICT) for education, during the period of health lock down in France in April 2020. It is based on the Pedagogical, Social and Technological affordance model, suitable for analysing online learning environments and situations. Selected factors are the presence and use of ICT in Education, as well as interactions and innovation. In order to identify these elements, a questionnaire was proposed and the data was processed quantitatively and qualitatively. The results tend to confirm existing studies that claim low affordability of technology in education. Previous experience seems to be a perception-amplifying factor, but it does not in itself ensure the transition from perception to action. However, under certain conditions and in the longer term, such a rich and constrained experience leads to expression of new training needs that could reveal new affordances in a richer professional development process.

KEYWORDS

Distance Learning, Learning Environment, Affordance, ICTE, Interaction, Teacher Professional Development

1. INTRODUCTION

Health lock down and the injunction of pedagogical continuity have created an unprecedented situation of distance education in primary and secondary education in France. How did we consider this specific situation as a professional development experience for teachers?

The disruption of the environment by the sudden need to use ICT could affect teaching activity and change the complex relationship between the teacher and the technologies. Beyond the question of the effectiveness of ICTE, we have chosen to focus on what teachers do in this constrained situation in order to try to perceive possible changes, from and through practice. Did confined teachers grasp ICT differently than usual, and does this open up new perspectives or even innovations? The term innovate is particularly appropriate as it implies the introduction of something new in a field. It raises therefore the question of the environment and its importance in learning. ICTE is an element of this environment. As practices are linked to the context in which they interact (Bru, 1991), a sudden evolution of this environment can then become a factor of change. But in order to study a change, it is necessary to know the previous state.

The starting point is the low level of use of ICT in education noted by the institutional surveys PROFETIC (Médiamétrie, 2018). The actions noted by these data show a use of ICTE mainly centred on the simple functions of these tools, in particular for the preparation of lessons and projection of documents in class. Thus, their place and role in education remains limited and sometimes their effectiveness and usefulness questioned (Cuban, 1982). At the same time, it should be mentioned the strong incentive of educational policies for a greater integration of ICT in education. The goal being to move towards so-called new skills such as collaboration or creation (*OECD Skills Outlook*, 2019).

In regular face to face classrooms, teachers can perceive live actions, productions and reactions of learners to engage them in a fluent interaction that scaffolds their knowledge construction and highlights their doubts and understanding. Such an interactive process can help the teachers to adapt the lesson to each of his/her pupils.

In confined mode, interaction becomes more scarce. There is a risk for teachers to concentrate their efforts on documents to deliver front transmission of knowledge and instructions for homework without direct feedback from their learners. This may lead to demotivation for some pupils. In this situation, the use of technology become necessary, which could lead teachers to glimpse new possibilities previously unexplored. Therefore, confined teachers could envisage new uses and perhaps lead to a shift in their representation of ICT. This is what we have chosen to analyse.

2. RESEARCH ISSUE AND QUESTIONS

This leads us to the following question: in what way had the situation of sanitary confinement made it possible to introduce new potentialities of action into teaching by constraining the use of digital technologies?

We try to understand who are the teachers who may perceive new potentialities and whether they drive them to action. But also whether their experience may generate new knowledge and perspectives.

Practically, we try to break down this main question into different sub-questions:

- Bringing their own experience and expectations: Do the teachers perceive new affordances of ICT for education in this context?
- Do they implement some of these new potentialities?
  From the many potentialities allowed by ICT, and according to the experience, needs and goals pursued by teachers, they might or might not perceive and implement a selection of these potentialities.
- What actions do they select in this context?
- What experiments do they carry out?
- Do they innovate?

Finally, what kind of new affordances does emerge in the French landscape of this lockdown period? With what effects on uses and practices?

In order to address these questions, let us present the theoretical background in the following section.

3. THEORETICAL BACKGROUND

The concept of affordance is proposed in 1950 by Gibson, an American psychologist, who defines it as the potential for action within an environment (Gibson, 1977). As an example, a door handle can suggest either an entrance or an exit and thus lead to a particular action (i.e.: pull or push the door). This concept leads to the study of relationships between humans, their activities and their environment with the ecological theory of development (Gibson, 1986). In this context, the ability to discover what can be offered by an environment stems directly from action. For this reason, experimentation is essential in the development process. Such an experimentation is itself a potential source of innovation. These affordances are objective, i.e. always available in the environment, subjective since they are visible only to the observing subject, and functional since everyone can see and implement them differently (Reed, 1993).

This notion of affordance is adapted to the ICT field by Norman in 1988. He distinguishes perceived and real affordances and adds the notion of utility and usability. Indeed, not only the tools must correspond to a desired function, but it has also to be easy to use, and thought for the user's satisfaction (Norman, 2002).

3.1 How do we Adapt into an Environment?

The complementary concept of the development niche (Super & Harkness, 1986) lights on the possibilities of adaptation and evolution of this environment, of humans and their activities, by taking into account the physical and social context, the practices, the beliefs of the individual and the group he or she belongs to. For example, these changes may be induced by the emergence of new tools, such as the possibility for confined teachers to teach lessons via videoconferencing or make use of other online working tools to bring their pupils to a different kind of interaction or production. Because technology is changing the environment we live in.

It provides new ways of doing things and allows us to adapt to new opportunities.

At the same time, however, we must take into account new constraints that are specific to this new environment. Therefore, each *niche* is unique and must take into account the particularities of everyone. For example, someone can have a bad Internet connection, particular needs or a specific experience that may help or impede him or her to take advantage of this *niche*. For the locked down teacher, the efficacy will depend on the ability to find the right information, adapted to his or her abilities, within his or her environment, his or her niche, by interacting, in order to extend it. And hopefully go as far as innovation.

3.2 Scientific Background

There are few studies on teaching in confined mode. For this reason, it seems important to look first at the concept of distance education to identify its specificities. The notion of distance should be understood not only as geographical or temporal, but above all as pedagogical and transactional (Moore, 1993). If distance learning is protean, it always brings out interaction needs to keep learners motivated and avoid drop-outs. Distance learning has to provide interaction between content and learners, between teachers and learners, between learners themselves and between technical devices and users (Swan, 2003). Then, interaction can be considered as a driving force for the success of fully online mediated learning and therefore an essential indicator to be taken into account when evaluating the effectiveness of the distance education system implemented. Finally, learning modalities have to be varied to offer different possibilities because everyone has different perspectives and perceives the new environment differently. Now, in such a short period of time, it is challenging to combine and articulate the appropriation of new digital tools with the variation of pedagogical approaches to build an environment that suits every actor of the learning situation.

The second area of study concerns learning environments. In her introduction on "Ethno theories, learning and contexts", Bril (2014) claims that "learning is trying to explore and exploit the constraints that organize the space of the activity". The verb "trying" emphasizes an operation whose results are not guaranteed. The success (i.e.: learning occurs) relies on the ability firstly to recognize in the environment, the components whose function can support the project and secondly to implement these functions. Such a presentation follows Norman's idea in 1988 that separates the perception and action phases.

3.3 What Model should be used to Observe Teachers in Confinement?

There is a need for a model capable of observing but also analysing learning environments that includes technologies. The pedagogical social and technological affordance: (PST) model presented by Kirschner (2002) allows us to keep the concept of affordance and niche, and the articulation of the learner-activity environment with the primacy of experimentation. It relies mainly on the support of interactions, which we have previously defined as essential. It relies on the principle that the potential of technologies can improve learning conditions by supporting pedagogical and social affordances. For example, the installation of a chat tool can make it possible to communicate directly and simultaneously in a group online.

Furthermore, this model includes a process to test the effectiveness of group e-learning modes. For this reason, this model can be used to study and assess the design of e-learning more generally.

Here, teaching combines technological, social and pedagogical affordances. It emphasises the importance of choosing an adapted pedagogy, taking into account the characteristics of the media used and their functionalities, including possible social interactions at a distance. In order to design and analyse these interactions, the model proposes to answer six questions which are all steps in an iterative system:

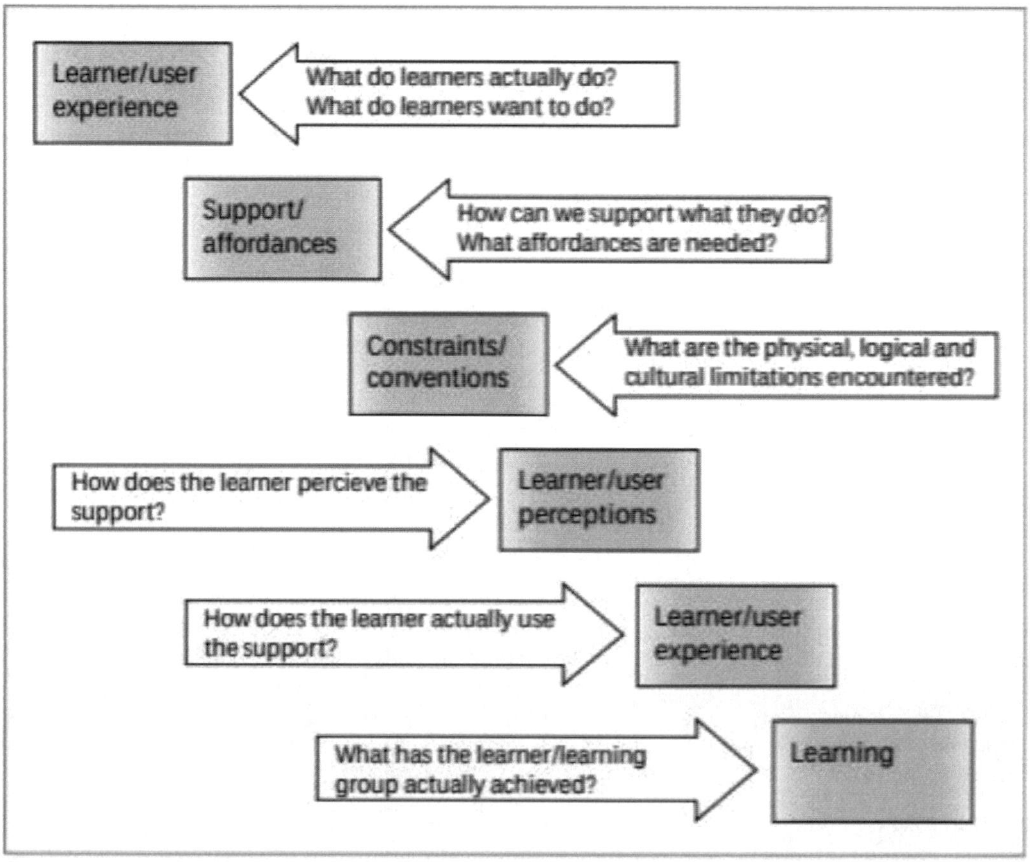

Figure 1. Interaction questioned by the PST affordance model (Kirschner, 2002, p. 33)

4. METHOD

We questioned the expectations, practices and emerging perspectives on ICTE of primary and secondary school teachers in France (i.e.: teachers of pupils aged 3-16 years). The questionnaire articulates closed and open-ended questions to determine the needs, means, organization facilities and perspectives perceived by confined primary and secondary school teachers, whether experts in ICT or not. It was distributed online to three different groups of teachers. This means that only connected teachers did answer our questionnaire.

The first group is made up of 100 experienced primary school teachers who are candidates for the trainer's certificate and who are present on social networks. The second is made up of 75 secondary school teachers who participate in online communities of practice. Both of these two first groups can be considered as experienced with ICTE, as they are active on exchange platforms. The idea was to have more opportunities to see innovative practices. The difference between these two groups helped to identify whether the level of the pupils (3-10 years old; 11-15 years old) could be an interesting variable. Finally, a third group consisted of 75 secondary school teachers of literature at the Besançon Academy, contacted through the disciplinary mailing list. This third and last group is not particularly experimented in pedagogy or in ICT. We consider this group as a control group, compared to the more experienced two other ones.

It is worth to mention that the questionnaire has been addressed during the third week of the lockdown period, i.e.: a relatively short period after the unprepared lockdown.

The data collected by this questionnaire are analysed with a mixed method. It is necessary to articulate quantitative and qualitative data and to elaborate grids to examine open-ended responses. This leads us to use content analysis method proposed by Bardin (2013), which consists of studying the comments collected to bring out a certain number of significant indicators in relation to the subject studied and the model, by coding and then categorizing this information using a lexicological study aided by the TXM software (Heiden et al., 2010).

The quantification criteria are based on the presence and level of use of ICT but also on indicators of perceived affordances in relation to: creation, differentiation, collaboration and autonomy. These choices are linked both to the PST model and to institutional expectations. It is not the purpose of this study to present these elements as central to education in general, nor to defend the effectiveness of ICTE.

5. DISCUSSION AND RESULTS

This study confirms a use of ICTE restricted to simple functions, in particular messaging and video proposed by the teacher to his or her pupils without interaction.

First, ICT are scarce in the comments collected. Among 250 teachers, 37% cite tools with limited capabilities, usually messaging. A quarter of teachers surveyed do not cite any tools. Only five teachers surveyed mentioned spontaneously they discovered a new tool during this period. Second, the tools chosen are used in their simplest functions such as communicating lessons or instruction and receiving assignments without feedback. Third, the interactive support for the activity is very limited: the so-called advanced functionalities of an online working environment, such as forums or personalized feedback are rare. The means generally offered by Distance Learning have not really been deployed by these teachers. They seem to ignore that more motivation is needed for learners at a distance and that some means are available to them to sustain this motivation.

We are at the beginning of lockdown when teachers fulfil the questionnaire and the vast majority of them are keeping with their routines and well mastered face to face practices. Most of them worry about how to adapt their practice to the new environment and very few try to find new opportunities to modify their teaching strategies. As a matter of fact, there are very few new experiments mentioned, and no significant perception of new training needs. Thus, the answers to question 1 "What are your needs, as a teacher, during this confinement?" indicate mostly modest needs. Only two answers receive a majority of votes. The answer "I need new tools" gets a small majority. And the answer "I need time" gets a very high score. In addition, in question 4, where confined teachers are asked to select among various expectations, only 28% of all respondents chose "to develop new skills".

This result applies for all three groups (primary or secondary school teachers, ICT experts or not), although the experience seems to be correlated with a better perception of affordances and a greater expectation of added value. Affordances are even more fragmented when the person did only recently test and manipulate ICT. Experience makes it possible to envisage new and more appropriate practices for the future. Even if this is not translated into action at this stage. The presence of sometimes negative affordances among non-experts should be also noted, e.g.: technical failures.

The main difference between primary and secondary school teachers concerns the use of ICT to communicate with parents this is why online messaging is cited 12% more by primary school teachers. The aim is to create the necessary link for young pupils to get to work. But they point out that this kind of coeducation is too time-consuming to be sustained afterwards. Primary school teachers also mention the use of online work plans and the implementation of challenges with a playful dimension.

The second part of the questionnaire, which is more prospective, outlines some forms of change in perceptions, more strongly among the group of experts. The main horizons identified, particularly in the free text areas of the questionnaire, are opportunities to work on:

- student autonomy, i.e.: the student is an actor of his or her own learning process, by providing young pupils numerous challenges;
- a greater use of audio, more multimedia creation;
- the need for a variety of approaches; active teaching methods; enriched teaching practices and
- the desire to learn.

They articulate pedagogical, technological and social affordances. However, these new affordances remain very limited and produced by only few (less than fifteen) respondents among our population.

- Creativity is generally restricted to video creation by the teacher,
- differentiation is at the desire stage and does not appear like an added value of the distance learning,
- collaboration is emerging mainly between teachers and finally,
- student autonomy remains to be built up.

The less experienced group does not perceive the confinement as being able to introduce a reflection on the proposed themes such as the construction of the courses or the expected skills. Moreover, teachers of literature perceive less added value in distance education. The difference varies up to 29%. The only item in which less experienced teachers have a higher score of 9%, but which is still in the minority, is 'facilitating exchanges'.

These main results lead us to answer our research question. Teachers have had little awareness of the potential of the tools available. Experiments are rare with no real perception of innovation and actions do not yet seem to lead to new knowledge after three weeks of this very unique situation.

However, in this unprepared situation, often uncomfortable, teachers were not strictly obliged to explore new possibilities. This is particularly the case if the means previously available keep working (according to them) or if they cannot consider other possibilities. Having resources and tools available, for those who have them, is not always a sufficient condition for action. Teachers also need to have a degree of (user) control over the task, i.e.: the users need to understand the process as a whole in order to control its evolution by their interaction as users. We have to take into account that people often limit themselves to what they think they can reasonably obtain (Sen, 1999). In addition, prerequisite knowledge is often necessary to perceive new potential and to learn how to exploit them. According to (Fernagu Oudet, 2012), a new resource must therefore be converted into a capacity for learning, which takes time.

In order to achieve this goal, interaction with the environment must be constructed by the learner (Brousseau, 2011) in a mutual, adaptive, continuous and interactionist process (Piaget, 1964). This implies for teachers to design their teaching by considering the new capabilities of the situation. In the specific context of a sudden confinement, they were critically unprepared.

Although teachers seem satisfied overall, their approach seems to lack effectiveness due to a lack of preparation, as the constraints and resources for e-learning activities are still little explored and little exploited.

6. CONCLUSION

This study has been implemented in the urgency that the sudden confinement imposed, and for this reason, we can recognize some limits to the results obtained. The teachers that answered this questionnaire cannot be considered as representative of the population of teachers in France. This study needs to be supplemented by others also because the qualitative data analysis is sometimes subject to interpretation and the study does shed light only on a limited number of elements of the teachers' environment. So it would have been helpful to also interviewed administrators of the same schools to complete the study and perhaps help them to meet future challenges. Finally, the study is based on the concept of affordance, which is evolving and whose value in the context of relationships between Human and ICT has yet to be consolidated.

Nevertheless, this study reinforces the observation that the use of ICT for education is limited, at primary and secondary schools, to basic functions of these tools. It confirms the necessity to reconsider time and scaffolding in distance learning. Beyond the initial hypotheses, one of this study's values is to underline the lack of knowledge for teachers on distance teaching and learning specificities: 46% of teachers want to be trained to distance teaching but 31% don't want to reconsider their teaching approach and 20% don't want to modify the content of their teaching. Our study shows the need for a specific training to prepare teachers for distance learning to emphasize the importance of redesigning their teaching as a whole, taking advantage of different communication tools to implement the needed interaction. The real expert is the one who is able to make the best use of his or her environment, to perceive the possibilities according to his or her own capacities and to realise them. For this reason, we may suggest teacher training to better observe their environment to capture the new opportunities to learn and to act for their own pedagogical practices. In any case, teaching in confinement is an experience that can be seen as a forced moment of training. The discrepancy between experts who are aware of the existence of new potential even if they do not take action and non-experts who, for the most part, do not perceive this new potential tends to show the need to first work on the question of perception before accompanying the implementation. We suggest that such an experience produced learning outcomes for teachers that the agenda of our study was not able to reveal.

7. FUTURE WORKS

This is why we can conclude that the situation of health confinement has not made it possible to reveal new affordances in teaching by introducing the use of ICTE, but that it has nonetheless made it possible to open up new perspectives in terms of innovative practices and, above all, training.

This may be an ideal time to start training, because if teachers are not taking full advantage of ICT it is also because, until now, they did not necessarily think they needed it. The continuing health situation may lead them to reconsider this position. It takes time and a great deal of experimentation to allow a shift to take place because the coupling of perception and action is not immediate when we are dealing with complex learning. It would be interesting to start from the new needs in order to make the available means visible or even to build new ones, because the technological world is evolving and can be a leaven of future innovations.

This is why affordance analysis can be a useful framework for rethinking the links between teachers and ICTE in order to help perceive and take advantage of the opportunities offered by ICT for possibly making new horizons appear and raising some innovations.

REFERENCES

Bardin, L. (2013). *L'analyse de contenu.* [Content analysis: in French] PUF. https://www.puf.com/content/Lanalyse_de_contenu

Bril, B. (2014, April 8). *Ethnothéories, apprentissages et contextes*. Supports mobiles et tactiles, contextes d'apprentissage chez les enfants [Ethno theories, learning and contexts, in Mobile and digital devices, learning contexts of children: in French], Lycée Henri IV, Paris. https://www.canal-u.tv/video/ehess/introduction_de_blandine_bril_ethnotheories_apprentissages_et_contextes.14701

Brousseau, G. (2011). La théorie des situations didactiques en mathématiques. *Éducation et didactique*, [Pedagogical Content Knowledge theory in mathematics. Education and Pegagogical Content Knowledge: in French] *5(1)*, 101–104. https://doi.org/10.4000/educationdidactique.1005

Bru, M. (1991). *Les Variations didactiques dans l'organisation des conditions d'apprentissage* [Pedagogical content knowledge variations when organising the learning conditions: in French]. Éditions Universitaires du Sud.

Cuban, L. (1982). Persistence of the Inevitable: The Teacher-Centred Classroom. *Education and Urban Society*, *15*(1), 26–41.

Fernagu Oudet, S. (2012). Favoriser un environnement « capacitant » dans les organisations. In *Former par le travail* [Foster an enabling environment in organizations. In *Training Through Work*: in French], (Bourgeois, E. & Durand, M. ed., pp. 201–213). Presse Universitaire de France.

Gibson, J. J. (1977). The theory of affordances. In *Perceiving, Acting and Knowing: Toward an Ecological Psychology* (Hillsdale, NJ: Lawrence Erlbaum Associates, Inc., pp. 67–82).

Gibson, J. J. (1986). The ecological approach to visual perception. Hills-dale. *NJ: Lawrence.*

Heiden, S., Magué, J.-P., & Pincemin, B. (2010). *TXM: Une plateforme logicielle open-source pour la textométrie - conception et développement.* [TXM: An open-source software platform for textometry - design and development: in French] *2*(3), 1021–1032. https://halshs.archives-ouvertes.fr/halshs-00549779

Kirschner, P. (2002). Can we support CSCL? Educational, social and technological affordances for learning. *Can We Support CSCL? Educational, Social and Technological Affordances for Learning*. https://www.academia.edu/2723181/Can_we_support_CSCL_Educational_social_and_technological_affordances_for_learning

Médiamétrie (2018). PROFETIC 2018 : Connaître les pratiques numériques des enseignants. [Learning about teachers' digital practices: in French]. Technical report, Consumer Insights Dpt, Digital & Médias, Mediamétrie, (2018). https://cache.media.eduscol.education.fr/file/ETIC_et_PROFETIC/65/7/Rapport_PROFETIC_2018_Synthese_1098657.pdf

Moore, M. G. (1993). Theory of transactional distance. In *Theoretical principles of distance education* (Keegan D., pp. 22–38). Routledge.

Norman D. A. (1988). *The psychology of everyday things*. Basic Books.

Norman, D. A. (2002). *The Design of Everyday Things*. Basic Books, Inc.

OECD Skills Outlook 2019: Thriving in a Digital World | en | OECD. (2019). OECD Skills Outlook 2019 : Thriving in a Digital World | En | OECD. http://www.oecd.org/publications/oecd-skills-outlook-e11c1c2d-en.htm

Piaget, J. (1964). *Six études de psychologie*. [Six psychology studies: in French], Gonthier Ed.

Reed, E. S. (1993). The intention to use a specific affordance: A conceptual framework for psychology. In *Development in context* (R.H. Wosniack & K.W. Fisher, pp. 61–92). Psychology Press.

Sen, A. (1999). La possibilité du choix social [The social choice possibility: in French]. *Revue de l'OFCE*, *70*(1), 7–61. https://doi.org/10.3406/ofce.1999.1691

Super, C. M., & Harkness, S. (1986). The developmental niche: A conceptualization at the interface of child and culture. *International Journal of Behavioral Development*, *9*(4), 545–569.

Swan, K. (2003). Learning effectiveness: What the research tells us. *Elements of Quality Online Education: Practice and Direction*, *4*.

IMMERSIVE VIRTUAL REALITY (VR) CLASSROOM TO ENHANCE LEARNING AND INCREASE INTEREST AND ENJOYMENT IN THE SECONDARY SCHOOL SCIENCE CURRICULUM

Dennis Choon Guan Pang
Riverside Secondary School, Singapore

ABSTRACT

This paper describes how an Immersive Virtual Reality (VR) Classroom in a secondary school in Singapore is used to enhance learning through visualization and deepen understanding of science and increase interest and enjoyment in science. The VR Classroom is a futuristic classroom that taps the affordances of VR and AR to enhance HCI (Human-Computer Interactions) through visualization and interactivity, as well as increase engagement and enjoyment in the school curriculum. About the size of a regular classroom, this VR Classroom has three units of Oculus Rifts coupled adorned with life-size wall Augmented Reality posters of the Coronavirus and cells. Drawing from the author's experience in implementing VR lessons as a part of everyday classroom practice, this paper aims to provide practical ideas for educators to leverage on the affordances of virtual reality technologies to plan and design VR lessons. The author will also share sample lesson ideas on how educators can use VR 360 degrees videos to reach out to their students during this COVID-19 pandemic to complement the inquiry learning experience. The immersive and interactive nature of VR makes it an ideal tool for differentiated instruction to cater to diverse learners and learning needs especially during this pandemic. Data from findings using grounded theory and quantitative studies on affective outcomes show that there is significant increase in students' enjoyment in learning science when immersive VR is used and that the use of immersive VR increases students' self-efficacy. These findings have implications on the pedagogical design of lessons that use immersive VR.

KEYWORDS

Immersive Virtual Reality, VR, Augmented Reality, AR, Visualisation, Science, Interest, Enjoyment, Oculus, VR Classroom, COVID-19, 360 Degrees Video

1. INTRODUCTION

The learning of science in secondary schools in Singapore is still largely teacher and textbook-centric. Most materials used in classrooms are two-dimensional (2D), such as textbooks and images or videos projected on the large screen. Models such as DNA, working of heart chambers and action of enzymes tend to have 2D 'imagination-caused spatial misunderstanding' that results in misconceptions in science. Interactions between teacher and student still largely didactic with dominance of teacher instruction. Such two-dimensional traditional media also does not offer any form of feedback to students in learning if wrong variables are inputted or if certain conditions are given to the system. Realistic 3D visualisation with feedback programmed through computer simulations can assist students to learn by inquiry scientific concepts and processes.

Immersive Virtual Reality (VR) offers the capabilities of dynamic representation of microscopic worlds such as cells and molecules that can give rise to a more accurate reasoning to explain scientific phenomena. They have the potential to revolutionise and improve the learning of science by enhancing visualisation, interactivity and realism, or presence. This is especially true for dynamic scientific processes that are either too dangerous, minute, or costly to observe, such as the fractional distillation columns in petroleum refinery, working of heart chambers and other body organs, and the minute environment of cells and unicellular organisms.

In Singapore, the current fourth ICT Masterplan for Education focuses on promoting active learning with technology, using technology to provide feedback to learners and enhance the ability of learners to collaborate and learn together. Singapore's Ministry of Education (MOE) has also rolled out the SLS (Student Learning

Space), an online platform for students' learning about three years ago. This is accompanied by the lesson design tool called the SLS Pedagogical Scaffold that is embedded within the SLS platform for educators to plan active learning using technology with the help of active learning processes for each step of the lesson. Immersive VR can also support differentiated instruction as some learners require more hands-on experiential or visual learning approaches to understand scientific concepts. Authentic learning contexts and immersive virtual experiences can help students see relevance in their learning. This increases the likelihood of students choosing science-related careers which is vital for Singapore's competitiveness.

2. LITERATURE REVIEW

2.1 Benefits of VR/AR Technologies

Immersive VR technologies allow multi-sensory interaction and learners can construct meaning from experience. It makes the teaching of complex or abstract ideas useful as it provides a means of visualization and allows natural hypothesis making (Christou, 2010). Research from the River City project in the US and Canada showed that immersive, authentic, and supportive virtual environments can produce substantial gains in knowledge and skills in scientific inquiry and problem-solving (Dede, 2009). Immersive virtual environments also support diverse profiles of students such as academically weak students or students who are comfortable with learning from digital technologies and builds their self-efficacy and confidence in performance tasks.

Immersive VR is a powerful tool for students can apply their scientific knowledge in realistic settings and increase transfer of learning to the real world. This is due to better generalisation of learning, which occurs when there is increased similarity between training and real-world tasks (Schultheis and Rizzo, 2001). An immersive VR software called VISE developed by Keio-NUS (National University of Singapore) CUTE Centre enables medical students to practice the skills of responding and handling patients injured in an emergency scenario (NUS, 2019). VR controllers are used to assess the conditions of casualties be it excessive bleeding, wound or even death. The simulation allows medical students to familiarise with the triage methodology process by going through the actual motions of assessing casualties (Figure 1).

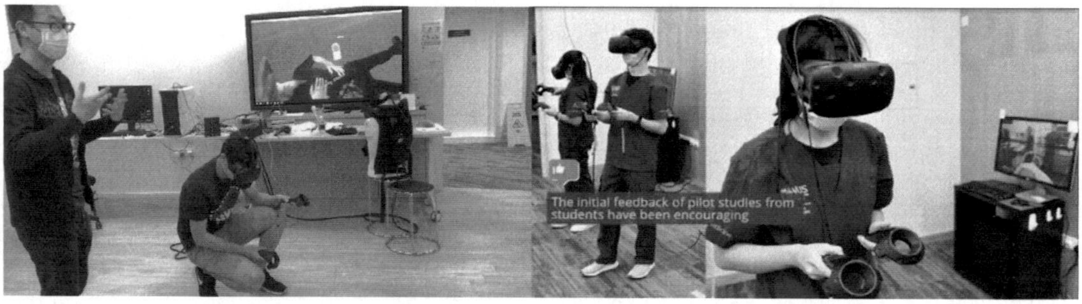

Figure 1. Vise immersive VR software used to train medical students

2.2 Immersive VR Classrooms

The VR School Research Project (Southgate et al., 2019) is a major project conducted in two government junior high schools in New South Wales (NSW), Australia that studied the affective, cognitive and safety aspects of using VR for children and teenagers. Findings include the need to translate the motivation to collaborate into pedagogy for on-task behaviour and respectful ethics in the use of VR Head Mounted Devices (HMD) including how to respond for example if the VR interactions got too intense or uncomfortable. The students had access to three Oculus VR headsets as they worked together to build virtual 3D objects in Minecraft VR. On the other hand, schools such as Cecil Hills High embarked on low-cost self-made immersive VR Cardboards to access VR 360 degrees videos to broaden their students' experiences as they go on virtual tours (NSW, 2020). A student reported that his marks improved because he became more engaged. Others felt that VR created a more empathetic feeling through videos presenting social issues. See Figure 2.

Figure 2. Immersive VR Classrooms in NSW, Australia

Liu (2020) researched on an Immersive VR Classroom (IVRC) in a middle school in China, whereby each student desk comes with a complete VR headset with tablet and screen. The immersive VR classroom students showed better science achievement compared to traditional teaching methods of using slides and video. The VR group showed better engagement in cognitive, behavioural, emotional, social domains. The research noted the importance of complementing IVRC with collaborative learning activities. See Figure 3.

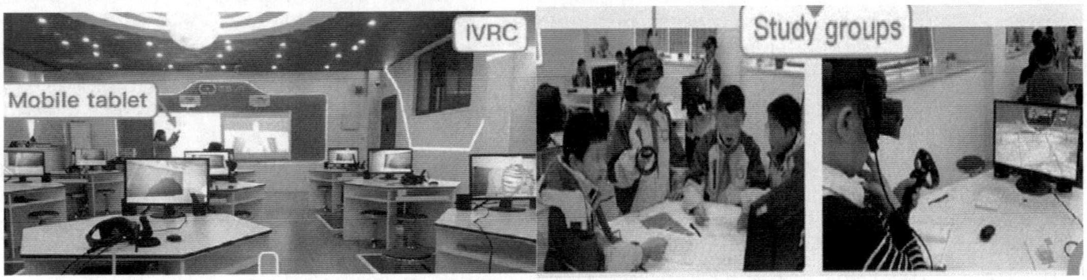

Figure 3. Immersive VR Classroom (IVRC) in a middle school in China

2.3 Effects of VR and AR on learning

With regards to the use of VR on the teaching of science at the secondary school level, Tan and Waugh (2014) found that immersive VR helped students to overcome frustration and lack of understanding in molecular biology, which caused some students to rely heavily on memorization in traditional 2D diagrams and models in textbooks and slides. These traditional media are insufficient to represent the DNA, proteins, and dynamic processes that take place in three-dimensional space in the cell. The study found significant increases in Molecular Biology achievement in male students. Data from interviews also found out and the visualization through immersive VR increased understanding leading to achievement.

Parong and Meyer (2018) carried out a study of undergraduates who learnt the biology of human body using immersive VR versus learning through didactic teaching with slides. The immersive VR group reported higher motivation, interest, and engagement than those being taught by slides. However, there was no differences in performance between VR and the slideshow group for conceptual items, and the VR group performed worse for factual items. The reason may be due to distraction by excitement and novelty of VR experience.

Pang (2021) carried out a between-subject study of two classes learning biology of enzymes. He obtained the effect size of 0.50 for the experimental class which indicates the VR has a positive effect on learning of the molecular representations of enzymes and their interactions. This suggests the possible impact of immersive technologies such as VR to enhance interest and achievement in science for topics such as enzymes in the high-school curriculum. Studies example by Tangaard (2019) also suggests that adding generative learning strategies such as enactment after the VR experience greatly increases the efficacy of VR on student learning and knowledge retention.

3. METHOD

3.1 Quantitative and Qualitative Studies

This is an ongoing study on lower secondary science classes (13-14 years old students) using pre-test post-test quasi-experimental design. There will be one experimental group (VR in learning science) and a control group (non-VR). In the first part of this study, the independent variable is the mode of learning science, either using VR or the traditional classroom approach. The dependent variable is students' performance based on whether there is significant increase in the pre- and post-tests' results. The second part of this study deals with one independent variable, the use of VR or traditional classroom approach, and the dependent variable, which is the enjoyment in learning science. To facilitate ease of implementation, intact classes. Each experimental and control group comprises of 80 students from the Express stream, total n=160.

All students will be given a pre-test (before intervention) and post-test immediately after the experiment. The pre- and post-tests each comprises two parts – an academic test and a self-rated questionnaire. The planned order between the pre-test and the treatment reduces learners' awareness of experimental observation and reduce test sensitization and hence improve test validity. In the next lesson immediately following the intervention, students are required to complete the post-test. The short time frame from intervention to post-test reduces interference from maturation factors such as consulting other reference materials. For the self-rated questionnaire, a second post-test to determine if the improvement is being sustained.

For the first part of the study, the analysis of variance (ANOVA) with between-subject factors would be used to examine their respective effects. The ANOVA will be done using the difference between the means of dependent variable, which is the increase in scores between the pre-test and post-test (academic test). If the p value obtained is less than 0.05 ($p < 0.05$), it confirms that there is a significant difference between the use of learning mode (with VR or without VR) on the performance of students. For the second part of the study, I will likewise use analysis of variance (ANOVA) to examine the effect of learning mode (with or without VR) on enjoyment of learning science based on the pre- and post-tests (attitudinal questionnaires). If the p value obtained is less than 0.05 ($p<0.05$), I can conclude that using VR leads to greater enjoyment in learning science.

Due to the impact of the COVID-19 pandemic which resulted in government measure that students do not need to attend school physically for close to three months in the year of 2020, the author was not able to carry the first part of the study. The author carried out a within-subject study on the impact of VR on students' science attitudes. The self-rated questionnaire is derived from ATSI or 'Attitudes towards Science Inventory'. Only the items specific to the variable of enjoyment of science is relevant and extracted for use, the 16 questions utilize the 5-level Likert response scale and probes students' enjoyment of science (Schruba, 2006).

3.2 Using Immersive VR as Part of Everyday Classroom Practice

My experience as a VR practitioner I have been integrating VR into science lessons In Riverside Secondary School for the past 4 years since March 2017. I have been using VR during science lessons to teach students in Secondary 1 on the topic of cells as well as in Secondary 3 in teaching topics such as enzymes. The VR/AR lessons take place in a specially designed and equipped VR Classroom in the school called 'VR Hub' to provide an immersive experience. The school obtained VR software from NTU through a collaborative partnership with Assoc. Prof. Cai Yiyu of NTU's VARTEL (Virtual and Augmented Reality Technology Enabled Learning) Lab. The rationale for using VR in our school is to harness the immersive and interactive nature of technology to enable students to improve learning of science. For example, in the topic of cells, students can visualize the microcosmic cellular environment, manipulate its organelles and even navigate the intra- and intercellular spaces through online VR games. As for the topic on enzymes, students are able to hold the enzyme molecule and see how it interacts with the substrate molecule. Such actions facilitate conceptual understanding as they transform abstract scientific concepts such as lock-and-key hypothesis into concrete experiences. See Figure 4.

Figure 4. Immersive VR lessons in the science curriculum, Riverside Secondary School

4. FINDINGS

Out of 16 ATSI-derived items, 2 items on "Science is something that I enjoy very much" (p value= 0.012) and "I feel at ease in a Science class" (p value=0.028) showed a significant increase in pre- and post-test scores for $p<0.05$. For the remaining items such as "I have a real desire to learn Science", "I do not do very well in Science" and "I would like a job that does not use any science" there is no significant increases shown. The pre-test was conducted was conducted on the first week of June and two post-tests were conducted, one immediately after the VR lesson in end-July and the other two months later in September 2020. The second post-test is necessary to determine if the improvement in scientific attitudes were sustained. Further analysis revealed high to moderate levels of correlation between the key attitudinal variable of "Science is something that I enjoy very much" to other variables such as "I would like a job not related to science" (negative correlation) and "I have a good feeling towards science", "Science is one of my favourite subjects" and "I have a real desire to learn science". This suggests that the impact of immersive VR on students' intrinsic motivation and their orientation towards future careers.

The author also carried out participatory inquiry using grounded theory study to determine "To what extent can the successes of one's virtual identity in immersive environments induce greater self-efficacy?" and "How does using VR cater to the varied learning styles of students in a differentiated classroom?". Analysis of line-by-line coding from interviews showed that the participants in general experienced a high sense of presence and immersion from the various VR experiences. One student who used immersive VR for biology shared that "VR has endless possibilities and capabilities, in that it allows us to travel to the other side of the ocean and still physical in our country…by merging VR and 3D objects, it allows users to get the same adrenaline rush as if they are physically doing the activity, we get to try out difficult things that seems impossible in real life, it not everyday that we get to look at cells and touch them." The increased sense of self-efficacy builds learner agency and self-directed learning.

Other students preferred "to learn science using VR as it is interactive so they can change values" and wanted more gamification elements because "it would be more fun if it were a game with scores." An immersive VR environment provides learners with 'embodied cognition learning experiences" (Barsalou, 2008) as they develop 'mental perceptual simulation' (Dede et al., 2017) to draw upon when retrieving or constructing knowledge. This is particularly useful for students with preferences in learning styles towards experiential or situated learning. In a related study, the same group of students who viewed 360 degrees videos on conservation of species using Google Cardboard reported the experience as immersive and real. Students were deeply engaged, and students expressed fear when the tigers or sharks approached them in the 360 degrees videos. See Figure 5.

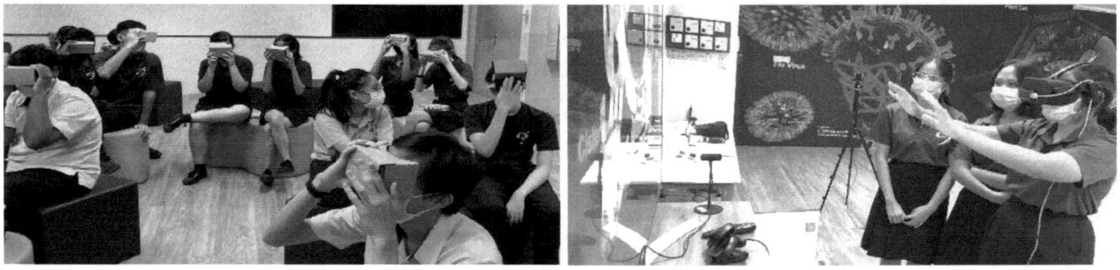

Figure 5. Immersive VR Classroom in Riverside Secondary School, Singapore

5. DISCUSSION

Results from this experimental study have provided empirical evidence that the use of immersive VR in teaching of science can lead to positive emotions such as enjoyment in learning science, which may translate into greater academic interest motivation and future career orientation. More research can be conducted on areas such as whether VR is more suited as a learning mode for which type of ability level or variety of learning styles. In addition, we need to find out where there are other moderator variables such as the characteristics of VR or the learning pedagogy that affects the efficacy of VR use. Immersive VR technologies can bring about greater understanding of science concepts by presenting educational content through more authentic, lifelike and visual representations of scientific models and concepts. It can also enhance user enjoyment leading to deeper engagement and greater interest in the learning of science. Using immersive VR in science not only increases the learner's scientific knowledge and skills, it also enhances their sense of self-efficacy (Dede, 2012).

From this experience of implementing VR in Riverside Secondary School, it is observed that many teachers still lack the understanding of immersive VR and AR technologies and the pedagogical content knowledge to use them proficiently to achieve curricular goals. It is therefore important to put in place a comprehensive professional development plan (Figure 6) to support teachers in their learning and use of immersive technologies and to provide ample support and opportunities for more experience VR practitioners like myself to handhold other teachers who are keen on trying immersive VR lessons but lack the pedagogical know-how or resources to begin. The ability to integrate VR into lessons to achieve learning and academic goals requires the teachers to be flexible and adaptive to harness the immersive nature of VR technologies, while ensuring that there is sufficient scaffolding of content and effective lesson enactment strategies to enable students to have a clear understanding of scientific theories and models. The ability to understand also depends on co-constructing knowledge and receiving feedback through collaborative work with peers.

Current research shows that school-based job-embedded learning and creation of learning communities are the most effective way for teachers to learn new pedagogical and technology skills to change classroom practice (Sparks and Hirsh, 1997). In view of the nature of the immersive VR technology, it would be better to focus on depth rather than scalability of implementation. This means that the PD efforts would entail a group of teachers who sign up and are enthusiastic about the use of immersive VR in science or other subjects' lessons.

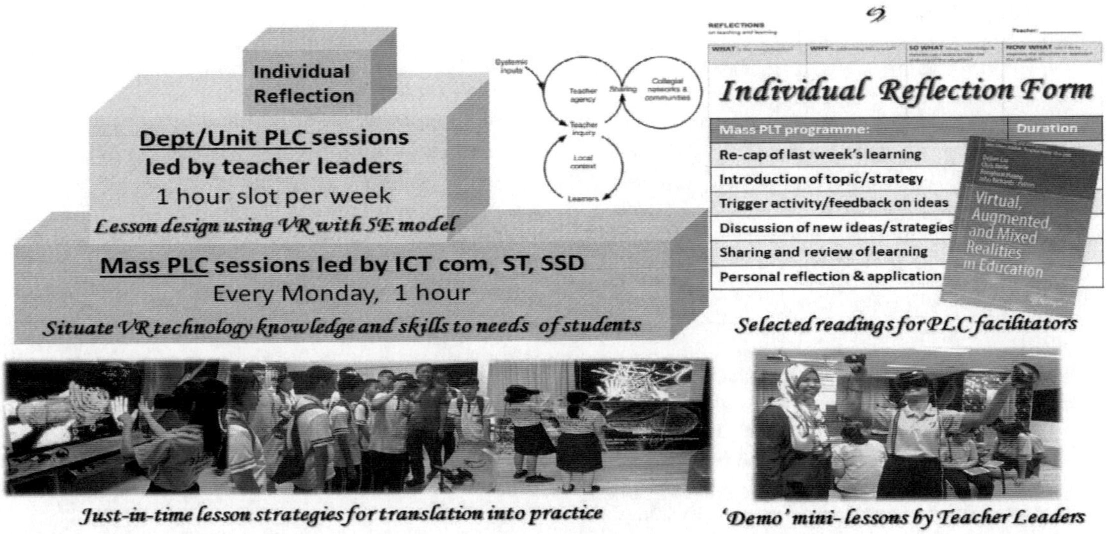

Figure 6. Suggested Professional Development plan to equip teachers with skills and pedagogical knowledge for VR

6. CONCLUSION

The use of VR and AR can provide more varied and authentic experience to enhance equity and opportunity for all students. More research will be needed to shed light on how to operationalize, using effective pedagogies and learning strategies, immersive VR in a secondary school/high school curriculum. Such strategies can also be adapted to primary/elementary schools. The use of immersive VR is *not* about the technology. What is important is a measured approach of integrating VR into lessons with specific learning intentions and learning outcomes in line with curricular goals that is aligned and suitable for Singapore's science curriculum. Riverside Secondary School, like many other schools in Australia, Europe, China, and Singapore, have been taking on the challenges of innovating e-pedagogies such as immersive VR to improving the teaching and learning in schools. Hopefully, more schools will come on board to share educational content and VR software, as well as lesson strategies and resources that will better support educators to embark on this exciting frontier of VR/AR powered by HCI and Artificial Intelligence, in the years to come.

ACKNOWLEDGEMENT

The author wishes to thank Miss Tham Yoke Chun, Principal of Riverside Secondary School and Derick Wong, Vice-Principal, for their valuable support for this VR Classroom project, Professor Yen Ching-Chiuan and staff at Keio-NUS (National University of Singapore) CUTE Centre for providing inputs to the portion of this paper on their VISE VR software and Professor Cai Yiyu of NTU (Nanyang Technological University) for the partnership in setting up the VR Classroom and provision of immersive VR software.

REFERENCES

Barsalou, L.W. (2008). Grounded cognition. *Annu. Rev. Psychol.* 2008. 59: 617–45.

Christou, C (2010). Virtual Reality in Education. In A. Tzanavari and N. Tsapatsoulis (Eds). *Affective, Interactive and Cognitive Methods for E-Learning Design: Creating an Optimal Education Experience*, pp. 228-243. IGI Global.

Dede, C. (2009). Immersive interfaces for engagement and learning. *Science*, 323, 66–69.

Dede, C. (2012). How Immersion in the virtual and augmented worlds help students in the real world. MIT Education Group. Retrieved Nov 9 2020.

Dede, C., Jacobson, J., & Richards, J. (2017). Introduction: Virtual, augmented, and mixed realities in education. In D. Liu, C. Dede, R. Huang & J. Richards, (Eds.). *Virtual reality, augmented reality, and mixed reality in education*, pp. 1-18. Hong Kong: Springer.

Liu, R., Wang, L., Lei, J. & Ren, Y. (2020). Effects of an immersive virtual reality-based classroom on students' learning performance in science lessons. *British Journal of Educational Technology*, 51(6):2034-2059.

NUS, National University of Singapore (2019). Virtual encounters with mass casualty incidents. https://news.nus.edu.sg/virtual-encounters-with-mass-casualty-incidents/ Accessed 5 December 2020.

Pang, D, Devi. S, Wong, D, Cai, Y.Y., Ba R. (2021). The Use of Immersive Virtual Reality Technology to Deepen Learning in Singaporean Schools (in press). Springer.

Parong, J. & Mayer, R. (2018). Learning Science in Immersive Virtual Reality. Journal of Educational Psychology.

Schruba, A. E. (2006). Evaluation of student attitude toward science and self-efficacy in a non-major college biology course. Masters Thesis. Texas Christian University. http://citeseerx.ist.psu.edu/viewdoc/download?doi=10.1.1.503.4915&rep=rep1&type=pdf Accessed 28 Feb 2020.

Schultheis, Maria & Rizzo, Albert. (2001). The application of virtual reality technology in rehabilitation. *Rehabilitation Psychology*. 46. 296-311. 10.1037/0090-5550.46.3.296.

Southgate, E., Smith, S.P., Cividino, C., Shane, S., Kilham J., Eather, G., Scevak, J., Summerville, D., Buchanan, R. & Bergin, C. (2019). Embedding immersive virtual reality in classrooms: Ethical, organisational and educational lessons in bridging research and practice. *International Journal of Child-Computer Interaction*, 19:19-29.

Sparks, D & Hirsch, S. (1997). A New Vision for Teacher Development. Alexandria, VA: Association for Supervision and Curriculum Development and National Development Council.

Tan, Sandra & Waugh, Russell. (2014). Use of Virtual-Reality in Teaching and Learning Molecular Biology. In Cai Y.Y (Ed). 3D Immersive and Interactive Learning. pp.17-43. Springer.

Tanggaard, L. (2019). Learning in Virtual Reality. Masters' Thesis. Aalborg University, Denmark. https://projekter.aau.dk/projekter/files/306328987/Master_s_thesis_nandre12.pdf Accessed 18 February 2020.

ICT TOOLS FOR FINAL QUALIFICATION ASSESSMENT SURVEY STUDY FOR EUROPEAN AND ORIENTAL LANGUAGES PROGRAMS

Rusudan Makhachashvili, Ivan Semenist and Anna Bakhtina
Borys Grinchenko Kyiv University
18/2, Bulvarno-Kudryavska-st., Kyiv Ukraine

ABSTRACT

The global pandemic and subsequent quarantine measures and restrictions have posed a challenge to the structure and procedure of university summative assessment process. Qualification assessment for Foreign Languages major programs in particular is a strict regimen process that involves different stages (oral and written exams, final project viva, internal and external review). This study seeks to analyze the practices of Borys Grinchenko Kyiv University digital qualification assessment for students of European (French, Italian, Spanish, English, German) and Asian (Mandarin, Japanese) Languages major programs, employed in the year 2020 due to quarantine measures. The survey and analysis of different ICT tools is used to translate real life qualification assessment practices into online blended format. The investigation also seeks to identify various groups of applied digital skills and collaboration skills, utilized through qualification assessment process by all parties (students, faculty and referees). Comparative results of ICT tools and practices efficiency for respondents of European and Oriental languages programs are provided.

KEYWORDS

ICT Tools and Practices in Education, Final Qualification Assessment, Digital Literacy, Blended Learning, European and Oriental Languages Acquisition

1. INTRODUCTION

The global pandemic and subsequent quarantine measures and restrictions have posed an array of challenges to the structure and procedure of university summative assessment process. Qualification assessment for Foreign Languages major programs in particular is a strict regimen process that involves different stages (oral and written exams, final project viva, internal and external review).

This study **objective** is to critically review the applied case and best practices of Borys Grinchenko Kyiv University Digital Final Qualification Assessment for students of European (French, Italian, Spanish, English, German) and Oriental (Mandarin Chinese, Japanese) Languages major programs, employed in the year 2020 due to quarantine measures. The survey and analysis of different ICT tools is used to translate real life qualification assessment practices into online blended format. The investigation seeks to identify various groups of applied digital skills (Dos Reis 2015; Eduventures 2020) and soft skills (Abbott 2013; Hymes 1972; Morze, Makhachashvili, Smyrnova-Trybulska 2016), utilized through qualification assessment process by all parties (students, faculty and referees).

In the educational sphere, according to our estimations, the result of the COVID-19 pandemic development was the need to take quick action in order to achieve such desirable results: to adapt the existent educational scenarios to digital, remote and blended formats; to boost ICT competence and digital literacy of all participants of the educational process. This study aims to identify, among other parameters, challenges for actual and underdeveloped skills (hard, technical and soft), that participants of the educational process encountered through Final Qualification Assessment in programs of European and Oriental Languages.

The study **design** included the following qualitative and quantitative methodological elements: 1) Educational activity profiling for Finale Qualification Assessment; 2) The online survey method (Dillman 2014) applied to assess The Final Qualification Assessment for European and Oriental languages programs, performed in digital and blended format; 3) the method of Final Qualification Assessment ICT tools efficiency ranking based on the user satisfaction quotient model.

According to the Law of Ukraine "On Higher Education" (Law 2019), Finale qualification assessment can be profiled as the establishment in compliance with learning outcomes (scientific or creative work) of higher education students with the requirements of the educational (scientific, educational and creative) program and / or the single state qualifying exam. The form of state certification of students is defined by the state standards of education and is reflected in the curricula of the Free Economic Zone. Usually state certification has two forms: 1. State exam; 2. Defense (viva) of Qualification (Bachelor's) paper/project.

In the situation of the COVID-19 pandemic lockdown all elements of the Final Qualification Assessment at Borys Grinchenko Kyiv University for European and Oriental Languages programs have been transformed to the digital, remote or blended format with the use of ICT tools. The qualification assessment regimen was adapted to digital format as a framework (a legal procedure that results in the degree confirmation of a student), the string of consecutive activities according to the legal procedure described in the profile above, the "ritual" scenario (and experience for the student that is emotionally uplifting and somber in nature, connects with the traditions of the university culture of Europe).

According to the law mandate, the following Qualification Assessment activities for European and Oriental languages programs at Borys Grinchenko Kyiv university have been transferred to digital remote mode: State exam conduct (introduction, oral answers, grading, discussion, results); State Exam card selection; State Exam assessment; State Exam results declaration and appeal; Bachelor's project submission; Bachelor's project review; Bachelor's paper/project viva; Bachelor's project assessment; Bachelor's project results declaration and appeal.

2. ICT TOOLS FOR FINAL QUALIFICATION ASSESSMENT FOR EUROPEAN AND ORIENTAL LANGUAGES: SURVEY STUDY

2.1 Questionnaire Overview

Based on the activity profile (Final Qualification Assessment) a survey was conducted among the participants of the Final Qualification Assessment at Borys Grinchenko Kyiv University Foreign European and Oriental languages programs (Spanish, French, Italian, English, Mandarin Chinese, Japanese major) in order to assess the efficiency of qualification assessment transfer into digital format via various ICT tools employed.

The survey comprised of 12 questions total (multiple choice and scoring), divided into such categories: 1) questions on overall experiences of Final Qualification Assessment participants in all procedures, conducted via ICT tools; 2) questions on digital literacy skills, required of Final Qualification Assessment participants; 3) questions on soft skills, required of Final Qualification Assessment participants; 4) questions, aimed to conduct Efficiency Ranking (Dos Reis 2017; Morze, Makhachashvili, Smyrnova-Trybulska 2016) of most widely used Final Qualification Assessment ICT tools.

2.2 Survey Results for European and Oriental Languages Programs

The following participants of the digital Final Qualification Assessment were respondents of the survey: students of senior year of Bachelor's program – 53,4% of respondents; assessment board members – 15,5%; faculty members (who took part in digital qualification assessment preparation and conduct) – 20,7%; Bachelor project referees and supervisors – 8,6%. Respondents of all groups took part in the survey – 59 total. The survey sample covers all the participants of Final Qualification Assessment in European and Oriental languages programs exhaustively, in the timeframe of the COVID-19 lockdown through the spring semester of 2020. The choice of respondent groups corresponded to the variation or similarity of tasks, performed throughout Final Qualification Assessment by representatives of European and Oriental languages programs and, subsequently, the variation and similarity of ICT tools used.

Respondents of all groups spanned the 4-year foreign language Bachelor's programs in proportional distribution measures: Spanish major program - 32,8%; Japanese major program - 19%; Mandarin Chinese major program - 22,4%; French major program - 15,5%; Italian major program - 15,5%; English major program- 8,6%. Students of all Bachelor's programs (senior year) surveyed had 4 years of the major foreign language training (European or Oriental) and 3 years of the minor foreign language training (European or Oriental). The spring (final) semester of foreign languages programs was conducted remotely in digital format due to country-wide quarantine measures.

The overall digital qualification assessment experience on the scale of 1 to 5 was defined as mostly agreeable (4) by 50% of respondents, most agreeable (5) by 29% of respondents and less agreeable (3) by 17% of respondents across all foreign language programs surveyed. Digital activities got overall rankings of 5-4 from respondents of European languages programs and 4-2 from respondents of Oriental languages programs.

The respondents identified all the ICT digital tools that they have to employ the most in digital qualification assessment process (Figure 1). The highest scoring ICT tools by all the groups of respondents of both European and Oriental language programs were: e-mail (93% of respondents), Google services (76% of respondents), videoconferencing services (84% of respondents), social media platforms (77% of respondents), automated testing systems and learning management systems (31% of respondents).

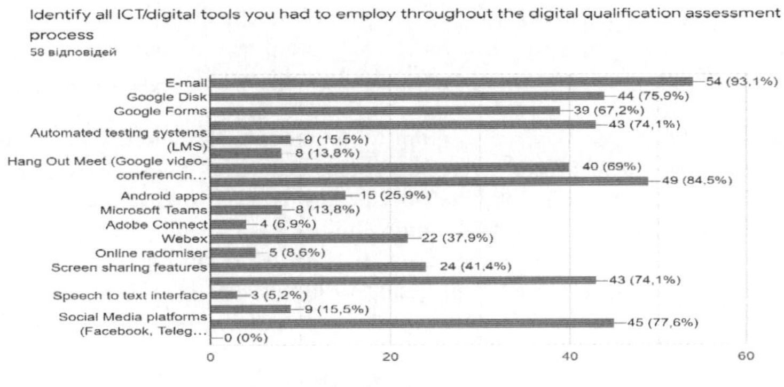

Figure 1. ICT tools identification through the digital qualification assessment

The ranking 1-5 of the ICT tools employed through digital qualification assessment process yields following tools getting the highest scoring (5 – most agreeable) among all ICT tools identified and used: email services; google forms; Zoom video conferencing services; screen sharing services; Microsoft Office tool-kit and various social media platforms.

The respondents identified the following most prominent activities across all ICT tools used throughout the digital qualification assessment process: Communication (synchronous); Communication (asynchronous); Collaboration; Information/file sharing; Summative assessment; Formative assessment; Peer review; Presentation; Speech quality assessment; Brainstorming.

Respondents from European languages programs identify Information sharing as and overwhelmingly prominent (59,1%) across all ICT tools employed for Final Qualification Assessment (Figure 2):

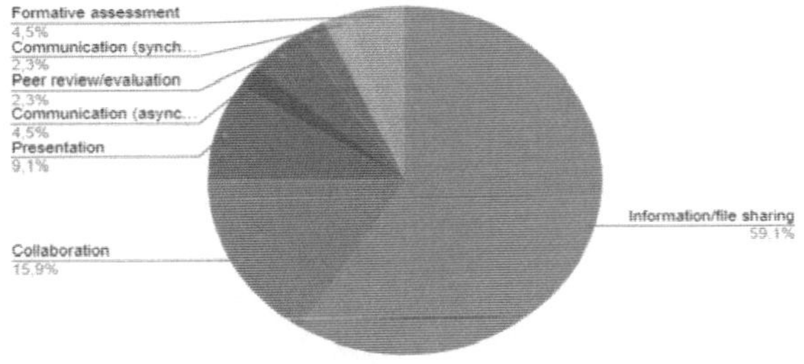

Figure 2. Activities prominent for ICT tools in Finale Qualification Assessment. European languages

For respondents of Oriental languages programs Speech quality assessment features as prominent as Information sharing across identified ICT tools (Figure 3). The following is inferred as being due to the phonetical and tonal features of Mandarin Chinese and Japanese languages being essential to meaning comprehension and decoding, which is hard to recreate and evaluate in a digital communicative environment.

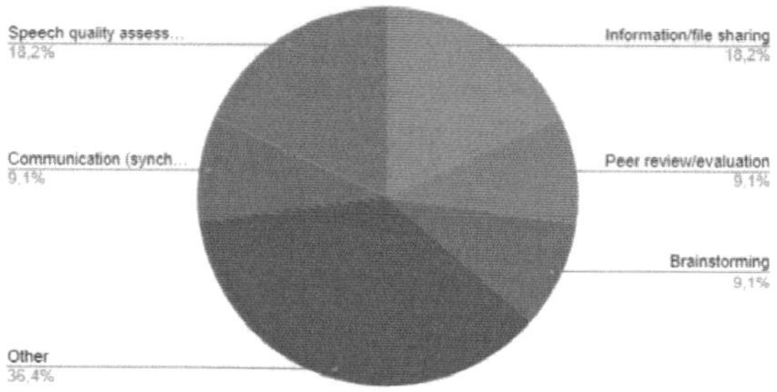

Figure 3. Activities prominent for ICT tools in Finale Qualification Assessment. Oriental languages program

Information sharing and presentation are considered prominent for such types of tools as email, Google services, Microsoft Office Toolkit. Both synchronous and asynchronous communication and collaboration is distributed proportionally among email services, learning management systems and various video conference services. The tools that feature summative assessment as a prominent activity are Google forms and LMS Moodle. Formative assessment as a type of activity features but does not dominate evaluation of ICT tools used qualification assessment process.

The *following technical and user requirements*, most prominent for ICT/digital tools employed throughout the digital qualification assessment process were identified: Bandwidth; Specialized software; Specialized hardware (webcam, mic, PC type etc.); Intuitive interface; Advanced digital literacy; Intermediate digital literacy; Elementary digital literacy; Customized training before use.

Respondents of the European languages program have assessed the dominant ICT tools requirements (Figure 4) being Intuitive interface (28,8%), elementary digital literacy (26,9) and specialized software (17,3%).

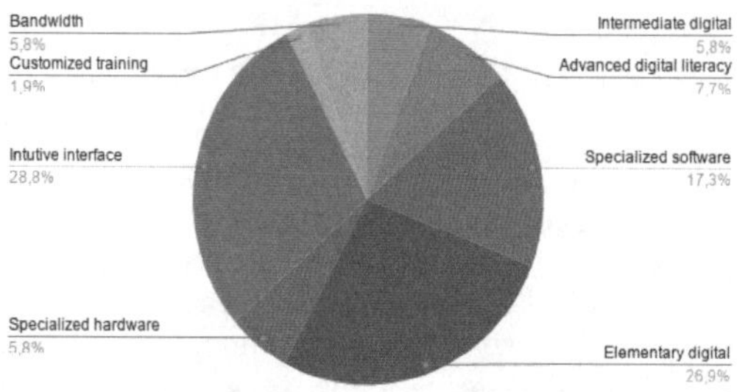

Figure 4. Technical and user requirements for ICT tools of qualification assessment for European languages

Respondents of the Oriental languages program have assessed the prominent ICT tools requirements (Figure 5) being Intuitive interface (31,8%), elementary digital literacy (31,8) and bandwidth and advanced digital literacy (9,1).

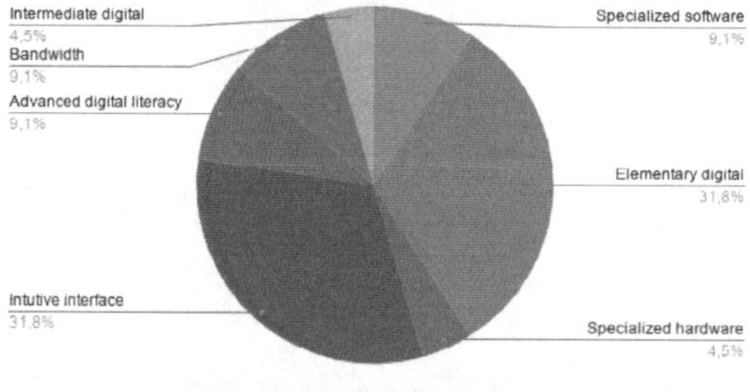

Figure 5. Technical and user requirements for ICT tools of qualification assessment for Oriental languages

It bears pointing out, that according to the status criterion in Final Qualification Assessment, different technical requirements are attributed importance by different respondents, regardless of the foreign language program (Figure 6 and Figure 7):

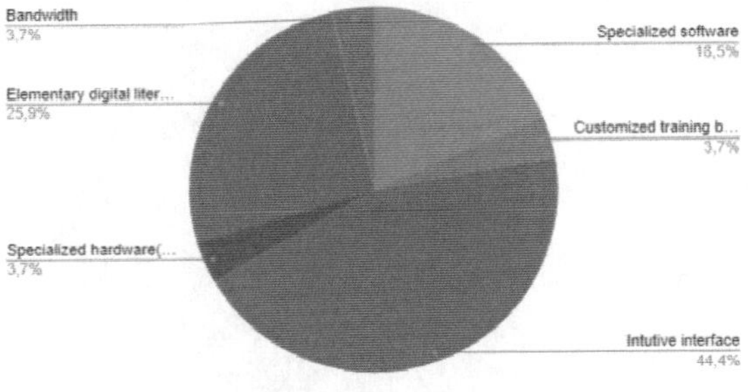

Figure 6. Technical and user requirements for ICT tools of qualification assessment for students

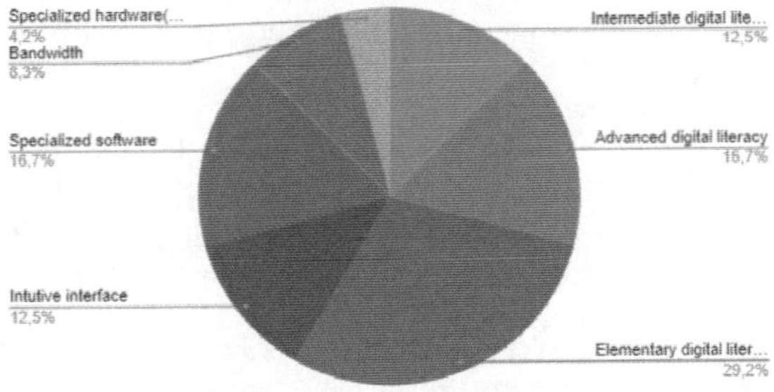

Figure 7. Technical and user requirements for ICT tools of qualification assessment for Assessment board members, Faculty members and referees

As can be seen in Figure 6, students rate Intuitive interface (44,4%) and Elementary digital literacy (25,9%) as highest necessary requirements. Assessment board members, Faculty members and referees (Figure 7) rate Advanced Digital Literacy (16,7%) and Intermediate Digital Literacy (12,5%) as proportionally prominent requirements to engage with the technical interface of ICT tools for Final qualification assessment. Intuitive interface ranks significantly lower as a requirement (12,5%) with Faculty and Staff than it does with students (average age 21-22 y.o.) Such distribution of technical requirement assessment testifies to the phenomenon of *digital divide* (TDD 2020), pervasive in various areas of educational activities in the framework of Covid-19 lockdown.

Across various ICT tools for the digital qualification assessment process the following skills and competences most widely implemented and practiced, drawn from various relevant 21st century skills frameworks (Davies 2011; Dos Reis 2015; EC 2020; Hymes 1972; UNESCO 2018; DGGSR 2019) have been identified: Communication; Collaboration; Team work; Digital literacy; Emotional intellect; Interdisciplinary skills; Critical thinking; Leadership; Flexibility and Adaptability; Decision making; Learning and Innovation skills. Different priorities in soft skills are identified for participants of digital Qualification assessment of the European languages program (Figure 8) and Oriental languages program (Figure 9):

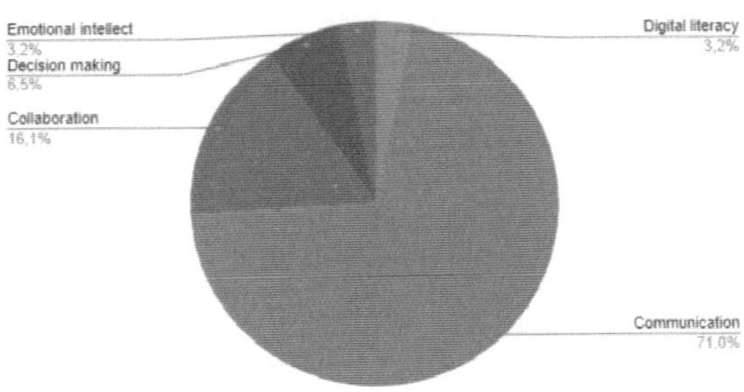

Figure 8. Soft skills for ICT tools in digital qualification assessment for European languages program

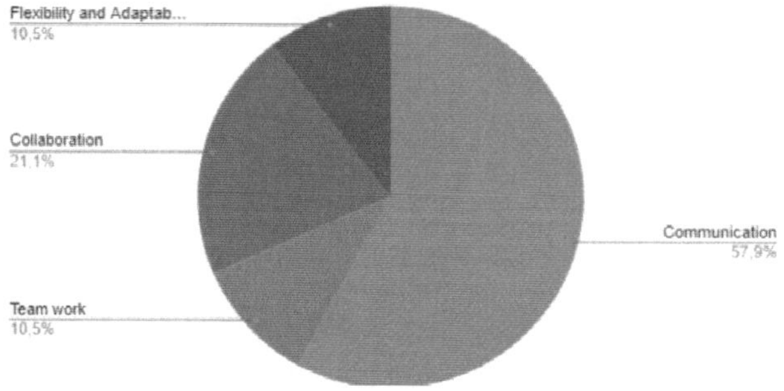

Figure 9. Soft skills for ICT tools in digital qualification assessment for Oriental languages program

Communication is identified as an overwhelmingly important soft skill for fulfilling Final Qualification Assessment via digital format (71% of respondents of European languages programs and 57,9% of respondents of Oriental languages programs). Collaboration as a skill ranks proportionally second across the board (16,1% of respondents of European languages programs and 21,1% of respondents of Oriental languages programs).

Yet respondents of Oriental languages distribute such soft skills as Team Work (10,5%) and Flexibility/Adaptability (10,5%) as proportionately activated in digital Final Qualification Assessment. Respondents of European languages programs distribute such soft skills as Decision making (6,5%), Digital literacy (3,2%) and Emotional Intellect (3,2%) as proportionately activated in digital Final Qualification Assessment.

Communication and collaboration rank as a type of skills most widely applied by respondents of all foreign language programs for the use of such instruments as email, Google services, video conferencing services and social Media platforms. Communication as a skill is ranked highest among respondents of the European languages program. Team work ranks second most prominent skill employed via the use of Google disk, learning management systems and video conferencing services. Team work and flexibility feature as top 5 priority skills among respondents of the Oriental languages program. Relevance is attributed to learning and Innovation skills in the use of such ICT tools as a learning management system (ranking second after interdisciplinary skills), automated Testing System (offline, online and cloud based), Android apps and Microsoft Office tools. Creativity as a skill ranks 3rd the use of Google services and ranks 1st in the use of Microsoft Office tools.

2.3 ICT Tools Final Qualification Assessment Efficiency Ranking

The Final Qualification Assessment ICT tools were subjected to Customer Satisfaction Evaluation Ranking (Dos Reis 2017). This ranking method features *the efficiency of ICT tools per education activity* as the main criterion. The CSER, as applied to various types of ICT tools in education process was approbated through the run of the IRNet framework project, funded by the People Program (Marie Curie Actions) of the European Union's Seventh Framework FP7/2007-2013/ (Morze, Makhachashvili, Smyrnova-Trybulska 2016).

For the ranking purpose the Final Qualification Assessment ICT tools were divided into 4 groups according to technical types and purpose in the Final Qualification Assessment process: 1) Google cloud services (Google Disc, Google Forms, G-mail); 2) Video conferencing services (Google Meet, Zoom, Webex); 3) Learning management systems (LMS Moodle, Automated testing systems); 4) Microsoft Office tools (Word, PPoint, Excel).

All respondents had to rank the activity importance 1-5 (1 = least prominent for the use of a tool type, 5 = most prominent for the use of a tool type) for the selected ICT tools type used. The activities, scored for each type of ICT tool for Final Qualification Assessment were presented in the following order: Communication (synchronous); Communication (asynchronous); Collaboration; Information/file sharing; Summative assessment; Formative assessment; Peer review; Presentation; Speech quality assessment; Brainstorming.

Figures 10-13 below exemplify the discrepancy in ranking score for one activity type - Communication (synchronous) – across all types of ICT tools for Final Qualification Assessment:

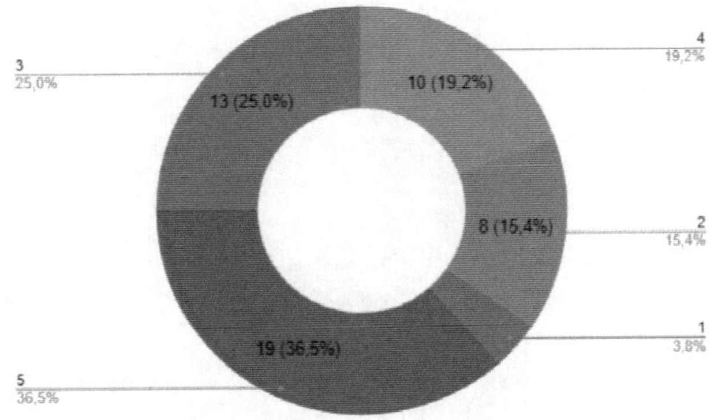

Figure 10. Evaluation of Tool Type 1 (Google Disc, Google Forms, G-mail). Sample ranking score card for Communication (synchronous)

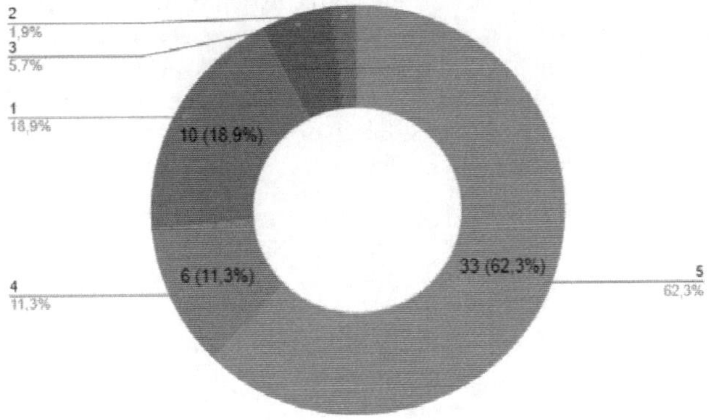

Figure 11. Evaluation of Tool Type 2 (Google Meet, Zoom, Webex). Sample ranking score card for Communication (synchronous)

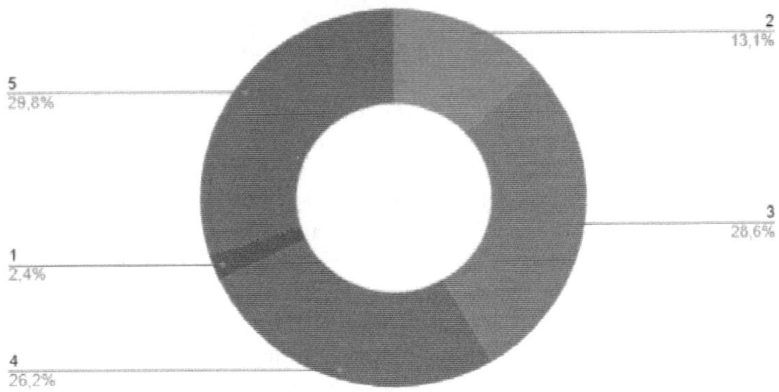

Figure 12. Evaluation of Tool Type 3 (LMS Moodle, Automated testing systems). Sample ranking score card for Communication (synchronous)

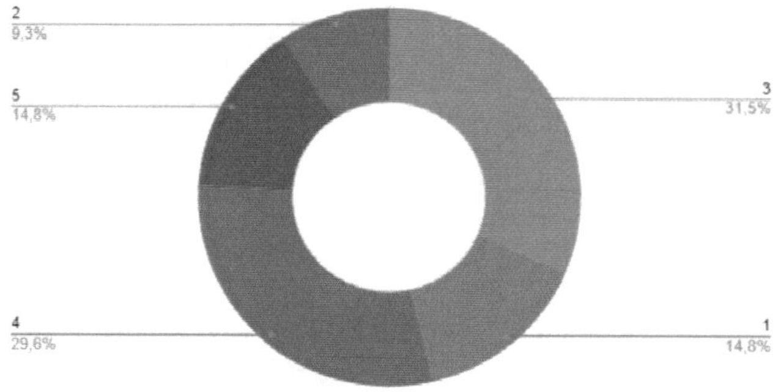

Figure 13. Evaluation of Tool Type 4 (Word, PPoint, Excel). Sample ranking score card for Communication (synchronous)

As apparent, Video conferencing services (**Google Meet, Zoom, Webex**) score the highest efficiency ranking for synchronous communication (62.5% for top score 5), but get a surprising ratio of lowest score as well (18,9% for lowest score 1). Learning management systems (29,8% for top score 1) and Google services (25%) get a proportional highest score 5 for efficiency in Synchronous communication in the framework of Final Qualification assessment across European and oriental languages programs.

This sample ranking testifies to the following suppositions: a) the specificity of ICT use for transference of Final Qualification assessment into digital mode for foreign languages programs that may not be encountered outside of this activity framework; b) the specificity of digital literacy, featured by participants of Final Qualification assessment for foreign languages programs.

3. CONCLUSION

All procedures and scenarios of the Final Qualification Assessment activities for foreign languages at Borys Grinchenko Kyiv university have been successfully transferred to digital remote format with the use of various sets of ICT tools in the framework of the COVID-19 pandemic adjustments. This transference could serve as a best practice model for other universities of Ukraine and European countries both as an adaptable measure for prolonged lockdown and as a way to further advance of blended learning and further digitalization and democratization of educational process.

The survey results conducted among all groups of participants of Final Qualification Assessment for European and Oriental foreign languages have yielded representative data as to the efficiency of various ICT tools implementation for rigorous assessment procedure scenario. Microsoft Office toolkit ranks highest in efficiency among respondents, presumably, due to the least digital literacy level adjustments required of users at a short notice to carry out the full spectrum of necessary activities for Final Qualification Assessment.

Various levels of digital literacy have been identified in the survey. *Advanced digital literacy* as the requirement for qualification assessment ICT tools efficiency is attributed to such instruments as learning management systems, Microsoft Office toolkit and social media platforms. *Intermediate digital literacy* is required predominantly for such instruments as Microsoft Office Toolkit, screen sharing interface, online randomizer, automated testing system, learning management system. *Elementary digital literacy* level is assessed as dominant for such tools as email, google disc, video conferencing, speech to text interfaces and social media platforms. Across the board, implementation of Final Qualification Assessment via various ICT tools requires of participants of educational process elementary to intermediate digital literacy. There's no significant discrepancy in digital literacy and ICT competence requirements between Final Qualification Assessment participants of European and Oriental languages program.

Communication, collaboration and team work are evaluated as crucial soft skills in various combinations within the scenario of digital Final Qualification Assessment. This results corroborate the correspondence between communicative competence and ICT competence components, adapted for Liberal Arts. Namely, the following components prove indispensable for all participants of Final Qualification Assessment in digital format: participation in group ICT initiatives, creating e-learning tasks, system using of ICT, presentation to the community the results of one's own research activities through the use of ICT.

The survey results will be furthered and implemented and explored in assessment of ICT tools efficiency and digital skills adaptability for separate groups of Final Qualification Assessment (students of foreign languages programs, Assessment board members, staff members, reviewers) according to roles and tasks performed, as well as according to age and entry digital literacy level (the distinction in efficiency assessment among digital natives and digital immigrants). The perspective of the study is in corresponding survey of digital qualification assessment experiences of students and faculty members of Asian (Oriental) countries and countries of Europe.

ACKNOWLEDGEMENT

The research methodology leading to these results was elaborated within the framework of the IRNet project, funding from the People Program (Marie Curie Actions) of the European Union's Seventh Framework Program FP7/2007-2013/ under REA grant agreement No: PIRSES-GA-2013- 612536. Empirical findings and survey procedures have been conducted under the auspices of Integrated Research Framework *European languages and literatures development in cross-communication context (0116 U 006607)* and Integrated Research framework *Oriental Studies development in the framework of Higher Education Internationalization (0116U007073).*

REFERENCES

Abbott S., 2013. *The Glossary of Education Reform.* Retrieved from: http://edglossary.org/hidden-curriculum (accessed July 2020).

Davies A., Fidler D. et al, 2011. *Future Work Skills 2020.* Institute for the Future for University of Phoenix Research Institute. Retrieved from: https://www.iftf.org/uploads/media/SR-1382A_UPRI_future_work_skills_sm.pdf (accessed October 2020).

Dillman, D. A., Smyth, J. D. et al, 2014. *Internet, Phone, Mail and Mixed-Mode Surveys: The Tailored Design Method*, 4th edition. John Wiley: Hoboken, NJ.

Dos Reis A., 2015. To Be a (Blended) Teacher in the 21st Century - Some Reflections. *International Journal of Research in E-learning, 1(1),* pp. 11-24.

Dos Reis A., 2017. Digital Storytelling and Technologies. *Electronic Scientific Professional Journal "Open Educational E-Environment of Modern University", 3,* pp. 106-112.

DQ Global Standards Report, 2019. *World's first global standard for digital literacy, skills and readiness launched by the Coalition for Digital Intelligence.* Retrieved from: https://www.dqinstitute.org/ (accessed July 2020).

Eduventures, 2020. *TechLandscape.* Retrieved from:https://encoura.org/2020-eduventures-tech-landscape-heres-what-to-expect/ (accessed July 2020).

European Commission, 2020. *European E-Competence Framework Guideline.* Retrieved from: https://www.ecompetences.eu/ (accessed July 2020).

Hymes, Dell H., 1972. Communicative competence. *Sociolinguistics: selected readings.* Harmondsworth: Penguin. pp. 269–293.

Law of Ukraine, 2019. *On Higher Education.* Retrieved from: https://zakon.rada.gov.ua/laws/show/1556-18#Text (accessed July 2020).

Morze N., Makhachashvili R., Smyrnova-Trybulska E., 2016. Communication in education: ICT tools assessment. *Proceedings from DIVAI*, Sturovo: University of Nitra, pp. 351-354.

Morze N., Makhachashvili R., Smyrnova-Trybulska E., 2016. Research in Education: Survey Study. *Information and Communication Technologies in Education*, 3, pp. 114-123.

The Digital Divide, 2020. *Project Overview.* Retrieved from: https://cs.stanford.edu/people/eroberts/cs181/projects/digital-divide/start.html (accessed October 2020).

UNESCO, 2018. *ICT Competency Framework for Teachers.* Retrieved from: https://unesdoc.unesco.org/ark:/48223/pf0000265721 (accessed July 2020).

LEARNER DEVICE PREFERENCE ACROSS AGE GROUPS

Peter Ilic
Center for Language research, School of Comp. Sc & Engineering, University of Aizu, Fukushima, Japan

ABSTRACT

In this study, a short survey was employed to understand better the learners' degree of technological adoption in relation to their educational activities. The first question this research seeks to identify is which technological devices are most popular with learners. The second question is to identify any differences in device preference across age groups. The data gathered can be applied to a later study to "map" learners' Digital Ecosystems in order to understand the present position occupied by Information and Communication Technologies (ICT) in the learners' educational activities. Digital Ecosystem refers to all the digital devices a student has at their disposal to leverage towards the learning goal. Today, it is still unclear to what degree students have embraced these technologies for educational purposes, and so it is uncertain what the impact of this Digital Ecosystem has on education in general. Results indicated the PC Laptop was the most popular device followed by the Smartphone for all age groups except 45 to 60 year-olds who preferred the Smartphone with PC Laptop second. The only device to have statistically significant variation across age groups was the Smartphone. This paper includes introduction, methodology, results and discussion, and conclusion sections.

KEYWORDS

Digital Ecosystem, Mobile Education, Curriculum Design, ICT

1. INTRODUCTION

In this study, a short survey was employed to obtain a better understanding of the participants' degree of technological adoption in relation to their educational activities. The first question this research seeks to answer is which technological devices are most popular with learners. The second question is to identify any differences in device preference across age groups. The data gathered can be applied to a later study to "map" learners' Digital Ecosystems in order to understand the present position occupied by Information and Communication Technologies (ICT) in the learners' educational life. Digital Ecosystem refers to all the digital devices a student has at their disposal to leverage towards the learning goal. Today, it is still unclear to what degree students have embraced these technologies for educational purposes, and so it is uncertain what the impact of this Digital Ecosystem has on education in general. This paper focuses on identifying devices employed for learning and differences across age groups as related to these tech devices. This is a preliminary study that will guide the development of a more extensive study designed to represent the Digital Ecosystem of learners visually.

This research will be of interest to curriculum developers and researchers interested in the affordance of ICT for education in general and especially in the opportunity to provide personalized learning opportunities. If educators can better understand an individual's ever-evolving technological learning environment, this information can inform the development of personalized learning. University students use varied e-resources and tools for learning while combining different subject learning, communication, entertainment, and personal interests, forming their personalized learning approaches (Ma, 2017). A better understanding of students' Digital Ecosystems will inform course design that better fits learner expectations instead of forcing them to adopt devices they do not use. For example, banning phones from the language classroom inhibits the perception that education is something students can integrate directly into their lives (Godwin-Jones, 2017) when the Smartphone can help to bridge the gap (Ilic, 2015) between school and life and encourage learning outside school (Byrne and Diem, 2014, Leis et al., 2018). It has been suggested (Whalley et al., 2019) that using mobile technologies should benefit from revising our pedagogy views, making it much more responsive to students' needs in education. It is this responsive pedagogy approach that will benefit from this mapping of the learners' Digital Ecosystems.

2. METHODOLOGY

This study employed a short survey consisting of a single question: "What technological devices do you use for your personal education?" Participants (n = 206) were encouraged to list all the devices they have used in the past ten years, specifically for learning. The survey was delivered online to a balanced random sample of participants. Since this data will be used to guide a larger study, the sample characteristics were purposefully broad in terms of household income, geographic location, age, and gender. However, the geographic location of participants was limited to the United States of America.

As shown in Table 1, the participants' average household income ranged from 0 to 200,000 US dollars, with the majority of respondents (49) at approximately $30,000.

Table 1. Household income of participants

Answer Choices	Response Percent	Responses
$0-$9,999	6.31%	13
$10,000-$24,999	13.59%	28
$25,000-$49,999	23.79%	49
$50,000-$74,999	18.93%	39
$75,000-$99,999	12.62%	26
$100,000-$124,999	6.31%	13
$125,000-$149,999	3.88%	8
$150,000-$174,999	1.94%	4
$175,000-$199,999	0.0%	0
$200,000+	5.83%	12
Prefer not to answer	6.8%	14

The participants were all located in the continental United States, as can be seen in Figure 1. The majority of the participants were located in the eastern sections of the continent, and a detailed breakdown of the location percentages is included in Table 2.

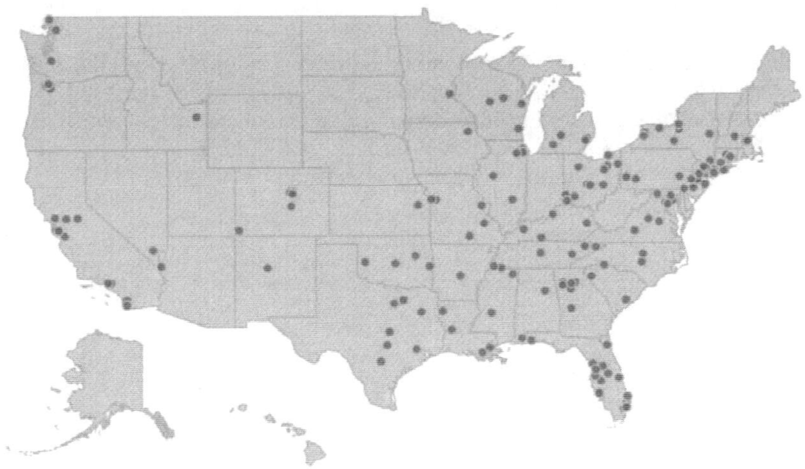

Figure 1. Geographic location of participants

Table 2. Geographic location of participants by percent

Answer Choices	Response Percent	Responses
East North Central	14.43%	29
East South Central	7.96%	16
Middle Atlantic	20.4%	41
Mountain	6.47%	13
New England	3.98%	8
Pacific	8.96%	18
South Atlantic	22.39%	45
West North Central	3.98%	8
West South Central	11.44%	23

The age of the participants is essential to the goals of this research. The average ages of respondents are detailed in Table *3*. Ages 45 to 60 make up the largest percentage of participants (68), with ages 30 to 44 following closely (55).

Table 3. Age distribution of participants

Answer Choices	Response Percent	Responses
< 18	0.0%	0
18-29	20.39%	42
30-44	26.7%	55
45-60	33.01%	68
> 60	19.9%	41

Finally, the age balance was 98 Male respondents (47.57%) and 108 Female respondents (52.43%). So overall, a well-balanced sample of 206 responses was collected. This data will inform the design of a future larger sample collection of 1000+ participants using a similar methodology. It is hoped that this future sample collection will improve the reliability and validity of the findings.

3. RESULTS AND DISCUSSION

Considering the first research question, Table *4* indicates that PC Laptop (39.81%) was the most popular device among the respondents. The second was the Smartphone (29.13%), and the third was PC Desktop (15.53%). The remaining devices, Tablet, E-Reader, and Computer Game were much less popular overall for educational activities. Other responses were not additional devices, but instead, the responses added brand name information only, so these Other responses were not considered.

Table 4. Devices reported as used for education

Answer Choices	Response Percent	Responses
PC Laptop	39.81%	82
Smartphone	29.13%	60
PC Desktop	15.53%	32
Tablet	7.77%	16
E-Reader	2.91%	6
Computer Game	1.46%	3
Electronic Toy	1.46%	3
Other	1.94%	4

The second research question asks whether there is a difference across age groups for device preference. In Figure 2, the device preference across the four age groups is represented. Considering the age groups, 18 to 29, 30 to 44, and >60 all prefer PC laptops with Smartphones as the second choice for educational activities. Only the 45 to 60 year-old group chose Smartphones with PC Laptop a close second. All groups chose PC Desktop as their third choice, but the 18 to 29 year-old group found this device less popular than the other groups.

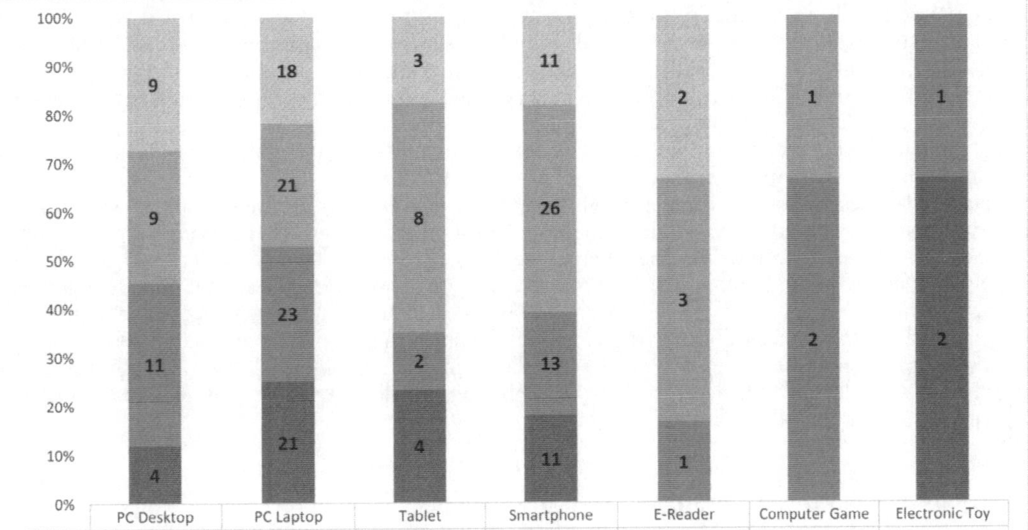

	PC Desktop	PC Laptop	Tablet	Smartphone	E-Reader	Computer Game	Electronic Toy
> 60	9	18	3	11	2	0	0
45-60	9	21	8	26	3	1	0
30-44	11	23	2	13	1	2	1
18-29	4	21	4	11	0	0	2

Figure 2. Primary device by age group

When looking at the device type and age group, the PC Desktop was most popular with 30 to 44, PC Laptop with 30 to 44, Tablet with 45 to 60, Smartphone with 45 to 60, E-Reader with 45 to 60, Computer Game with 30 to 44, and Electronic Toy with 18 to 29. The PC Desktop was least popular with the 18 to 29 age group, which may be explained by the device's lack of mobility. The popularity of PC Laptops and Smartphones as learning devices may be explained by their greater computing power and mobility, which offer a more ubiquitous learning experience. However, a clear explanation will require a more extensive study. The Chi-squared test was performed on the results in figure 2. The data was group into four columns, including the top three most popular devices and the remaining devices grouped into one. The top three popular devices in order were Pc Laptop, Smartphone, and Desktop PC. The remaining combined devices were Tablet, E-Reader, Computer Game, and Electronic Toy. The result for all four columns across the four age groups was not significant at $\chi^2(9, n=206)=9.112$, $p=0.426$. When the Chi-squared goodness of fit test was performed on the four device columns individually, the results were not significant for PC Laptop ($p=0.875$), PC Desktop ($p=0.394$), or the combined devices ($p=0.256$). However, the result for the Smartphone was significant $\chi^2(9, n=61)=9.19$, $p=0.020$. This seems to indicate that the Smartphone as a learning device has greater differentiation across the age groups.

4. CONCLUSION

The relatively stable traditional classroom learning context includes common resources, consistent schedule and location, and usually a single instructor following an agreed curriculum (Kukulska-Hulme et al., 2011). So, when technology is incorporated, it is essential that it does not create a completely separate space but adds to the continuum of learning (Cinque, 2013) and bridges the moments of learning (Ilic, 2014). Theories always change more rapidly than practice, so when a new cognitive theory is developed that may guide the use of educational technology, there is an inevitable lag in adoption of these theories by instructional designers (Winn, 2004). There is also a widespread lack of awareness (Richardson, 2011, Jones, 2004) of the educational affordances offered by ICT. All stakeholders planning to integrate technology into education should have an understanding of learner technology use and place within current theory. To this end, this research provides insight into the digital ecosystem available to the learners to inform the integration of technology in a way that maximizes benefits with minimal disruption.

First, this research sought to identify which technological devices are most popular with learners. The second question was to identify any differences in device preference across age groups. The PC Laptop was the most popular device followed by the Smartphone for all age groups except 45 to 60 year-olds who preferred the Smartphone with PC Laptop second. There was a significant difference for the Smartphone across age groups. In the future, this study will be expanded to include a larger sample size with greater cultural diversity. The small sample size and lack of follow-up interviews make it challenging to understand the reasoning behind the device preferences, so these issues will be remedied in a future large-scale study to map learners' digital ecosystems. This "map" of device availability and preference will help educators design course materials that fit with learners' preferred devices.

ACKNOWLEDGEMENT

This research was supported by a grant from the Japanese Ministry of Education (MEXT).

REFERENCES

Byrne, J. & Diem, R. 2014. Profiling mobile English language learners. *JALT CALL Journal,* 10.

Cinque, M. 2013. The "Reflective Student": The use of Mobile Devices Through Seamless Educational Spaces and Authentic Learning Scenarios. *In:* BERGE, Z. L. & MUILENBURG, L. (eds.) *Handbook of Mobile Education.* New York, NY: Routledge.

Godwin-Jones, R. 2017. Smartphones and language learning. *Language Learning & Technology,* 21, 3-17.

Ilic, P. 2014. The Relationship between Students, Mobile Phones and Their Homework. *In:* Kalz, M., Bayyurt, Y. & Specht, M. (eds.) *Mobile as a Mainstream – Towards Future Challenges in Mobile Learning.* Springer International Publishing.

Ilic, P. 2015. The Effects of Mobile Collaborative Activities in a Second Language Course. *International Journal of Mobile and Blended Learning (IJMBL),* 7, 16-37.

Jones, A. 2004. A review of the research literature on barriers to the uptake of ICT by teachers. *ICT Research.* 1 ed.: British Educational Communications and Technology Agency (BECTA).

Kukulska-Hulme, A., Pettit, J., Bradley, L., Carvalho, A. A., Herrington, A., Kennedy, D. M. & Walker, A. 2011. Mature Students Using Mobile Devices in Life and Learning. *International Journal of Mobile and Blended Learning,* 3, 18-52.

Leis, A., Tohei, A. & Cooke, S. D. 2018. Smartphone-Assisted Language Learning and Autonomy. *Handbook of Research on Integrating Technology Into Contemporary Language Learning and Teaching.*

Ma, Q. 2017. A multi-case study of university students' language-learning experience mediated by mobile technologies: a socio-cultural perspective. *computer assisted language learning,* 30, 183-203.

Richardson, J. W. 2011. Challenges of Adopting the Use of Technology in Less Developed Countries: The Case of Cambodia. *Comparative Education Review,* 55, 8-29.

Whalley, B., France, D., Park, J., Mauchline, A. & Welsh, K. Developing Active Personal Learning Environments on Smart Mobile Devices. Proceedings of the Future Technologies Conference, 2019. Springer, 871-889.

Winn, W. 2004. Cognitive perspectives in psychology. *In:* JONASSEN, D. H. & DRISCOLL, M. (eds.) *Handbook of research for educational communications and technology: A project of the Association for Educational Communications and Technology.* 2 ed. New York: Taylor & Francis.

ORAL FLUENCY: BASIS FOR DESIGNING A COMMUNICATIVE COMPETENCE STRUCTURED MODULE

Charito G. Ong and Eunice Villegas
University of Science and Technology of Southern Philippines
CM Recto Avenue, Lapasan Highway, Cagayan De Oro City, Philippines

ABSTRACT

This study analyzed and observed the oral discourse of Local Community College students. A descriptive analysis was conducted to find out the communicative competence level among the one hundred fifty randomly chosen respondents. A triangulation method was initiated to ensure the legitimacy of the gathered data. *Focus Group Discussion*, *Classroom Observation*, and *Individual Interview* were used to collect and validate the data gathering procedure. Results showed that one hundred five out of one hundred fifty respondents belong to the unconscious incompetence level while the remaining forty-five fall under the conscious competence level. The study concluded with the findings that the design of a communicative competence based module was necessary to develop oral fluency. The paper recommended for students to be constantly exposed to communicative activities in their classes to further develop their communication competencies.

KEYWORDS

Communicative Competence, Fluency, Module

1. INTRODUCTION

Oral fluency is one the most important markers of proficiency in second language but undeniably it is a neglected component in a communicative classroom. The greatest achievement of a learner is to be proficient in a language as communication is part of everyday life. Language is more than an external expression; it is also an exchange of internal thoughts through formulated expression ranging from independent verbalization to non-verbalization. Sirbu (2015)posits that language is essentially a means of communication among the members of a society. Indeed, it is through language that people understand each other in a social interaction.

In a country like the Philippines, which aims to participate meaningfully in international affairs, learning the English language has a special place(Ong, 2017). Alongside Filipino, English is used as an official language mainly in publications, media and the academe. Knowing the language increases people's chances of getting a good job. However, according to Ella (2018), learning a language is a *complex task* as it involves several imperative processes. It requires not only learning grammar structures and acquiring vocabulary but also developing communication skills. Yet, Oberg (2013) strongly believes that oral fluency can be taught by means of providing communicative activities. Hence, the researcher in this study looked into classrooms and sought to find out the communicative competence level of the college students in a Local Community College.

Tuan (2017) cited Dong (2007) in a research conducted in Vietnam that their English needs are elementary and that is thought to be problematic, thus disadvantaging and demotivating those aiming to achieve higher English levels. The situation described that learners consider English irrelevant for their purposes. They did not understand English lectures. They did not communicate in English in daily or professional situations. Students failed to read their professional reading materials texts. Furthermore, they were not able to write in English. Therefore, although their motivation to learn English was high, they achieved very little. The situation in the research locale of this paper was quite similar. The college respondents were hesitant to communicate and write in English. When asked, they fall back to their first language. Survey questions requiring opinions were likewise answered in their first language.

According to Tuan (2017), with the cited situation in Vietnam; the National Foreign Language 2020 Project was implemented. The project expanded its influence and training programs to the majority of teachers of English at all levels. Several training workshops were similarly conducted by the different organizations and institutions to enhance the teachers' teaching skills. This paper sought to do the same. A communicative competence based module which covers areas of discourse, strategic, grammatical and linguistic competencies was designed and developed to train teachers and students.

According to McGuire & Larson-Hall (2017), the primary purpose of teaching discourse fillers to second language users is to facilitate fluency and proficiency of target language. Oral fluency is often a neglected component in a communicative classroom. Rossiter et al. (2009) believes that oral fluency is one of the most salient markers of proficiency in second language. Universities focus more on the development of students' writing and reading skills, whereas the speaking and listening skills are relatively neglected. Prime importance should be placed in using the target language. Hence, the teachers' intervention methods in emphasizing oral fluency were considered highly significant in developing students' speaking skills. Majority of the student-populace today fail to express their ideas, thoughts and emotions verbally to particular events or situations. Consequently, speaking skills and vocabulary learning have become worse and have greatly deteriorated. The researcher looked into this scenario through classroom observation, focus group discussion and interview.

2. THE THEORETICAL FRAMEWORK

Figure 1 below presents the conceptual framework of this study. Krashen's (1994) Second Language Acquisition theory and Wray's (2002) integrated model of Discourse Fillers were basis in creating the framework of this paper.

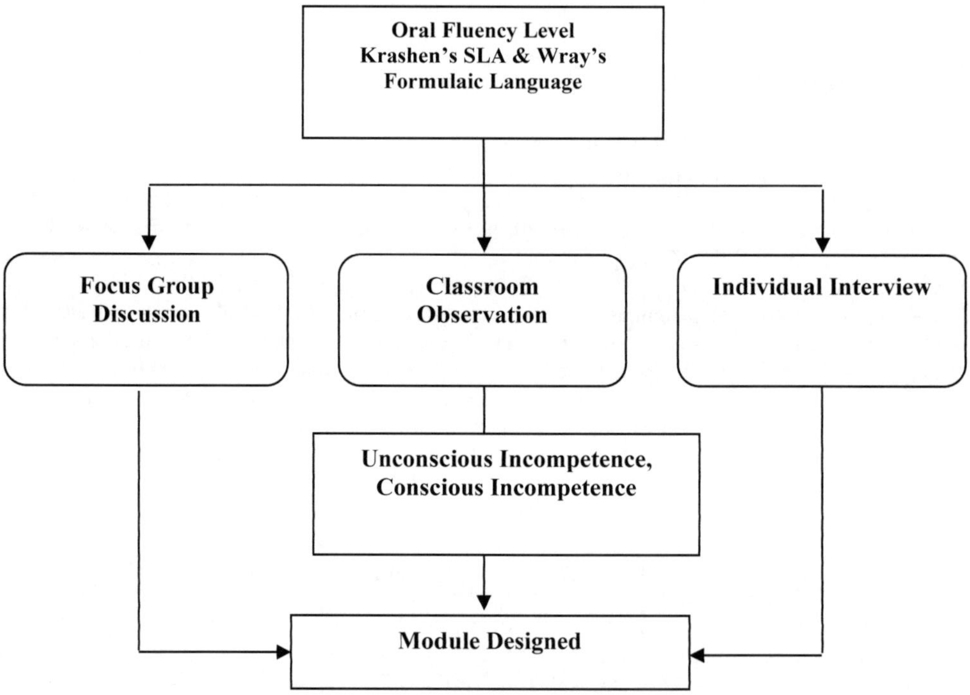

Figure 1. Framework of the Research

Generally, students are diverse in language competencies particularly in academic performance. Hence, finding out their individual communicative fluency level is deemed vital as this manifests spontaneous expression of thoughts and ideas. A strong command of English language will place them in good employment when they graduate. As a communicative classroom is an important component in developing the said speaking competency, this study was conducted. In particular, this study sought to identify the communicative competency level of the respondents, their engagement in communicative activities in the classrooms and the design of module to address the competency level. As shown in figure 1, the researcher did triangulation to identify the communicative competence level of the respondents then designed the module to address their unconscious incompetence.

3. METHODOLOGY

This study used both the qualitative and quantitative research methods to investigate the communicative competence level of the research participants. The qualitative research method was found suitable for the study as a means of exploring the individuals in their environment (Creswell, 2009). The research further targeted to identify and observe the College students in a Local Community College and the word fillers that helped them in the communication process. The students as the important core in the classroom became recipients of substantive information from the teachers. However, engaging these students in classroom discussion and activities is vital to foster learning. The Descriptive analysis was likewise used in this study for it consists of systemic observation and description of the characteristics and classroom events to discover the use of word fillers. This was supported by Gall et al. (2006) who stated that the goal of descriptive research is to describe a phenomenon and its characteristics. The paper was more concerned with 'what' rather than 'why' something has happened. Hence, observation and survey tools were used to gather data.

Furthermore, the study aimed to provide a qualitative description of the respondents' experiences in the classroom environment. Their non-engagement to communicative activities in their classes was basis for the development of the communicative competence based module.

4. RESULTS AND DISCUSSION

To address the first research problem, the researcher based the research questionnaire from Krueger (2002) and Coopman's(2016) guided structural questions. Hence, the stages of questioning in the identification of word fillers among the college students included: (1) Open-ended questions, (2) Questions to get more information, (3) Questions to clarify a point, and (4) Questions to compare perspectives. The activity was videotaped apart from the separate notes made by the researcher. The objective of the Focus Group Discussion was linguistic-based with emphasis on the word fillers generated from the students in their oral discourse. In introducing the focus group discussion, Hennink's (2015) recommendation was subsequently followed as: (1) Welcome, (2) Overview of the topic, (3) Ground rules, and (4) Question and Answer. These were the phases utilized in the Focus Group Discussion.

The evaluation and note taking of the commonly used word fillers was done during this process. However, other forms of research tools were used to determine and measure oral fluency based on the triangulation method. This was supported by (Golafshani, 2003) that a triangulation method can be used in a quantitative research to test the reliability and validity but can also illuminate some ways to test or maximize the validity and reliability of a qualitative study.

The tabular results that follow show the communicative competence level of the College respondents in a Local Community College during the Focus Group Discussion, individual interview and classroom observation. The rating scale for each instrument was given a corresponding weight value with one as the lowest and ten as the highest (according to the scale in Philippine educational system). Descriptive equivalents or verbal descriptions were also provided for the interpretation of result.

The scale that follows, adapted from Tuan (2017); was used to determine the respondents' communicative competence in discourse. This was used during the focus group discussion. Using the FGD prompts, the competency level of the one hundred fifty research subjects was derived. Table 1 shows that majority of the College students in the Local Community College belong to the modest user of English. These respondents uttered un-English sentences, faulty grammar and sentence construction. They likewise were observed to have difficulty in expressing themselves using the English language. Most of the time, they would fall back to their first language when asked to respond to the questions directed to them in a question and answer activity.

Table 1. Communicative Competence Level of the Respondents

Number of Respondents	Score Interval	Competence Level
2	8-10	Very Competent User of English
18	7-9	Competent User of English
25	4-6	Fair User of English
105	1-3	Modest User of English

To derive the score intervals, Rowland's (2014) communication matrix of the communicative competence level of language use was employed. It is subsequently represented.

Table 2. Communication Matrix employed for Individual Interview

Level of Competence	Description
Pre-intentional	Pre-intentional or reflexive behavior that expresses state of subject. State (eg., hungry, wet) is interpreted by observer.
Intentional Proactive Behavior	Behavior is intentional, but is not intentionally communicative. Behavior functions to affect observer's behavior, since observer infers intent.
Non-conventional Pre-symbolic Communication	Non-conventional gestures are used with intent of affecting observer's behavior.
Conventional Pre-symbolic Communication	Conventional gestures are used with intent of affecting observer's behavior.
Concrete Symbolic Communication	Non-conventional gestures are used with intent of affecting observer's behavior.
Abstract Symbolic Communication	Limited use of abstract (arbitrary) symbols to represent environmental entities. Symbols are used singly.
Formal Symbolic Communication	Rule-bound use of arbitrary symbol system. Ordered combinations of two or more symbols according to syntactic rules.

The study further used Hargie's (2011) multiple stages of competence to assess as the respondents they communicated in the classrooms. This is depicted in the tabular presentation reflected as table 3. The data shows that the population studied mostly belong to the unconscious incompetence stage.

Table 3. The Respondents' Stage of Competence

Stage of Competence	Description	Number of Respondents
Unconscious Incompetence	Being unaware of communicating in an incompetent manner	105
Conscious Incompetence	Learning more about communication and having a vocabulary to identify concepts, knowing what is to be done, realizing what is done is not as well as it could have	25
Conscious Competence	Knowing that he/she is communicating well in the moment, which will add to the bank of experiences to draw from in future interaction	18
Unconscious Competence	Communicating successfully without straining to be competent	2

Before building up a rich cognitive knowledge base of communication concepts and practicing and reflected on skills in a particular area, speakers may exhibit unconscious incompetence. One hundred five out of one hundred fifty College respondents belong to this category. They were unaware of communicating in an incompetent manner. Majority of them code mixed and code switched when they respond to their teachers. They manifested anxiety in using English, and were not able to complete one utterance using the target language; English. There were a few who were noted to stammer when they recite. Furthermore, twenty-five of the respondents exhibited conscious incompetence. They knew and were conscious of their utterances. They were likewise aware that they were not doing well as they could. This was triangulated when the individual interview was conducted among them. However, there were eighteen whose communicative competence fall under conscious competence. They were aware of communicating well during the classroom observation and individual interview and focus group discussion. The two respondents who reached the stage of unconscious competence, just spoke naturally; as if native English speakers; without straining to be competent. The ideas they shared were full of content.

According to Hargie (2011) reaching the stage of unconscious competence does not mean that the person will always stay there. Factors such as facing new communication encounters regularly will help one ladder to the next level. However, it will take a few instances of conscious incompetence before the advancement to later stages is achieved.

With these results, the researcher designed and developed a training module composed of five academic parcels. Each parcel contained topics and activities which address communicative competence difficulties. The modules confirmed that the areas of linguistic, sociolinguistic, discourse, strategic and grammatical competence were given sufficient activities for the students' training. Word fillers was one of the subtopics under discourse competence. This was one area found to help the respondents in their communicative acts. They similarly established this during the focus group discussion.

Furthermore, the modules were evaluated using the evaluation instrument developed by Ong (2017). Before the development of the academic parcels, they went through a thorough assessment by three experts in the field of language teaching. Additionally, appraisal was during the development phase. The research adviser carefully scrutinized the academic packets 'content.

5. CONCLUSIONS

Communicative competence among 150 respondents at a local community college is an element of diverse factors. Primarily, the unconscious incompetence and modest competence among these learners were influenced by a brief English language exposure. The implementation of English language use was not firmly employed. English language was thus literally seen as a foreign language, not a second language. Such approach among language classes hinders the development of language proficiency of the learners in the

English language. Specifically, the command of language use spelled out diverse communicative competence levels of the learners. Though majority of the respondents fall under one low category. Finally, grammatical and discourse competence among the learners was influenced by usage of word fillers. The more word fillers they used, the higher their communicative competence level reached.

6. RECOMMENDATIONS

These recommendations are suggested to enhance the communicative competence of students in the English Language. Colleges and Universities may strictly implement use of English as a second language. Policies which will motivate teachers to use communicative and collaborative activities may be considered among classes. An enhanced English language communication program maybe designed to sustain existing language programs. Teachers may likewise be sent for trainings quarterly.

REFERENCES

Ella, F., Hooper, J., & Mitchell, R. (2013). Rote or Rule? Exploring the Role of Formulaic Language in Classroom ForeignLanguage Learning. Language Learning. https://doi.org/10.1111/0023-8333.00045

Nekrasova, T. M. (2009). English L1 and L2 speakers' knowledge of lexical bundles. Language Learning. https://doi.org/10.1111/j.1467-9922.2009.00520.x

Nurmasitah, S. (2010). A Study of Classroom Interaction Characteristics in a Geography Class conducted in English. Semantic Scholar, 1–107.

Oberg, K. (2013). Formulaic Sequences for Improving Oral Fluency [University of Wisconsin-River Falls]. https://minds.wisconsin.edu/bitstream/handle/1793/65364/KristopherOberg.pdf?sequence=1&isAllowed=y

Ochs, E. (2002). Becoming a speaker of culture. In Language acquisition and language socialization: ecological perspectives.

Ong, C. G. (2009). A Training Scheme for College Communicative Teaching. JPAIR Multidisciplinary Research. https://doi.org/10.7719/jpair.v2i1.67

Ong, C. G. (2017). Digital Story Creation: Its Impact towards Academic Performance. International Association for Development of the Information Society.

Onoda, S. (2014). An exploration of effective teaching approaches for enhancing the oral fluency of EFL students. In Exploring EFL Fluency in Asia. https://doi.org/10.1057/9781137449405

Pangket, W. F. (2019). Oral Communication Proficiency in English of the Grade 5 Pupils. International Journal of Humanities and Social Sciences. https://doi.org/10.26803/ijhss.11.2.4

Park, C. (2003). Engaging students in the learning process: The learning journal. Journal of Geography in Higher Education. https://doi.org/10.1080/03098260305675

Parupalli, S. R. (2019). The importance of speaking skills in english classrooms. March.

Patton, M. Q. (2002). Qualitative research and evaluation methods. In Qualitative Inquiry. https://doi.org/10.2307/330063

Rowland, H. (2017). Qualitative and descriptive research: Data type versus data analysis. In Language Teaching Research. https://doi.org/10.1177/1362168815572747

Tuan, A., & Syder, F. H. (2017). Two puzzles for linguistic theory: Nativelike selection and nativelike fluency. In Language and Communication. https://doi.org/10.4324/9781315836027-12 A case study. Canadian Journal of Applied Linguistics.

Woods, P. (2006). Successful writing for qualitative researchers. In Successful Writing for Qualitative Researchers. https://doi.org/10.4324/9780203001721

Wray, A. (2000). Formulaic sequences in second language teaching: Principle and practice. Applied Linguistics. https://doi.org/10.1093/applin/21.4.463

Wray, A. (2002a). Formulaic Language and the Lexicon. In Formulaic Language and the Lexicon. https://doi.org/10.1017/cbo9780511519772

Wray, A. (2002b). Formulaic Language in Computer-supported Communication: Theory Meets Reality. Language Awareness. https://doi.org/10.1080/09658410208667050

Wray, A., & Perkins, M. R. (2000). The functions of formulaic language: An integrated model. Language and Communication. https://doi.org/10.1016/s0271-5309(99)00015-4

Xu, Y., & Filler, J. (2008). Facilitating Family Involvement and Support for Inclusive Education. School Community Journal.

Yang, Y. I. J. (2014). Is speaking fluency strand necessary for the college students to develop in the EFL class? Theory and Practice in Language Studies. https://doi.org/10.4304/tpls.4.2.225-231

Yasuda, S. (2010). Learning phrasal verbs through conceptual metaphors: A case of japanese EFL learners. TESOL Quarterly. https://doi.org/10.5054/tq.2010.219945

Yilmaz, K. (2013). Comparison of quantitative and qualitative research traditions: Epistemological, theoretical, and methodological differences. European Journal of Education. https://doi.org/10.1111/ejed.12014

Zabelkova, M. (2009). The Phrasal Expressions in Business Texts [Tomas Bata University in Zlin]. http://hdl.handle.net/10563/11013

Zaremba, A. J. (2014). Speaking Professionally. In Speaking Professionally. https://doi.org/10.4324/9781315700656

CHANGES IN THE TEACHING METHODOLOGY AND THE STUDY OF THE ADAPTATION OF STUDENTS TO THE NEW TECHNOLOGY: FROM THE CANVAS METHODOLOGY TO THE ACCENTUATION OF THE FLIPPED METHODOLOGY

María Teresa Bendito Cañizares[1] and Francisco Javier Sánchez Botas[2]
[1]*Profesora-UNED, Facultad de Derecho-UNED, C/ Obispo Trejo 2, 28040 Madrid, Spain*
[2]*Ingeniero informático-INTECCA-UNED, C/Juan del Rosal, 12. 28040 Madrid, Spain*

ABSTRACT

The purpose of this article is to highlight two educational notions implemented in CANVAS, an Enriched Electronic Book used in the study of the subject of "Civil Law III: Real Estate and Registration Rights" of the Law Degree, CANVAS, Enriched Electronic Book. (EEB). Firstly, CANVAS makes use of two learning and teaching methodologies: the "Neuronal System", understood as a set of several OARS strategically connected in a "neuronal-like" structure detailed by the teaching staff; and the "Scenario System", which portrays the topics on the subject in a solar system representation. The intended outcome of this first axis is to promote autonomous and multipurpose teaching, study, and self-evaluation. Secondly, these methodologies revalue others such as Flipped Class-Room (FCR) or "flipped class". This methodology, in the current teaching of law subjects, tends to be based mainly on providing videos to students for the preparation of their flipped activities.

CANVAS, through its FCR approach and the Neuronal and Scenario systems, provides a set of connected teaching materials that mitigate feelings such as limited time-wasting or unnecessary effort, found in both teaching staff and students. Indeed, teachers benefit since, by using CANVAS' materials, they only have to guide students in the flipped activities. Thus, they will not always be required to give master classes guided by a single basic book and in a unidirectional way. As far as the students, CANVAS promotes the "flipped class", and establishes and enhances "peer to peer" feedback as well as a "content creator-content receptor" relationship in the creation of electronic educational didactic materials.

KEYWORDS

CANVAS Methodology, Neuronal System, Scenario Methodology, "Flipped-Class-Room" Methodology, Tutorial Methodology, OARs

1. INTRODUCTION

It is essential at current the development of new learning and teaching methodologies in the subject the Professor is responsible for. Two reasons lead to this affirmation: First, the shortage of time granted institutionally for the full explanation of the Program; and second, distance's students' profile: an adult working student who frequently does not have much time to study and/or attend to Associated Centers where face-to-face teaching is used by professors called Tutors.

We start with CANVAS, a pilot developed at the Nacional of Distance Education University (UNED) in 2018 to explore and coordinate the production of an EEB in a law subject "Derechos reales e inmobiliario registral" (Real State and Registry law), which combines the educational resources needed, thus providing a comprehensive, versatile, customized, easy to update and all in one learning and teaching method; thus, the target group is the UNED-students undergoing the Degree of Law.

CANVAS, still under development in other UNED-platform title e-Online[1], has allowed the use of the Flipped methodology in classrooms of distance university's Associated Centers. Currently, the development of new technologies makes the appearance of a more flexible (or blended and/or hybrid methodology) teaching method no longer a desideratum. The unidirectional teaching approach used in Universities does not always seem to favor student learning. Thus, giving the chance to reverse the usual teaching roles is, at least, worth the shot. CANVAS, along with all of its telematic materials, makes it possible. This is a new experience that supposes a revolution to, at least, Distance University, where tutors do not share the notion that the alumni can collaborate at some point in the teaching of their subjects.

Thus, let's appreciate the insight into this new teaching method that CANVAS gives us with its original structure and methodologies. Let's comprehend the "Flipped" methodology and its byproducts, as well as its influence on CANVAS. And let's open our mind to a new project that posits its faith in the more efficient transmission of concepts and law institutions, which tend to be hard to comprehend.

2. FROM CANVAS METHODOLOY AND SCENARIO METHODOLOGY TO FLIPPED METHODOLOGY

Due to different OARS, the project (CANVAS) uses two methodologies: CANVAS (or neuronal) ethodology and Scenario methodology. These two, permit the experimentation with other methodologies, such as the Flipped Methodology.

Professors need a tool that combines the educational resources needed to provide a comprehensive, versatile, tailored, easy to update, and all-in-one learning and teaching method. The tool for this is CANVAS. Two basic notions inspired this pilot project. Firstly, the need for methodologies that permit a holistic overview of the subject in a short time. And secondly, the current development of EEBs. EEBs, contrarily to those resources that simply allow browsing, note-taking, and consultation, permits the integration of OAR disjointed multimedia resources (such as videos, radio conferences, links).

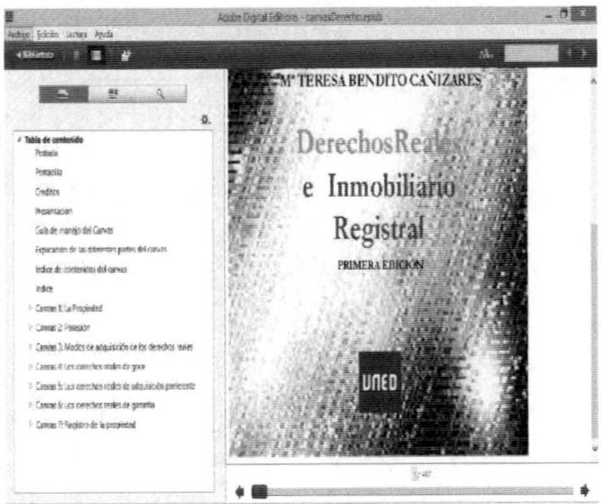

Figure 1. CANVAS e-pub frontpage

Two different, but complementary, methodologies are brought together under the heading "CANVAS": CANVAS (or Neuronal) methodology, and Scenario methodology. CANVAS' structure might seem obvious, but the use of both Neuronal and Scenario systems makes it a revolutionary and cohesive tool in the teaching of law subjects.

2.1 CANVAS Methodology: Neuronal System

CANVAS' structure, apparently common, is a didactic learning experience that tries to resemble the brain structure. By this, it is meant that the EEB provides students with "neuronal connections" all over the book itself and external "stimuli" (OARS such as websites, external documents, class video-room, questions…). As in the brain, students start from one "stimuli" or topic. To gain knowledge of this topic, students are able to choose which pathways to follow. For example, student A may go from the summary table to an article, which will lead to a certain case, and student B might start in another section of the topic and explore its own pathway. These two students can reach different degrees of knowledge of the subject of study according to their starting point (previous experiences, studies, cognitive skills ...), but both will reach the minimum amount of study required to achieve a fruitful evaluation of their knowledge.

The book is made up of seven "Canvasses" (chapters), each divided into four parts. The core of each Canvas is the lecture content itself, displayed in tables. Above this summary table, we find a "tab-like" structure with three tabs. The first one is the Frequently Asked Questions tab (FAQ). This section includes questions and answers concerning the matter developed in the specific Canvas. The FAQ section aims to answer common concerns and issues that students have repeatedly asked professors in forums. The second section is the "¿Qué hemos aprendido?"(What have we learned?) tab (QHA). This module evaluates the newly learned knowledge acquired using didactic, entertaining, and active exercises (v.gr., serious legal games). It's also used as a strategy to facilitate information retainment. Finally, the Various tab (VV) is used as an annex that includes all the articles, jurisprudence, and comments mentioned in the summary section. Likewise, it includes extra information that the student can consult at any time for further understanding.

2.2 Scenario Methodology

"Real State and Registry law" is a complex matter that needs to be taught in an especially short period of time (only one semester). In order to provide students with a comprehensive and graphical overview of the subject, the Scenario methodology was developed. This method represents the Real State and Registry law matters as a Solar system (Figure 2). In this universe, the Sun, or Property (the main right in rem), is surrounded by three planets, the other derived rights in rem. Likewise, the Possession is represented by the moon, which bathes the rest of the planets with its light. Finally, observing most of these elements, is the telescope, the land register, or property registration. This "Solar System of Real State and Registry law" displays a concise and interconnected representation of the subject.

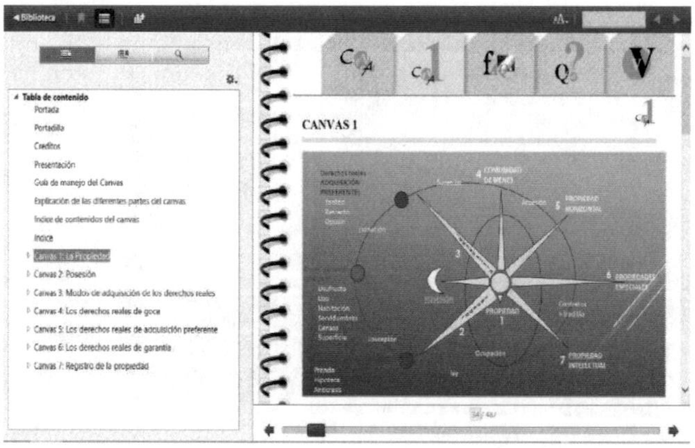

Figure 2. CANVAS chapter starting page showing methodological components

2.3 Benefits of the Methodologies

The merging of both methodologies provides considerable benefits to the learning and teaching experience. We can highlight the following:

1) Individualized or personalized study. The main benefit of CANVAS. Many pathways are built into the Neuronal system by the author. Using these, students decide their **own pathways** way to study, producing a more tailored and autonomous form of study.
2) All-in-one system. Students don't need to use other tools to prepare the subject, apart from the civil code. All information cited (mortgage act, horizontal property law, jurisprudences and other documents) are available at a click. Thus, students save time and money. Importantly, teachers are not perceived as owners of the subject, but facilitators or mediators who make knowledge acquisition plausible for students.

3) Update of the subject. EEBs allow to keep the knowledge fresh and up to date through the update of the book from time to time.
4) Personalized assessment. Like students, professors are able evaluate students in a more personalize way. Instead of using a rigid form of evaluation, the table format allows students to answer questions in exams from different perspectives. The teacher then can understand where these interpretations are coming from.
5) Elaboration of material. Provides the necessary materials to be used by both the student and the teacher or tutor responsible for the subject. This set of materials will be the key to promoting the use of the Flipped methodology.

2.4 Conclusions

An in-depth analysis of our personal experience during the production process of CANVAS leads us to several conclusions. In February 2019, a final report, collecting a list of conclusions, was presented in the form of 5 Guidelines and condense these needs:

- The content must be analysed by a multidisciplinary commission to check the feasibility of the project.
- This multidisciplinary team should be an integrated and interconnected group of heterogeneous professionals: computer developers, designers, accessibility advisors, publishers, etc. These should work together when necessary, and not in a phase-like manner (as usual).
- In our case, ADE is not a suitable or convenient software for producing epubs3. Therefore, institutions should test or research new operative systems to produce this type of didactic materials more efficiently. Currently, UNED has adapted CANVAS into a new platform named e-Online.
- Research over the accessibility of these materials for people with disabilities should be performed.
- There is a need for the development of guidelines and behaviour patterns.
- The urge of determining a balance of cost-benefits of the project and the prices of the EEBs.
- The update schedule is still pending. The tool for professors to independently (without relying on the technical team) update the EEB has not been developed yet.

3. FLIPPED METHODOLOGY ALONGSIDE CANVAS: IT IS THE MOMENT

To allow the constant update of the ebook and the recurring income of material-production, a Research Project "Proyecto de Investigación Docente" (PID) called "*Un discente a otro discente para la transmisión del conocimiento del Derecho o metodología "Flipped" (Flipped Teaching Metodology-FTM)*" has been initiated.

The purpose of the project is the development of telematic materials (audiovisual and / or auditory) for the course, found in CANVAS. In general, online teaching denotes a change from a teacher-centered approach to a student-centered approach. To do so, the project proposes the "Flipped Teaching Methodology" (hereinafter, Flipped learning or FTM) which includes the "Flipping the Class-Room" (FCR) method.

Although the Flipped methodology will be explained more thoroughly in the following chapter, a general view is described below.

1- All the information to be taught is found in CANVAS.
2- As some parts of the subject are difficult, the teacher proposes the "Flipped Teaching".
3- The teacher asks a student to explain to the rest of their classmates, in their own words, a difficult topic. In the distance learning field, the formula must be accompanied by telematic means of communication, such as mini-videos or podcasts.
4- The teacher provides that student with the instructional material necessary. This includes localization of the difficult matter in the CANVAS, determination of articles, jurisprudence, and other resources that the student needs to use in their teaching day. All this information is found on CANVAS. The availability of materials permits agility in adopting the FCR methodology. Thus, professors, who

usually run short on time, do not have to spend time collecting the materials to guide the student, since that material is already found inside CANVAS.

5- The day in which the student has to present the topic, the student undertakes over the role of teacher, and transmits the knowledge by using the telematic means at their disposal (mainly videos and radio broadcasts).

6- The experience is evaluated by collaborators in the Flipped Project, by the author of CANVAS and by the rest of students.

7- If the teaching experience provided by the student is suitable, their audiovisual material would be cited and included in CANVAS. It's important to note that this is a voluntary action and the pupil can decide whether or not the team can use their material in CANVAS.

This provokes that, now, students are teaching students. Besides, the teachers, move away from their usual role and give the opportunity to their students to do so. Thus, each part of the teaching process (educators and students) adopt atypical roles. By "flipping", a suitable learning of the subject is achieved, under the support of the teacher and the design of new didactic materials. This method is about learning from the other side of the "teaching omelet", by putting students in the spotlight and giving them the active role in the teaching process. Indeed, the utility has already been investigated. Several meta-analyses reveal that students in flipped classrooms achieve higher learning outcomes compared to non-flipped classrooms, or when quizzes were added in the flipped classrooms (Van Alten, D., Phielix, C., Janssen, J.& Kester, L., 2019). Nevertheless, the "Flipped" strategy seems to find its limitations over the professors themselves, who see their original methodology break down. Likewise, students suffer from this role-change, which again, poses a limitation to the implementation of FCR.

3.1 Objectives of Flipped Classroom

The general objective of the PID is the approach of knowledge of the subject "Real estate and Registry Law" that is studied in 3rd of the Degree in Law to the students through other students who, playing the role of educators, take the load of the understanding of the concepts, cases and particular problems of each of the lessons that are combined in the program of the subject to other students, to a telematic format (video or audio) in which they are the protagonists.

Including these student-produced didactic materials into CANVAS permits overcoming three main issues: 1) Overcoming the unidirectional, conventional manner of teaching; 2) Reduce teachers' overload, allowing them to save time in the orientation phase of the FCR; and 3) Progress through the program more quickly. The digital revolution here mentioned can offer law educators the opportunity to return to the Langdellian Model and the implementation of the Socratic Method (Schaffin, K.T.).

Professors' concerns about negative evaluations from alumni, which ultimately can affect professors' job promotion, will not be due to their performance as "flipping teachers" per se, but rather based on their inability to evoke feelings of satisfaction towards the new methodology. Academic rewards (extra points for example) are a way to do so.

The set of mini-videos and mini-audios (MVM and MAM, respectively), will serve for the learning of a subject loaded with technicalities that is also under constant review by our legislator. Its use in the virtual course on the platform and outside of it in the Associated Centers by the Tutors is beyond doubt because they will have material that will help them transmit learning with the FTM. Thus, students can make possible the conversion of unidirectional education (from the tutor to the student), in two-way (from the student to the educator and vice versa).

The production of videos and or audios on definitions, basic concepts to remember or review, norm extracts or capital rules in the learning unit, or theories and practical cases, pursues the following objectives:

Facing the student:

1) Understanding those parts of the program that are more difficult due to their technicality or because of their not obvious relationship with other parts of the program or other civil law subjects.

2) The arrival of those students with some degree of visual or hearing disability. For example, MVMs can be done with subtitles.

On the teacher's side, the student's feedback will enable:

1) The discovery of new formulas, methods, etc. to explain the subject proposed by the student-teacher
2) The deepening of those parts of the program that always remained residual due to lack of time
The ideal structuring of scientific knowledge.

3.2 Why have we chosen Mini-Videos Modulares (MVM and MAM)? Because of Analyse of Backgroud and State of the Art

The 10-minute modular videos and audios designed by the teachers for the students are the basis of the Flipped Material used in many educational systems (Schaffin, K.T.) and this is a model of teaching and learning so common practical in EEUU and in particular, in Law field (Upchurch, A. 2013).

"Flipped" Lectures do not have to follow a determined structure, it is not only about the videos. The use of MVMs has been discussed and developed by our teacher-groups, who thought about what format was the appropriate to implement the "Flipped" paradigm. The use of videos involves two things: 1) MVMs imply the implementation of the "Flipped" methodology; 2) MVMs can be, later on, used and incorporated as revised material in both CANVAS and other "Flipped" classrooms. Nevertheless, it is essential that the person in charge of the class who must think about its structure and where to apply it. This person must devise a plan (which includes the production time, technologies to use, collaborators, or partners…). During this preparation period, there should be an emphasis on the acknowledgment that the "Flipped" program requires the management of different technological tools. In CANVAS, for example, we have tried to gather and display all the tools required. In our PID, based on the current state of the scientific-technical knowledge of the Distance University, we have concluded that the production of modular videos is easier because even the Teachers of the Computer Science school of the Distance University are trying to extend the production of mini-videos to other Teachers through MOOCs (Letón, E. 2017); The director of this PIE is in fact as a student of one of them called Modular teaching mini-videos to design a MOOC (MDM); but although these videos offer in themselves an innovation in the learning of scientific knowledge, the particularity that they are carried out by the students themselves for other students, is a plus in this halo of teaching innovation.

Starting by guiding students in the materials to use and by giving them the responsibility and the challenge of materializing their own work in videos that their classmates will use is a good manner to begin promoting a methodological renewal of tutorials at the Distance University (Bendito, M.T. 2019) as well as the interest of students. Sometimes, this experience has already been tested previously when students were proposed to participate in a contest on Radio, for instance, "Concurso-Juegos Jurídicos-UNED" (Bendito, M.T. 2018).

3.3 Where to apply Flipped Methodology?

The starting hypothesis to achieve the proposed objectives could be described as follows: we would place the FTM in the classrooms of the Associated Centers, in which the Prof. Tutor has to face in a very short time (more in this subject than in the study plans goes from being annual to quarterly), to a very extensive program and perhaps the most technical and difficult of those that currently make up civil law. The usefulness of the material (MVM and MAM), in which students have explained the concepts, and cases that are more difficult to understand, is important for other students who will go to class with said knowledge and in the classroom they will go almost directly to the useful discussion of themselves and their relationship with others. The effort of occupying the role of the preparation of the classes carried out by the students is less with the material that wants to be done in this PID.

3.4 Benefits of the Flipped Methodology for Students and Teachers

The benefits that have been highlighted would be more evident if the dissemination and explanation of the prepared material were done from the University itself, with one of these three actions:

1) the preparation of a prize for the participation of the students who have intervened;

2) an academic compensation that could be related to, for example, the exemption from having to take an exam from that part of the subject in which you helped to prepare the MDM or MAM.

3) in the participation of the International Conference to which this PIE will be presented as a result.

Project Benefits: The change of roles of the students and teachers will produce:

a. These benefits for the Teacher:

1) The feedback of the students regarding the specific understanding of the contents of the program, so that the Teacher may correct (increase or decrease the explanations) the study materials.

2) The student's feedback regarding the understanding that the matter of real and real estate registration rights is difficult and difficult to fit into a semester. It would create trust in the Faculty.

3) Increase of the explanations in the classroom of the subject with other materials since it is assumed that the basics will be treated in the classrooms with the MVM and MAM.

b. These benefits for the student:

1) The face-to-face class would become a true forum for discussion and support for students who could attend, and with the increase in explanations, the best interests of some students would be satisfied.

2) To alleviate the lack of content and explanations that logically suffer from the recommended manual because it has to be coupled to new study plans in which the Civil Law III subject is restricted to a semester.

3) The MVM and the MAM would serve as telematic material for those students who could not attend the classrooms now converted into face-to-face forums.

4) If the associated center could record said sharing of the matter in the classrooms, in turn, other telematic material would be generated for everyone, for the students attending the forum, and for those who cannot attend.

This last point 3) is directly related to the PIE results since the MVM and / or MAM would be presented as Univesity material in any of the national or international conferences deemed pertinent. Specifically, through EADTU, this material would be presented to the Universities that are part of the EMPOWER project. Thus, a greater diffusion would be achieved than, on the other hand, it would be requested, as is obvious, from the University itself.

4. PILOT DEVELOPMENT AND TECHNICALITIES

The fundamental technical tasks that have been carried out during this second stage of methodological changes are:

Flipped Classes:

1. The coordination and support of the tasks for the application of the Flipped-Classroom methodology (Bergman, Y. & Sam, A. 2014), in the Civil Law III course of the Law Degree at Distance University.

Canvas Scenary:

2. The preparation of a Test to collect information about the Acceptance of Technology from users, used in the new bibliographic materials in each of the different groups involved (students and tutors).

4.1 TAM-UTAUT

Applying in a combined way the Technology Acceptance Model (TAM Technology Acceptance Model) (Covadonga, et al. 2017) and the Unified Theory of Acceptance and Use of Technology (UTAUT Unified Theory of Acceptance and Use of Technology) (Martín, A. V., García del Dujo, Á., & Muñoz, J. M., 2014) a test must be obtained with all its questions classified within the following constructs:

1) Individual characteristics (CI0)

Specified as gender, age, experience (training and professional orientation) and voluntary use.

2) Expectation of performance (ED1) or results (ER1)

The degree to which an individual believes that the use of the system will help them realize a performance benefit.

2.1. Perceived utility (PU)

The degree to which an individual believes that using a system will help improve performance.

2.2. Extrinsic motivation

Source of behavior caused by each person's need for external rewards.

3) Expectation of effort (EE2)

The degree of ease of use associated with the system

3.1. PEoU Ease of Use Perception

Degree of belief of a person in the level of effort required to use a system.

3.2. Apprehension

Anxiety towards the use of a new medium, system or technology. to the source of behavior.

4) Social Influence (IS3)

The degree to which an individual perceives that others will value the use of the system.

4.1. Social pressure

Source of behavior or individual motivation based on the belief that with it we will obtain a superior social status or that it improves our prestige.

5) Facilitating Conditions (CF4)

The degree to which an individual considers that the organizational and technical structure exists to help him adopt the system.

A test of between 10 and 20 questions will be generated where users will be able to express their agreement and disagreement in a range and a 5-point Likert scale (HYOSUN STELLA KWON, & CHIDAMBARAM, L. 2000): from 1 (Very unfavorable) to 5 (Very favorable).

4.2 Surveys

Survey questions have been grouped under two headings 'Content' and 'Format'. They were published in the Distance University learning environment (aLF) at a date close to the mandatory face-to-face tests of the subject and remained open throughout the course.

2.2.1. Tutors:

A 28-question test was created.

2.2.2. Students:

14 questions were written for the test.

4.3 Results

4.3.1 Tutors

During the 2019/20 academic year none of the tutors of the partner centers of all Spain has responded to the survey. So, these results should wait for future calls.

4.3.2 Students

During the 2019/20 academic year, 101 of the 1168 students from partner centers across Spain responded to the survey. So, these results, over 8% of participation, should be presented for this call as a reliable statistical.

Among students, in general, the acceptance of technology has been quite balanced and distributed, around 50% in all fields and constructs, divided between acceptors and detractors, considering that more than 70% of these students had not had previous performance experience with this type of enriched material.

Most of the difficulties raised were about the technical format used to generate the material (ePub) and the tool used to deploy the publication (Adobe Digital Editions) that conditioned the results negatively.

Only one exception: the use of these new information technologies in teaching materials had increased participation in the academic forums of the subject.

The content and development effort of the new book has been positively valued at 61% of respondents, especially in the case of audiovisual's materials, which are the most valued.

4.4 TAM Conclusions

The realization and implementation of an initiative like this, has required, first of the help of an educational institution of recognized international solvency such as Distance University, despite the absence of funding; second of the participation of a multidisciplinary team that has worked altruistically and finally of the clear determination that improving the materials, methodology and motivation of students should result in better academic results in a shorter time.

But when this effort is not rewarded with a majority acceptance by the recipients, due to the format and technical execution, it must also be considered. For this reason and again with the help of the institution, the author has made the decision to migrate this ePub content the next course, abandoning this format in complex and enriched electronic materials like this and deploying it on MOOC-based learning platforms such as OpenEdX[1].

3. The preparation and publication of the "Informed Consents" (Buthta, 2004) to allow the computer processing of the information collected in these personalized tests for each group involved and further Machine Learning treatment.

It has been divided into a first information part, two specific parts about the automated processing to be carried out with the data, as well as a final part focused on collecting, in a justified and in accordance with Spanish/European legislation, the user's consent.

Despite the Distance University' extensive research experience in automated processing of content and materials outside the institution, surprisingly, there was no legally grounded initiative for these internal information processing, to the point that many of them were either abandoned or difficult to publish for this reason.

This initiative thus aroused the interest of the departments involved as it can be considered the first effort to provide justification within the legal framework of Spanish and European Data Protection for the automated processing of the information of the content collected in the learning environment of the institution (aLF).

5. FINAL CONCLUSIONS

The final objective of knowledge transmission in the world of Law Science, is not to obstruct any path, that is, to be open to any form or methodology of teaching and learning. Nowadays, with the use of new technologies, CANVAS has been able to collect telematic materials and design teaching pathways for teachers that are far from old-fashioned, as it tends to happen in basic paper-based books methodologies, where knowledge is corseted in epigraphs. Furthermore, the methodology presented not in a "linear" or "unidirectional" manner, since CANVAS breaks down the unilateral teaching direction (teacher-student).

CANVAS, an enriched electronic book that combines all kinds of telematic materials along with its Neuronal and Scenario systems, breaks with the tightness and unidirectionality of the conventional teaching paradigm. Thus, in this new freedom of the student's handling of materials, the "inverted class" surges, allowing teachers to plan more effectively classes, and at the same time, improving CANVAS, with the incorporation of the "*mini-videos*" produced by students.

Using the didactic materials of "Flipped", CANVAS will get this feedback, producing the rise of new learning pathways that are different from those already constructed by the author. Thus, the author benefits, simultaneously, from an enhancement of the ebook. Accordingly, this blend will also make it easier for the teacher to rely part of their work on their students, which in turn, will produce among students a higher degree of commitment and will to study the subject. Similarly, reinforcing CANVAS with the materials produced by the flipped class, such as mini-videos on some legal concept or practical cases, challenges the main disadvantage pointed out by the authors of the FCR methodology, which is that only students who perform flipped will benefit from the experience, thus leaving the rest of students in the same unidirectional learning experience as before.

Obviously, as alumni's participation in LEE increases, the authors' work will be to achieve harmony in three directions. The first one involves working with the teachers in their involvement in flipped, acknowledging the increase in their teaching workload and the possibility of being poorly evaluated by

[1] https://eonline.uned.es/courses

students. Making this counseling work less complex and arduous for them, both in and outside the class, is challenging and depends on the content found in the LEE. The second axis revolves around the materials per se. The newly produced contents in the LEE cannot become a simple collection of materials and increase without a sense of time and space. Finally, authors should ensure that all "flipped-students" have compensations in their final grade, in order to avoid their demotivation and criticism towards the teacher who proposes the Flipped methodology. All in all, we conclude that a flipping the classroom approach is a promising pedagogical approach when appropriately designed by LEE, as in CANVAS.

REFERENCES

Arza, G. (2012). Validación de la Teoría Unificada de Aceptación y Uso de la Tecnología UTAUT en castellano en el ámbito de las consultas externas de la Red de Salud Mental de Bizkaia.

Bendito, M. T. (2012). "Juegos jurídicos" como modalidad de gestión del talento en el estudio, medida paliativa que fideliza al estudiante" sin aula" y al profesor de Metodología a Distancia, y proyecto que escapa de las manos del profesor co-autorizando a otros profesionales. In *Innovación docente universitaria en entornos de aprendizaje enriquecidos: I Jornadas Internacionales de Innovación Docente Universitaria en Entornos de Aprendizaje Enriquecidos: libro de actas (pp. 8-10).* UNED, Universidad Nacional de Educación a Distancia.

Bendito, M.T. (2012) "Juegos jurídicos" como modalidad de gestión del talento en el estudio, medida paliativa que fideliza al estudiante "sin aula" y al profesor de Metodología a Distancia, y proyecto que escapa de las manos del profesor co-autorizando a otros profesionales" (2012), Libro de actas de las I Jornadas Internacionales de Innovación Docente Universitaria en Entornos de Aprendizaje Enriquecidos, UNED, Madrid, 19-21 de septiembre 2012, Pp. 8-10, ISBN: 84-695-8245-3.

Bendito, M.T. (2016), *Gamification in the traditional education environment*, <http://www.slideshare.net/EADTU/gamification-in-the-traditional-education-environment>

Bendito, M.T., (2018), *Juegos Jurídicos 2017: la hipoteca*, podcast, Radio UNED, Madrid, <https://canal.uned.es/video/5a6faddfb1111f50318b456a>

Bendito, M.T., 2019, *CANVAS: ¿Renovación metodológica de las tutorías?*, streaming video, Canal UNED, Serie Serie: CANVAS: La nueva metodología de aprendizaje de los derechos reales y el sistema registral español, Madrid. <https://canal.uned.es/video/5d394d0fa3eeb0914e8b458b>

Bendito, M.T., García Serrano & Botas, F.J.S. (2019) "Connecting educational resources to "all in one" distance learning and teaching: the CANVAS pilot project" , into *Blended and online education within European university networks*, Overview of papers on Higher Education for the Future as presented during the Online, Open and Flexible Higher Education Conference (OOFHEC), Madrid, October 2019, Editors George Ubachs, Pp. 101-111. https://pure.coventry.ac.uk/ws/portalfiles/portal/27637722/Proceedings_OOFHEC2019.pdf#page=113

Bergmann, J. & Sams A., Flip Your Classroom: Reaching Every Student in Every Class Every Day, 1st Edición., Retrieved from http://legaledweb.com/flipping-a-law-school-course/

Bidarra, J. (Universidade Aberta) Y Rusman, H. (Open Universiteit), *A pedagogical model for science education through blended learning* http://www.slideshare.net/EADTU/a-pedagogical-model-for-science-education-through-blended-learning-63327944

Botas, F. J. S., & Yuste, Á. R. (2019). Analyzing Academic Forums from Different Perspectives. Selección de atributos (Foros aLF). The Online, Open and Flexible Higher Education Conference, "Blended and online education within European university networks", 16. EADTU.

Buthta, Z., *Más allá del consentimiento informado*, Boletín de la Organización Mundial de la Salud, Retrieved from https://www.who.int/bulletin/volumes/82/10/bhutta1004abstract/es/

Engerhard, N. (FernUniversität in Hagen) *Training and qualification* (http://empower.eadtu.eu/fields-of-expertise/ict-media-and-educational-support-services/introduction

Igniting Law Teaching Conference 2014, Flipping a Law School Course, Retrieved from http://legaledweb.com/flipping-a-law-school-course/

Kalles, D. (OHU) *Onlabs: 3d game for distance laboratory* (http://empower.eadtu.eu/fields-of-expertise/ict-media-and-educational-support-services/introduction

Letón, E., 2017, *Características de un MDM*, Serie Mini-videos docentes medulares, (2017), Canal UNED, <https://canal.uned.es/video/5a6f883cb1111f4c618b46f9>

Martín, A. V., García del Dujo, Á., & Muñoz, J. M., 2014. Factores determinantes de adopción de blended learning en educación superior. Adaptación del modelo UTAUT*. *Educación XX1*, 17(2). https://doi.org/10.5944/educxx1.17.2.11489

Rodrigo, C., García-Serrano, A. & Sánchez-Elvira, Á. (2017). Narrative design combined with a TAM survey to achieve a multisensorial museum user-experience for people with disabilities. The Online, Open and Flexible Higher Education Conference, "Accelerating and Strengthening Innovation", 248. EADTU.

Schaffin, K.T., ( ). Learning Outcomes in a Flipped Classroom: A Comparison of Civil Procedure II Test Scores Between Students in a Traditional Class and a Flipped Class, *The University of Memphis Law Review*, Vol. 46, https://www.memphis.edu/law/documents/schaffzin46.pdf

Upchurch, A. (2013), Flipping the Law School Classroom: Optimizing the law School Classroom, *Conference "Hybrid Law teaching"* held at Washburn University of Law (Topica-Kansas) in June 7-9 2013.

Van Alten, D. , Phielix, C., Janssen, J., Kester, L., (2019), Effects of flipping the classroom on learning outcomes and satisfaction: A meta-analysis, *Educational Research Review* https://reader.elsevier.com/reader/sd/pii/S1747938X18305694?token=00BE87589FF0834533AA7293F6C6AAAE9BF99665A5BE6C5BF4D721997A297CA8660F55D75D83B4EE896CBF8AA72D6804

Wolff, L-C. & Chan, J., (2016), Flipped Classrooms for Legal Education, *Springfinger Briefs in Law*, https://www.springer.com/gp/book/9789811004780#reviews

Yosun Stella Kwon, et al., 2000. A test of the technology acceptance model: The case of cellular telephone adoption. *Proceedings of the 33rd Annual Hawaii International Conference on System Sciences*, 7 pp. vol. 1. https://doi.org/10.1109/HICSS.2000.926607

AN INVESTIGATION OF TEACHER PERSPECTIVES ON INTEGRATING CHINESE CULTURE INTO CHINESE-AS-A-FOREIGN-LANGUAGE CURRICULUM

Xuan Song[1] and Lih-Ching Chen Wang[2]

[1]*Doctoral Student, Urban Education Ph.D. Program with a Specialization in "Teaching Chinese as a Foreign Language"*
College of Education and Human Services, Cleveland State University
2121 Euclid Ave., JH215, Cleveland, OH 44115-2214, U.S.A.
[2]*Ph.D, Professor, Educational Technology in the Department of Curriculum and Foundations*
Director/Founder, Chinese Teacher Licensure M.A. Program
Coordinator/Founder, Urban Education Ph.D. Program with a Specialization in "Teaching Chinese as a Foreign Language"
College of Education and Human Services, Cleveland State University
2121 Euclid Ave., JH386, Cleveland, OH 44115-2214, U.S.A.

ABSTRACT

During recent decades, Chinese as a Foreign Language (CFL) education has been booming worldwide, but not without difficulties. One criticism is that current CFL curricula largely ignore the role of foreign languages in cross-cultural communication and understanding. Current models that heavily emphasize grammar and conversation typically lack support for CFL teachers to incorporate culture into their classes, and as a result, many Chinese teachers are either reluctant to teach culture or don't know how to integrate culture in their CFL classes (Wang, 2007; Hu, 2010; Fung & Wang, 2012; Cheng, 2015; Attaran & Hu, 2015; Wei, 2017). Meanwhile, using culture to facilitate foreign language education has been widely utilized in teaching English as a foreign language (Kramsch, 1993; Byram & Morgan, 1994). This study proposes to gain a better understanding of the relationship of currently working Chinese-as-a-foreign-language teachers to the incorporation of Chinese cultural elements into their teaching, and to explore ways in which they might be encouraged to include more emphasis on Chinese culture as part of their language instruction pedagogy. This study will use a qualitative approach grounded in Interpretive Phenomenological Analysis (IPA), employing interviews and documentary analysis. The subjects of the study will be native Chinese-speaking teachers currently teaching Chinese to students in American schools.

KEYWORDS

Mandarin Chinese, Foreign Language Instruction, Chinese as a Foreign Language, CFL, Chinese Culture

1. INTRODUCTION

During the past three decades or so, Chinese as a Foreign Language (CFL) education has been booming worldwide. However, traditional CFL curriculum places a heavy emphasis on grammar and conversation, while content addressing Chinese culture is often not emphasized as part of CFL instruction. As a result, many CFL teachers are either reluctant to teach culture or don't know how to integrate culture into their CFL classes (Wang, 2007; Hu, 2010; Fung & Wang, 2012; Cheng, 2015; Attaran & Hu, 2015; Wei, 2017). There is a need to better understand the potential role of Chinese cultural content as a component of CFL education, as well as the needs involved in moving forward were it to be implemented in practice.

2. CONTEXT

Most existing CFL materials and curricula continue to emphasize grammar and conversation while largely excluding cultural content that might be helpful in developing cross-cultural understanding. Cheng and Li (2019) pointed out two reasons for this dilemma: 1) the uncertain goal of culture in CFL education; and 2) the lack of theoretical principles and pedagogical guidance for teaching culture in CFL curriculum. Meanwhile, using culture to facilitate foreign language education has been widely utilized in teaching English as a foreign language (Kramsch, 1993; Byram & Morgan, 1994).

There are many reasons to consider incorporation of culture into foreign language instruction. Stainer (1971) found that studying another culture gives students a reason to study its language as well bringing meaningfulness to the study of a second language. Gardner and Lambert (1972) stated that the study of culture not only increases learners' curiosity and interest in target countries but also boosts their motivation. A number of theories in the foreign or second language area also support incorporating culture into foreign language education, including Schumann's acculturation model (1978), Krashen's comprehensible input theory in second language acquisition (1985), Swain's output hypothesis (1993) and Long's interaction hypothesis (1981).

The pedagogical concept of conceptualization has practical significance for foreign language teachers seeking to put theory into practice. A country's culture provides the context within which a language evolves and functions. Shulman (1986), the developer of Pedagogical Content Knowledge (PCK), stated that one could hardly hope to achieve meaningful learning without connecting knowledge to familiar context. Mackay and Tymon (2013) considered contextualization as "an active and deliberate process of exploration and discovery, involving a periodic stepping back to consider meaning and the connection between experience and learning" (p. 649). Another approach to the integration of culture and language instruction in one curriculum is the model of Systemic Functional Linguistics (SFL) created by Liddicoat, Papademetre, Scarino, and Kohler (2003). SFL is an approach that guides teachers to develop intercultural language learning in a systematic manner through five phrases, including: activating construction, making connections, interacting learning, developing intercultural sensitivity, and reflecting learning. SFL offers a linguistic foundation for second language acquisition and provides an instrument for teachers to place language education in a cultural context (Hyland, 2015). Both PCK and SFL provide practical guidance on integrating culture into CFL, though debates remain on which kinds of cultural materials are eligible and precisely how they should be integrated (Hadley & Terry, 2001).

We propose to study the experience of CFL teachers currently working in the United States with respect to questions of culture, curriculum, and CFL pedagogy. Our intent is to explore the problems and possibilities from Chinese teachers' perspectives including their current practices and needs. The goal is to understand, describe, and interpret their real- world experiences regarding CFL instruction and a potential cultural component. We hope to understand two things: the experiences of CFL teachers in using culture as a part of their CFL classes, and their perceived needs in the area of developing curriculum and materials that integrate culture with language instruction. In other words, we hope to explore Chinese teachers' relationship to incorporating culture into their CFL classes, and also to investigate possible theories and approaches that Chinese teachers might adopt in integrating culture into CFL education.

Given the focus on understanding CFL teachers' experiences and needs, a qualitative approach was chosen for this study, and the research is being conducted under the paradigm of social constructivism in qualitative research. Denzin and Lincoln (2011) contended that qualitative researchers "study things in their natural settings, attempting to make sense of or interpret a phenomenon in terms of the meanings people bring to them" (p. 3). Social constructivism theory argues that knowledge is a product of humans and it is socially and culturally constructed (Creswell, 2013). Green and Piel (2010) expressed that knowledge is built through the negotiation of meaningful dialogue with the target language in its socio-cultural contexts. Social constructivism supports constructing knowledge in a cultural perspective, and it is important in curriculum development, because culture provides a context for language acquisition including listening, speaking, reading, and writing as a total entity. Integrating culture into the foreign language learning process helps students increase their language proficiency (Schaub, 2012). It is important to understand whether the real-world experience of CFL teachers supports this concept, and if so how they might be assisted in further developing materials and curriculum to further advance its use.

As this research aims to seek the essence of the experiences of Chinese teachers with respect to developing a culture-language integrated CFL curriculum, interpretative phenomenological analysis (IPA) has been chosen as an appropriate qualitative research design to guide data collection and analysis. Brocki and Wearden (2006) argued that IPA is an ideographic approach to qualitative research which aims to offer insights into how a given person, in a given context, makes sense of a given phenomenon.

This study will be conducted in a state-supported university located in a large metropolitan area in the Midwestern United States. Participants will be Chinese teachers who are currently teaching in K-12 schools, and are recruited through a local professional affiliation with the World Language Association of Chinese. A purposeful sampling method (Patton, 1999) will be used to sift the most qualified participants. Data will be collected via individual interviews with the CFL teachers. All interviews will be conducted using a standard interview protocol, and due to the COVID-19 pandemic they will be conducted online. Data will be analyzed, transcribed and coded in three categories: descriptive, summative, and holistic codes, then these codes will be evolved into categories, concepts, themes, and patterns. Once the coding is complete, member checking will be employed to ensure fidelity of the results.

3. CONCLUSION

In a complex world of global interaction, understanding multiple cultures can be as important as understanding multiple languages. In many ways, the prevailing culture of teaching Chinese as a Foreign Language has failed to acknowledge this fact, and has retained a tendency to teach the Chinese language as separate from Chinese culture. There is considerable support in the literature for the idea that incorporating culture into foreign language instruction has positive effects not only in promoting cross-cultural understanding but also in improving language performance on the part of students. This study proposes to gain a better understanding of the relationship of currently working Chinese-as-a-foreign-language teachers to the incorporation of Chinese cultural elements into their teaching, and to explore ways in which they might be encouraged to include more emphasis on Chinese culture as part of their language instruction pedagogy.

REFERENCES

Attaran, M., & Hu, Y. (2015). Teacher education curriculum for teaching Chinese as a foreign language. *The Malaysian Online Journal of Educational Science, 3*(1), 34-43.

Brocki, J. M., & Wearden, A. J. (2006). A critical evaluation of the use of interpretative phenomenological analysis (IPA) in health Psychology. *Psychology & Health, 21*(1), 87–108.

Byram, M., & Morgan, C. (1994). *Teaching and learning language and culture*. Great Britain: WBC.

Cheng, A. (2015). Teaching Chinese in the global context: Challenges and strategies. *European Review, 23*(2), 297–308.

Cheng, C., & Li, Y. (2019). Study of cultural introduction to teaching Chinese as a foreign language. *Modern Linguistics, 7*(1), 7-14.

Creswell, J. W. (2013). *Qualitative inquiry and research design: Choosing among five approaches* (3rd ed.). Thousand Oaks, CA: SAGE Publications, Inc.

Denzin, N. K., & Lincoln, Y. S. (2011). *The SAGE handbook of qualitative research* (4th ed.). Thousand Oaks, CA: SAGE Publications, Inc.

Fung, A. S., & Wang, M. W. (2012). Retrospective and prospective: development of teaching materials for writing for teaching Chinese as a foreign language (TCFL) in the last two decades. *Quarterly Journal of Chinese Studies, 4*(1), 46-50.

Gardner, R. C., & Lambert, W. E. (1972). *Attitudes and motivation in second-language learning*. Rowley, MA: Newbury House.

Green, M. G., & Piel, J. A. (2010). *Theories of human development: A comparative approach*. Pearson Education, Inc.

Hadley, A. O., & Terry, R. (2001). *Teaching language in context*. Boston, MA: Heinle & Heinle.

Hu, B. (2010). The challenges of Chinese: A preliminary study of UK learners' perceptions of difficulty. *The Language Learning Journal, 38*(1), 99-118.

Hyland, K. (2015). *Academic publishing: Issues and challenges in the construction of knowledge*. Oxford, UK: Oxford University Press.

Kramsch, C. (1993). *Context and culture in language teaching*. Oxford, UK: Oxford University Press.

Krashen, S. D. (1985). *The input hypothesis: Issues and implications*. London, UK: Longman.

Liddicoat, A. J., Papademetre, L., Scarino, A., & Kohler, M. (2003). *Report on intercultural language learning*. Commonwealth Department of Education, Science and Training, Commonwealth of Australia.

Long, M. H. (1981). Input, interaction, and second-language acquisition. *Annals of the New York Academy of Sciences, 379*, 259-278.

Mackay, M., & Tymon, A. (2013). Working with uncertainty to support the teaching of critical reflection. *Teaching in Higher Education, 18*(6), 643-655.

Patton, M. Q. (1999). Enhancing the quality and credibility of qualitative analysis. *Health Services Research, 34*(5, Part II), 1189–1208.

Schaub, S. (2012). Acquiring second-languages through constructivist and communicative approaches in literacy collaborative schools. Retrieved from http://lcosu.blogspot.com/2012/04/acquiring-second-languages-through.html

Schumann, J. H. (1978). *The Pidginization process: A model for second language acquisition*. Rowley, MA: Newbury House.

Shulman, L. S. (1986). Those who understand: Knowledge growth in teaching. *Educational Researcher, 15*(2), 4-14.

Stainer, F. (1971). Culture: A motivating factor in the French classroom. In C. Jay & P. Castle (Eds.), *French language education: The teaching of culture in the classroom* (pp. 28-37). Springfield, IL: State Department of Public Instruction.

Swain, M. (1993). The output hypothesis: Just speaking and writing aren't enough. *The Canadian Modern Language Review, 50*(1), 158-164.

Wang, S. C. (2007). Building societal capital: Chinese in the US. *Language Policy, 6*, 27–52.

Wei, B. (2017). Issues in teaching Chinese characters and strategies for foreign learners outside the Chinese character culture circle. *Gdańskie Studia Azji Wschodniej, 11*, 98-111.

ASSESSMENT OF ONLINE EXAM SYSTEM PERCEPTION IN COVID-19 PANDEMIC ERA

Meltem Eryılmaz[1] and Ahu Genis-Gruber[2]
[1]*Computer Engineering, Atilim University, Ankara, Turkey*
[2]*University of Applied Sciences Upper Austria, Steyr, Austria*

ABSTRACT

The swift conversion of courses to online exams has labelled the recent Covid-19 pandemic era. In educational agenda, all educators in the globe have faced the obstacles of abrupt adoption of distance education learning methods. Although distance education methods have been exercised in the past decade, the usage was not common. The pandemic has brought not only the sudden transformation of education format, but also online security issues. The online exam solution in e-learning techniques, tools and adoption has been a popular topic to research. Recent literature review shows various analyzes in the field, however the outcome of the research proves that the challenges are similiar in the globe. The aim of this research is to determine the essential problems and develop solutions based on the students` perception of online exams which became compulsorily transitioned during the pandemic process. The custom-made survey was conducted on 165 students to have an insight on their approach to e-learning and online exam. Descriptive statistics method is used to describe the features of the data in the study.

KEYWORDS

e-Learning, Online Exam Perception, Covid-19, Exam Efficiency

1. INTRODUCTION

With the sudden Covid -19 pandemic in the globe, the educational agenda in the world had to swift rapidly to online or TV based distance education in all levels. Many universities experience an unexpected and rapid transition from traditional face-to-face education to online or distance education. Distance education had gained vast importance in the education system over the years with the accelerating research and development in technology. However its importance has increased with Covid-19 pandemic, and whole educational system had to transform rapidly into distance or online education all over the world, which forced the lecturers to offer the courses online. This unexpected swift has presented numerous challenges as preparing an online course content requires developing detailed course plan design, audio and video content, technical support equipment. Most faculty members faced hurdles in terms of online teaching experience, technical support issues, and early preparation issues (Bao,2020).

The general purpose of the exams is to test students` knowledge (Elliott, 2008). Thus, exams and assessments are an important component of the learning process. In distance education, online exams have accelerated, which are not completely reliable yet. Researchers try to develop new models and algorithms in this field (Özden et.al.,2004). There are different online platforms, like Blackboard, Schoology, Moodle, ZOOM, MS-Teams and some social media platforms and mobile applications are used as well (Dhyab et.al.,2018). Most of these platforms have their own online exam modules offering various exam techniques. Through automatically evaluation process, online exams offer an effective way to increase objectivity (Frankl et.al., 2012). However, ensuring the security of online exams is an ongoing problem of distance education. The development of automated exam tracking and control models is of great importance for the reliable execution of distance education systems. Although both the preparation of online course videos and materials and the lecture explanations through video conferencing systems are mostly conquered, the system development to detect and prevent cheating attempts is still pending. Attempted systems have been developed to take exams in places where the students reside with camera being observed by monitoring camera images during the exam.

One of the most important components of distance education is the measurement and evaluation process of online exams. The main challenges of the process are classified as safe exam environment, identity check, cheating and suitable exam type for the course. The aim of this research is to determine the problems and to develop solutions based on the opinions of the students about the online exams that are compulsorily transitioned during the pandemic process.

1.1 Online Exams

Assessment is important to measure the students' learning capacity and to analyze the grasp of the course content. Throughout their studies, the students need to know what they have learned, what they should do and how to evaluate themselves (Chickering et.al., 1994). Assessment methods work best when they match learning outcomes, are shared with students and when the assessment criteria are agreed (Brown et.al.,1995). Online assessment is a fact of all fields of education, such as university, business life and industry. In the literature, there are many studies showing that online exams decrease the workload of the educators. Recent literature review shows various analyzes in the field, however the outcome of the research proves that the challenges are similiar in the globe; security in online exams, cheating possibilities (Hylton et.al., 2016), learning for online exam hurdles (Ilgaz et.al.,2020), effective measurement of students`knowledge in online exams, increasing workload of educators, implementation challenges of courses to online classes (Milone PharmD et.al., 2017). The online exam solution in e-learning techniques, tools and adoption has been a popular topic to research (Muzaffer et.al.,2020). Online exams have many advantages with instant feedback, automatic scoring, diversity of exam methods, questions from the question bank (Hewson, 2012; Marriott, 2009; Anakwe 2008). These features increase student participation, as well as reduced costs and provides more flexibility compared to traditional methods. Meanwhile, online exams increase efficiency and ease teaching workload and management. Feedback plays an important role in evaluation processes and is an important element of the learning process. Online exams enable time-saving, student self-assessment and participation in the learning and teaching process with both standardized and personalized feedback opportunities (Chickering et.al., 1990; Hewson, 2012). In online assessments, communication, interaction with embedded graphics, video and animation tools within questions and collaboration are possible by the use of the Internet compared to traditional classes. Features in online assessments include collaborative projects, case studies conducted in teams, online discussions, multiple choice questions and self assessment. Online exams enable learners to take responsibility for their own learning by providing immediate feedback and identifying areas for review. It also assists teachers to identify problem areas (Brown et.al., 1995). However, online exams are critical because of their online features, so they face a number of challenges like cheating, technical problems and lack of technological skills (Hewson, 2012; Hylton et.al., 2016). Limited bandwidth, technological limitations, managing test scoring and accessing problems can be counted among other issues. It is certain that the need for a general security methodology will increase when using online assessment in online learning. Confidentiality, Privacy, Integrity, Authorization, Non-repudiation, Authentication are the general requirements concerning security in online assessment (Ilgaz et.al., 2020).

2. METHODOLOGY

2.1 Participants

The study was conducted on total of 165 students taking online courses and writing online exams via Moodle at 2020 winter semester. At the end of the study, the questionnaires of 108 students were evaluated. Incomplete or unsubmitted responses are not considered.

2.2 Data Collection

During the course of application, students attended the course online. Material sharing, forum, exam, text, picture and video supported lesson summaries parts are included in the online learning environment. The standard exam module was used. A custom-made satisfaction survey about students` perception of online exams has been applied to the students after the exam. The survey, which evaluates the online examination system, was composed of a structure with four factors with 12 items in total. Accordingly, the factors were learning, use of tool, assessment and technical issues. On the 5 point Likert type scale, the numbers stand for some adverbs of frequency. That is, strongly agree (5), agree (4), neutral (3), do not agree (2), and strongly disagree (1).

2.3 Data Analysis

In order to examine the survey's validity, factor analysis technique is used. To determine the reliabilities internal coherence coefficient (Cronbach Alpha) is calculated and reported as 0.92. Descriptive statistics is used to describe the features of the data in the study.

3. RESULTS AND CONCLUSION

According to survey results, students participating in the study, a ratio of 32.4 % stated that they agree that the online tests are a good tool to help students evaluate their level of knowledge (Figure 1). Most of the students stated that they agree with a ratio of 36.1 % and strongly agree with a ratio of 17.6% that the online exams conducted without using a secure exam software, are secure (Figure 2). Some students proposed the university to act toward integrating such software into the online assessment procedures. However, it was observed that knowing that an exam security software was used in the exam, increased the anxiety level of students and is considered to imply a negative attitude towards online education.

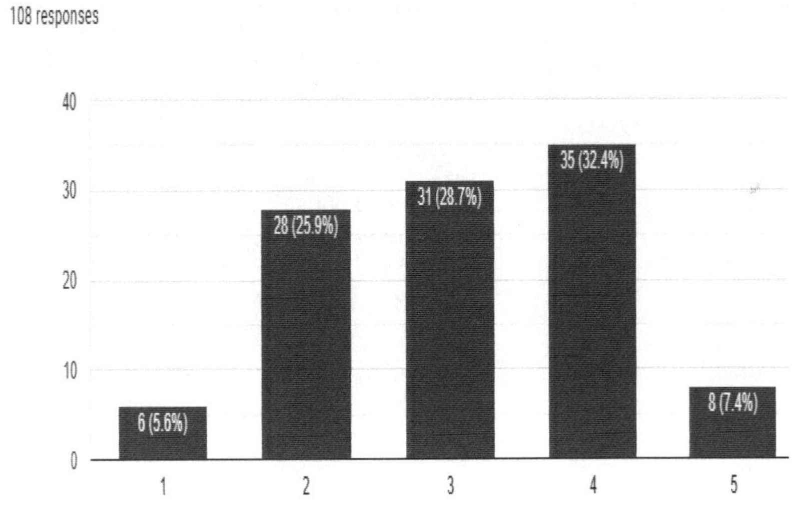

Figure 1. Online tests are a good tool to help students evaluate their level of knowledge

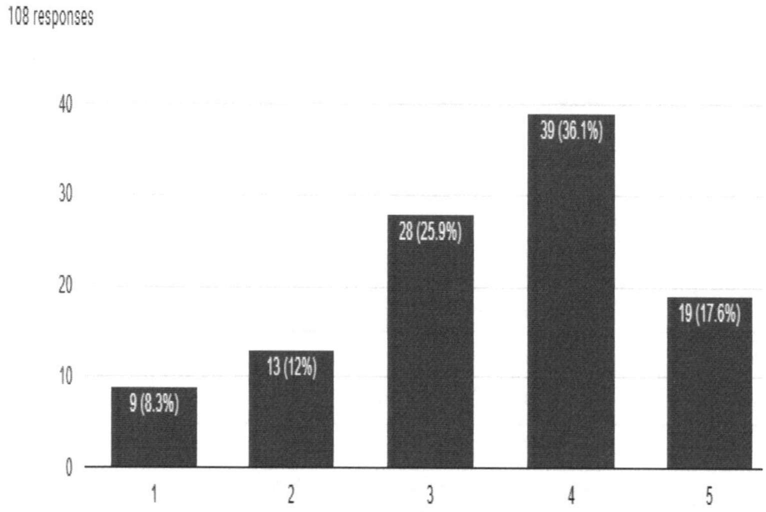

Figure 2. Online exams conducted without using a secure exam software are secure

According to the item "The structure and test scheduling (number of questions, duration, time, etc.) are adequate", the students stated that they agree with 24.1 % and do not agree with a ratio of 31.5%. They reported that the time pressure was the biggest problem and effected their motivation negatively. For the technical issues factor, poor internet connection was stated as the disadvantage. On the other hand results showed that the students had the opportunity to examine the questions in different scenarios and answered them according to their own response time. Immediate feedback that provided to each student at the end of the exam was very helpful for their learnings. Taking the same exam at the same time despite being in different locations was stated as the superior aspect. It has been seen that unlike the traditional exams, assessments, communication, interaction with embedded graphics, video and animation tools within questions and collaboration have become possible by the use of the Internet in online exam.

Although the students stated that they thought the online exam environment to be safe without security software, they were uncomfortable because of cheating issues. In this case, it can be suggessted that exam security softwares can be used which locks the internet environment for a short time.

REFERENCES

Abdul Wahab M.; Muhammad T.;Muhammad W.A.; Qaiser C.; Shamaila R.M. (2020) "Systematic Review on Online Exams Solutions in E-learning: Techniques, Tools, and Global Adoption" Computers and Society, arXiv:2010.07086v2

Anakwe, B. (2008) "Comparison of Student Performance in Paper-Based Versus Computer- Based Testing," Journal of Education for Business, No. October, p. 13-18.

Bao W. (2020) "COVID-19 and online teaching in higher education: A case study of Peking University", Hum Behav & Emerg Tech., 2, p.113–115.

Brown, S., & Knight, P. (1995) "Assessment in higher education", London: Kogan Page.

Chickering, A.W. & Ehrmann, S.C. (1994) "Implementing the Seven Principles", American Association for Higher Education Bulletin, 49 p.3-6.

Dhyab, R. & Varol, A. (2018) "Distance Education Features using Facebook", International Journal of Interactive Mobile Technologies, 12(6), p.19-34.

Elliott, B. (2008), "Assessment 2.0: Modernising assessment in the age of Web 2.0," Scottish Qualifications Authority, Retrieved May 16, 2019, from http://www.scribd.com/doc/461041/Assessment-20.

Frank, l, G. & Schratt-Bitter, S. (2012) "Online Exams: Practical Implications and Future Directions", The Proceedings of the 11th European Conference on e-Learning (Academic Conferences International (ACI); H. Beldhuis.

Hewson, C. (2012) "Can online course-based assessment methods be fair and equitable? Relationships between students' preferences and performance within online and offline assessments," Journal of Computer Assisted Learning, 28(5), p.488-498.

Hylton Kenrie, Yair Levy, Laurie P. Dringus (2016), "Utilizing webcam-based proctoring to deter misconduct in online exams", Computers & Education, V 92–93, p.53-63.

Ilgaz, H., Afacan Adanır, G.(2020) "Providing online exams for online learners: Does it really matter for them?", Educ Inf Technol. V 25, p.1255–1269.

Marriott, P. (2009) "Students' evaluation of the use of online summative assessment on an undergraduate financial accounting module," British Journal of Educational Technology, 40 (2), p. 237-254.

Milone PharmD A.S., Angela M. C., Rebecca L. B., Amy L. P., (2017) "The impact of proctored online exams on the educational experience", Currents in Pharmacy Teaching and Learning, 9(1), p.108-114.

Özden, M. Y., Ertürk, I., & Sanli, R. (2004) "Students' Perceptions of Online Assessment: A Case Study", Journal of Distance Education, 19(2), p.77.

EASY TECHNOLOGY DESIGNS FOR INNOVATIVE LEARNING

Marc Beutner[1] and Rasmus Pechuel[2]
[1]Prof. Dr., Chair of business and human resources education II, University of Paderborn
Warburger Str. 100, 33098 Paderborn, Germany
[2]CEO Ingenious Knowledge
Friedrich-Karl-Str. 200, 50735 Cologne, Germany

ABSTRACT

In this text we describe a technology-based approach which uses just a small set of technological requirements to offer innovative learning within the DISK-Online approach. In times of pandemics it is crucial to provide solutions for education which are easy to access. Teachers and trainers need solutions which let them connect to their learners without having to be experts in technology and without having to use too much special equipment. This is especially important in the field of vocational education and training (VET). In this article we provide insights into the approach and some impressions gleaned from first tests in the field of VET.

KEYWORDS

DISK-Online, Innovative Learning, Technology, Hybrid Learning, COVID-19, Streaming

1. CHALLENGES IN THE FIELD OF TECHNOLOGY IN EDUCATION IN TIMES OF COVID-19

The COVID-19 pandemic affects the whole world and many countries have implemented safety regulations. People have to make sure that they keep their distance, observe hygiene and in many cases use a mask every time they leave their homes. This influences our daily lives with particular emphasis on work and education.

With regard to education we can see different ways of dealing with the challenges. Some countries focus on home schooling and digital approaches, some on small groups and keeping distance at school. With all of these approaches digital solutions have become more important than ever for schools and education providers.

One of the key concerns besides the digital and didactical competencies needed by teachers and trainers is the technical equipment of the school or education provider. Technology is shifting and schools are struggling to keep up with the equipment they need in order to stay in contact with the learners via online technologies. This means a school or an education provider needs a stable and fast internet connection and fast and accessible Wi-Fi. For teachers and trainers it is very challenging to teach in a digital way, when not every classroom offers internet access. The simple exchange of files doesn't have very steep technological requirements. Sharing a pdf file can easily be accomplished with low bandwidth. However more complete pedagogical and didactic approaches, such as interactive apps that connect audio and video, may have much greater requirements than are typically available to an instructor.

Interaction between teachers / trainers and learners is crucial. In the learning process feedback and immediate response are very important as well as the ability to form a connection though visualization with the person teaching the topic. Here broadband is needed. This need goes hand in hand with the need for technical equipment such as computers, laptops, tablets and interactive whiteboards. Having this equipment readily available allows the instructor to use them directly within the learning process.

In addition to that, data security is becoming extremely important due to the fact that we are dealing with personal data and individual learning processes.

The learners must also have access to a computer, a laptop, a tablet or a smartphone, plus internet access at home to allow for schooling at home and online learning to work. Today, many learners have access to smartphones but the restrictions of such technical environments, such as small screens (Maniar and et. Al. 2008), also affect the available methods of teaching. 3PLearning states that it is one of the most important issues to "assess whether your students have reliable access to technology" (3PLearning 2020) before eLearning gets started.

Moreover the learners or students often encounter technical difficulties that such platforms are apt to have. For schools, education providers and especially teachers and trainers this means that they have to be able to react to such technical questions and provide ways to find a solution.

Mehdipour and Zerehkafi in 2013 listed technical challenges for M-Learning, including:

- Connectivity and battery life
- Screen size and key size [...]
- Meeting required bandwidth for nonstop/fast streaming
- Number of file/asset formats supported by a specific device
- Content security or copyright issue from authoring group
- Multiple standards, multiple screen sizes, multiple operating systems
- Reworking existing E-Learning materials for mobile platforms
- Limited memory [...]
- Risk of sudden obsolescence [...]" (Mehdipour & Zerehkafi 2013, 97)

All these aspects are cost intensive and solutions are needed which don't put a financial burden on learners. Solutions should not require more than a browser for the learner which makes it easier to handle and access. Ease of access is also an important consideration for teachers. We therefore offer the following approach, which combines low technological requirements with easy access and maintaining the human face of teaching.

2. THE DISK-ONLINE APPROACH - EASY TO HANDLE HYBRID LEARNING

A possible solution we created in 2020 is the DISK-Online approach (Beutner & Pechuel 2020). The DISK-Online approach is focused on hybrid learning (Beutner & Pechuel 2020b) and therefore offers opportunities for eLearning which combines face-to-face learning with online learning via a streaming concept (Beutner & Pechuel 2020c).

DISK-Online stands for Didactic Interactive Streaming Know-how and this approach is designed for dealing with the challenges of COVID-19 and the technologic challenges at schools and education.

Our DISK-online approach is a basic approach which can be expanded. In its core setting it comes with four DISK implementation stages. These stages address different sets of increasing blended interaction, beginning with a first stage, where interaction is quite low and focused on the teacher and goes up to the fourth stage, where interaction is learner-centered and moderated by the teachers and trainers. To accomplish this DISK-Online uses streaming of lessons, courses and lectures via a streaming platform and the use of an easy to handle streaming tool like Streamlabs OBS.

Before we have a closer look at the technical issues we would like to introduce you to the DISK-Online approach and the step-by-step process to implement and enhance hybrid learning and teaching. DISK-Online makes it possible for a teacher to be separated from the learners who are all connected online. However, usually the concept works with a group of learners who are on site while there are other groups of learners who are not in the classroom. Hybrid learning offers the chance to use technical equipment and smart pedagogic designs to cope with challenges which we are currently facing in schools. The DISK-Online approach offers education with increasing levels of interaction via digital tools. This increasing interaction is described from DISK 1 (low teacher centered interaction) to DISK4 (learner centered interaction) and can be used at different schools to adjust the teaching to technical restrictions and digital teaching competences. The following paragraphs provide an overview on the increasing interaction from DISK1 to DISK4:

DISK1

In the first implementation stage which we call DISK1 students are split into an in-class group and an online group. Interaction between learners and the teacher takes place in the classroom. The lesson is made available via streaming on the Internet. For the online learners there will be no two-way interaction at this point. The teacher can also decide to make the stream available as a video. In this case learners can choose to watch the video at their own convenience depending on their personal schedules. Again, this method doesn't have any interaction. It is recommended that learners who follow the stream online take extensive notes to interact with the teacher when groups are switched and they become the in-class group.

DISK2

The second implementation stage, DISK 2, offers Interaction on a local level in the classroom and online via the Internet. The teacher offers the lesson via live streaming and the online students are able to communicate in real time with the teacher, just as the students in the classroom do. The online learners use easy to access tools such as the chat available in the streaming service or other messaging services to talk to their teachers. This allows the students to make comments or ask questions, allowing them to make the same sorts of contributions to learning as they would in the classroom. The stream can still be recorded and made available later for on-demand viewing, but in that case there is no additional interaction.

DISK3

Within the third implementation stage, called DISK 3, interaction takes place both in the classroom and via the internet as in DISK 2. Online students continue to be able to engage in real-time interactions with the teacher. However, in this stage, online students will be able to interact with each other using chat or voice chat or video chat options. The learners are collaborating and the role of the teacher transforms from presenting and lecturing to monitoring and guiding the interactions of the peers. The entire lesson will be available via stream and all learners, regardless of location, can interact with the teacher and with their group. The learning process is enhanced with both questions as well as engaging in discussions. In this stage the stream can also be recorded for later viewing just as previously, without the ability to interact, of course.

DISK4

Implementation stage 4, called DISK4, offers the highest level of interaction. In addition to the interaction opportunities of DISK 3 the learners in the classroom now also get the opportunity to discuss and interact with the online learners. The teacher role is now completely shifted to a moderator role which supervises and fosters the learning processes. The lesson is available via streaming on the internet and the learners are active in the learning process and involved in the structure of teaching and learning. The learners are working together in mixed groups which can include on-site and online learners. Optionally, the stream can be available as a video. Usually this is means that interaction will happen via mail or via comments over a longer time period.

3. TECHNICAL REQUIREMENTS AND RESTRICTIONS WITHIN THE DISK APPROACH

From a technical point of view, it is possible to provide a system in which everything is preconfigured in such a way that teachers only have to start the devices and switch them off after their lessons. Especially at the DISK1 level the necessary technical knowledge of teachers is reduced to a minimum. This means that existing devices can be integrated without any problems.

From a technical point of view the following technical components are necessary:

Hardware:

1. Internet Connection

It is important for schools to have a fast internet connection in order to be able to stream videos. The upload speed is particularly important for streaming. Streaming videos requires a minimum of 5 Mbit / s. It should be noted, however, that the official figures given often do not correspond to the speed available in practice. There are a number of websites that can be used to test actual speed. The important key figure here is the upload speed. Note that multiple streams running at the same time (which would happen if multiple teachers were streaming at the same time) must share the available Mbps (megabits per second) between the different streams.

If the school already has fast Wi-Fi, no device is required. Otherwise it is recommended to install a powerful wireless router to make connecting easier. The role of a wireless network is to connect devices such as tablets to the school's internet connection without the need of connecting cables. It is highly recommended not to open the Wi-Fi network used for streaming to students. As with internet connections, too much traffic can slow down a Wi-Fi network. Wi-Fi routers are now standard, and are usually installed when the school is connected to the Internet. There is a wide range of wireless routers available. The most important requirement is that teachers get a good signal from the network when streaming (full bars if possible) and that the router offers a speed higher than the speed of the internet connection.

2. Projection in Classroom

Ideally, classrooms will have projectors that are ceiling-mounted and have a wireless connection. In the simplest case, projection walls can be a white wall, but corresponding projection surfaces increase the image quality. There are many modern projectors that support wireless connections. This means that a teacher can connect very quickly and share the screen with the projector so that the students in the classroom can follow the lesson. However, it is also possible to connect projectors to tablets with cables. In most cases the teacher only needs an adapter to the HDMI cable of the projector.

The role of the projector is to make the screen of the tablet visible to the students in the classroom. If no students are present, the projector can be ignored. When choosing projectors, the light intensity is particularly important. The required light intensity depends on the size of the projection surface. A value of around 500 lumens / m^2 is recommended (if you have an area of 4 m^2, the brightness should be around 2000 lumens). In addition it is advantageous to use projectors that can transmit images wirelessly, so that teachers do not have to spend a lot of time setting up and therefore do not lose time unnecessarily.

3. Tablet and Digital Pen

When it comes to tablets there is a wide variety available and teachers should choose the tablet that they are comfortable with. Almost all tablets are suitable for streaming. From entry level Android tablets to higher level tablets like the iPad Pro or even touch-sensitive screens with integrated computers running Windows 10, there are many choices for teachers. A big screen size is a plus, making it easier for the teacher to use the tablet like a blackboard/whiteboard. When it comes to choosing the tablet, the operating system plays a big role. From a maintenance point of view Android and iOS are a lot easier than Windows. In general teachers should choose the system that works well for them though. Of course, streaming can also be done with computers or laptops, it is just not as comfortable as using tablets.

Choosing the digital pen is very important and teachers are encouraged to try out which pen works best for them. There are big differences in quality. Some pens are worse than drawing with a finger on the screen while some modern pens achieve results that resemble writing with real pens.

4. Microphone

A good microphone is also essential. Many tablets are good at picking up sound with their internal microphones but viewers can usually feel the difference between internal microphones and external microphones that are connected to the device. For teachers the easiest solution could be a simple microphone that clips to the shirt and has a wire that plugs into the microphone port on the tablet. Sometimes an adapter is needed, depending on the tablet. For teachers who move around a lot there are wireless microphone solutions available that usually connect to the tablet via Bluetooth.

Software

1. Streaming Software

The role of the streaming software is to send the content of the tablet screen to a streaming platform as encoded video. A simple and free solution for this would be the program Streamlabs OBS, one of the most popular choices used by many streamers world-wide. The program is available as an app for iOS and Android and already comes with pre-configured settings to connect to some of the most popular streaming platforms. However, there are other choices for streaming software, especially if teachers decide to developer greater skills in this area. Streamlabs OBS covers everything that is needed though and allows full customization of the streaming layout so that teachers can even add chats and other elements of interaction.

2. Streaming Platform

The role of the streaming platform is to make the video stream available to the viewers through browsers. Teachers who want to stream need to register an account at a streaming platform (which is normally free). When it comes to choosing streaming platforms, there are also a few choices. The biggest streaming platforms are YouTube and Twitch. Both can be used freely and without requiring the students to register. However, they also don't offer good solutions for protected environments ich which teachers can easily limit the classes to their students. Considering topics such as data security and preserving a protected learning space calls are getting louder for school authorities or ministries to provide a streaming platform solution for schools that takes the difficult decision of how to deal with the aspect of student data on the internet out of the hands of teachers.

3. Whiteboard Software

Strictly speaking no special software is needed, however, it can support the teacher greatly. The easiest solution would be using any drawing program with a white background that the teacher can write on. More and more apps offer writing support for digital pens though, and they have the advantage of making it easier to save the screens or quickly open screens the teacher prepared in advance. There are specific blackboard /whiteboard apps that have more support functions but these are generally not free. Of course, apart from writing on a blank surface there are countless opportunities to use other apps, such as presentation apps, maps, videos, mathematical apps, etc. that can be integrated into the lessons.

When aiming for the higher DISK levels the following advanced components become necessary:

1. Video Camera

Most tablets come with a video camera. If teachers choose to be visible to the students, they can add a video of themselves to the stream, thus making it easier for the learner to relate to the teacher. Streaming software like Streamlabs OBS makes it easy to overlay a small image of the presenter over the screen presentation (in one of the corners, for example).

2. Chat Software

Chat software is a great help in making streaming more interactive. Some streaming platforms (like Twitch) already have integrated chat systems that can be used directly. However, it is also possible to integrate other chat systems, such as Discord. Discord is freely available and allows users to create chat servers for private groups with topic-related threads. Thus it could be an ideal tool to support group work.

3. Voice Chat / Video Chat Software

Voice chat software could greatly support the connection between remote students, especially in group work. There are many voice chat systems available, such as Google Hangouts, Skype, Google Meet, Zoom, Telegram, Slack and many others. Discord also supports voice chat for large groups. If seeing each other is important students could also use video connections. However, teachers need to tread carefully in order not to be accused of being too careless with the security of student data when it comes to sharing images and videos of the students themselves.

4. Advanced Learning Systems

There are learning system that structure interaction between students and teachers and can greatly support remote teaching. When these systems support interaction, they are a valuable addition to achieving the higher levels of the DISK approach. One example is a systems like Microsoft Teams which supports text, voice and video communication and sharing of files and assignments. Another example is Google Classroom which also structures assignments and supports group work. Another system that was specifically developed for schools in Germany by the Hasso Plattner Institute with data protection in mind is Schul-Cloud. While these systems all have the potential to greatly enhance interaction and structure the online learning process it will probably still take a while until teachers and schools are ready to use them on a greater scale.

4. TEACHERS' FEEDBACK CONCERNING TECHNICAL EQUIPMENT AND INTERNET CONNECTIVITY

In October 2020 we conducted a survey concerning technical equipment and internet connectivity at school. 104 teachers at VET schools answered a short questionnaire concerning their technical environment at school. All teachers came from Germany and therefore only provide insight into the current German situation. 33 of the teachers came from North-Rhine-Westphalia (31,7%), 25 from Rhineland Palatinate (24 %), 24 from Hesse (23,1%), 18 from Brandenburg (17,3%) and 3 from Bavaria (3,8%). Therefore, not all German member states (Länder) were involved and the Western part is slightly overrepresented. Nevertheless the results are very similar in the different regions. 49 teachers were female (47,12%) and 55 teachers male (52,88%).

When asked about the quality of the internet connection the following answers painted a clear picture of the situation in schools:

'At school the headmaster / the administration of the school has connection to the internet' – 99% (103 teachers) agreed and one person did not answer.

'At school, we have PC rooms without connection to the internet' – 46 persons agreed (44,2%).

'At school, we have PC rooms with connection to the internet' – 84 teachers agreed (80,7%).

However, when it came to the item 'At school, all teachers have connection to the internet', only 52 teachers agreed which is exactly 50% of the responding teachers.

And regarding the item 'At school, all classrooms have connection to the internet' only 6 teachers (5,77%) could agree.

With regard to Wi-Fi the positive answers are not much better. Only 7 teachers (6,73%) stated that there is Wi-Fi at school ('At school, we have Wi-Fi').

Moreover, concerning the learners, 12 teachers (11,54%) agreed with regard to the item 'At school, all learners can access the internet'.

The teachers were also asked to estimate how many learners have access to the internet via smartphones, tablets, PCs or laptops from home (regardless if this is their own device). The mean of the estimate of the 104 teachers is 87%, which means that the teachers think that on average 87% of the learners have access to the internet. This is lower than the results of a survey of STATISTA 2020 which found that in 2019 97 % of youths in the age range of 12 to 13 as well as 97% of youths of the age range of 14 to 15 and 97% of youths of the age range of 16 to 18 have access to the internet. In the survey of 2014 the number was even higher (2014: 98% of youths of the age range of 12 to 13; 99% of youths of the age range of 14 to 15 and 100% of youths of the age range of 16 to 18).

Therefore, it seems that teachers estimate the number of learners who can access the internet too low.

With regard to equipment 48 teachers (46,15%) stated that they have laptops at school, 35 teachers (33,65%) agreed to the fact that they have smart boards at school. Moreover, 93 teachers have their own laptops or PCs which is 89,4% of the teachers responding in our survey.

5. CONCLUSION

These numbers show that there is a need to support schools and provide them with good internet access and equipment to foster the learning and teaching processes. The political will to provide schools with better learning technology seems to be heading in the right direction but efforts must be intensified. However it is not only the technical equipment, but it is crucial that the competences of the teachers are strengthened to know how to use these tools, software and hardware to their best advantage. There is a need to train teachers, to provide them with in-service training and to support them. For the future it is crucial to have good equipment combined with didactic and pedagogical knowledge of how to use it effectively in learning processes. The DISK approach is a way to combine technical requirements which can be handled with a pedagogical and didactic approach which supports learning and teaching in hybrid scenarios step-by-step. More research has to be done in the field of improving the digital competences of teachers. With regard to the DISK-Online approach additional scenarios can be tested and implemented.

REFERENCES

3PLearning (2020). *5 Challenges of Online Teaching (and How to Rise Above Them).* Retrieved from: https://www.3plearning.com/blog/5-common-pitfalls-distance-teaching-avoid/, access date: 18.10.2020

Beutner, M. & Pechuel, R. (2020a). *DISK-ONLINE - Basiskonzept für die Gestaltung von Online-Unterricht mit neuen Medien durch Lehrkräfte an Schulen - Einfache Umsetzungsmöglichkeiten im Rahmen von COVID-19.* Köln / Paderborn: Ingenious Knowledge.

Beutner, M. & Pechuel, R. (2020b). DISK Online Streaming Concept for hybrid learning – Dealing with the challenges of COVID-19 in learning settings. *Proceedings of Innovate Learning Summit 2020 Online. USA 2020.* Currently in Print.

Beutner, M. & Pechuel, R. (2020c). The use of streaming for online lessons – A basic implementation option in the context of the COVID-19 situation. *Proceedings of SITE Interactive Online 2020.* Currently in Print.

Mehdipour, Y. & Zerehkafi, H (2013). Mobile Learning for Education: Benefits and Challenges. *In International Journal of Computational Engineering Research.* Vol. 3, No. 6, pp. 93-100.

Maniar, N., Bennett, E., Hand, S. & Allan, G. (2008). The effect of mobile phone screen size on video based learning. *In Journal of Software.* Vol. 3, No. 4, pp. 51-61.

Statista (2020): *Anteil der befragten Kinder und Jugendlichen, die zumindest gelegentlich das Internet nutzen, nach Altersgruppen in Deutschland in ausgewählten Jahren von 2014 bis 2019.* Retrieved from: https://de.statista.com/statistik/daten/studie/298170/umfrage/internetnutzung-von-kindern-und-jugendlichen-in-deutschland/, Access date: 18.10.2020

PODCASTS TO PADLETS: WRITING AND SPEAKING IN NEW DIGITAL PLATFORMS

Sandra L. Guzman-Foster[1] and Alyssa S. Cortes-Kennedy[2]

[1]Ph.D.

[2]MAA

University of the Incarnate Word

4301 Broadway, CPO #293

San Antonio, TX 78209, USA

ABSTRACT

The authors of this proposal explain the process of understanding new education technology formats or digital platforms in higher education, specifically podcasts and padlets. The scholars go on to explain the importance of technology driven educational platforms and alternative communication opportunities students enrolled in college level courses can utilize. Platforms such as these are an intricate part of facilitating course content and promoting dialect among peers. It is important to understand how to implement new learning platforms and technologies is the first step in this new virtual learning venture. The opportunity to learn why two or more different ways of content facilitation can create a new digital learning space for both the facilitator and the student(s) during a standard or shortened college semester is vital. Learning to be flexible with course dialect and/or content does not mean to eliminate important assignments, but as a facilitator knowing when the delivery is or is not being absorbed. Hence, recognizing the importance and different ways education technology can improve content delivery and enhanced student communication and interactions. A variation of outcomes and opportunities stem from this experience of podcast and padlet platform application and surely other experiences in the future. The significance of this proposal is shown through the implementation of podcasts and padlets which bring a new visionary way to facilitate course material and if anything, enhance the student learning experience(s) during the process.

KEYWORDS

Digital Platforms, Higher Education, Pandemic, Podcasts, Formats

1. INTRODUCTION

The 2020 global pandemic was an additional push for facilitators in higher education to further their use of new formats or digital platform integrations in the classroom. The additional factors of a pandemic push had facilitators and instructors alike, scrambling to create new and improved course content to finish out the 2020 spring semester and hopefully start the summer semester(s). The experience was nothing less than this in South Central Texas for one professor and her teaching assistant. Broadening the significance of the course content for her graduate level research course over a period of 10 weeks via the virtual summer semester. Prior experience and background in a flipped class pedagogy background help to understand that keeping learning techniques and platforms "fresh" and "engaging" for learners is a revolving challenge (Balzotti et al, 2016). Building content for a summer "core" research course at the graduate level was no exception. Many new technical challenges were being discovered, sketchy internet signals, time management issues, reduced student attention spans, and stress of the unknown in both faculty and students. Understanding the importance of communication at all levels of academia are most important to the success of the students and the content they are learning. However, how the content is expressed whether visibly or verbally will vary greatly amongst facilitators. Even though technology surrounds many college students throughout their academic journey there are a significant number of individuals (facilitators and students) who do not utilize the different types of digital learning resources available to them. It is important to note, facilitators spend a profound amount of time and energy to build course content often on a complex deadline. Leaving less time for critical reflection, preparation, creativity, flexibility, and recognition which are needed to make the learning process worth wild. In 2020, facilitators and students faced a new world of learning to which many outcomes and opportunities were learned and further developed through virtually learning environments. Podcasts and Padlets were two methods used to engage students, create opportunities for critical thinking, develop new ways of communication amongst peers, and being flexible in how students decided to integrate core and supplemental learning modules into their daily schedule.

2. BODY OF PAPER

According to Knowles, Holten, and Swanson (1998) adult learners learn differently than children. Therefore, courses designed for adults should tap into their social contexts and experiences. With the new normal and remote learning increasing across the country, especially in higher education, educators must be comfortable with using different types of technology and how to best utilize them in a learning environment when working with adults. Adult learners learn best when the information presented to them is relevant and useful. Since adults possess a mature mindset, they are often better at creating solutions related to real-life issues/scenarios as opposed to simply memorizing and regurgitating information. Problem-solving, immediate application, and performance-based tasks are all pillars of effective instruction when it comes to working with adult learners. In practical terms, andragogy means that instruction for adults needs to focus more on the process and less on the content being taught. Strategies such as case studies, role playing, simulations, and self-evaluation are most useful. Additionally, the educator takes on the role of facilitator or resource rather than lecturer.

As Schwandt (1998) noted, "the terrain of constructivist approaches is marked by multiple uses of the term" (p. 237). Moreover, Schwandt (1998) described Guba and Lincoln's early use of the term "constructive paradigm" as "a wide ranging eclectic framework" (p. 242). Utilizing a constructivist paradigm (Mertens, 2014), students are constructing their own understanding in a shared social setting by using Podcasts and Padlet. These technological tools provide an opportunity for students to contribute their own response, to engage with content from within their normal communication channels, and to articulate their understanding. Students who would normally have reservations in participating in class now have a platform for their voice. Using tools like Podcasts and Padlet can help to encourage a growth mindset as students reflect on their own learning. By using these tools, students become active participants. New topics and ideas create an environment where both students and teachers embark on a learning journey together, which fosters a growth mindset in the classroom. Padlet was also used so students could have a platform where they could practice writing the language of the course content. Podcasts and Padlet provided a platform for students to make personal connections to the curriculum, which helped make the activity more meaningful.

Students were required to listen to biweekly podcasts and pose questions via Padlet to elicit a higher-level thinking and deeper understanding of the content. Students were asked to respond to their facilitator's podcasts via Padlet, so there is genuine interaction, not just asynchronous understanding of the material. According to Fox and Cayari (2016), it is common to see facilitators use group work in graduate classrooms. Furthermore, group work enhances student learning and understanding via constructivist means, assisting in helping students with their critical thinking and problem solving skills as well as collaborative skills.

2.1 Digital Platforms

Flipped classrooms have been used by facilitators for many years (Berrett, 2012). Although, whether facilitators do or do not integrate digital learning technology/platforms into their syllabi is questionable. Recent global events have shed light on how education technology can be used to facilitate course material in a richer and much needed context. While many students become tech savvy early on, educational technology such as, material preparations and course integrations can be stressful and misdirected, if adequate time is not invested into the complex developmental process. Whether it is a concern of funding, time to develop and create modules, or a lack of continual training, using digital platforms as a learning tool remains relatively low in such an advanced age. A sentiment share by many but explored and implemented by even less. But what if we told you that is far from reality? Montgomery (2018) suggested digital platforms offer a "low-cost, low-barrier engagement to increase connections and participation" between people (p. 2). Therefore, thinking beyond our free learning management systems (LMS) such as blackboard and canvas which are often provided by our institution, awaits a different opportunity to engage students in a different context and light. Not only do digital platforms raise the bar of learning course material they also produce a cognizant thought of sustainability, creativity, and global ecological awareness (Dieck-Assad, 2018). In our case maintaining social distance guidelines implemented by our University during a pandemic was an essential part of being able to continue learning in the year 2020. Creating physically safe spaces, via virtual learning was essential but unpredictable in terms of learner outcomes. By integrating additional learning resources, such as a podcast and padlet, we could supplement a lack of class time via zoom for students to continually engage in course dialog.

2.2 Digital and Verbal Communication

Different digital and verbal platforms of communication do much more than create dialect in a traditional or virtual classroom. These types of learning platforms play a significant part in helping learners become more marketable and versatile in their future roles and organizations (Baepler, et al. 2014, Dieck-Assad, 2018, NASM Committee, 2018). For example, having students communicate digitally and verbally can be considered to be more equitable because they open up participation to students who may be experiencing issue with their internet connection, who have schedule conflicts, or who may be uncomfortable engaging with the full class. Students were asked to pose clarifying and probing questions after listening to the podcasts, which helps students improve their communication skills by practicing and applying higher order questioning. The goal is to inspire deep reflection on what they heard on the podcasts and ask questions to clarify their understanding as well as to provide opportunities for problem solving based on the content of the podcast.

2.3 Flexibility and Recognition

Recent research by Counselman Carpenter & Redcay (2019) emphasized that students who used virtual classroom learning expressed thankfulness in how it allows them to access course content in their own time and how it best supports their learning format (via computer, laptop, smartphone or tablet). Being accessible to students is not just being an email away but now goes further into how and when a facilitator lectures, even if not in "real" time. Podcasts allow more room for self-paced learning opportunities and create a type of flexibility possible through listening on one's own time (Luttenberger, et al. 2018). It is important to note, previous studies have shown no difference in students learning outcomes when listening to a lecture via podcast vs. face to face (O'Bannon et al. 2011, Traphagan et al, 2010). Podcasting also allows alternative perspectives and conversation for intricate topics (Carmelina Films, 2010). With complex material, such as introduction to inquiry, a graduate level course which focuses on research design, implementation, analysis, and synthesis it is nearly impossible for any facilitator to cover all the material in one lecture. With podcasting it introduced a "casual" conversation of the subject matter by having the hosts speak of their scholarly experiences on and off the research field. In addition, talk about how methodology is applied and utilized in certain scenarios of real- life experiences.

2.4 Experimentation and Implementation

During the summer 2020 term a core curriculum course focused on the foundations of research design and designated for masters and doctoral level students were tasked with the challenge(s) to experiment with new forms of technology. Due to the state of the global pandemic, face to face learning was unavailable and forms of connecting course material, student peers, and course material became difficult to comprehend and apply because of the lack of social interaction. Like many facilitators of knowledge at multiple stages of learning we were challenged to experiment with how knowledge was distributed and implemented for retention. These came in the form of virtual, recorded, written, live and remote classroom demonstrations.

The first experimental platform was a podcast. The implementation and introduction was done within the first few weeks of the semester and meant as supplemental methodology to cover in-depth course material i.e. theoretical and methodological material. A series of podcasts were created to outline research methodology and theoretical perspective through casual researcher conversations. Which included explaining the methodology from a scholarship definition, sharing a real life experience using this type of research, and finally using comparing analysis to apply to real events happening in the world. Students were free to listen unlimited, in their own time and space as fit to their schedule. Students reactions were positive to the experience, in that it allowed a true asynchronous learning experience, based on the stresses of covid-19 living conditions, opportunities to feel a part of a real case scenario, and it created somewhat of a "stress-free" learning zone, meaning the pressure to comprehend the entirety of research methods was eliminated to a certain degree.

The second platform was experimental towards communication and virtual peer interaction. Implementing the platform was simplistic by creating hyperlinks for students to connect on and structuring the virtual writing tool by having specific topics and/or points to discuss and quite possible debate. Padlet became a way for students to socially interact with their peers about specific topics, postings, or podcast listening sessions. A second way to supplement for the lack of classroom interaction which includes peer conversation and/or discussion padlet was a significant tool to allow these social interactions to discuss course material. The goal: hold a back and forth interactive discussion. Students' responses were generated by personal thoughts, comments, feelings, and even a emoji or photo representation. This generated a deeper-critical thinking aspect to the material covered and how they began to apply it as a novice researcher themself and other events happening locally and globally.

2.5 Point of View

From our point of view, students can become empowered when they can reflect and connect curriculum with authentic activities through the application of digital tools via technological platforms such as Podcasts and Padlet. These tools can support learning if utilized effectively. Therefore, the intent of this paper is to help further explain opportunities for engagement in reflection and articulation of one's understanding of course content beyond the traditional face-to-face classroom walls when utilizing tools such as Podcasts and Padlet.

3. CONCLUSION

Technology has the power to transform learning by introducing new ways to teach adult learners. With new ways of teaching, facilitators are able to provide opportunities for adult learners to apply what they have learned to the real world. Utilizing Podcasts and Padlet as an instructional tool, contributes to educational benefits for all adult learners. It enhances students' ability to think critically; be authentically engaged with the content that is delivered; make connections with multi genre materials, as well as cross-curricular connections; create original published works; and communicate via academic discussions and writings with both the facilitator and their peers.

REFERENCES

Baepler, P. et al, 2014. It's Not About Seat Time: Blending, Flipping and Eficiency in Active Learning Classrooms. *In Computers and Education*, Vol. 78, pp. 227–236.

Balzotti, J. M. et al, 2016. Using Digital Learning Platforms to Extend the Flipped Classroom. *In Business and Professional Communication Quarterly*, Vo. 79, No. 1, pp. 68-80.

Berrett, D., 2012. How 'Flipping' the Classroom Can Improve the Traditional Lecture. *In The Education Digest*, Vol. 78, No. 1, p. 36.

Carmelina Films, Films for the Humanities & Sciences, & Films Media Group, 2010. *Podcasting in the Classroom*. Films Media Group, New York, N.Y., USA.

Counselman Carpenter, E. 2019. Understanding the Role of the Brick-and-Mortar Classroom in Course Design and Implementation of the "Flipped" Classroom: An Exploratory Case Study. *In Journal of Teaching and Learning with Technology*, Vol. 8, No. 1, pp. 42-59.

Dieck-Assad, F. A. 2018. Digital Teaching: In Search Of An Effective Paperless Platform For Classroom Activities. *In Journal of International Education Research*, Vol 14, No. 2, pp. 1-8.

Fox, H. L. et al, 2016. Graduate Students' Readiness and Perceptions of the Pedagogical Application of Collaborative Video Logs. *In Tech Trends*, Vol. 60, pp. 585-590.

Knowles, M.S., et al., 1998. *The Adult Learner* (5th Edition). Butterworth-Heinemann Publishers, Houston. USA.

Luttenberger, S. et al, 2018. Different Patterns of University Students' Integration of Lecture Podcasts, Learning Materials, and Lecture Attendance in a Psychology Course. *In Education and Information Technologies*, Vol. 23, No. 1, pp. 165-178.

Montgomery, B. L. 2018. Building and Sustaining Diverse Functioning Networks Using Social Media and Digital Platforms to Improve Diversity and Inclusivity. *In Frontiers in Digital Humanities*, Vol. 5.

National Academies of Sciences, Engineering, Medicine. Committee on How People Learn II: The Science Practice of Learning, 2018. *How People Learn II: Learners, Contexts, and Cultures*. Consensus study report.

O'Bannon, B. W. et al, 2011. Using Podcasts to Replace Lecture: Effects on Student Achievement. *In Computers & Education*, Vol. 57, No. 3.

Schwandt, T. A. 1998. Constructivist, Interpretivist Approaches to Human Inquiry. In N. K. Denzin, & Y. S. Lincoln (Eds.), *The Landscape of Qualitative Research: Theories and Issues* (pp. 221-259). SAGE, Thousand Oaks, CA, USA.

Traphagan, T. et al, 2010. Impact of Class Lecture Webcasting on Attendance and Learning. *In Educational Technology Research and Development*, Vol. 58, No. 1, pp. 19–37.

OPPORTUNITIES AND CHALLENGES FOR TEACHING AND LEARNING INNOVATION IN A GLOBAL PANDEMIC: THE CASE OF THE EPICA ePORTFOLIO SOLUTION

Lourdes Guàrdia, Marcelo Maina, Derek Clougher and Federica Mancini
Universitat Oberta de Catalunya, Spain

ABSTRACT

The impact of the COVID-19 pandemic is undeniable in terms of how it has changed the way we live and learn. A direct area affected by the consequences of the pandemic includes how to consistently deliver high quality level education in higher education institutions when faced by these and other similar taxing situations. Pedagogical innovation and technology provide a potential response to these challenges through the use of new and innovative educational tools. The ePortfolio solution, designed under the EPICA project, aimed at bridging the gap between higher education institutions and the workplace by helping students to showcase their employability skills is a core example of pedagogical innovation. Although the implementation of the solution was severely affected by the unprecedented arrival of the pandemic, successful adaptive measures were taken to ensure that it could respond to the demands to move to online learning. Said adaptations meant that despite a reduction in initial participation numbers, engagement with the ePortfolio remained satisfactory. Results demonstrating this success are presented. Opportunities and challenges are discussed in relation to the use of the ePortfolio.

KEYWORDS

Higher Education Technology, ePortfolio, Pedagogical Innovation, COVID-19 Pandemic

1. INTRODUCTION

The global COVID-19 pandemic has greatly impacted higher education, generating debate about the methods of education and their efficacy in response to the challenges. In these unprecedented times questions regarding universities' capacity to continue providing high-quality education have emerged (Bates, 2020). The effectiveness of 'emergency remote education' (Bozkurt et al., 2020) has received mixed reviews in terms of course design, development and delivery. The aforementioned difficulties are primarily related to the fact that the usual planning time was cut short by the rapid arrival of the pandemic (O'Keefe et al., 2020), and the issue that many teachers had no/little experience in an online environment (Johnson et al., 2020a). To respond to these issues, pedagogical innovation (PI) and technology can be used as they "solve problems higher education is facing today" (Henderikx & Jansen, 2018; p. 3).

A prime example that PI can be successfully fostered is through the development of new educational tools (OCDE, 2016) that support a shift from traditional educational paradigms to emerging pedagogical approaches that are often learner-centred and constructive processes (Licht et al., 2017). EPICA, the H2020 project presented in this article, was based on this approach in its use of an ePortfolio solution in both a European and African context across three areas of impact which included the transition between higher education and the workplace, the use of micro-credentials for employability and the articulation of employability skills for prospective employers. The overarching aim of this solution was to bridge the gap between higher education institutions and the workplace using ePortfolios as a transitional tool. Specifically, EPICA identified: a new methodology for employability skills assessment and micro-credentialization to make employability skills visible to prospective employers.

The project was affected by the current COVID-19 circumstances. The aim of this paper is to present the solution developed at the UOC, with a specific focus on the changes made during the pilot study in which it was implemented to adapt to the unprecedented situation generated by the pandemic. We propose that the ePortfolio, and the methodology enhancing its use, are a robust solution that can be used in response to the demands to move F2F activities online, enhance remote support to students, simplify the workflow and use new communication channels. Therefore, the EPICA ePortfolio represents an opportunity to ensure that high quality education remains in the face of the challenges which forced higher education institutions to adapt to the emergency with limited resources.

2. EPICA ePORTFOLIO SOLUTION

This section describes a solution including a competency-based ePortfolio designed under the EPICA project and a specific methodology, with a focus on how it was adapted and successfully implemented during the COVID-19 pandemic in four of the partner universities: Maseno University (Kenya), Makerere University (Uganda), Open University of Tanzania (Tanzania) and Open University of Catalonia (Spain). Firstly, the format and composition of the ePortfolio are described. Then, the changes for its use in the pandemic are outlined.

2.1 Design of the Solution

The EPICA competency-based ePortfolio was designed to embed employability skills into the curriculum as a core aspect of learning, and was implemented as a reflective, professional and transitional tool to encourage the showcasing of graduates' employability skills.

The specific methodology designed under the project took inspiration from the following successful initiatives: (1) Deakin University's Professional Practice Credentials, (2) University of Waterloo's UWaterloo curriculum vitae project, WatCV, (3) VALUE rubrics by the Association of American Colleges and Universities (AACU) and (4) the Comprehensive Learner Record from the American Association of Collegiate Registrars and Admissions Officers (AACRAO). Their influence in the project provided a multi-perspective overview of how graduate skills are approached and understood, and allowed EPICA to create a unique methodology combining the strengths of the aforementioned initiatives, adapted to the context of the present research. The solution envisaged a multi-collaborative approach and a double articulation design which involved both academic assessment (Articulation 1) and employer appraisal (Articulation 2) of students preparing to graduate. This approach in the use of the ePortfolio was implemented and tested during the pilot study at the four participating universities between February and July 2020. It is important to note that the solution was designed to be implemented in universities that used blended and/or online learning delivery mode with three of the four universities that participated in the pilot adopting it to their blended mode. However, the COVID-19 pandemic forced all participating institutions to adapt to fully online mode in all activities causing challenges for the overall process of the solution implementation.

2.2 Implementation's Planned Procedure

Prior to the emergency situation the following procedure, presented in Table 1, was planned to implement the solution.

Table 1. Planned procedure for implementation

Stage	Procedure
1	1. Local coordinators introduce list of skills to be implemented at institution 2. Lecturers participate in self-training on Moodle 3. Lecturers create and design assignment activities in ePortfolio 4. Assessment rubrics uploaded to ePortfolio

2	1. Pilot launch 2. Intervention 1: Lecturers introduce study aims/activities to students 3. Students access ePortfolio, check assigned activities and download assessment rubric
3	1. Students participate in micro-credential process e.g. provide evidence for curricular, co-curricular, extracurricular and professional experiences to demonstrate each skill they showcase in their ePortfolio for an academic environment (Articulation 1). Articulation approach was based on the Catalyst Framework on High Impact ePortfolio Practice (Eynon & Gambino, 2017), which encouraged them to inquire, reflect and integrate each of their selected evidence presented in the ePortfolio. 2. Lecturers provide formative feedback via optional Intervention 2 3. Lecturers assess submissions and provide personalised feedback via the ePortfolio, including action points for students to improve their work 4. Final student submission includes reflective narrative to help students purposefully link their coursework and other academic, co-curricular and extracurricular activities with their chosen skills. 5. Lectures use rubric to evaluate each submission and any students who successfully demonstrate their showcased skill receive a micro-credential on their ePortfolio in the form of a digital badge
4	1. Successful students from initial phase invited to customize their ePortfolio for the workplace (Articulation 2) 2. Lecturers offer third intervention to introduce the STAR method of interviewing and articulation of skills for the workplace 3. Students provide another evidence for an employability skill in the ePortfolio given that the showcased skill/s is/are relevant to the workplace. This submission is aimed at employers and students include a video testimonial directed at said employers to explain their evidence. 3. Employers partake in following steps: (1) review the video testimony, (2) review all evidence submitted, (3) review the student profile, (4) appraise students by completing appraisal form, (5) provide qualitative feedback, and (6) write, if they saw fit, a commendation for those students who showed outstanding potential in the public message space of the ePortfolio, thus concluding the process.

2.3 Materials

Different generic support materials were elaborated (see: EPICA Employability Skills Kit, 2020) to guide participants in the step-by-step micro-credential process. Each resource was followed and/or adapted to each context accordingly. To allow for this, all materials were provided in editable format so that they could be readapted if and as necessary according to the pedagogical and organisational needs. For example, handbooks were provided for lecturers, students and employers containing information about the conceptual framework of the pilot's methodology. Simulations in the form of screenshots were also included to illustrate the way to perform the workflow within the EPICA ePortfolio and ePortfolio tutorials highlighting its features, modules and components. Importantly, the materials designed to assist and guide the participants also included two assessment instruments. The first, for lecturers, was the employability skills rubrics. This was used to assess the students' showcased skills. It was provided in .xlsx format and included the employability skills from the Skill Up Project - Good Practices in Connecting Workplace and Learning in Higher Education (Ornellas et al., 2019). The second was the student's appraisal scale, also provided in .xlsx format, which was designed to be completed by the employer(s) in order to appraise whether the student had successfully demonstrated their employability skill(s) as well as their professional persona.

3. ADAPTATIONS DUE TO THE COVID-19 PANDEMIC

The spread of the COVID-19 virus led to the closure of universities globally and was reflected in a large number of dropouts of the participating students leading to the need to adapt the implementation procedure. Connectivity difficulties were encountered for those students who continued in the project when they were forced to work from home, especially in some areas of Africa where internet in private homes represents a challenge. Therefore, given the issues that the pandemic presented for the project, the original pilot implementation underwent significant changes in order to provide a suitable response to the new situation while aiming to reach the project aims. It was particularly important to apply an attitude of understanding toward students' engagement given the difficulties they were faced with. As such, the implementation of the solution had to be scaled down to a reduced number of students. To provide further insight into the actions taken to address the challenges the specific reorganization of the study at each university is presented in Table 2.

Table 2. Reorganization of work for each university to adjust to COVID-19

University	Adaptation measures implemented
Makerere	1. Blended courses moved to fully online delivery mode 2. All meetings/communication held via Zoom, emails and WhatsApp. 3. Teachers motivated students to participate via continuous and targeted messages/support.
Maseno	1. Blended courses were moved to fully online delivery mode 2. Students contacted via SMS and Whatsapp, with one lecturer physically visiting a student. 3. Extra internet data provided to students to facilitate their work from home.
OUT	1. Students motivated to participate by phone/whatsapp/sms follow-up. Also given extended deadlines to submit their work. 2. Lecturers/students provided with extra internet data from the project to facilitate ePortfolio completion 3. F2F orientation day for employers led via Zoom
UOC	1. Students offered to participate voluntarily in the pilot (previously mandatory) and numbers decreased. Second round of pilot using another group organized in response. 2. Lecturer involvement maximised. Students received continuous and targeted attention to foster participation and minimise further dropouts.

4. RESULTS

As aforementioned, the high dropout rate due to the challenges caused by the COVID-19 pandemic meant that many adaptations had to be made in an effort to ensure sufficient participation. Despite the reduced participation, the pilot study was performed with a sample of 248 participants across the four aforementioned universities demonstrating that although the pandemic presented challenges, the ePortfolio was successfully implemented. The breakdown of participants per profile is provided in Table 3.

Table 3. Breakdown of participant per profile

	Employer(s)	Lecturers	Local Coordinator(s)	Students
Total	31	16	4	197

The ePortfolio engagement enabled students to showcase a set of generic skills to employers in their desired sector, which in turn provided them with a useful appraisal in terms of their professional development. Results are presented in Table 4.

Table 4. Employability skills presented and articulated per institution

	Makerere	Maseno	OUT	UOC	Total
Communication and interpersonal skills	16	82	41	20	159
Creative thinking skills	22	98	41	15	176
Digital skills	0	0	40	13	53
Problem-solving	0	68	40	8	116
Teamwork	16	62	0	0	78

The EPICA solution has been used to generate pedagogical innovation in higher education institutions during the global COVID-19 pandemic as it is a flexible and adaptable tool when used in online environments providing many opportunities for educators and education administrators alike. Of equal importance to note are the challenges that arose from the solution. Below, both the opportunities and challenges are discussed as a point of final reflection.

5. OPPORTUNITIES & CHALLENGES

One of the most important opportunities that the EPICA ePortfolio solution provided was the fact that it acts as an innovative pedagogical solution to reduce the skills gap in the demand and supply of skills even during a global pandemic. Despite the aforementioned challenges that arose and complicated the implementation of the solution, a successful pilot study was conducted. Therefore, the ePortfolio could be seen as a flexible, adaptable and scalable innovative solution that can be implemented in situations that generate limitations similar to those witnessed by COVID-19 and this pedagogical innovative solution could be seen as forming part of other technological advances that offer the chance to solve the challenges that higher education faces (Henderikx & Jansen, 2018).

Challenges were also observed. For example, many of the teachers felt that they experienced difficulties with digital competence and thus needed extra support throughout the implementation of the ePortfolio. This was amplified by the fact that all the training needed for the teaching staff to effectively carry out the study protocol, as well as the need for extra support, had to be rethought and optimised for the online environment while remaining scalable enough to accommodate the high volume of users. In a pandemic situation, reliant on emergency remote education, the lack of these skills impacts negatively. In fact, the absence of digital fluency and a positive experimental attitude towards technology for learning may present a challenge in regards to the future effective adoption of the solution. In both the European (Cruz-Jesus et al., 2016) and the African context (ITU, 2017) the aforementioned constraints could further contribute to the already evident digital divide. Moreover, connectivity problems could further hinder the opportunities that the solution has to offer as poor internet connection prevented students from engaging with the ePortfolio within the initially planned time frame. Consequently, efforts to make broadband more accessible and affordable are needed in order to foster the development of digital skills so that the EPICA solution can be adopted as an innovative pedagogical method that can be successfully delivered by higher education institutions.

REFERENCES

AACRAO, 2019. *Comprehensive Learner Records (CLRs)*. https://www.aacrao.org/signature-initiatives/comprehensive-learner-record

Association of American Colleges and Universities (AAC&U), 2009. *Inquiry and analysis VALUE rubric.* https://www.aacu.org/value/rubrics/inquiry-analysis

Bates, T, 2020 April 1. *Advice to those about to teach online because of the coronavirus*. Tony Bates. https://tinyurl.com/y8s2wpv2

Cruz-Jesus, F. et al, 2016. The education-related digital divide: An analysis for the EU-28. *Computers in Human Behavior*, *56*, 72-82. https://doi.org/10.1016/j.chb.2015.11.027

Deakin University, n.d.. *Professional Practice credentials.* Retrieved from https://www.deakin.edu.au/credentials

EPICA, 2020. *EPICA Employability Skills Kit*. https://www.epica-initiative.com/employability_skills_kit.php

Henderikx, P., & Jansen, D, 2018. *The changing pedagogical landscape: In search of patterns in policies and practices of new modes of teaching and learning*. EADTU. https://tinyurl.com/CPLreport2018

International Telecommunication Union, 2017. Measuring the Information Society Report 2017. *International Telecommunication Union.* http://www.itu.int/en/ITU-D/Statistics/Documents/facts/ICTFacts-Figures2017.pdf.

Licht, A.H et al, 2017. *Open Book of Educational Innovation.* European Schoolnet, Brussels.

OECD, 2016. *Innovating Education and Educating for Innovation: The Power of Digital Technologies and Skills*. OECD Publishing, Paris.

Ornellas, A et al, 2019. Enhancing graduates' employability skills through authentic learning approaches. *Higher Education, Skills and Work-Based Learning, 9*(1), 107–120. https://doi.org/10.1108/heswbl-04-2018-0049

University of Waterloo, n.d. *Bridging the Articulation of Skills Gap through WatCV: Career and Competency ePortfolios.* https://uwaterloo.ca/centre-for-teaching-excellence/bridging-articulation-skills-gap-through-watcv-career-and

PIANO STUDENTS' PERSPECTIVES AND EXPERIENCES WITH REMOTE PIANO INSTRUCTION

Gwendolyn C. Jefferson
Ed.D.,
Bowie State University, 14000 Jericho Road, Bowie, MD USA 20715

ABSTRACT

This qualitative phenomenological study explored student perspectives and experiences with remote piano instruction during COVID-19. Ten participating students responded to 13 original, vetted questions via phone/video conferencing or Google form, an online application for uploading responses to questions. The findings indicated that the students believed they benefitted from continuing their piano instruction via remote piano instruction. Research findings also revealed the students had to manage and cope with audio/video technological interruptions and socio-emotional issues associated with remote piano instruction. The research findings further indicated the students' use of their preferred virtual communication application to interact, see, hear, and maintain their established teacher/student relationship helped offset the problems associated with remote piano instruction. All ten students felt that they have continued to progress with their piano performance and music reading skills via remote piano instruction. The findings would benefit and encourage piano instructors, researchers, and technology developers to conduct more research, both qualitative and quantitative, to determine the best measures for improving students' and teachers' experiences with remote piano instruction.

KEYWORDS

Remote Piano Instruction, Virtual Communication, Webcam, Audio/Video Apps, Piano Students' Perspectives

1. INTRODUCTION

Before March 2020, the researcher for this study was providing traditional, private (individual and group) in-person piano lessons to students. The students were making good progress with their piano performance and music reading skills due to their consistent lessons and practice schedules. The students had previously performed in annual piano recitals and had always worked hard to master specially selected piano solos for these recitals. However, the coronavirus pandemic (COVID-19) and the resulting lockdown and social distancing requirements caused the students' piano lessons to come to a screeching halt in March 2020. Some students wanted to continue their piano instruction; thus, remote piano instruction became a viable alternative to the traditional, private in-person piano instruction. Remote piano instruction enabled interested piano students an opportunity to interface with their piano instructor via virtual modes of communication to not only keep up their music reading and piano performance skills but also to maintain their established teacher/student relationship.

Remote piano instruction is a type of online piano instruction that has been effectively implemented by piano instructors during private and group piano lessons (Dumlavwalla, 2017). Remote piano instruction involves the following: the piano teacher provides the lessons from a distance whereby the piano instructor is not physically sitting beside or in the physical presence of the students (Comeau, et al., 2019). The piano instructor and the piano students use technological devices such as laptops, desktops, iPads, Chromebooks, and smartphones with audio/video applications (apps), microphones, speakers, and webcam capabilities (Dumlavwalla, 2017). These technological devices enable the piano instructor and piano students to see, hear, and communicate with each other similar to how interactions occur during traditional, in-person piano instruction (Pike & Shoemaker, 2015).

Due to Covid-19, piano instructors have had to alter their mode of piano instruction to include technology to teach online (McAlister, 2020). The online teaching can include remote instruction and virtual instruction (Kim, 2016). Remote instruction requires the piano instructor to use technology to see, hear, and interact with piano students during the piano lessons; virtual instruction involves piano students accessing software programs that teach piano performance and music reading skills (Kim, 2016).

According to Wachter (2017), the use of piano instruction software programs can often be attractive to some piano students since these software programs are usually free and available on YouTube Piano Tutorials. This online instruction allows students to experiment with learning to play piano for personal fulfillment (Wachter, 2017). Also, online piano instruction can be attractive to some piano students since online piano instruction connects students with their familiarity and use of technology (Jutras, 2014). Although online piano instruction can be an attractive venture for some students, Wachter (2017) indicates that online piano instruction cannot compete with the teacher/student interactions of private and group piano instruction. Pike and Shoemaker (2015) reveal that since the teacher and student can see, hear, and interact with each other during remote piano instruction, this type of online piano instruction continues to foster viable teacher/student relationships. Thus, remote piano instruction helps piano instructors use technology while promoting teacher/student interactions and relationships.

Pike and Shoemaker (2015) further indicate that remote piano teachers can continue using traditional materials of instruction such as leveled piano instruction books. Many of these piano instruction books include classic piano pieces in levels and forms that stimulate students' piano performance and increase the students' gratification with playing the piano (Story, 2011). Due to the variety of leveled piano instruction books on the market, piano teachers can select books that best address their students' abilities and interest in playing the piano (Bakkum, 2010).

Remote piano instruction also involves eliminating distance and travel associated with piano instruction. Campbell (2004) indicates that remote piano instruction can be a viable option when traditional in-person piano instruction presents obstacles due to distance and time constraints. Campbell further reveals that remote piano instruction enables the piano student to continue their piano instruction remotely from a piano instructor of their preference from a distant location. Thus, remote piano instruction enables students to keep up their piano performance and reading skills despite distance restrictions, such as with COVID-19.

Since the advent of COVID-19, the researcher/piano teacher implemented remote piano instruction as an alternative to traditional in-person piano instruction. Three phases occurred with the lesson activities: phase one – before the lesson, phase two – during the lesson, and phase three – after the lesson.

Phase one: The piano instructor engaged in the following: (a) collaboration with students and their parents to identify the technological device and virtual communication application with audio/video capabilities to be used, (b) purchase and use of same music books assigned to students during instruction, and (c) positioning of the piano instructor and student technological devices and keyboard/piano at the beginning of each lesson to enable teacher and student to see each other's face, fingers on the piano keys, books, and seating position. These preliminary steps, corroborated by Pike and Shoemaker (2015), promote productive remote piano lessons.

Phase two: The piano instructor engaged the students as follows: (a) performing scales and technical studies, (b) sight-reading and identifying musical notation, (c) counting/clapping note values and rhythms of piano pieces, (d) practicing and performing piano pieces in their music books, (e) questions/answers and discourse between teacher and students about musical notation, musical terms, and history of composers of the musical compositions, and (f) assessing the performance of students' assigned piano pieces. According to Hyry-Beihammer (2010), teacher/student interactions and discourse about musical notation, musical terms, piano performance, and music history, associated with the narrative approach to piano instruction, enhance students' musical knowledge and performance skills.

Phase three: The piano instructor engaged in the following: (a) assigning students scales/technical studies and piano pieces to practice between piano lessons, (b) receiving verbal feedback from the students about their experience with remote piano instruction, and (c) providing feedback to the virtual communication platform about technical experiences with the piano instruction. Dumlavwalla (2017) indicates that these efforts enhance self-efficacy, musical knowledge, and piano performance.

While remote piano instruction can be a viable alternative to traditional piano instruction, the researcher/piano teacher observed various problems and obstacles the students encountered with remote piano instruction. To address the problem of how piano students were adjusting to remote piano instruction during COVID-19, the researcher/piano teacher conducted a qualitative phenomenological research study to gather and analyze data based on the perceptions and lived experiences of the students with remote piano instruction. The purpose of the study was to determine how are piano students faring with receiving private piano remote instruction from their piano teacher via virtual modes of communication. The question for this study was: How do piano students manage and cope with remote piano instruction in their efforts to continue learning to play the piano despite the social distancing restrictions of the coronavirus pandemic?

2. METHODS

2.1 Research Context and Participation

The researcher, who conducted this qualitative phenomenological study, was also the private piano instructor of the study. The researcher/piano instructor is currently certified in music education, early childhood education, special education, and administration/ supervision/educational leadership.

The research study occurred on the East Coast of the United States via virtual modes of communication due to the social distancing restrictions of the coronavirus pandemic. The study participants included ten private piano students who chose to continue their piano instruction via remote piano instruction. The students' ages ranged from ages 7 to 62 and included only one adult piano student. The students were identified as Student A, B, C, D, E, F, G. H, I, and J to maintain their anonymity for this study.

The researcher used the qualitative phenomenological research design to explore the piano students' perspectives and life experiences with remote piano instruction. The students' responses to 13 original research questions, created by the researcher, revealed the phenomenon of how the researcher's piano students were managing and coping with remote piano instruction amid COVID-19. The 13 original questions were validated (vetted) by expert professionals certified in music education and licensed to practice school social work. The researcher consulted these expert professionals throughout the research to provide credibility to the study.

2.2 Methods Used for Data Collection and Analysis

The researcher used qualitative methods to collect and analyze data.

Due to the social distancing restrictions of COVID-19, the researcher used virtual modes of communication to collect data from the students. The researcher presented the 13 original, vetted questions to students aged 11 to 62 via an online Google form with the uploaded questions. The students were required to respond to the questions and submit their responses to the Google form platform. For the younger students aged 7 (grade 1) and 8 (grade 2), who were not able to respond to the questions on the Google Form, the researcher video conferenced or phone conferenced with the students and recorded the students' verbatim responses on the Google form. The researcher recorded their responses in a verbatim format to ensure that the younger students' actual words were a part of the evidence collected. The older students' verbatim responses also were included in the evidence. Therefore, the students' responses have some grammatical errors. To provide credibility to the study and eliminate researcher bias, the researcher did not change or correct any of the students' grammatical errors.

After collecting the data, the researcher analyzed the data using codes to categorize the data. The codes became the basis for the triangulation of the data. The triangulation of the data was conducted to determine similarities and differences among the data derived from the students' responses to the 13 questions. The triangulation of the data led to the emerging themes or major ideas that substantiated the research findings.

3. DATA ANALYSIS AND FINDINGS

3.1 Research Questions and Responses

All of the students' verbatim responses are provided below:

Research Question 1: *What is your grade level or highest level of education?*

Student A: Grade 1, Student B: Master's Degree, Student C: Grade 12, Student D: Grade 2, Student E: Grade

2, Student F: Grade 6, Student G: Grade 7, Student H: Grade 6, Student I: Grade 11, and Student J: Grade 9

Research Question 2: *How old are you?*

Student A: 7 years old, Student B: 62 years old, Student C: 17 years old, Student D: 8 years old, Student E: 8 years old, Student F: 11 years old, Student G: 12 years old, Student H: 11 years old, Student I: 17 years old, and Student J: 14 years old

Research Question 3: *What music book are you currently using for piano lessons?*

Student A – Michael Aaron Primer, Student B – Alfred's Basic Adult Piano Course, Student C – Michael Aaron book 3, Student D- Michael Aaron book level 1, Student E – Piano Adventures level 1, Student F – I am currently using the Michael Aaron Piano Course Lessons Grade 2 book, Student G- Michael Aaron Piano

Course Lessons Grade 2 book, Student H- Michael Aaron Grade 2 book, Student I -John Thompson Modern Course for the Piano Second Grade book, and Student J-Michael Aaron Piano Course Lessons Grade 3 book.

Research Question 4: *Explain why learning to play the piano is important to you.*

Student A: Because I love piano!

Student B: I've always admired piano players. Played cello during my primary education. Wanted to learn something new, to enhance brain function.

Student C: Learning to play the piano is important to me because it's something I've been doing for majority of my life and it's a part of me now. I can't imagine not playing the piano.

Student D: Because I like music.

Student E: Because I like to play music. I like how the piano sounds. I want to play piano.

Student F: Playing the piano is important to me because when my grandparents used to have a piano, I would pretend to play on it whenever I went over there. By pretending to play I mean banging on random keys. My parents thought it would be a good idea to sign me up for piano lessons so that I could actually learn how to play properly. So, they signed me up and I have gotten pretty good at it. I enjoy learning new pieces and playing them for my family. Piano lessons have improved my patience because sometimes I do not learn a piece in one day and I have to keep trying until I get it completely right. It is also a good skill to learn for the future because it could help me get a part-time job at a church or teaching piano if I take it seriously. It can also count as a useful skill to help me get into college or a music program at school.

Student G: It's important to me because I like to play to calm down and I like to use my fingers and fiddle with them so it helps with that too.

Student H: Playing piano is important to me because I always wanted to play and learn a new musical skill that I haven't learnt before.

Student I: Learning to play piano is important to me because it's a fun hobby.

Student J: Learning piano is important to me because it is a fun and useful skill to have that I can use in the future.

Research Question 5: *Why did you choose to have your piano instructor to provide you with remote piano instruction?*

Student A: Because I like my piano teacher

Student B: Convenience.

Student C: I wanted to continue my lessons despite the fact that they would be online because there is no end date to this pandemic and I didn't want to wait it out. I want to continue to improve my skills and what I know regardless of if I am able to see my teacher in-person or not.

Student D: Because of coronavirus.

Student E: Because the iPad is fun. So, it is easy to touch things on the tablet iPad.

Student F: I chose to have my piano instructor provide me with remote piano instruction because she recommended it to my parents after not being able to meet with her in person anymore due to COVID19. I was tired of playing the same songs repeatedly while waiting for the pandemic to end and wanted to learn fresh, new songs to play.

Student G: Because I didn't want to fall behind in learning piano.

Student H: Due to COVID-19, we have to practice social distancing and stay indoors so that we can stay safe during this time and I chose to have my piano instructor to help me with remote piano instruction because it's easier to hear my piano instructor play and show me the examples so I can improve my piano skills.

Student I: I chose to have my piano instructor provide me with remote piano instruction so that I can continue to develop my piano skills.

Student J: Because I want to keep up with my piano skills and learn new material.

Research Question 6: *What virtual communication mode are you using for your remote piano instruction?*
Student A: WhatsApp, Student B: Google Duo, Student C: WhatsApp, Student D: Google Duo, Student E: Google Duo, Student F: Zoom, Student G: Zoom, Student H: Google Duo, Student I: Zoom, and Student J: Zoom

Research Question 7: *Why did you choose this particular virtual mode of communication?*
Student A: My mommy's phone has WhatsApp.
Student B: It is what my instructor uses and it is a free application on my device.
Student C: It seemed easiest to do and so far has worked really well.
Student D: I didn't choose. Mommy chose.
Student E: Because Zoom sometimes freezes and Google Duo works better and does not freeze so much.
Student F: I chose Zoom because that is what I also use for virtual learning online for school.
Student G: It was easier for me.
Student H: I chose to do this type of virtual mode so that it can be easy since you can call and communicate through a video call.
Student I: Zoom is the easiest to navigate in my personal opinion.
Student J: My teacher and I both know how to use it.

Research Question 8: *What do you do during and after your remote piano lessons to improve your music reading skills and piano playing?*

Student A: Practice and listen to my teacher.

Student B: Practice, practice, practice.

Student C: I make sure to pay attention and I take notes during my lesson so I can know exactly what to practice and how to practice. I also make sure to practice everyday along with practicing my entire repertoire.

Student D: I practice. I listen.

Student E: I never give up. I try harder to get the notes, music, and counting right. I count and sometimes I use the metronome for steady counting. I practice my piano pieces and count.

Student F: I practice my piano at least 30 minutes daily to improve my piano playing and music reading skills.

I also pay attention to my teacher during lessons when she corrects me if I play a wrong note so I can fix my mistake.

Student G: I practice.

Student H: After I am done with my remote piano lessons, I always practice every evening so that it would be easy for me to move on to the next song.

Student I: I practice my music pieces in the book and learn other piano pieces from YouTube videos.

Student J: During the lesson I start by playing scales then we move into the piece we were last working on in my book. If I'm learning a new piece my teacher has me read and play the notes at first glance, we go section by section. Afterwards I practice the section/sections I'm supposed to so next lesson we can move on or I can play it with no mistakes for a grade.

Research Question 9: How does your piano teacher help you with improving your music reading skills and piano playing during remote piano instruction?

Student A: When I play a wrong note and key, my piano teacher helps me to play the right note and key. My piano

teacher can see my piano when I play and that helps me.

Student B: She takes incremental steps to learning, reducing the lesson from overwhelming to attainable.

Student C: My piano teacher always answers my questions I have and makes sure that any confusion on mypart is cleared up before my lesson is over.

Student D: She helps me to practice my piano pieces and she gives me corrections.

Student E: My teacher tells me to count steady and look at the grand staff to figure out the letter name of notes.

I ask questions about the treble and bass clef to help figure out the letter name of notes. If I'm wrong, she tells me the correct letter name of the note and key. She tells me to look at the clefs.

Student F: She helps me read the notes if I need help and corrects me if I accidentally play the wrong notes and/or I can't figure out what I did incorrectly.

Student G: She tells me to slow down and to read over what I am about to play.

Student H: My piano teacher helps me to improve my music and reading skills by doing my scales so that if I am doing a new song, I can know where to put my hands in the position.

Student I: My piano teacher helps me improve my music reading skills and piano playing by having me review my chords and make sure that I'm playing the correct notes in every piece of music.

Student J: If I make a mistake with a note or play the wrong chord, she'll correct me and if I don't understand why she'll explain.

Research Question 10: *Do you think remote piano instruction is helping you to keep up your piano playing skills? Why or why not?*

Student A: Yes, my piano teacher sees me through the camera. I think I'm getting better because I'm learning new things.

Student B: Absolutely

Student C: I think my remote piano instruction is without a doubt helping me keep up with my piano [playing skills]. Instead of taking a break from the piano because of COVID-19, I have continued to learn and expand my skills.

Student D: Yes, I am keeping up. It does the same thing as when the teacher is here.

Student E: Sometimes it helps because I feel like I'm learning new pieces.

Student F: I think that remote piano instruction is helping me to keep up with my piano playing skills. At the start of the pandemic, I was repeating the same songs over and over again because my parents stopped my lessons because of social distancing rules. This did not help me because eventually I memorized the songs and I wasn't challenging myself and I soon became bored. Remote piano lessons have allowed me to continue to learn new pieces, while keeping safe.

Student G: Yes, because of all the skills that I learn in the Michael Aaron book.

Student H: I think that remote piano lessons is helping me because when there is a group of people who do piano lessons on the same day I do it in-person [group piano], there is a lot of noise that doesn't let me hear what I am playing.

Student I: Yes, remote piano instruction is helping me keep up my piano playing skills because it reminds me to set time aside during the week to practices pieces that I'm learning during remote piano lessons.

Student J: Yes, it is helping me keep up my skills because I'm more likely to practice a new piece that I've learned so that I'm ready to play it the next lesson.

Research Question 11: *What do you like about remote piano instruction?*

Student A: I like it because I can still see my teacher.

Student B: Technology allows for the convenience of a home instruction. I don't have to drive anywhere. Comfort of being home. I can have a lesson in my PJs. No worries regarding social distancing.

Student C: I like that I am able to sleep in and no longer have to have so much of my Saturday taken up from my mom driving there and back home from my lesson.

Student D: I like that it does the same thing as when the teacher is at my home.

Student E: I like that I get to draw happy faces on the book to show that I played the piano piece correctly.

Student F: I like that I can finally continue to learn new and exciting piano pieces again instead of playing the same songs repeatedly. I like that we have the option to use technology since we cannot have instructions in person because of the virus. If we couldn't meet remotely, I would have had to stop taking lessons until it was safe to do so again in person.

Student G: I like how I still get to learn every Saturday.

Student H: I like remote piano instruction because it is easier for me to do things like having a nice area that I can hear myself play.

Student I: I like that remote piano instruction is very convenient and how you don't have to worry about being late or on time due to external factors.

Student J: It helps me keep up my piano skills.

Research Question 12: *What do you dislike about remote piano instruction?*

Student A: I'm not sitting next to my teacher.

Student B: I have no dislikes; this has been a very pleasurable experience.

Student C: Sometimes it's hard to communicate and show my teacher when I'm confused.

Student D: Sometimes it glitches. The tablet sometimes freezes and I can't see the teacher moving and I can't hear the teacher.

Student E: That when the teacher says a letter name of note, I think she is saying another letter. I can't always hear the teacher really well. Freezing – the teacher stops moving and I can't hear her speak. It sometimes sounds scratchy.

Student F: I dislike that sometimes our computers freeze which puts a delay to the lesson. I also do not like the fact that she cannot physically correct me by moving my hands when I make a mistake or am in the wrong position.

Student G: I don't like how my instructor can't physically help me or show me if I play a note wrong.

Student H: The thing I dislike about remote piano instruction is that I am not used to it because I am used to doing piano lessons in person more than online or virtual.

Student I: Sometimes the audio will cut out and sometimes it's hard to tell what note is being played over Zoom.

Student J: Sometimes the piano [sound] cuts out or I can't hear my teacher properly.

Research Question 13: *When the coronavirus pandemic is over, which type of piano instruction would you prefer?*

Student A: traditional in-person piano instruction, Student B: remote piano instruction, Student C: remote piano instruction, Student D: traditional in-person piano instruction, Student E: traditional in-person piano instruction, Student F: traditional in-person piano instruction, Student G: traditional in-person piano instruction, Student H: traditional in-person piano instruction, Student I: traditional in-person piano instruction, and Student J: traditional in-person piano instruction.

3.2 Analysis of the Data

Codes were developed and used to triangulate the data. The data were the students' responses to the research questions. Themes emerged from the triangulation of the data and were the basis for the findings.

Codes were as follows: piano performance/music enjoyment and fulfillment, positive teacher/student relationship, usefulness, user-friendly, virtual communication applications, continuity of instruction, COVID- 19 social distancing restrictions, positive teacher/student interactions, incremental instruction, remote instruction-convenient and safe, piano practice, no dislikes, technical interruptions, behavioral/socio-emotional effects, and enhancement of piano performance skills.

The triangulation of the data indicated that there were some similarities and differences among the students' responses. The similarities involved all ten students believed the following: (a) piano playing is an enjoyable and fulfilling endeavor, (b) their choice and use of a virtual communication device were based on being user friendly, (c) improving piano performance and music reading skills requires personal practice and positive teacher/student interactions/relationship during remote piano instruction, and (d) remote piano instruction is safe and allows continuity of piano instruction despite COVID-19 social distancing restrictions.

The triangulation of data revealed differences among the responses of some of the students to various questions. Student H (age 11) believed that remote piano instruction eliminated distractions and unwanted noise from traditional in-person group piano instruction. Only Student B (age 62) felt no dislike for remote piano instruction, while 6 of the students disliked the freezing of the computer screen and problems with audio. Student A (age 7), Student F (age 11), and Student G (age 12) disliked the inability of the teacher to be in their physical presence during remote piano instruction. Student H (age 11) disliked remote piano because she is just not used to this form of instruction. Four students viewed piano instruction as a useful venture as follows: (a) Student B (age 62) helps with brain function, (b) Student G (age 12) calms her and enables the fiddling of her fingers productively, and (c) Student F (age 11) and Student J (age 14) is a useful skill to have in the future. Finally, only 2 students indicated that they would prefer remote piano instruction once COVID-19 is over, while the other 8 students indicated that they wanted to resume traditional in-person piano instruction.

The themes that emerged from the coding and triangulation of the data were: Remote Piano Instruction during COVID-19 involves: (a) Opportunities for Continuous Piano Instruction (b) Fosters Continuity of Positive Teacher/Student Interactions and Relationships (c) Managing and Coping with Using Technology for Piano Instruction; and (d) Opportunities for Continuous Improvement with Piano Performance and Music Reading Skills.

4. DISCUSSION, RECOMMENDATIONS, AND CONCLUSIONS

4.1 Findings

The findings indicated that the student responses provided the evidence to answer the research question: How do piano students manage and cope with remote piano instruction in their efforts to continue learning to play the piano despite the social distancing restrictions of the coronavirus pandemic? The emerging themes provided evidence that focused on what remote piano instruction during COVID-19 involves from the participating piano students' perspectives. The emerging themes are discussed below:

Theme A: Opportunities for Continuous Piano Instruction. The triangulation of the data indicated that all of the students believed that remote piano instruction provided them with the opportunity to continue their piano instruction with their traditional in-person piano teacher and use of leveled music books. All ten students expressed a desire to play the piano. The ten students indicated that remote piano instruction is helping them to continue to learn new piano pieces. The ten students also revealed that remote piano instruction is a viable alternative to traditional in-person piano instruction during the social distancing restrictions posed by COVID-19.

Theme B: Fosters Continuity of Positive Teacher/Student Interactions and Relationships. The triangulation of the data indicated that remote piano instruction enabled the students to continue positive, established interactions and relationships with their piano instructor as a result of the following: (a) being able to still see and hear the teacher, (b)incremental instruction, (c) teacher/student question-answer segments, (d) verbal assistance from the teacher with identifying and playing correct notes and piano keys, and (e) teacher's requirement for students to count, sight-read music, play scales, and play chords. Positive teacher/student interactions and relationships during remote piano instruction have helped to make this a viable alternative to traditional in-person piano instruction.

Theme C: Managing and Coping with Using Technology for Piano Instruction. According to the triangulation of the data, the piano students' use of virtual modes of communication for remote piano instruction presented some obstacles. These obstacles included: (a) freezing of the video, audio, and microphone features, (b) not being able to hear the piano teacher well, and (c) not being in the physical presence of the teacher during instruction. Using a preferred virtual communication mode and continued teacher/student interactions helped students to manage and cope with using technology during remote piano lessons. Only 2 students revealed that they prefer to continue remote piano instruction once COVID-19 is over, while the other 8 students indicated that they prefer to resume traditional in-person piano instruction.

Theme D: Opportunities for Continuous Improvement with Piano Performance and Music Reading Skills. The triangulation of the data indicated that all ten piano students experienced an increase in their piano performance and music reading skills as a result of continuing their piano instruction remotely. Also, all ten students believed that their piano teacher helps them learn new skills and piano selections since they can still see, hear, and interact with their piano teacher during remote piano lessons. According to the students, remote piano instruction has enabled them to continue piano lessons with their piano teacher and progress despite COVID-19.

4.2 Implications, Recommendations for Future Research, and Conclusions

The findings of the study indicated that piano students continued to increase their piano performance and music reading skills via remote piano instruction.

Based on the piano students' perspectives and experiences explored in this study, the findings revealed that the students benefitted from remote piano instruction. However, the findings revealed that the students had to manage and cope with the accompanying technological and socio-emotional issues. The findings also revealed that the students' use of a preferred mode of virtual communication and the opportunity to interact with their piano teacher helped to make remote piano instruction a successful venture. These findings imply that there is a need for piano teachers, researchers, and technology developers to explore viable ways to improve technology and remote piano instruction from students' perspectives. Iwaguchi (2012) corroborates these findings since Iwaguchi indicated that student perspectives of lesson outcomes help improve piano instruction. Future research, both qualitative and quantitative, should be continued to explore and enhance the technological and socio-emotional aspects associated with remote piano instruction. Future research should reflect the perspectives and experiences of piano students.

This qualitative phenomenological research study revealed the perspectives and lived experiences of piano students with remote piano instruction during COVID-19. Continued research, adjustments to piano instruction, and improvements with technology should occur and be based upon student perspectives and lived experiences with remote piano instruction. Using student perspectives and lived experiences, researchers, piano instructors, and technology developers can improve their efforts to eliminate technological interruptions and promote better teacher/student interactions and relationships during remote piano instruction.

REFERENCES

Bakkum, K., 2010. Life Got Easier. *Clavier Companion*, Vol. 2, No. 5, pp. 35-36. Available at: http://search.ebscohost.com.proxy-bs.researchport.umd.edu/login.aspx?direct=true&db=a9h&AN=53957803&scope=site (Accessed: 20 January 2021)

Campbell, C., 2004. Remote Piano Lessons in Real Time. *New York Times,* 11 March, Vol. 153, No. 52785, p. G4. Available at: http://search.ebscohost.com.proxy-bs/researchport.umd.edu/login.aspx?direct=true&db=a9h&AN=12711825&scope=site (Accessed: 8 December 2020)

Comeau, G., Lu, Y. & Swirp, M., 2019. On-site and Distance Piano Teaching. An Analysis of Verbal and Physical Behaviours in a Teacher, Student, and Parent. *Journal of Music, Technology & Education,* Vol. 12, No.1, pp.49-77. https://doi-.proxy-bs.researchport.umd.edu/10.1386/jmte.12.1.49_1

Dumlavwalla, D., 2017. Transitioning from Traditional to Online Piano Lessons: Perceptions of Students, Parents, and Teacher. *MTNA E-Journal,* Vol. 8, No. 3, pp. 2-20.

Hyry-Beihammer, E., 2011. Narratives in Teaching Practices: Matti Raekallio as Narrator in His Piano Lessons. *Music Education Research*, Vol.13, No. 2, pp. 199-209. doi: 10.1080/14613808.2011.577767.

Iwaguchi, S., 2012. From Student Evaluations to Teacher Performance: A Study of Piano Class Instruction. *Music Education Research,* Vol. 14, No.2, pp. 171-185. Available at: https://doi-org.proxy-bs.researchport.umd.edu/10.1080/14613808.2012.685562

Jutras, P., 2014. The Future of Piano Teaching: Changes and Constants. *Clavier Companion*, Vol. 6, No. 6, pp. 16-20. Available at: http://search.ebscohost.com.proxy-bs.researchport.umd.edu/login.aspx?direct=true&db=a9h&AN=9920449&scope=site (Accessed: 20 January 2021)

Kim, J., 2016. Online class piano instruction: Challenges and opportunities. *MTNA E-Journal,* Vol. 8, No. 2, pp. 20-21.

McAlister, A., 2020. Class Piano and COVID-19. *Piano Magazine: Clavier Comparison,* Vol.12, pp. 29-30.

Pike, P. D. & Shoemaker, I., 2015. Online Piano Lessons. *American Music Teacher,* Vol. 65, No. 1, pp. 12-16.

Story, D., 2011. Piano Fun for Adult Beginners: Recreational Music Making for Private or Group Piano Instruction. *American Music Teacher,* Vol. 67, No. 1, p. 56.

Wachter, M., 2017. YouTube Piano Tutorials: The Art of Teaching and Lypur. *Clavier Companion,* Vol. 9, No. 3, pp. 22-24. Available at: http://search.ebscohost.com.proxy-bs.researchport.umd.edu/login.aspx?direct-true&db=a9h&AN=124105931&scope=site (Accessed: 20 January 2021)

AN INITIAL SUSTAINABLE E-LEARNING AND GAMIFICATION FRAMEWORK FOR HIGHER EDUCATION

Aidrina Sofiadin and Muna Azuddin
Faculty of Information and Communication Technology, International Islamic University Malaysia

ABSTRACT

The movements towards achieving sustainable goals among many countries have risen throughout the years. A part of the sustainable goals – the COVID-19 pandemic has forced many universities to move to online learning to sustain students' education. Indeed, e-learning has been delivering through the website since 1960. There is a need to develop new e-learning models that transform education to support sustainable development goals and achieve education's objectives. Interestingly, e-learning needs to integrate gamification context to increase learners' engagement and passion while promoting lifelong learning. To identify the relationship between e-learning and gamification, this paper examined and assessed various e-learning and gamification models and frameworks, specifically in sustainability, to develop an initial sustainable e-learning and gamification framework for higher education. The framework intends to assist higher education institutions in designing a gamified e-learning that promotes better learning engagement, education equity, skill development, social engagement, well-being, and lifelong learning among their learners. Thus, enabling a sustainable education throughout surviving the pandemic.

KEYWORDS

Lifelong Learning, E-learning, Gamification, Sustainable Development, Sustainable Education

1. INTRODUCTION

Since the announcement of the 17 sustainable goals by the United Nations Summit Post (President of United Nations General Assembly 2015), many higher education institutions (HEI) are working towards achieving sustainable development goals, especially in terms of providing eco-friendly campus environments and delivering sustainable education through courses. Also, Covid-19 crisis has impacted HEI to shift to online education as an alternative to resume learners' learning. Higher education institutions play a significant role in promoting e-learning to be an effective platform to deliver education. The decision to shift to online education has forced academicians to develop online learning materials and conduct online classes. However, the use of e-learning unable to sustain learners' participation and engagement. Thus, to survive this pandemic crisis, higher education institutions need to deliver education through e-learning that can increase learners' participation and learning engagement, promote skill development, social engagement, and lifelong learning.

Higher education institutions have invested much money in e-learning development to make it successful in being implemented. Most higher education institutions (HEI) focus on the five trends of e-learning implementation, which are e-learning policy, e-learning governance, Learning Management System (LMS), e-learning training, and e-learning integration into teaching and learning (Al-rahmi, Othman, and Yusuf 2015). HEI also focused on developing knowledge and skills among learners throughout their experience using e-learning. However, learners' participation and engagement using e-learning seemed to be lower than expected. The HEI should aim to provide an online learning initiative that can develop learners' passion for learning, and at the same time to increase learners' participation and engagement.

Gamification has become a technique to transform learning experiences into a game. In contrast, game-based learning refers to games' integration into a learning process to develop specific skills (Scepanovic, zaric, and Matijevic 2015). Game technologies create opportunities for HEI to redesign and innovate their e-learning models that able to sustain learning experiences among learners. Thus, gamification is a potential technique to increase learners' participation and engagement, which HEI should innovate the e-learning models and strategies that could also promote lifelong learning.

2. GAME-BASED LEARNING AND GAMIFICATION

2.1 The Concept of Gamification in E-Learning

The concept of gamification was introduced in 2008, and many studies on gamification in various contexts have been published (edulearning2 2015). Gamification offers rewards, personal achievements, and challenges as ingredients of game success. These ingredients will motivate students learning engagement through e-learning (Smiderle et al. 2020). From the educational perspectives, game-like rule systems, entertainer skills, and characters are used for the development of gamification (Su & Cheng, 2013). Most educational games were developed for primary schools compared to higher education institutions.

2.2 Gamification and Sustainability in Recent Years

There were several studies reported on gamification in higher education (Table 1).

Table 1. Studies on Gamification on Different Sustainability Context

Authors	Year	Sustainability Dimensions			
		Strategies	Education	Consumption	Practice
Lu and Ho	2020	x			
Mahmud et al.	2020		x		
Romero-Rodriguez et al.	2019		x	x	
Mattila	2019	x	x		x
Schiele	2018				x
Chui and Wai	2017				x
Nordby et al.	2016		x		
Polyak	2016		x		
Huber and Hilty	2015			x	
Hamari et al.	2014		x	x	x

The outcomes of the studies reported in Table 1 show that gamification was mostly found to be positive influenced for the learners which the learners showed increased motivation, engagement, and enjoyment in their learning. The inclusion of gamification in e-learning promotes the quality in education that can increase learners' motivation, experience, and engagement and achieve greater learning success (Strmecki et al, 2015).

2.3 Existing Studies on Gamification Framework

In general, gamification is about designing game elements in a non-game context to promote user engagement (Susan, 2015), motivation (Roy & Zaman, 2018), and satisfaction (Urh, Vukovic, Jereb & Pintar, 2015). The key elements in gamification (Dale, 2014) are:

- Game mechanics - describes the use of elements such as points, badges and leader boards that are common to many games.
- Experience design - describes the journey players take with elements such as game play, play space and storyline.
- Gamification - is a method to digitally engage, rather than personally engage, meaning that players interact with computers, smartphones, wearable monitors, or other digital devices rather than engaging with a person.
- The goal of gamification - is to motivate people to change behaviors or develop skills.
- Gamification focuses on enabling players to achieve their goals. When organizational goals are aligned with player goals, the organization achieves its goals because of players achieving their goals.

Palamino et al. (2019) separated the gamification framework in education into two; structural and content framework. Structural elements are focusing on game mechanics and content elements are concentrating on the narrative concept. They found out that narrative characteristics resembled user experience, which is important to influence engagement among learners.

The use of gamification in e-learning also has connection between learners' learning style, achievements, and behaviors (Zaric, Scepanovic, Vujicic, Ljucovic & Davcev; 2017). Gamification in e-learning does have a positive impact on learners' engagement, however, one of the primary concerns with gamification elements is the inability to induce motivation among learners (Hassan, Habiba, Majeed & Shoaib; 2019). Dale (2014) and Sailer and Homner (2019) found the combination of structural elements and social interaction among others were effective in fostering behavioral learning outcomes. The social interaction can be conducted by combining competition with collaboration among other learners, which can motivate the learner to learn.

According to Majuri, Koivisto, and Hamari (2018), they found that behavioral outcomes were comprised of grades, participation in a system, and speed of conducting tasks and assignments. This is in line with the educational context which the aim is to achieve learning objectives that have been set by an organization (Dale, 2014). Figure 1 shows a summary of gamification elements in the e-learning context.

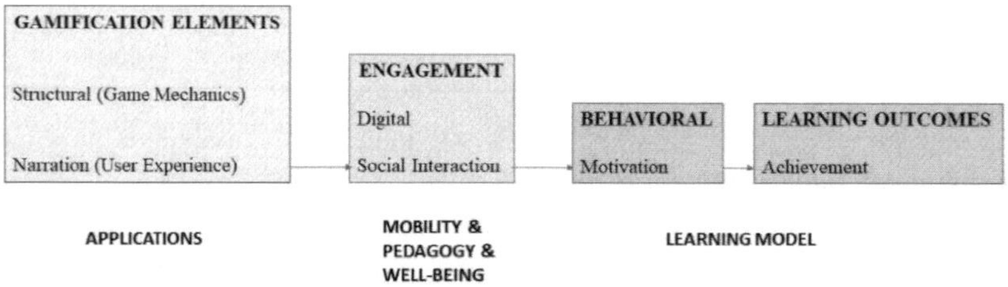

Figure 1. Studies on Gamification on Different Sustainability Context

3. SUSTAINABLE E-LEARNING

Sustainability is defined as a long-term innovation process that benefits the triple bottom line; people, environment, and economy (Foo, 2013). One of the sustainable development goals (SDG) listed by United Nations is Quality Education. In response to the pandemic issues, UNESCO has launched the COVID-19 Global Education Coalition – to ensure learners have access to continuous learning. The Global Education Coalition aims to assist "countries in mobilizing resources and implementing innovative and context-appropriate solutions to provide education remotely, leveraging hi-tech, low-tech and no-tech approaches" (UN.org). This shows that from now onwards, to sustain education is by providing "innovative and context-appropriate solutions" through remote or e-learning platform - for the learners to continue their learning in higher education institution to avoid drop-out.

It is important to define sustainable e-learning since sustainability has a broad meaning in a different context. According to Gunn (2010), sustainability in e-learning is achievable if 1) the e-learning design has been developed and implemented within a course, 2) the e-learning concept, design, system, or resources can be adopted by other development, and 3) the maintenance and improvement of the e-learning concept, design, system, or resources are independent. Sustainable e-learning aims to ensure education quality is maintained while minimizing the cost and environmental impact (Sofiadin, 2013). In 2020, sustainable e-learning is defined as e-learning system that supports the sustainability dimensions while ensuring the learning goals development and sustainable practice (Sofiadin, 2020).

3.1 Existing Sustainable E-Learning Framework

There are various existing e-learning frameworks that focused on e-learning quality, content, implementation, and governance (Georgouli et al., 2008; Yunus and Salim 2008; Chatti et al.2010; Alkhattabi et al.,2010; Sumranwong, 2011; Glancy and Isenberg, 2011; EPSA, 2011; Fang et al. 2012; Ramakrisnan et al. 2012; Hadullo et al. 2017). However, there are a few existing studies on sustainable e-learning framework.

In 2013, a sustainable e-learning framework was developed for higher education institutions in Malaysia (Sofiadin, 2013). The initial framework consists of four main categories that intend to support sustainability. These categories are:

a) Teaching and learning principle: refer to meeting the learner's needs through lifelong learning.
b) Technology: focuses on the technology that will reduce, recycle, and reuse e-learning resources.
c) Application: This is related to the application that will promote mobility and learning personalization.
d) Sustainable development: refers to delivering sustainable education and e-learning environment.

The sustainable e-learning framework will provide a good basis for the study to integrate the gamification approach in higher education, which it should be extended to include gamification dimensions that could promote lifelong learning and sustainable e-learning. The gamification in e-learning platform able to promote engagement among learners to continue learning and at the same time, to avoid drop-out or lessen other issues of conducting learning.

4. METHODOLOGY

Design thinking can be described as a development of artifacts (Simon, 1969) and meanings (Johansson and Woodilla, 2010), this study adopted the design thinking approach. This approach consists of five stages that involve understanding the users, problem-definition and problem-solving, brainstorming new ideas, developing prototypes, and testing (HSG, 2018; Lewrick et al., 2018). Design thinking promotes the innovation of new models that intend to improve and visualize creative processes conducted by multidisciplinary teams (Clemente et al. 2016). Thus, this study started by understanding the users' problems and generate new ideas through literature review. Literature research can be considered as a comprehensive summary of existing literature and could lead to a new framework developed for the specific area of study (Vom Brocke et al., 2009). As a result, this study proposed a framework for sustainable e-learning by adding the gamification aspect to the framework. However, this paper does not conduct the testing phase. The testing phase will provide results that rethinking one or more problems. The proposed framework will be tested and validated by e-learning stakeholders through surveys and online interviews and will be reported in another paper.

5. THE PROPOSED SUSTAINABLE E-LEARNING AND GAMIFICATION FRAMEWORK

Based on the literature review, there are a few criteria (see Table 2) that will assist the researchers in developing the initial sustainable e-learning and gamification framework for higher education. The initial framework (see Figure 2) represents the element in designing the framework, which needs to be focused on transforming education as part of surviving the pandemic. The components of initial sustainable e-learning and gamification framework.

Table 2. Components of Gamification Sustainable E-Learning Framework

Key Element	Components	Description	References
Teaching and Learning Principles	Curriculum	The curriculum is intended to develop knowledge and skills among players through online quizzes, assessments, and learning activities. Play metrics can be captured to differentiate instruction and assessment that can be personalized to a learner. The gamified course curriculum should improve learner's engagement and enjoyment. A Teacher-centred curriculum defines learner ability through technique expertise, understanding of rules, and game participation. Leaner-centered curriculum is where the students will determine what and how it is processed and how it is learned. The curriculum should focus on learning content design to learning experience that is motivating and captivate to learners.	Doyle, 1978; Udosen and Ekpo. 2016

	Pedagogy	Pedagogy approaches include constructive, collaborative, critical thinking, problem-solving, reflective, and inquiry-based learning. Pedagogical knowledge practices such as project-based group work can be used as game-based teaching.	Nousiainen et al. 2018; Hanghøj 2013.; Becker.2009
	Learning Model	Use of the Game Achievement Model that defines the learning objectives for the game and define the storyline that will encompass these objectives. It should promote intrinsic motivation for the learners to play.	Amory and Seagram. 2003
	Sustainable Education	Provide interactive game-based learning that promotes sustainability literacy skills and sustainable practices.	Cheah, Wei, Kee, and Mohamad. 2013; Emblen-Perry. 2018.
Technology	Simulation	Simulation can create students' mental models of complex situations and their strategies in problem-solving.	Gredler 2002
	Virtual reality	Provide a safe environment to experiment with the curriculum concepts. Virtual reality intends to increase learner's satisfaction, enjoyment, creativity, audio, and graphics quality.	Rizzo et al. 2011; Pallavicini et al 2019; Shelstad et al. 2017
	Artificial intelligence	Artificial intelligence (AI) is used for various parts of the game and aspects of nonplayer characters. AI is applied in behavior modeling aspects such as situation analysis, target selection, resource allocation, learning, and simulated perception.	Tozour. 2002; Prakash, et al. 2009
	Mobility	Smartphones offer more practical, easy access, and easy to carry anywhere. Mobile devices allow learners to play mobile game anywhere at any time.	Schmitz et al. 2012; Nuryanti, 2015; Rojas-Mancilla et al. 2019
	Game Engines	Provides a powerful utility that helps in game development such as player interaction, graphics, animation, artificial intelligence, modeling, and networking.	Prakash, et al. 2009
Applications	Points	Points are the rewards collected based on what learners earned during gameplay when they achieve a certain goal.	Byl. 2013; Dale, 2014
	Levels	A game level represents a story chapter, a set of challenges, or a separate subdivision in a game environment. Levels refer to a reward for loyalty where players received gifts, privileges, and benefits.	Deterding, Khaled, Navke, and Dixon. 2011; Byl. 2013
	Badges	Badges can be earned through positive effort that present recognition and status of completed challenges.	Antin and Churchill 2011; Deterding, Khaled, Navke, and Dixon. 2011. Byl. 2013
	Quests	A quest refers to the sub-tasks that need to be completed as part of the ultimate goal of the game.	Byl. 2013
	Social network	The game should be designed for social interaction elements.	Deterding, Khaled, Navke, and Dixon. 2011; Byl. 2013

	Leaderboards	Based on the accumulated points, the game leaderboards will display a list of high scores in a game.	Deterding, Khaled, Navke, and Dixon. 2011; Dale, 2014
Security & ethics	Cheating	Illegal activity that leads to security threats that may impact other players.	Robles et al. 2008
	Well-being	User passion on learning more skills, competition, social interaction, healthy lifestyle and skill development.	Kim and Werbach (2016)
	Social justice and equality	Game design should be intended for both males and females. Also, the game should be designed for players with cognitive disabilities.	Earp et al. (2018)

Table 2 shows that gamification can be applied in all four key elements of the initial framework: Teaching and Learning Principles, Technology, Applications, and Security and ethics. These all four key elements require support not only from the management of higher education but also from the lecturers, learners, and government. The implementation of sustainable e-learning and gamification is the innovative solution that intends to promote education equality among learners, lifelong learning, and lower the drop-out rates.

Table 3. The Key Elements Sustainable Dimensions

Key Element	**Sustainable dimensions (supporting SDGs)**
Teaching and Learning Principles	SDG#4. Quality education- to comprehensive and equitable to quality education
Technology	SDG#4. Quality education- to ensure equitable access to quality education SDG#5. Gender equality – learning games should be designed for both men and women. SDG#9. Foster innovation – transform e-learning to game infrastructure. SDG#10. Reduced inequalities – accessing e-learning through an interactive mobile game.
Applications	SDG#4. Quality education- promote lifelong learning through motivations
Security & ethics	SDG#3. Promote well-being – develop learning passion through interactive learning games.

To become sustainable, the key elements of the framework need to support the sustainable dimensions. In the paper, the key elements aim to support the SDGs (see Table 3). As shown in Table 3, the main SDG for this paper is on quality education. This is to ensure that e-learning provides comprehensive and equitable access to quality education through the gamification approach. Due to the COVID-19 pandemic, many learners have experiencing stress and depression issues due to the lockdown and restricted movement. Therefore, this framework aims to improve learners' well-being by proposing interactive e-learning through gamification, which also intends to support SDG on promoting well-being. Since games were mostly designed for males, it should also be designed for females. Thus, this will support the SDG on gender equality. The SDG on foster innovation can be supported through a transformation of e-learning to game-based learning. Due to a number of learners who afford to own a smartphone than a desktop or a laptop, the idea of gamified e-learning intends to reduce inequalities by offering e-learning access through an interactive mobile game. In conclusion, the initial framework (see Figure 2) shows the elements of designing the sustainable e-learning and gamification framework for higher education.

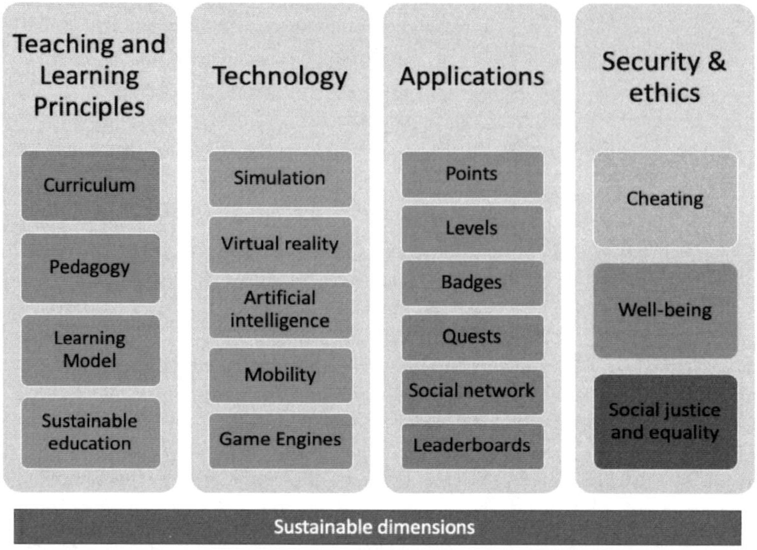

Figure 2. The Proposed Sustainable E-Learning and Gamification Framework

6. CONCLUSION

The paper presents gamification in e-learning platform can increase learners' engagement and motivation during their learning process. The initial sustainable e-learning and gamification framework clarifies that gamification can be implemented in higher education institutions to sustain and provide quality education among learners, especially during the pandemic. In order for gamification to be operationalized in a real education setting, gamification ingredients such as badges, rewards, and personal achievements should be integrated into e-learning to motivate students learning. Thus, the proposed framework intends to provide a guideline and recommendations on how teaching and learning principles, technology, applications, security and ethics can be used to achieve sustainable e-learning through gamification. In addition, the framework intends to support SDGs on promoting well-being, gender equality, innovation, and inequality reduction. Based on the literature review, there is slight or no research on developing an initial sustainable e-learning and gamification framework. The framework should be further tested and validated by conducting the test stage of the design thinking approach to identify more problems that may lead to improvements. In conclusion, this research will develop and evaluate a sustainable e-learning and gamification framework that will transform e-learning for new norms.

REFERENCES

Alkhattabi, M., Neagu, D. and Cullen, A. 2010. Information Quality Framework for e-Learning Systems. Knowledge Management & E-Learning: An International Journal, 2, pp. 340-361.

Amory, A. and Seagram. R. 2003. Educational game models: conceptualization and evaluation. South African Journal of Higher Education Vol.17(2), pp. 206 – 217.

Becker, K. 2009. Video Game Pedagogy: Good Games=good Pedagogy. In Games: Purpose and Potential in Education, edited by Christoper Thomas Miller, pp.73–125. New York: Springer.

Bekker, T., Sturm, J. and Barakova, E. 2010. Designing for social interaction through physical play. Personal and Ubiquitous Computing, Vol. 14(5), pp. 281-283.

Byl, P. 2013. Factors at Play in Tertiary Curriculum Gamification. International Journal of Game-based Learning. Vol. 3(2), pp. 1-21.

Cathy G.2010. Sustainability factors for e-learning initiatives. Journal Research in Learning Technology. Vol.18 (2), 89–103.

Chatti, M. A., Agustiawan, M. R., Jarke, M. and Speeht, M. 2010. Toward a Personal Learning Environment Framework. International Journal of Virtual and Personal Learning Environments, Vol.1, pp. 66-85.

Cheah, W., Wei, T. Z., Kee, B. H., and Mohamad, F. S. 2013. Sustainability education for fun: An interactive mobile learning system. Proceedings of the International Conference on Informatics and Creative Multimedia. Kuala Lumpur, Malaysia.

Clemente, V, Vieira, R and Tschimmel, K. 2016. A learning toolkit to promote creative and critical thinking in product design and development through Design Thinking. In: International Conference of the Portuguese Society for Engineering Education (CISPEE), Vila Real, pp. 1-6.

Dale, S. 2014. Gamification: Making work fun, or making fun of work? Business Information Review, Vol. 31(2), pp. 82–90

Design Thinking at HSG, http://dthsg.com/phases/, last accessed July 2018

Deterding, S., Khaled, R., Nacke, L. E., and Dixon, D. 2011. From Game Design Elements to Gamefulness: Defining Gamification. Proceedings of the 15th International Academic MindTrek., Tampere, Finland., pp.9-15.

Doyle, W. 1978. Paradigms for research on teacher effectiveness, in: L. Shulman (Ed.) Review of research in education, pp.163-198.

Earp, J. Persico, D., Dagnino, F. M., Passarelli, M., Manganello, F., and Pozzi, F. 2018. "Ethical Issues in Gaming: A Literature Review" Proceedings of the 12th European Conference on Games Based Learning. SKEMA Business School. France. Editor: Ciussi, M. pp.54-61.

Edulearning2 .2015. A brief history of gamification: part III – the definitions, online blog: http://edulearning2.blogspot.com/2014/03/a-brief- history-of-gamification-part.html, last accessed July 1, 2015

EmblenPerry, K. 2017. Promoting Education for Sustainability through game-based learning: Using the Sustainable Strategies Game to improve students' knowledge and skills of sustainable business practices. In: Leal Filho W. (eds) Handbook of Sustainability Science and Research. World Sustainability Series. Springer, Cham., pp. 849-866.

EPSA.2012. EPSA Implementation Framework. In: (INTAN), I. T. A. N. (ed.). Malaysia.

Fang, L., Chow, S. H. and Soo, W. M. 2012. Framework for Evaluation Blended Learning in a University Public-Speaking Course in Singapore. Journal IGI Global Snippet.

Foo, K. Y. 2013. A vision on the role of environmental higher education contributing to the sustainable development in Malaysia. Journal of Cleaner Production, pp. 1-7.

Georgouli, K., Skalkidis, I. and Guerreiro, P. 2008. A Framework for Adopting LMS to Introduce e-Learning in a Traditional Course. Journal Educational Technology & Society, Vol (11), pp. 227-240.

Glancy, F. H. & Isenberg, S. K. 2011. A conceptual e-learning framework. European, Mediterranean & Middle Eastern Conference on Information Systems 2011. Athens, Greece.

Gredler, M. E. 2002. Educational Games And Simulations: A Technology In Search Of A (Research) Paradigm.

Hadullo, K., Oboko, R., and Omwenga, E. 2017. A model for evaluating e-learning systems quality in higher education in developing countries. International Journal of Education and Development using Information and Communication Technology (IJEDICT), Vol.13(2), pp. 185-204.

Hanghøj, T. 2013. Game-based teaching: Practices, roles, and pedagogies. In New Pedagogical Approaches in Game-enhanced Learning: Curriculum integration. IGI Global., pp.81-101.

Ho Su, C. and Hsue Cheng, C. 2013. A mobile game-based insect learning system for im- proving the learning achievements. IProcedia-Social and Behavioral Sciences, Vol.103, pp. 42–50.

Johansson, U. and Woodilla, J. 2010. How to avoid throwing the baby out with the bath-water. An ironic perspective on design thinking. European Group for Organization Stud-ies Colloquium, Lisbon, Portugal.

Nousiainen, T., Marjaana, K. Jenni, R. and Mikko, V. 2018 Teacher competencies in game-based pedagogy. Teaching and Teacher Education Vol.74(2018). pp. 85-97.

Nuryanti, F.H.P. 2015. Mobile Game Effectiveness for Game Enthusiasts Who Have Little Spare Time to Play Games. Sisforma. Vol.2(1), pp.10-12.

Pallavicini, F., Pepe, A., and Minissi, M. E. 2019. Gaming in Virtual Reality: What Changes in Terms of Usability, Emotional Response and Sense of Presence Compared to Non-Immersive Video Games? Simulation & Gaming. pp.1-24. Sage publisher.

Palomino, P.D., Toda, A. M., Oliveira W., Cristea, A. I. and Isotani, S. 2019 Narrative for Gamification in Education: Why Should you Care? 2019 IEEE 19th International Conference on Advanced Learning Technologies (ICALT), Brazil, 2019, pp. 97-99, doi: 10.1109/ICALT.2019.00035.

Prakash, E., Brindle, G., Jones, K., Zhou, S., Chaudhari, N. S., and Wong, K. 2009. Advances in Game Technology: Software, Models, and Intelligence. Simulation & Gam-ing. Vol. 40(6), pp.752-801. Sage publisher.

Ramakrisnan, P., Yahya, Y., Hasrol, M. N. H. and Aziz, A. A. 2012. Blended Learning: A Suitable Framework For E- learning in Higher Education. Procedia Social and Behavioral Sciences, Vol.67, pp. 513-526.

Rizzo., A., Lange, B., Sums, E.A., and Bolas, M. 2011. Virtual Reality and Interactive Digital Game Technology: New Tools to Address Obesity and Diabetes. Journal of Diabetes Science and Technology. Vol. 5(2), pp. 257-264.

Robles, R. J., Yeo, S., Moon, Y., Park, G., & Kim, S. 2008. Online Games and Security Issues. Editors: Ahmad, D. & Arce, I. Attack Trends. IEEE Security & Privacy. pp. 76-79. IEEE Computer Society Publisher.

Rojas-Mancilla, E., Conei, D., Bernal, Y.A., Astudillo, D. and Contreras. Y. 2019. Learn-ing Histology Through Game-Based Learning Supported by Mobile Technology. Int. J. Morhol. Vol.37(3), pp.903-907.

Roy, R. V., and Zaman, B.2018. Need-supporting gamification in education: An assessment of motivational effects over time, Computers & Education,Vol.127(2018), pp.283-297.

Sailer, M and Homner, L. 2019. The Gamification of Learning: a Meta-analysis. Educational Psychology Review (2020) Vol, 32, pp.77–112

Sandusky, S. 2015. Gamification in Education. Educational Technology Graduate Pa-pers. The University of Arizona.

Scepanovic, S. zaric, N. and Matijevic, T.2015. Gamification in higher education learn-ing- state of the art - challenges and opportunities. Conference in e-Learning, Serbia.

Schmitz B., Klemke R., and Specht M. 2012. Mobile Gaming Patterns and Their Impact on Learning Outcomes: A Literature Review. Ravenscroft A., Lindstaedt S., Kloos C.D., Hernández-Leo D. (eds) 21st Century Learning for 21st Century Skills. EC-TEL 2012. Lecture Notes in Computer Science, Vol. 7563. Springer, Berlin, Heidelberg.

Shelstad, W.J., Smith, D.C., and Chaparro, B.S. 2017. Gaming on the Rift: Virtual Reality Affects Game User Satisfaction. Proceedings of the Human Factors and Ergonomics Society 2017 Annual Meeting. pp. 2072-2076.

Simon, H.1969. The Sciences of the Artificial, 1st eds, MIT Press, Cambridge, MA.

Smiderle, R., Rigo, S.J., Marques, L.B., Coelho, J.A.P.M., and Jaques, P.A. 2020. The impact of gamification on students' learning, engagement and behavior based on their personality traits. Smart Learning Environment, Vol. 7(3). https://doi.org/10.1186/s40561-019-0098-x

Sofiadin, A. 2020. Defining Sustainable e-learning: A meta-synthesis. Journal of Information Systems and Digital Technologies, Vol.2(2), pp. 72-84.

Sofiadin, A.2013. Development and Evaluation of a Sustainable E-Learning Framework for Higher Education Institutions in Malaysia. International Conference on Sustainability, Technology and Education.

Strmečki, D. Bernik, A. and Radošević, D.2015. Gamification in E-Learning: Introducing Gamified Design Elements into E-Learning Systems. Journal of Computer Sciences, Vol.11(12), pp. 1108-1117.

Sumranwong, D.2011. An eLearning Model Application for AS9100 Standard. 2011 International Conference on Information Management, Innovation Management and In-dustrial Engineering. Shenzhen, China.

Udosen, A.E. and Ekpo, U. S. 2016. Instructional Games: Implications for Curriculum and Instruction. Equatorial Journal of Education and Curriculum Studies. Vol. 1(1), pp. 24-42.

Urh, M., Vukovic, G., Jereb, E., and Pintar, R. 2015. The model for introduction of gamification into e-learning in higher education. Procedia - Social and Behavioral Sciences 197. pp.388 – 397

Brocke, J.V., Simons, A. Niehaves, B., Riemer, K., Plattfaut, R., and Cleven, A. 2019 Reconstructing the Giant: On the Importance of Rigour in Documenting the Literature Search Process. Information systems in a globalising world: Challenges ethics and practices; ECIS 2009 17th European Conference on Information Systems. Italy.

Yunus, Y. and Salim, J.2008. Framework for the Evaluation of E-learning in Malaysian Public Sector from the pedagogical perspective. Information Technology. International Symposium, 2008. Universiti Kebangsaan Malaysia, pp. 1-8.

Zaric, N., Scepanovic, S., Vujicic, T., Ljucovic, J. and Davcev, D. 2017. The Model for Gamification of E-learning in Higher Education Based on Learning Styles. International Conference on ICT Innovations, pp. 265 – 273.

PRE-SERVICE TEACHER TRAINING FOR REALITIES OF 21st CENTURY CLASSROOMS

Osman Sadeck, Moses Moyo, Nyarai Tunjera and Agnes Chigona
Faculty of Education, Cape Peninsula University of Technology, South Africa

ABSTRACT

Pre-service teacher training (PTT), programs are required to emphasise the importance of enhancing the theory practice nexus and on constantly developing a sense of teacher identity and teaching competencies (Liu & Low, 2015) for the 21st Century learners. The 21st Century Curriculum Research Project (21CP) sought to explore how pre-service teachers could be adequately equipped with 21st Century skills for ICT integration. This paper reports on the development and implementation of a technology integration curriculum conducted with pre-service teachers at a university in the Western Cape, South Africa.

The findings of the study have highlighted that a curriculum grounded in a sound theoretical base can yield desired outcomes in f2f/online context. It argues that the theory-practice nexus could be bridged through experiential learning from carefully designed activities. Furthermore, it suggests that cognitive access is crucial in the design and presentation of any curriculum.

KEYWORDS

Curriculum Design, ICT Integration, TPACK, SAMR, Pre-Service Teacher Training, 21st Century Skills

1. INTRODUCTION AND BACKGROUND

The expectation is that PTT will graduate new teachers with 21st century knowledge and skills and the know-how to plan and implement the integration of information and communication technologies (ICTs) in their classroom practice. Recent evidence shows that newly qualified teachers (NQTs) are joining the teaching professional not fully prepared for realities of the 21st Century classroom. PTT programs are required to emphasise the importance of enhancing the theory practice nexus and on constantly developing a strong sense of teacher identity and teaching competencies (Liu & Low, 2015).

An educator must have knowledge of how technology, pedagogy and content are interconnected, i.e. Technological Pedagogical and Content Knowledge (TPACK-Mishra & Koehler, 2006). However this is not sufficient to enable teachers to plan and present appropriate technology integrated learning activities and to teach with technology. This calls for a PTT curriculum that is appropriate and implementable so as to mediate constructive alignment through TPACK and the Substitution, Augmentation, Modification, Redefinition (SAMR) framework.

The 21CP study is a pedagogically focused digital literacy PTT program located within the curriculum studies subject as part of PTT. It sought to develop pre-service teachers with ICT integration competencies for teaching and learning. A curriculum was developed in alignment with the requirements and recommendations in provincial and national policies and guidelines for ICTs in education. All aspects of the planned blended f2f/online implementation were catapulted into exclusive online engagements on account of emergence of Covid-19 since March 2020. We reconceptualise our interaction and support with/for students and further had to revise the curriculum in terms of the number of activities and tasks.

2. PROBLEM STATEMENT, RATIONALE, AIMS AND RESEARCH QUESTION

The 21CP is viewed through an educational lens (theory-practice nexus). The situation we considered was: What is best suited to address the apparent disjuncture between the pedagogical-technology connections for teaching in a 21st Century classroom, and, how does PTT respond to these needs?

Based on literature and our experiences in PTT and continuing teacher professional development (CTPD), we focused on the following identified gaps to action: knowledge, understanding and skills: for planning and developing pedagogically sound technology integrated activities for learner engagement; for teaching with technology; to use technology to develop educationally sound learning objects. Given the above, the aims of the project focused on:

1. Developing a curriculum for PTT to effectively plan and integrate ICTs into curriculum delivery.
2. Equipping pre-service teachers with technological understanding, knowledge and skills to integrate these into their planning and teaching.
3. Determining the extent to which the design and implementation of the 21CP curriculum addressed the development of the necessary knowledge, skills and understanding for ICT integration.

We approached the study through a focused research question (RQ): How can the theory-practice nexus of 21st Century digital literature skills be enhanced in PTT through curriculum design?

3. THEORETICAL BACKGROUND

3.1 ICTs in Education

There is a strong belief in this millennium by developed and developing countries that ICTs are powerful tools that can help bring about transformation in education (Fu, 2013). In South Africa, research has also shown that, the use of digital technologies while integrating 21st Century knowledge and skills for teaching and learning has both direct and indirect impact on economic development. Meador (2014:1) argued that in this century "technological advances have exploded. Schools have not been left out in these advancements with classroom technology becoming increasingly more popular with "...technological tools ... [that] provide teachers with methods in which they can actively engage their students in the learning process".

Current methods used in teaching with technology, to digitally savvy students, are proving to be ineffective. PTT providers have the responsibility to adequately equip graduating students with 21st century knowledge and skills to integrate technology into teaching and learning. This, according to Skoretz (2011:12), is complex as it involves much more than just learning how to use technology and adding technology-related activities to an existing curriculum.

Evidence (Sherman & Howard, 2012; Chigona 2015) show that NQTs are joining the teaching professional not fully prepared for realities of the 21st Century classrooms. Researchers have argued that for effective integration of technology into the curriculum, an educator must not only have knowledge of technology, pedagogy and content but have knowledge of how these three elements are interconnected (Koehler, Mishra, Akcaoglu & Rosenberg, 2013). Integration of ICTs implies that teacher should have knowledge, skills and understanding of technological pedagogical and content knowledge (TPACK) so as to enact SAMR in the teaching learning environment. Research has further shown that an educator's perception of his or her knowledge of ICTs for curriculum delivery coupled with the capacity to integrate them into the classroom has a direct impact on [attitudes, motivation] and self-efficacy beliefs (Moore-Hayes, 2011). Given the complexities of ICTs in education, the next sections set out the theories and frameworks to substantiate a theoretical framework of this study.

3.2 Illeris Levels of Learning

Learning is a transactional activity between a learner and the environment (Illeris, 2003:396). Illeris (2003:402) identifies four levels of learning: 1. "cumulative or mechanical learning"; 2. "assimilative or learning by addition"; 3. "accommodative or transcendent learning", and 4. "transformative or expansive learning". In effect what this refers to is, the opportunities to learn along the 4 levels of Illeris is given life through Puentedura's SAMR framework. Laurillard's conversational framework and the Biggs's constructive alignment assist in understanding how this theory can take place in practice.

3.3 Laurillard's Conversational Framework

Laurillard's (1993) conversational framework maintains that there are constant interactions between the student-teacher and student-student. Laurillard (2002:29-30) identifies four kinds of activity for learning to take place: 1. 'discursive' - discussion between teacher and student; 2. 'interactive' - task/action/feedback cycle operating in the world of the content; 3. 'adaptation - description and task by teacher, and description and action by student; and 4. 'reflection' - on student performance by the teacher, and on experience by the student". This means that for a student to understand knowledge from the teacher or constructed themselves, the student must be able to experience it by practical applications in the real world – then the student has to reflect on this and through dialogue with the teacher/peers, they adapt the way they act on situations (Laurillard, 2002).

3.4 Biggs Constructive Alignment

Biggs's (1996) constructive alignment alludes to the constant interaction necessary among learning outcomes-activities-assessment, for effective learning, aiming to support students in developing as much meaning and learning as possible. Congruency of this is explicitly achieved when there is good alignment between a curriculum's intended learning outcomes, teaching and learning activities, and assessments of student learning.

3.5 Theoretical Framework

A synthesis of the theoretical framework literature yields a graphic flow (figure 1). It informs us of how the curriculum was designed and implemented, and for what purpose.

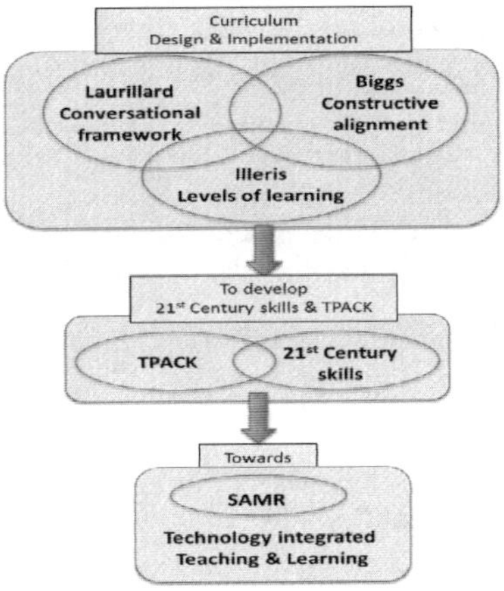

Figure 1. Authors conceptualisation of the theoretical framework

4. PRESENTATION OF THE CURRICULUM

4.1 21CP - Content and Design of Materials

Our approach to the curriculum design used 'backward mapping' as the method for developing a reliable curriculum aligned with Wiggins & Mc Tighe (2005). The 21CP curriculum comprises 5 modules: 1. 21st Century skills/Digital literacy; 2. Tools and technologies; 3. TPACK/SAMR; 4. Integration-planning;

5. Integration-strategies/techniques. The curriculum context drew on TPACK; SAMR; Laurillard's learning events; SA national policy and the Western Cape Education Department (WCED's) ICTs in education technology affordances. Student's subject specialisation provided the content for activity applications.

The curriculum was delivered through a blend of instructivist, constructivist and connectivist methodologies using a blended f2f/online mode. New content was addresses when necessary and the task expectations were discussed. The f2f/online blended mode required students to continue and complete work via the LMS. All resources (physical and human) were made available: resource materials; surveys; journal and forums were available through the LMS via links; personal support was enabled through a specific help (Q&A) forum; peer support via their own back channels; personal WhatsApp groups; e-mail and a student-lecturer WhatsApp group.

The materials were designed in alignment with Illeris's levels of learning (2003); Laurillard's conversational framework (1993) and Biggs's constructive alignment (1996). Our reason for combining these three was to: enable depth of knowledge and engagement progressively; to provide opportunities for learning through collaborative means; and to provide realistic and authentic alignment among the outcomes, activities and assessment. The following sections provide brief insights into the content, and how each of the frameworks/theories (table 1) featured in, and informed the design of the 21CP curriculum. Table 2 provides some examples of how the theoretical framework was operationalised for developing TPACK and SAMR.

Table 1. Theory / framework key concepts

Key Concepts		
Illeris levels of learning	**Laurillard's conversational framework**	**Biggs's constructive alignment**
1. Cumulative/mechanical	A. Discursive	i. Outcomes
2. Assimilative/by addition	B. Interactive	ii. Activities
3. Accommodative/transcendent	C. Adaptation	iii. Assessments
4. Transformative/expansive	D. Reflection	

4.1.1 Illeris Levels of Learning

(Modules built on one another to achieve progressive scaffolding)

1. *Cumulative/mechanical*: Selective tasks required basic-moderate use of technologies to (re)produce their understanding of the lessons and content. Students had to learn/know mechanically and through construction/collaboration certain content that was factual (e.g. Mind map of technologies and extending to individual affordances of the technologies).
2. *Assimilative/by addition*: Activities/tasks were ordered so that prior knowledge, skills and understanding could be used and built on for each successive module (e.g. Micro-ICT lesson plan built on learning events and SAMR).
3. *Accommodative/transcendent*: Inclusion of tasks based on higher order engagements (creating new knowledge (non-reproduction) (e.g. 4IR Forum discussion; Digital learning object creation).
4. *Transformative/expansive*: Extending learning to create something new aligned with redefinition in SAMR (e.g. LMS built on the 21CP design).

4.1.2 Laurillard's Conversational Framework

(Module design used combinations)

A. *Discursive*: We facilitated through constructivism and collaboration with minimal instructivism. Students constructed meaning through f2f and virtual interactions and discussions.
B. *Interactive*: We approached the task/action/feedback cycle with feedback (verbal/written) as well as with clarity of tasks and concepts –resources and help you files were made available to supplement teacher-student interaction.
C. *Adaptation*: Detailed guidelines and module information was made available (see Biggs below). Surveys and task assessment criteria were designed to encourage reflective engagement.
D. *Reflection*: Focus was on both cognitive (surveys) and affective (surveys and journal). At the end of each module students were expected to complete a survey on their learning. The journal was available throughout the course for reflections on their understanding, learning and feelings about the course and its implementation.

4.1.3 Biggs's Constructive Alignment

(Curriculum alignment with some examples)

I. *Outcomes*: Each module included Module outcomes (MO) and Student learning outcomes/indicators (LO) which emphasized and stated explicitly what was to be achieved and demonstrated (e.g. MO: develop knowledge and awareness of different types/affordances of various technologies/systems/services; LO: demonstration of collaborative abilities and technological understanding of the interrelationships and affordances of tools/technologies by creating a wiki (group work).

II. *Activities*: Engagement through the teaching (T) and learning (L) activities attended to the practical implementation of the modules (e.g. (T) overview of TPACK & SAMR videos (concepts/interrelationships) – (T/L) mediated time stamped discussions of above (focus-core concepts and application); (L/T) discussion of tools/technologies / apps / programs/software / systems/services using animated presentation).

III. *Assessments*: Tasks were organised aligned with SAMR and included assessment (for, of, as) (e.g. demonstrate knowledge and understanding by synthesising discussions/notes in a WIKI on the interrelationships between TPACK and SAMR; demonstrate information literacy skills by sifting and analysing a range of data and synthesising into a document outlining the teacher/learner promoting / prohibiting factors for ICT integration).

Guidelines: We additionally provided guidelines for all activities/assessments to hedge the chances of success towards the outcomes (e.g. when posting comments...address the challenge practically and logically. *First* make your opening comment on your own thoughts on the challenge *and then* ensure that you make reference to how you will plan and also how you will deliver accordingly - *Thereafter* you ...do not simply comment that you agree or disagree...etc.; e.g. purpose of this module is to give you the opportunity to use easy to access technologies... It seeks to develop conceptual understanding that you can apply in any context).

Table 2. Operationalised theoretical framework for TPACK/SAMR

Task	Task: Context	Task: Digital Literacies Focus & Activity Emphasis	Task: Application	TPACK Targeted	SAMR Targeted
Forum discussions	4IR hype - Mobile phones/ tablets not permitted in class	· Information & Technological literacy focus. · Interrogate information and provide argumentative / deep thinking with responses to colleagues.	*Student Application*	TPK TCK	SAMR
Using technologies to create learning objects/resources	3 Digital Literacies - Subject specific context - Tools and technologies	· Information, Technological & Media literacy & Pedagogical focus. · Creating a quiz through intermediate use of application & developing documents with freeware.	*Student Application*	TPK TK	SAMR SAMR
Planning ICT integrated e-Lessons	Subject specific context	· Information, Technological & Media literacy & Pedagogical focus. · Plan & develop ICT integrated lessons - cumulative application.	*Student Application*	TPACK	SAMR
Completing journal & surveys	21CP course specific - 5 X 21CP module specific	· Information, Technological & Media literacy & Pedagogical focus. · Reflect on learning, teaching, course, etc. and key-takeaway of each module.	*Student Application*	TPACK	SAMR SAMR

5. RESEARCH DESIGN AND METHODOLOGY

This study is underpinned by an interpretivist philosophy to gain rich insights into the complex issue of ICT integration professional development for PTT. We used the phenomenological tradition to guide the research focus. A qualitative research method was used.

A purposive sampling method was used. The population numbered 244 final year (4th year) pre-service teachers. Data was available from 166 respondents who agree to data collection. Clean usable data was available from 90 of the 166 students. These 90 students were invited for classroom observations, individual and focus group interviews.

Primary data specifically for this paper was collected through surveys and journal entries. Both open and closed questions were included in the surveys closed questions required selection of appropriate leads and/or rating of leads. Journals were completely open-ended requiring students to reflect on the curriculum, their learning experiences and feelings about learning in an online environment.

6. DATA ANALYSIS AND FINDINGS

We used iterative inductive and deductive reasoning for thematic analysis. Our process was to inductively atomise and assign codes to the data under the most relevant themes and categories (e.g. Effects of the curriculum design: on implementation (modality); on learning (pedagogical/competencies)). Deductive analysis comprised deductions from data aligned with existing theories/frameworks (e.g. Curriculum alignment: outcomes, activities, assessment, materials, engagement and facilitation). Our codification method was organised to provide us with findings related to the outcomes of the curriculum (effects) and of the design of the curriculum (alignment). The findings and analysis in this paper are confined to the theme of *Curriculum alignment* and will briefly present some related aspects of the *Effects of implementation modality* theme only.

6.1 Theme - Curriculum Alignment

The data revealed prior experiences of technology-integrated learning were not widespread among students. They commented that the layout of the curriculum on the LMS was useful and developmental.

"We were not exposed to these in High schools that is why sometimes it takes time for us - intimidated because I have not been exposed to the opportunity to self-mediated learning from subject/course outlines and working it out for myself - I have not been exposed to seeing what is expected and going to happen all at once...I am not used to reflecting on my learning after each day/session - It is kind of difficult not to sit in a classroom and being taught the content...we are familiar with someone physically teaching us - There is a need for students [to be] inducted from 1st year to an on-line environment."

"All the information for the course is provided and broken down for students...the new and improved setup created an organized and simple program layout - Module outline with the guidelines for the tasks are useful to manage and take charge of my own learning through knowing what is coming up in the following modules...the online elements of this curriculum provide an advantage to continue uninterrupted learning at your one's own pace - It was useful to know and see the different modules' learning outcomes upfront...I'm starting to realize that this module is extremely well structured and planned...resources were quite helpful - I enjoy coming to the classroom for that reason and it shows how prepared the lectures are...the assessment tasks sufficiently covered a range of ways to assess learning."

Many acknowledge that the curriculum layout and presentation was useful to enable learning especially as the Covid-19 context severely changed the course of instruction and learning. Lack of prior engagement in a technological environment appeared to be a factor that resulted in newer experiences from a blended f2f/online curriculum for students. Student's appeared to 'enjoy' the learning experiences and inclusive nature of the curriculum.

6.2 Theme - Effects on Implementation

Reactions to the modules and the amount of effort and work required were mixed. The data highlighted that some students felt the cognitive level was extremely challenging and that it was overloaded with little time to complete all the work.

"The module has been paced well enough for me to gain an understanding of the different facets - it takes too much time as all students have other tasks and responsibilities - The modules were not as easy as I thought they will be...I faced some challenges in completing them."

Notwithstanding reservations of some students, the majority appeared to find a value-laden element of usability and applicability in the modules. These include the engagement with activities and pedagogical benefits for them. There appeared to be a progression in student's knowledge and skills.

"The learning materials/resources for the whole course are useful in informing my understanding of the work - has developed my understanding as to how ICT can be integrated into learning and teaching - I enjoyed engaging in the on-line discussion forum to verbalize my opinion - I am really happy with the activities and task of this modules, they motivate teachers to be more technological - I would make use of this knowledge."

"I have learned new techniques and strategies - gained more skills that i can use during planning and executing of tasks - I know now that when I plan a lesson I should think about what skills - I'm now getting more equipped with knowledge that will help me."

Aspects of student's pedagogical reflection came to the fore in the data. There appeared to be a satisfaction in the methodologies used during the course.

"There is a great inclusion of technology and a learner centred method in the way the teaching takes place - I know exactly what to do when it comes to my assignment because it was discussed in depth - This is collaborative learning at its best and it allows students to think in a critical manner - I am being exposed to new ways of using ICT for learning as opposed to the use of ICT for social means."

The reflective activities appeared to have stimulated student's thinking beyond their previous experiences. The nature of activities and f2f/online engagements appeared to have set a base for bridging the theory-practice disjuncture.

"...made me realise that there is more to the sessions than just the content...provoked my thinking - Made me to look at the integration of ICT in schools differently - This module of ICT has prepared me to use technology in everything that i do."

As the curriculum progressed students began to acknowledge the intensity of the content in justifying its relative heaviness. Student's preferred learning styles emerged through the data. They specifically referred to the need and preference for the 'teacher' explaining/teaching a lesson - where they could interact and see on a 'whiteboard' (share board). Implied in the data were student's take on self-paced and self-determined learning. There are some indications in the data that students are not used to taking charge of their own learning and learning on their own. The data showed that students were reflecting on their learning in different ways.

7. CONCLUSIONS

7.1 Curriculum Design and Implementation

The overall presentation and design of the curriculum for f2f/online was considered useful and sound for student's development. Student's prior experiences or rather lack thereof to operate in an 'e' environment can be debilitating in that it diminishes access to learning. This, coupled with institutionalised traditional methods at many universities, shapes the varying learning styles, attitudes and self-efficacy beliefs of students. We believe that our attention to the alignment of the elements of the theoretical framework contributed to promoting cognitive access.

We acknowledge that the number of tasks could be less heavy, but we do not believe that they were unreasonable. The particular challenges, which lead to this situation, were that we were tasked with completion within 6 months and Covid-19 upturned the planned run. Our response, to the concerns and Covid-19 imperatives, was to reduce the number of tasks while maintaining the integrity of the content and reworked or supplemented our materials to be more online appropriate.

Overall, students' notions show an acceptance of the contribution of the 21CP curriculum towards the use and prospective integration of various ICTs for teaching and learning. Most of the comments indicated that regardless of the challenges faced by the students, the modules/topics and various activities were valid, useful and beneficial in developing essential knowledge and skills. The curriculum provided opportunities to bridge the gap of a theoretical knowledge of ICT integration and practical knowledge through experiential learning. This was evident in the data when students noted that they were learning new 'things' by doing tasks that they now believed could be used by them.

Beliefs about gains are rational thoughts that we believe emanated out of the level of critical thinking of students. This could be attributed to number of opportunities to reflect that we presented and the method of delivery. We argue that sufficient quality opportunities to reflect on learning are a sound methodology to encourage critical thinking. This is aligned with (Bain et al., 2002) five elements of: Reporting, Responding, Reasoning, Relating and Reconstructing.

The 21CP curriculum appears to have equipped students with sufficient skills to plan for the use of technology effectively in classroom situations. One could conclude that, besides developing and enhancing: technological knowledge and skills, integration knowledge and skills, the 21CP reinforced positive attitudes of using ICTs among students.

7.2 21CP Outcomes

Our reflections on the 21CP are summed up through students' acknowledgment that the approach to the curriculum for ICT integration was of use to them and that they found value and derived benefits. Many of the students further acknowledged that it assisted them in thinking and doing beyond the normal with technology and as such opened them to newer possibilities.

There is a high probability that the university (where the research was conducted) will realign its curriculum to progressively incorporate the 21 CP curriculum from 1st to 4th year. The 21CP curriculum has additionally been adopted by a university (in a different province) for its PTT and is being researched in a doctoral study.

Given the findings thus far, we offer the following recommendations:

- The 21CP curriculum should be integrated in all subject offerings to students so as to synergise the different approaches to subject specific planning that does not currently give adequate attention to ICT integration.
- The curriculum should be offered from the 1st year of university. It should be sensibly spread over year at a time. This is to pay more attention to Illeris's levels of learning and progressively induct the students into an ICT integrated world.
- The next step of this work that would greatly benefit the implementation of this curriculum would be additional systematic evaluation that include but not limited to: Teacher educator preparedness to integrate ICTs in instruction; an exclusive on-line delivery mode and adaptability of the curriculum to different context.

REFERENCES

Ajzen, I. and Fishbein, M. 2005. The Influence of Attitudes on Behavior. In Albarracín, D. Johnson, B.T. and Zanna, M.P., eds. The handbook of attitudes, pp.173–221. Lawrence Erlbaum Associates Publishers.

Bain, J.D. et. al., 2002. Reflecting on practice: Student teachers' perspectives, Post Pressed: Flaxton, Qld

Biggs, J. 1996. Enhancing teaching through constructive alignment. Higher Education, 32(3): 347-464.

Chigona, A. 2015. Pedagogical shift in the twenty-first century: Preparing teachers to teach with new technologies, *Africa Education Review*, 12(3): 478-492, DOI: 10.1080/18146627.2015.1110912

Eickelmann, B. and Vennermann, M. 2017. Teachers' attitudes and beliefs regarding ICT in teaching and learning in European countries. European Educational Research Journal, 16(6): 733–761.

Fu, J. S. 2013. Complexity of ICT in education: A critical literature review and its implications. *International Journal of Education and Development using Information and Communication Technology (IJEDICT)* 9 (1): 112–125.

Illeris, K. 2003. Towards a contemporary and comprehensive theory of learning. International Journal of Lifelong Education, 22(4):396-406.

Koehler, M., et. al., 2013. The Technological Pedagogical Content Knowledge Framework for Teachers and Teacher Educators.

Laurillard, D. 2002. Rethinking University Teaching in the Digital Age.

Laurillard, D. 1993. Rethinking university education: a framework for the effective use of educational technology. London: Routledge.

Liu, W.C. and Low, E.L. 2015. Editorial: teacher education for the 21st century. Educ Res Policy Prac 14:189–191. https://doi.org/10.1007/s10671-015-9188-x

Meador, D. 2014. Classroom technology that every teacher needs. Available at: http://teaching.about.com/od/tech/a/Technology-In-The-Classroom.htm

Mishra, P. and Koehler, M.J. 2006. Technological pedagogical content knowledge: a framework for teacher knowledge. Teachers College Record, 108(6):1017-1054.

Moore-Hayes, C. 2011. Technology Integration Preparedness and its Influence on Teacher-Efficacy. Canadian Journal of Learning and Technology 37(3)

Puentedura, R.R. 2009. Learning, Technology, and the SAMR Model : Goals, Processes, and Practice.

Richardson, V., 1996. The role of attitudes and beliefs in learning to teach. In Sikula, J. ed. Handbook of research on teacher education (2nd ed., pp.102-119). New York: Macmillan.

Sherman, K. and Howard, S.K. 2012. Teachers' Beliefs about First- and Second-Order Barriers to ICT Integration: Preliminary Findings from a South African Study. In P. Resta (Ed.), *Proceedings of SITE 2012--Society for Information Technology & Teacher Education International Conference.* Association for the Advancement of Computing in Education (AACE). March 5-9, Austin, Texas (pp. 2098-2105).

Skoretz, Y. M. 2011. A Study of the Impact of a School-Based, Job-Embedded Professional Development Program on Elementary and Middle School Teacher Efficacy for Technology Integration. Theses, Dissertations and Capstones. Paper 150.

Straub, E.T. 2009. Understanding technology adoption: theory and future directions for informal learning. Review of Educational Research, 79(2), pp. 625-649.

WCED. 2016. e-Education Strategy. Cape Town.

Wiggins, G. and Mc Tighe, J. 2005. Understanding by Design. Alexandria, VA: Association for Supervision and Curriculum Development.

PROBLEMS AND OBSTACLES OF DISTANCE LEARNING IN THE POINT OF VIEW OF PRIMARY SCHOOL TEACHERS IN THE "COVID PERIOD"

Zuzana Svobodova, Martin Kursch and Jaroslav Veteska
Department of Andragogy and Educational Management
Faculty of Education, Charles University in Prague
Myslíkova 7, 110 00 Prague 1
Czech Republic

ABSTRACT

The COVID-19 pandemic period confronted schools with new challenges related to school closures and the transition to distance learning, which brought with it several problems and obstacles that schools had to overcome. The main objective of our study is to qualitatively explore the problems and obstacles of distance learning at the first level of primary schools. We were based first on a document of the Czech School Inspectorate and their evaluation of distance learning and other foreign publications dealing with obstacles in distance learning. Based on a qualitative survey based on eight semi-structured interviews, we sought an answer to the research question: "What problems do teachers perceive in the implementation of distance learning?". The analysis of the interviews identified three basic categories; 1) Technical problems; 2) Socialization; 3) Widening the gap; We elaborated these three categories in detail in the results section and illustrated with authentic statements of respondents. As an overarching topic that was intertwined with all the interviews, we identified the issue of teaching effectiveness, which was the actual goal in overcoming the identified obstacles.

KEYWORDS

Distance Education (Distance Learning), Efficiency of Learning and Education, Teacher and Pupils of Primary School, Primary School, COVID-19 Pandemic, Czech School Inspectorate

1. INTRODUCTION

Distance learning is a form of teaching that has been the subject of research for recent years. At the same time as this boom, the advantages and disadvantages of distance learning are more obvious, across all levels of education according to ISCED. The main objective of our study is to qualitatively explore the problems and obstacles of distance learning at the first level of primary schools (ISCED 1, the first level of primary schools includes school attendance from 6 to 10 years of age).

We are based on published documents of the Czech School Inspectorate (ČŠI, 2020),which comments on the findings from questionnaires commissioned as part of full-time inspection activities during the month of September and the first half of October 2020, which was attended by 1,767 pupils and 602 teachers from a total of 66 primary schools located in different regions of the Czech Republic. Focusing on the shortcomings of distance learning, the most important factor was the absence of social personal contacts with classmates, which was expressed by 55 % of respondents. A worrying result was that 16 % of 1st grade respondents declared that they had no online teaching and did not take place at all. From the point of view of grade 1 teachers, obstacles were cited such as a reduction in the successful performance of the role of class teacher at the time of distance learning, content reduction (although surprisingly low, only 17 %), the lack of quality digital technology, (38 % of teachers) and the lack of training of teaching staff to work with digital technologies (42 % of teachers). (Pavlas, Zatloukal, Andrys, Pražáková and Šlajchová, 2020).

Available foreign studies dealing with obstacles to distance learning report problems with IT infrastructure, internet availability and frequent outages (Utomo et al., 2020). The Zan et al. study (2020) found that 61 % of students were unable to participate actively in distance learning courses due to computer or tablet problems, and 40.3 % had internet connectivity problems. The advantages were characterized by technological difficulties, cultural and regional differences, evaluation and scoring, unplanned shifting of hours, the problem of discipline and the inability to focus on the problem. (Zan et al., 2020). Constructive feedback from the teachers (Tsodikova et al., 2020) is an important factor in alleviating the shortcomings of distance learning. Nenko (2020) points to the lack of qualifications of some teachers, conservatism, psychological barriers and unpreparedness for online education. It also underlines the rigidity towards the innovation, the low incentive level for the development of distance learning courses, technological inadequacy of teachers, excessive bureaucracy of distance learning, passive access by teachers to applications on the Internet, low awareness of distance learning opportunities and a lack of adequate technical equipment and internet access for students living in rural areas.

The effectiveness was a central identified topic, which in a way contains all the texts (Veteška et al., 2020). It includes, on the one hand, a view of effectiveness by the teacher (e.g. Wilson and VanBerschot, 2014, Jurkowski and Müller, 2018, Neifeald and Nissim, 2019, Rabin, 2020) as well as a student view (e.g. Puttonen, 2014, Strogilos, King-Sears, 2019). The view of effectiveness by teachers is usually the basis for revision of the methods used or modification of a course. Based on a pilot study, the teachers reflect the entire teaching process, finding the positives and negatives on which it is based when adjusting the course or educational activity to its final form (Kim et al., 2007, Wilson and VanBerschot, 2014, Neifeald and Nissim, 2019).

Problems and prospects for improving distance learning are being explored around the world. It is clear that the development of distance learning for both students and teachers requires adjusting some aspects of its implementation in order to meet the needs of the educational process and to increase the effectiveness and educational process of this unexplored form of teaching. We agree with the statement of Kryshtanovych et al. (2020) that each and the analysis of accumulated experience of teachers from different disciplines, summarizing the results of pedagogical, didactic and methodological problems and their context, will significantly contribute to the future improvement of the quality of distance learning. We join with our qualitative study, which summarizes obstacles and problems in distance learning based on controlled interviews with teachers of the 1st grade.

2. BODY OF PAPER

2.1 Methods

An exploratory and descriptive qualitative approach was chosen. The goal of qualitative description research is to provide a rich description of the experience displayed in an easy-to-understand language. The authors try to discover and understand the phenomenon, process, perspectives and opinions of the people involved. A qualitative descriptive approach offers an opportunity to collect authentic descriptions of a phenomenon little is known about. As part of the process, the researcher tries to stay close to the "surface of data and events", where the experience is described from the perspective of participants (Bradshaw et al., 2017). Research of this type focuses on authentic "what", "who", "where" and "why" experienced events or experiences (Neergaard et al., 2009). Qualitative descriptive approach does not require highly abstract data rendering compared to other qualitative designs (Lambert & Lambert, 2012), but of course some interpretation logically occurs (Sandelowski, 2000, Bradshaw et al., 2017). The data was collected in an authentic first-grade elementary school[1] environment (i.e. ISCED 1 education period) in autumn 2020 (September-November) using semi-structured interviews and analysed using content analysis.

[1] This is an elementary school that is involved in the TAČR project. The aim of the scoping review is to analyze and summarize the most important knowledge on selected topics of co-teaching as a starting point for further research work within the Project Technology Agency of the Czech Republic (TAČR: TL03000133) entitled *New Method of Education for the 21st Century: Virtual-Co-Teaching* solved in the 2020-2023.

2.2 Participants

A total of 8 semi-structured interviews were conducted with first-grade teachers (ISCED 1) at the school involved in the TAČR project. The criterion for inclusion in the study was essential: teaching only in the ISCED 1 period in the Czech Republic (i.e. pupils up to the age of 10 years), active use of distance learning tools and experience with distance learning already from the period of the first lockdown (spring 2020). Participants in the study were recommended by the school head based on this criterion. Teachers of different subjects (English, German language, main subjects, subjects of educational orientation) were selected, these were only women, given that no man works as a teacher in the school.

2.3 Data Collection

The data was collected using semi-structured interviews conducted during autumn 2020 (i.e. during the second school closure period), it was recorded, repeatedly listened to and the main parts were written down. In view of the restrictions associated with the Covid-19 pandemic, the conversations were conducted in a virtual environment (hangouts meet, phone, facetime). The talks lasted between 20-30 minutes. At the beginning, all participants were asked the introductory question: "What problems do you perceive in distance learning?". To understand the context communicated to them, the participants were asked even more additional questions: "Can you tell me more about what you mean? How do you feel about the situation? Do you see the difference between spring 2020 and the current situation? What does this mean for you?". The interviews were conducted by one of the authors of the study (Zuzana Svobodova).

2.4 Data Analysis

The analysis utilized inductive and deductive content analysis, as described by Graneheim, Lindgren and Lundman (2017). Content analysis is a method that is based on the analysis communicated through coding and categorization, and which is suitable for determining the opinions, ways, behaviours and experiences of individuals or groups (Mayring, 2000, Hendl, 2016). The analysis process included a series of successive steps that were regularly discussed by the research team (authors of the text). The participants' communications in the interviews were thematically broader than relevant for the research, however, only their relevant communications regarding obstacles and problems with distance learning were included in the data analysis. Interviews were repeatedly listened to by the research team (authors) in order to understand the content and to identify the obstacles and problems that respondents experience in the implementation of distance learning. The first phase of analysis was inductive. Categories and meanings related to the research question (objectives of this study) have been identified. These codes were subsequently grouped into subcategories based on significant similarities (Hendl, 2016). The next phase was deductive. Subcategories were classified under the categories identified in the previous study (Veteška et al., 2020). The subcategories and categories that emerged during the analysis are shown in Table 1.

2.5 Results

Distance learning, however challenging, allows pupils to participate in education even at the time of school closures. As we mentioned in the introduction, the level of compensation and the problems they had to overcome were different. In the autumn of 2020, schools experienced a second closure, when they switched to distance learning in the Czech Republic completely from 14.10.2020. Problems and obstacles to distance learning can be summarised under three key areas: 1) technical problems, 2) socialisation and 3) widening differences. Similar problematic categories were identified in a previous study of authors focused on co-teaching opportunities in a virtual environment (Veteška et al., 2020). The overarching term for these three categories is “education effectiveness” which should also be the same category identified for the previous study of the authors (Veteška et al., 2020). The result part is structured according to individual categories, each category being discussed from the point of view of the participants and related to the effectiveness of teaching. Participants were quoted literally to ensure their authenticity.

Table 1. Subcategories and categories

Categories	Subcategories
Technical problems	Technical problems of pupils Technical problems of teachers Cameras versus icons
Socialization	Focus on the curriculum Communication and relationships
Widening the gap	Children with specific educational needs Ability to be independent

2.5.1 Technical Problems

Initial reaction of all study participants to the introductory question asked, *"What problems do you perceive in distance learning?"* was essentially similar and involved a "*sigh*" over technical problem. Overall, they rated distance learning positively in the first place and saw it as an opportunity to educate and be with pupils even at this difficult time (*"better online than nothing"*), but immediately there were complaints about technical difficulties, which make this positive aspect difficult for them , one participant aptly remarked: *"The beginning is difficult, the children immediately report technical problems, this doesn't work, this doesn't work and before I put it together, then the hour is actually gone", "before the class starts, we say hello ten times, we have technical problems, we have 30 minutes education and during that we connect for five minutes".*

At the same time, technical problems **make it difficult** for pupils to concentrate at the beginning of class, when teachers were able to get their attention easily during normal teaching. Now if something is not going well, which is almost always the case, the attention is immediately gone and it is difficult to get it back and the effectiveness of teaching decreases significantly: "*Children do not learn so much, I cannot expect outputs that would be from normal teaching, I am completely annoyed by it*"

Technical problems of pupils

Technical problems of pupils depend not only on technical equipment and signal quality, but above all on their age. Participants of the study perceive as a turning point the third year of basic education, i.e. age about 8-9 years, when pupils are able to independently operate platforms for distance learning and parents are not needed as technical support: *"Younger ones simply cannot put together work with a camera, shared screen, textbook and so on"*. At the same time, they perceive that when pupils are so-called on their own, they don't have parents in the same room, the lessons run better even with minor technical difficulties than when the parent is present and tries to technically help: *"I had to teach parents that they should not intervene immediately, if the child cannot mute the microphone, we would not get anywhere, I try to explain to them that they should not be at the lessons and that if I need them I will call them myself*".

Technical difficulties in first- to third-grade students stem primarily from the fact that it is first necessary to teach them how to operate the necessary equipment and operate on the platform. So the curriculum was turned back at the beginning, and the teachers preferred targeted behavioural training in a virtual environment: "*The first lessons were just about how to turn on the microphone and turn off the microphone, I did not teach anything*". They perceived the constant presence of parents in teaching as challenging: "*I am not used to being looked at all the time by a parent, I want to be alone with my pupils for a while".*

On the other hand, younger children perceive that the presence of a parent helps to maintain the concentration of pupils: *"third-graders can technically handle something on their own, but they can't keep their attention at all, but if they have parents there, they can convince them"*. It is therefore a constant balancing act of independence, of help from parents versus the need to teach without them, of practicing the control of technology, directing and solving various small things, which is of course a great obstacle to the realization of effective teaching. One of the interviewed teachers said that it is a pity that companies did not come up with products designed specifically for teaching younger children, where the control would be adapted to their maturity: "*It's a pity that there is no laptop for the youngest, the products for seniors are, but no one is thinking about first-graders' education*".

Technical problems of teachers

The technical problems of the pupils were mainly based on the inability to control the necessary applications for distance learning, rather than on real technical problems. Teachers solve problems of different nature – they are considering how to transfer the activities they did in the classroom to the online environment, as well as how to combine their work with family and their own children in online teaching (and their technical problems). The foreign language teacher perceives the inclusion of listening as very problematic, because it is not of enough quality to play it directly into the online lesson and the solution to this problem will take almost an entire class. So she went back to the old way of playing CDs, which leads to better quality than playing directly on the computer: "*I have a problem with listening, it takes too long to get connected and thirty minutes is a short time, then it doesn't work and the hour is ruined. So, I'd rather play it from the cassette player, not much, either, but at least something, it's a lot about improvisation*"

A big complication for teaching **is the need** to provide for their own children, the respondents consistently stated that basically their own child is directly participating in the learning, that it is really challenging, and it complicates their work significantly. At the same time, they often do not have strong enough internet connection, because the whole family is at home and online: "*home Wi-Fi does not catch up, their own child is at home learning, so it is really impossible*".

A specific technical problem is **the absence of a comprehensive concept of materials** and technical equipment that would be suitable distance learning: "*the problem is that we follow a normal textbook, and something isn't viable doing online*". Teachers need to "digitize" the materials they used in full-time teaching, which is of course time-consuming, and not always in the conditions and possible with the equipment they have: "*textbooks are not ready for it, I have to invent myself, create new digital materials and do everything again, and it is very demanding to prepare*".

Cameras versus icons

The issue of on or off cameras is actually on the border of other categories, because it is also related to the area of socialization and educational problems, however, due to the prevailing technical character, it was classified in this category and due to its overlap is described separately. The interviewed teachers made it clear that it was extremely difficult for them to teach icons and wished that pupils had their cameras turned on. On the other hand, they realize that it is necessary to share one Wi-Fi in families with more children, and the cameras turned on are, of course, more demanding on the quality of transmission. None of the respondents knew how to deal with this problem, whether to handle it with parents, with children, with other teachers, whether to proceed with sanctions, if the pupil refuses to turn on the camera or whether to accept this fact and put up with it: "*I do not know how to deal with it, they say they have a bad signal, but they say it all the time, I do not know if it is true*". At the same time, they feel that seniors may be conducting inconspicuous truancy, and children avoid teaching in this way "*especially the fourth and fifth grades, they pretend that their sound does not work, they turn off their cameras, I do not know if I should believe it*".

Teaching icons is unpleasant for teachers, they lack facial expressions, responding to pupils' expressions and overall the atmosphere of the class to which everyone was used: "*When I look at icons, I don't really know if they enjoy it, I know that maybe it does not matter, but still, when I see a face, I can react, say something differently, but I don't know how, the icon still looks the same*". One respondent said that when she started class, she always remembered the previous class, which does not work in the virtual class "*when I see them in the classroom, I remember what I actually wanted and I do not remember it online, because, as I cannot see them, I do not know*". Another problem of teachers not seeing pupils is different screen sharing and switching to other applications, then really everyone is referred only to auditory sensations without facial expressions, "*I want to share a screen and show them something, but then I actually lose them all*".

2.5.2 The issue of Socialization

Socialization, relationships and personal contacts are limited in all areas nowadays. Of course, human contact is essential for quality development in childhood, and socialization is an important part of school education, which is very difficult to transfer to the online environment of distance learning. It is always difficult, however with younger pupils everything is complicated by the above-mentioned technical difficulties and overall problematic control of the necessary devices. Distance learning is therefore concentrated on mastering the teaching, communication and relationships instead of complex development of the child's personality.

Focus on the curriculum

Teachers perceive that they had to reduce socialization activities for distance learning and focus essentially only on mastering the teaching. They have smaller time subsidies for online teaching, part of the curriculum is solved in the form of separate tasks and the achievement of socialization courses of education has disappeared almost completely "*it is just about discussing the curriculum, that's all we can do*". At the same time, they perceive that the curriculum is essentially given to children in a frontal way , and online lessons are very instructional, it is impossible to realize playful activities that were typical for the full-time form of teaching younger children: *"it is more monotonous than in full-time teaching", "didactic games associated with movement cannot be replaced, it would normally help to maintain concentration and experience of the curriculum"*. It is therefore clear that children of younger school age actually experience a significant reduction in what is normally happening in schools and focusing on facts only is not appropriate for this age, and as one respondent has said, children are also *"losing their hard-earned work habits"*.

Communication and relationships

All respondents consistently stated that children of younger school age lack a lot of group dynamics in teaching, lack contacts with classmates and teachers, lack friends and relationships, and none of this can be replaced by technology. They perceive that the lack of these stimuli leads to a loss of attention and reduces interest in the curriculum *"children begin to lack internal motivation"," young children would need to go to school, they lack friends, the longer it lasts, the worse it gets"*. Children are also beginning to be uncertain in teaching because they lack immediate feedback from the teacher, they do not have additional visual and auditory support, and for some it is very difficult: *"there is no immediate feedback from the teacher, smiles, nod, this simply cannot be replaced by the technique"*

A specific problem in the area of communication and relations was reported by one respondent, who was taken aback by the fact how strange it is that some teachers do not want to learn to work in distance learning and boycott the whole process a little, which complicates the work in other classes and groups and disrupts the relationships in school: *"Colleagues do not want to learn anything new, this is absurd, the teacher should be the one who likes to learn when she teaches others"* and then added: *"Now it turns out that schools are backward and should, on the contrary, give direction"*.

2.5.3 Widening the Gap in Acquired Knowledge

Our respondents expressed their comments in a similar way, as also shown by the findings of the Czech School Inspectorate of the Czech Republic (ČŠI, 2020) informing about the widening differences in pupils' knowledge. They perceive different family backgrounds, different help from parents and different abilities of individual pupils. They realise that it is extremely difficult to develop all children equally in the conditions of distance learning and that the situation in individual families and their involvement in teaching is much more accentuated *"the difference between the weaker pupils and the class's best pupils is much more accentuated and you can see who is being helped at home and who is on their own", "weaker pupils are less concentrated and they don't catch up with the curriculum, the best pupils overtake them"*.

Children with specific educational needs

Surprising fact for respondents was that for some children with special educational needs (SEN), is the distance learning better, however, they realize that they cannot really accurately evaluate it, but feel that they are doing better: *"some children with ADHD do not nudge themselves in the classroom and are alone, so they concentrate better, no one disturbs them"*. Unfortunately, most SEN pupils do not manage the online learning environment and there is no way to activate them properly and involve them in teaching. In the classroom and during personal contact, the teachers immediately saw when a child started to be at loss in class or did something else, during the online transmission they logically miss this *"I just do not see the children, so I do not know if they are with us or doing something else or nothing"*.

Teachers are also not sure whether the tasks are actually done by children and if they understand the teaching, or it is the work of parents and their help *"I really do not know who did the task, I never knew with homework, but the point is that a lot of the curriculum is actually homework now, so I can't be sure that the pupils can really do it and with some it is really strange"*. This is a fact that cannot be checked within the next class. According to respondents, children who are hypoactive are problematic, i.e. those who still need to be motivated and encouraged to work in class, which is not possible now: *"children who have their world and stare around, no one will adage them, no one will tell them anything, they are staring and not working, this would not happen in the classroom"*.

Ability to be independent

The development of independency logically does not happen equally for all children , and in the classroom it is easy to individually support children in this regard, in an online environment it is very difficult: *"children are not very independent and still need to make sure that they are doing something right, so they are in discomfort and someone keeps asking questions, in full-time teaching I can regulate it by gesture and not disturb others, here it is impossible".*

Respondents clearly identified differences in pupils' ability to work on their own and adapt to new educational conditions. One of those interviewed said that this method of teaching would clearly show who has **study prerequisites** and is ripe to go into the academic educational mainstream and who does not: *"I think that in this way of teaching it will come out quickly enough, then we do not need any entrance exams, it is simply clear that who can organize a curriculum like this, is ready to study independently even in grammar school", "in this way there would be no need to take entrance exams – who does independently in online, can go straight to grammar school, we could tell them straight away".*

Regarding the **effectiveness of teaching**, as an overarching term for defined problematic areas of distance learning, there were also reflections focusing on the overall meaning of the curriculum. One respondent said that she perceived that the curriculum, as defined now, constitutes an obstacle to quality distance learning. She perceives that she is very focused on memorising facts and even the tests she uses to verify knowledge are focused on information that pupils can easily find in distance learning. She perceives that she is therefore in the stage of thinking about the meaningfulness of what he teaches and does not really know what to do with it: *"We are referring to the problem of pedagogy itself – whether the pedagogy is supposed to be, that children should have fun or biff something, I really do not know, for example, in the language, words have to be biffed, they can look it up elsewhere, but then they are unable to use it".*

3. CONCLUSION

Distance learning is an opportunity not to interrupt the education process at the time of school closures, but its implementation faces a number of problems. This study gives an overview of these problems and experiences by looking at eight teachers of the first level of primary school in the Czech Republic. Inductive and deductive content analysis identified three main categories that were continuously related to the question of teaching effectiveness.

The results of this study show that the area of technical problems is not only based on the technical equipment of schools and families, but also relates to other aspects – such as maturity and age of pupils, family situation during lessons and overall personal settings and willingness to learn something new. The study reaffirmed that personal contacts and standard full-time teaching are irreplaceable for this age group of pupils and its absence leads to a further widening of the gap between pupils and complicates the already demanding education of children with special educational needs.

A deeper understanding of the needs of teachers and pupils, which would lead to overcoming some of the identified obstacles, would be appropriate to carry out further research investigations and to rely on more qualitative data to lead us to a clearer understanding of the issues pursued – i.e. the effective implementation of distance learning.

ACKNOWLEDGEMENT

The authors would like to thank the participants for their willingness to share their experiences of distance learning. The authors would also like to thank the cooperating primary school for selecting participants and thereby facilitating data collection. This study was supported by the Technology Agency of the Czech Republic (TAČR: TL03000133).

REFERENCES

Bradshaw, C., Atkinson, S. and Doody, O., 2017. Employing a Qualitative Description Approach in Health Care Research. *Global Qualitative Nursing Research*. https://doi.org/org/10.1177/2333393617742282

Graneheim, U.H., Lindgren, B.-M. and Lundman, B., 2017. Methodological challenges in qualitative content analysis: A discussion paper. *Nourse Education Today*, 56, 29-34. https://doi:10.1016/j.nedt.2017.06.002

Hendl, J., 2016. *Qualitative research: basic theories, methods and applications*. Prague: Portal.

Krysthanovych, M., Gavrysh, I., Khltobina, O., Melnychuk, I. and Salnikova, N., 2020. Prospects, Problems and Ways to Improve Distance Learning of Students of Higher Educational Institutions. *Romanian Journal for Multidimensional Education /Revista Romaneasca pentru Educatie Multidimensionala* [online], pp. 348-364.

Lambert, V. A. and Lambert, C. E., 2012. Qualitative descriptive research: An acceptable design. *Pacific Rim International Journal of Nursing Research*, 16, pp. 255-256.

Mayring, P., 2000. *Qualitative Inhaltsanalyse* [online]. 1 (No. 2). Retrieved from: https://www.ph-freiburg.de/fileadmin/dateien/fakultaet3/sozialwissenschaft/Quasus/Volltexte/2-00mayring-d_qualitativeInhaltsanalyse.pdf

Molnár, Z. et al. *Advanced methods of scientific work* [online]. Prague: Profess Consulting. Retrieved from: http://lsa.vse.cz/kniha.html

Montgomery, M. and Akerson, A., 2019. Facilitating Collaboration through a Co-Teaching Field Experience. *Networks: An Online Journal for Teacher Research.* Vol. 21, Iss. 1, pp. 1-21.

Neergaard, M. A., Oleson, F., Anderson, R. and Sondergaard, J., 2009. Qualitative description – The poor cousin of health research? *BMC Medical Research Methodology*, 9, Article 52.

Nenko, Y., Kybalna, N. and Snisarenko, Y., 2020. The COVID-19 Distance Learning: Insight from Ukrainian students. *Revista Brasileira de Educação do Campo* [online], pp. 1-19.

Pavlas, T., Zatloukal, T., Andrys, O., Pražáková, D. and Šlajchová, L., 2020. *Experience of primary school pupils and teachers with distance learning in the second half of the 2019/2020 school year Summary*of selected findings and recommendations for the following period: Thematic report. Czech School Inspectorate.

Sandelowski, M., 2000. Focus on research methods: Whatever happened to qualitative description? *Research in Nursing & Health*, 23, pp. 334-340.

Strogilos, V. and King-Sears, M., 2019. Co-Teaching Is Extra Help and Fun: Perspectives on Co-Teaching from Middle School Students and Co-Teachers. *Journal of Research in Special Educational Needs,* Vol. 19, No. 2, pp. 92-102.

Tsodikova, O., Korzh, O. and Hyria, M., 2020. Information and Communication Technologies in Postgraduate Training of Primary Care Doctors: A New Look at the Problem of Using Online Resources During the COVID-19 Pandemic. *Technium Social Sciences Journal* [online], Vol. 8, No. 1. https://doi.org/10.47577/tssj.v8i1.661

Utomo, M. N. Y., Sudaryanto, M. and Saddhono, K., 2020. Tools and Strategy for Distance Learning to Respond COVID-19 Pandemic in Indonesia. *Ingénierie des Systèmes d'Information* [online], Vol. 25, No. 3, pp. 383-390.

Veteška, J., Kursch, M., Svobodová, Z., Tureckiová, M. and Paulovčáková, L., 2020. Longitudal co-teaching projects – scoping review. *17th International Conference On Cognition And Exploratory Learning In Digital Age*, pp. 115-123.

Zan, N. and Zan Umut, B., 2020. Koronavirüsile Acil Durumda Eğitim: Türkiye'nin Farklı Bölgelerinden Uzaktan Eğitim Sistemine Dahil Olan Edebiyat Fakültesi Öğrencilerine Genel Bakış. *Electronic Turkish Studies* [online], Vol 15, No. 4, pp. 1367-1394.

ON DUAL TECHNOLOGY INTEGRATION FOR EFFECTIVE TEACHING OF DIGITAL ACCOUNTING IN A TECHNOLOGY-RICH, ONLINE LEARNING CONTEXT

Marina Thomas
TAFE NSW
183 Narellan Rd
Campbelltown NSW 2560 Australia

ABSTRACT

In recent years, the development of digital accounting technologies has been increasingly transforming the accounting profession. At the same time, emerging digital educational technologies have revolutionized the way accounting education is delivered. Therefore, embracing digital technologies and enhancing technology integration is an important mechanism for improving teaching effectiveness, providing students with new opportunities, and promoting lifelong learning in accounting education. Drawing on various streams of accounting education and professional teacher competence literature, the paper introduces the concept of dual technology integration and proposes directions for its investigation.

KEYWORDS

Accounting Education, Digitalization, Dual Technology Integration

1. INTRODUCTION

This research is concerned with the problem of improving accounting faculty's preparedness for effective teaching of digital accounting in a technology-rich, online learning context. Embracing digital technologies and enhancing technology integration is seen by accreditation agencies and accounting professional bodies as an important mechanism for improving teaching effectiveness, providing students with new opportunities and promoting lifelong learning (Islam 2017; AACSB 2018). Developing a capacity for integrating digital accounting content into accounting education and delivering it with the most effective use of emerging educational technologies and digital pedagogies is critically important for today's accounting educators (O'Connell et al. 2015). Despite a growing body of international research on technology integration, very little of it is specific to accounting education. In addition, specific competencies required for effective teaching of digital accounting content in technology-enhanced learning environments are not well defined and understood (Watty et al. 2016).

2. TECHNOLOGY INTEGRATION TYPE I AND TYPE II

The literature review in this paper is organized around two key dimensions of digital technology integration in accounting education that are labelled in this paper as Type 1 and Type 2.

- Technology integration Type 1 is related to incorporating digital accounting and business technologies, such as blockchain, data analytics, EPR, Excel, XBRL in the subject matter of accounting disciplines (Kreher et al. 2017; AACSB 2018; Lawson 2018; Kruskopf et al. 2019).
- Technology integration Type 2 deals with the use of emerging educational technologies and digital pedagogies in accounting disciplines (Watty et al. 2016).

The distinction between Type 1 and Type 2 is important, because each type of digital technology integration, as shown in the review, is associated with a distinctly different set of accounting faculty's competencies. Therefore, to effectively teach digital accounting with the use of emerging learning technologies and digital pedagogies accounting faculty must develop a complex set of specific competencies which includes knowledge, skills and abilities for both types of technology integration (collectively referred to hereafter as "dual technology integration").

3. ACCOUNTING DIGITALIZATION AND ACCOUNTING EDUCATION

Technology Integration Type I. Recent advances in the development of digital technologies, such as artificial intelligence, blockchain, cloud computing, and data analytics, are transforming accounting practices, methods, and procedures (Kreher et al. 2017; Pincus et al. 2017). To keep up with accounting digitalization, professional accountants are being forced to adapt or risk losing their jobs (Zhang et al. 2018; Kruskopf et al. 2019). The new set of information technology (IT) competencies necessary for accounting professionals to successfully perform in the new environment is often referred to as digital accounting (Lawson, 2018; Kruskopf et al. 2019). Extant research reveals significant gaps in accounting graduates' IT knowledge and skills including automatic identification systems, enterprise resource planning (ERP), eXtensible Business Reporting Language (XBRL), analytical programming and data mining tools and techniques (Pan & Seow, 2016).

Responding to the industry call, professional accounting bodies and accrediting institutions have called for integrating IT knowledge and skills into accounting education (The Pathways Commission 2012; Birt et al. 2018). In 2018, the American Association of Collegiate Schools of Business has introduced Standard A5 "Information Technology Skills, Agility and Knowledge for Accounting Graduates and Faculty" which defines technology integration as "the ability of both faculty and students to adapt to emerging technologies" (AACSB 2018). The standard highlights some specific IT elements that need to be integrated in accounting curriculum such as information systems, business processes and data analytics; also, it emphasizes "developing information technology agility among students and faculty" (ibidem). While integrating digital technology into accounting curriculum at large and specific courses in particular have received significant attention in the literature (Sledgianowski et al. 2017; Dzuranin et al. 2018; Richardson & Shan 2019; Andiola et al. 2020), the issue of faculty preparedness and training necessary to meet the profession's future technology competency demands remains largely unexplored (Gamage 2016; Brands & Elam 2019).

Technology Integration Type I and Accounting Teacher Professional Competence. When discussing a competency-based approach to increasing teaching effectiveness of accounting academics, Smith and Emerson (2017) recommended focusing on their role as professional accounting *teachers*, rather than accounting *researchers*, or teaching *accountants*. For identifying variables affecting technology integration in accounting education, Thomas and Chukhlomin (2020) suggested to draw from the modern literature on teacher training. Following Shulman (1986) approach to teacher knowledge, the co-developers of the COACTIV project in Germany integrated various streams of literature on professionalism and competences and developed the teacher professional competence framework (Baumert & Kunter 2013). Teacher professional competence (or teacher competence) which is the central concept of the framework is defined by Kunter et al. (2013) as "the skills, knowledge, attributes, and motivational variables that form the basis for mastery of specific situations" (p. 807). The teacher competence literature follows Shulman (1986) in sub-dividing teacher competence into three distinctive bodies, namely content knowledge (CK), pedagogical knowledge (PK), and pedagogical content knowledge (PCK) where PK is "an interdisciplinary knowledge about teaching methods, learning strategies and classroom management" (Förtsch et al. 2016, p. 2), CK is knowledge about subject matter and its conceptual understanding (Shulman 1986), and PCK is "the transformation of subject matter knowledge per se into subject matter for teaching" (Park & Oliver 2008, p. 262). PK, CK and PCK are separate knowledge dimensions (Förtsch et al. 2016). There is empirical evidence that it is the teachers' PCK (and not as much as their PK or CK) that is a main predictor for instructional quality and student achievement (Förtsch et al. 2016).

In addition to identification of the main subset of variables affecting teacher professional competence for teaching any type of subject matter content (CK, PK and PCK), various sub-streams of teacher training literature can be instrumental for identifying specific variables dealing with teaching digital content. For example, Ball et al. (2008) developed a conceptual framework for teaching digital content in mathematics. Tabach and Trgalová (2020) further modified this framework by introducing specialized digital content knowledge (labeled here for consistency as C_dK). According to Tabach and Trgalová (2020), specialized C_dK presents "specificities related to the mathematics embedded in technology" (p. 224).

The implication of the above analysis for accounting education is that by way of identifying and examining the constituent components of CK, PK, PCK and C_dK (Park & Oliver, 2008; Tabach & Trgalová, 2020), accounting faculty, administrators, and educational researchers can better understand teaching and learning of digital accounting content in various contexts which may improve teaching effectiveness. However, the constituent components of CK, PK PCK and C_dK for accounting educators are yet to be determined and explored (see also Thomas & Chukhlomin, 2020).

4. THE IMPACT OF DIGITAL EDUCATIONAL TECHNOLOGIES

Technology Integration Type II. In the last two decades, technology-enhanced learning environments have been increasingly replacing traditional classrooms in accounting education (Guthrie et al. 2013; Morris et al. 2015; Watty et al. 2016). Among powerful forces that drive this change and force accounting faculty to increasingly adopt digital educational technologies are the emergence of digitally native learners that are looking for anytime, anywhere learning opportunities (Morris 2015; Watty et al. 2016; Al-Htaybat et al. 2018); the push for efficiency by educational institutions competing in the evolving online marketplace (Guthrie et al. 2013); and, most recently, COVID-related events.

While the mainstream accounting literature devotes significant attention to the formation of accounting graduates' competencies including a range of IT knowledge and skills (Lawson et al. 2014), it is largely silent on the issue of faculty competence base for teaching in a technology-rich learning context (Brands & Elam 2019). As noted by Bryant et al. (2005) in an early review of distance learning in accounting education, there is a variety of important research questions related to teacher issues in technology-rich learning environments that remain to be investigated including "which skills are needed to effectively teach a distance education course in accounting [and] how these skills are different from those required to teach a traditional accounting course" (p. 266). In a more recent review of the state of accounting education in Australia, O'Connell et al. (2015) concluded that "redesigned accounting courses or units that embrace the potential of learning technologies will challenge the existing perceptions and digital competencies of many accounting academics" (p. 88). One of the key recommendations of the report was to complement the knowledge base of accounting faculty by employing "instructional designers with experience in key enabling [digital learning] technologies to assist accounting academics with the deployment of relevant technology in their teaching" (p. 94). This recommendation in the O'Connell et al. (2015) report is noteworthy because it opens an avenue toward extending the competence base of accounting teachers by adding new skillsets such as developing an understanding (or a working knowledge) of instructional design. The need to further investigate the emerging competencies of accounting academics is supported by a broader literature on technology-enhanced learning environments and online learning which emphasizes new academic roles and required skillsets such as instructional design, learning content design, online facilitation, coordination of online learning (Anderson 2008).

5. CONCLUSION

Keeping in mind a growing importance of online learning and MOOCs in accounting education (Guthrie et al. 2013), it is imperative to develop a better understanding of accounting faculty competence formation in a technology-rich, online learning environment. To do so, researchers need to focus on revealing the benefits and challenges of integrating digital educational technologies in teaching digital accounting: a) in general and b) in specific online learning contexts. For example, how do accounting faculty perceive their current and desired levels of professional competence for dual technology integration in the online learning context? How do they identify and evaluate possible dual technology integration competency gaps? How do they use professional development to eliminate dual technology integration competency gaps? What factors do participants perceive help and what factors impede their competence development for effective dual technology integration?

REFERENCES

AACSB 2018, *2018 Eligibility Procedures and Accreditation Standards for Accounting Accreditation*, AACSB International, https://www.aacsb.edu/accreditation/standards/accounting>.

Al-Htaybat, K, von Alberti-Alhtaybat, L & Alhatabat, Z 2018, 'Educating digital natives for the future: accounting educators' evaluation of the accounting curriculum', *Accounting Education*, vol. 27, no. 4, pp. 333-57.

Anderson, T 2008, *The theory and practice of online learning*, Athabasca University Press.

Andiola, LM, Masters, E & Norman, C 2020, 'Integrating technology and data analytic skills into the accounting curriculum: Accounting department leaders' experiences and insights', *Journal of Accounting Education*, vol. 50, p. 100655.

Ball, DL, Thames, MH & Phelps, G 2008, 'Content knowledge for teaching: What makes it special', *Journal of teacher education*, vol. 59, no. 5, pp. 389-407.

Baumert, J & Kunter, M 2013, 'The COACTIV model of teachers' professional competence', in *Cognitive activation in the mathematics classroom and professional competence of teachers*, Springer, pp. 25-48.

Birt, J, Wells, P, Kavanagh, M, Robb, A & Bir, P 2018, 'ICT Skills Development: Education'.

Brands, KM & Elam, DA 2019, 'A case study on accounting faculty's perceptions of technology in accounting classes', *International Journal of Entrepreneurship and Innovation Management*, vol. 23, no. 5, pp. 513-29.

Bryant, SM, Kahle, JB & Schafer, BA 2005, 'Distance Education: A Review of the Contemporary Literature', *Issues in Accounting Education*, vol. 20, no. 3, pp. 255-72.

Dzuranin, AC, Jones, JR & Olvera, RM 2018, 'Infusing data analytics into the accounting curriculum: A framework and insights from faculty', *Journal of Accounting Education*, vol. 43, pp. 24-39.

Förtsch, C, Werner, S, von Kotzebue, L & Neuhaus, BJ 2016, 'Effects of biology teachers' professional knowledge and cognitive activation on students' achievement', *International Journal of Science Education*, vol. 38, no. 17, pp. 2642-66.

Gamage, P 2016, 'Big Data: are accounting educators ready?', *Journal of Accounting and Management Information Systems*, vol. 15, no. 3, pp. 588-604.

Guthrie, J, Burritt, R & Evans, E 2013, *'Challenges for accounting and business education: blending online and traditional universities in a MOOC environment'* (Doctoral Dissertation, Institute of Chartered Accountants Australia; Centre for Accounting, Governance and Sustainability, University of South Australia)

Islam, MA 2017, *Future of Accounting Profession: Three Major Changes and Implications for Teaching and Research*, International Federation of Accountants (IFAC), https://www.ifac.org/global-knowledge-gateway/business-reporting/discussion/future-accounting-profession-three-major>.

Kreher, M, Sellhorn, T & Hess, T 2017, 'Digitalisation in Accounting: Study of the Status Quo in German Companies', https://home.kpmg/content/dam/kpmg/de/pdf/Themen/2017/digitalisation-in-accounting-en-2017-KPMG.pdf>.

Kruskopf, S, Lobbas, C, Meinander, H, Söderling, K, Martikainen, M & Lehner, O 2019, 'Digital accounting: opportunities, threats and the human factor', *ACRN Oxford Journal of Finance and Risk Perspectives*, vol. 8, pp. 1-15.

Kunter, M., Baumert, J., Voss, T., Klusmann, U., Richter, D., & Hachfeld, A. (2013). Professional competence of teachers: effects on instructional quality and student development. *Journal of Educational Psychology*, 105(3), 805-820

Lawson, RA, Blocher, EJ, Brewer, PC, Cokins, G, Sorensen, JE, Stout, DE, Sundem, GL, Wolcott, SK & Wouters, MJ 2014, *'Focusing accounting curricula on students' long-run careers: Recommendations for an integrated competency-based framework for accounting education'*, Issues in Accounting Education, vol. 29, no. 2, pp. 295-317.

Lawson, R 2018, Management Accounting Competencies: Fit for Purpose in a Digital Age? *Institute of Management Accountants*, https://www.imanet.org/insights-and-trends/the-future-of-management-accounting/management-accounting-competencies---fit-for-purpose-in-a-digital-age

Morris, M., Burnett, R., Skousen, C., Akaaboune, O. 2015, 'Accounting Education and Technology: A Study of the Long Term Effects', *The Accounting Educators' Journal*, vol. 25, pp. 67-93.

O'Connell, B, Carnegie, GD, Carter, AJ, de Lange, P, Hancock, P, Helliar, C & Watty, K 2015, 'Shaping the future of accounting in business education in Australia', *Melbourne, Australia: CPA*.

Park, S & Oliver, JS 2008, 'Revisiting the conceptualisation of pedagogical content knowledge (PCK): PCK as a conceptual tool to understand teachers as professionals', *Research in science Education*, vol. 38, no. 3, pp. 261-84.

Pan, G, & Seow, P.S. 2016, 'Preparing accounting graduates for digital revolution: A critical review of information technology competencies and skills development', *Journal of Education for business*, *91(3),* pp. 166-175.

Pincus, KV, Stout, DE, Sorensen, JE, Stocks, KD & Lawson, RA 2017, 'Forces for change in higher education and implications for the accounting academy', *Journal of Accounting Education*, vol. 40, pp. 1-18.

Richardson, VJ & Shan, Y 2019, 'Data Analytics in the Accounting Curriculum', *Advances in Accounting Education: Teaching and Curriculum Innovations (Advances in Accounting Education, Vol. 23), Emerald Publishing Limited*, pp. 67-79.

Shulman, LS 1986, 'Those who understand: Knowledge growth in teaching', *Educational researcher*, vol. 15, no. 2, pp. 4-14.

Sledgianowski, D, Gomaa, M & Tan, C 2017, 'Toward integration of Big Data, technology and information systems competencies into the accounting curriculum', *Journal of Accounting Education*, vol. 38, pp. 81-93.

Smith, KJ & Emerson, DJ 2017, 'An Analysis of Professional Competence Indicator Possession among U.S. Accounting Faculty', *Issues in Accounting Education*, vol. 32, no. 2, pp. 17-38.

Tabach, M & Trgalová, J 2020, 'Teaching Mathematics in the Digital Era: Standards and Beyond', in Y Ben-David Kolikant, et al. (eds), *STEM Teachers and Teaching in the Digital Era: Professional Expectations and Advancement in the 21st Century Schools*, Springer International Publishing AG, Cham, pp. 221-42.

The Pathways Commission 2012, *Chapter 7: Constructing a Foundational Body of Knowledge. Initial Step: Assembling Accounting Competencies*, Charting a National Strategy for the Next Generation of Accountants, <http://commons.aaahq.org/posts/a3470e7ffa>.

Thomas, M., & Chukhlomin, V. (2020). Supporting Faculty Development in Technology-Enhanced Accounting and Business Education: A TPACK-Powered, Competence-in Action Framework. *Journal of Accounting and Finance*, 20(7).

Watty, K, McKay, J & Ngo, L 2016, 'Innovators or inhibitors? Accounting faculty resistance to new educational technologies in higher education', *Journal of Accounting Education*, vol. 36, pp. 1-15.

Zhang, CA, Dai, J & Vasarhelyi, MA 2018, 'The Impact of Disruptive Technologies on Accounting and Auditing Education: How Should the Profession Adapt?', *The CPA Journal*, vol. 88, no. 9, pp. 20-6.

REDUCING LEARNING DISCONTINUITIES BETWEEN ACADEMIC AND VOCATIONAL SUBJECTS IN FRENCH VOCATIONAL HIGH SCHOOLS

Valérie Théric, Hélène Cheneval-Armand, Alice Delserieys and Pascale Brandt-Pomares
ADEF, Aix-Marseille Université, France

ABSTRACT

The French vocational training system uses both academic and vocational teaching. This design-based research studies how vocational and academic teachers devised a co-teaching device to help students transfer their skills and knowledge from one type of teaching to the other.

It was found that the device is strongly shaped by external factors, and that teacher's professional identity is called into question in co-teaching. The results were used to create an analytical framework adapted to the context of vocational education and training.

KEYWORDS

Vocational School, Co-Teaching, Interdisciplinarity

1. INTRODUCTION

In France, vocational training for students aged 15 to 18, is mainly carried out in vocational high schools. The syllabus is based on four axes: academic subjects (mathematics, physics, languages, etc.), vocational subjects, support and guidance, and training periods in workplaces. This system thus brings together two different types of teachers (academic and vocational) with two distinct syllabi. Going from one learning context to another creates many learning discontinuities (Veillard, 2017). Students must therefore create the links between these different contexts themselves, which is exceedingly difficult for them.

2. RESEARCH QUESTION

The notion of links between different school subjects thus refers to the concept of interdisciplinarity. According to Lenoir & Hasni (2016, p.2446) "Professional (or vocational) interdisciplinarity, for its part, has to do with the integration of a set of processes and knowledge (academic and practical) to develop the skills and competencies required by a given occupation. It requires going beyond the usual characteristics of interdisciplinarity".

Teachers' interdisciplinary work is well documented in other contexts, but there is a lack of knowledge about interdisciplinarity in vocational high schools. This research then focuses on the way academic and vocational teachers think about and organize interdisciplinarity together. Thus, the research question is: how do academic and vocational teachers try to create links and reduce learning discontinuities between their school subjects, in the context of vocational training?

3. RESEARCH METHODOLOGY

The experiment took place in France in a vocational high school that educates young people aged 15-18 years. The research was conducted over two academic years (2018-2020), in the context of a new institutional recommendation: academic and vocational teachers do not only have to teach their own school subjects, but they are also required to co-teach for one hour a week (MEN, 2019).

A mixed method research (Johnson et al., 2007) was used.

First, in a case study format (Yin, 2003), a design-based research (Barab & Squire, 2004) was carried out. The twofold objective was to accompany teachers in co-designing an educational device, and to study how teachers envisaged, devised, and set up this interdisciplinarity. A working group was set up, composed of two vocational teachers (VT), two mathematics-physic-chemistry teachers (MPCT) and two researchers. Ten 3-hour meetings were organized, 4 meetings to analyze the problem together, 5 meetings to co-design an educational device, and 1 meeting to discuss the first results of the researchers' analysis with the teachers.

Two types of analysis were then carried out: a qualitative and a quantitative one. The corpus was first decontextualized. In order to manage the high amount of speech extracts, the software NVivo (QSR International) was used (Richards, 1999). The speeches were segmented and categorized using a directed approach of content analysis (Hsieh & Shannon, 2005). The aim of this approach is to extend the theory linked to teachers' practice of interdisciplinarity to the context of vocational training (Hsieh & Shannon, 2005). The first coding was done a priori i.e., the categories used to create nodes were taken from the literature. Then, the corpus was analyzed horizontally. In addition, a lexicometric analysis was carried out, using the free software IRaMuTeQ (R Interface for Multidimensional Text and Questionnaire Analysis) (Loubère & Ratinaud, 2014).

Then, based on these first-phase results, hypotheses were formulated, concerning how teachers deal with interdisciplinarity in vocational training.

Finally, a questionnaire is currently being made to test these hypotheses on a larger sample of teachers.

4. WORK DONE SO FAR

4.1 Most Important Results

4.1.1 An Asymmetrical Design

Thanks to the content analysis, the input activities of the different teachers were separated into two groups: Vocational Teachers (VT) and Mathematics Physics Chemistry Teachers (VT). It appeared that in the context of our study, input activities are almost exclusively carried out by VT. Concerning the epistemics of the interventions, a dissymmetry can be noted: MPCT interventions fall into the academic category or are cross-category (i.e., transversal skills). Only a few indeed really deal with vocational subjects, and therefore cannot be put into the vocational category. On the opposite, VT interventions may be related to the vocational category, the trans-category, but also to the academic category, depending on their contents.

In the last meeting, when the results were presented to the teaching team, and when the dissymmetry of the proposal activities was pointed out, one of the MPCT explained that he had not done any proposal activities to follow the institutional instructions. He explained: "*During the inspectors' training days, we were told we had to base our lessons on vocational teaching activities. That is exactly what is written in the institutional text. So, this is where the ambiguity lies, you see? You asked us to co-design the class, but the official instructions tell us to base our lesson on a vocational activity.*"

4.1.2 An Educational Device Strongly Shaped by External Factors

The educational device strongly evolved during the co-design phase of the experiment. Indeed, different educational devices were proposed by the teaching team over the sessions, and his form were influenced by personal or externals factors. The first forms were clearly more influenced by teachers experience or abilities than by the institutional framework. Teachers tried to adapt what they already did in their courses. A strong influence of external factors on teachers' choices had also be observed. The determining variables in the context of our study have been the number of students and the positions of the school teaching group.

The number of students was a blocking constraint, especially for vocational teachers; this question recurs regularly in the speeches, particularly those of vocational teachers. Indeed, workshop constraints mean that most of the time they teach in front of twelve students, whereas their colleagues in academic courses teach much more regularly in front of twenty-four students. "*When we heard we will co-teach, we said: that's great! Twelve students, and we'll be two teachers! Ah no no no, you didn't understand: it's not twelve, it's twenty-four. So, we will be two for twenty-four students, I don't really see the benefit...* "says VT1.

The second variable, which strongly influenced the device shape, is the positions of the school teaching group. Indeed, one of the devices proposed, consisted in annualizing the co-teaching weekly hour over a group of hours. According to the co-design team, longer teaching sessions, would have allowed a more immersive project-based learning for students. However, this organization (permitted by the framework text for co-teaching (MEN, 2019)), raised fears among the other teachers in the high school of a precedent that could have modified their working conditions. The organization and content of the co-designed device therefore had to be modified. "*The schoolteacher's group doesn't want to. So if they don't want to, it's dead...*" says VT1. "*There were collective positions. At the beginning there were openings, but now it is very blocking.*" added MPCT1.

4.1.3 Teachers Professional Identity is Called into Question by Working in Co-Teaching

Teachers who participated in the experiment described co-teaching as a stressful way of teaching. One of them said: "*With co-teaching, we feel morally interdependent with each other. It's weird.*"

For Audigier (1997) indeed, teacher professional identity strongly depends on his or her school subject. He thus offered a framework for professional identity related to the school subject, in the context of the history/geography subject. This framework takes several parameters into account, such as class duration, groups of students, how knowledge is conveyed by the teacher, syllabus, methods, and textbooks. When transposed to vocational education, these parameters were quite different for both vocational and academic teachers. Matching them to create a co-teaching device that satisfies both types of teachers is therefore extremely complicated.

4.2 A New Analysis Framework and Hypothesis

The above results showed that in the vocational training context, specific variables were involved. For example, "Professional identity related to the school subject" is not the same for academic teachers and vocational teachers. This variable played a strong role in the experiment, and it must therefore be considered.

Thus, the case study has made it possible, on the one hand, to build a new theoretical framework, adapted to the links between academic and vocational subjects. Table 1 shows the different selected variables, organized along four axes.

Table 1. Axes for the links between academic and vocational subjects

Personal Axis	Didactic Axis	Epistemological Axis	Organizational Axis
Form of cooperation Symmetry in cooperation Field of teaching Professional identity related to the school subject	Importance of the link within the class syllabus Subject integration strategy Use of the link Conducive didactic organization Creation of the link through the teaching approach	Type of knowledge involved Learning goals Interdisciplinary approach Purpose of the link	Favorable teaching organization Interactions with other teachers Material requirements Interpersonal requirements

On the other hand, the case study has made it possible to put forward some hypotheses based both on the results described in the previous paragraph, and on the study by (Theric et al., 2019) which shows that vocational teachers used educational approaches as inquiry-based learning.

Hypothesis 1: The "institution" variable can be used to modify all axes.

Hypothesis 2: Creating links between academic and vocational subjects forces teachers to redefine the part played by their professional identity.

Hypothesis 3: The scientific approach may be a means of reducing learning discontinuities between academic and vocational subjects.

A questionnaire is currently being made, to test the previous hypotheses on a larger sample of academic and vocational teachers.

5. CONCLUSION

Our work has led us to conclude that co-teaching in the vocational training context is specific, compared to other co-teaching situations. Supplementing the case study with quantitative data will help to improve the reliability of our results. However, one of the remaining limitations is that the questionnaire only shows what teachers say they do, not what they actually do.

The results of this study could improve educational training by making both academic and vocational teachers aware of the difficulties encountered by their students in vocational high schools. Our work would also make it possible for teachers to help their students change from one learning context to another. Indeed, according to Clark & Wallace (2015, p.247), "disciplinary knowledge is necessary but far from sufficient for effective professional practice. Integrative skills via interdisciplinary method are essential to effectiveness in problem solving". Vocational and academic teachers must work together to help students to develop integrative skills, and they should be trained to do so.

ACKNOWLEDGEMENT

We would like to thank the Rectorat d'Aix-Marseille (French National Education) and the Federation of Research Laboratories (Sfere) for founding this project.

REFERENCES

Audigier, F. (1997). Histoire et géographie : Un modèle disciplinaire pour penser l'identité professionnelle. *Recherche & formation*, *25*(1), 9–21.

Barab, S., & Squire, K. (2004). Design-Based Research : Putting a Stake in the Ground. *Journal of the Learning Sciences*, *13*(1), 1-14. https://doi.org/10.1207/s15327809jls1301_1

Clark, S.G., Wallace, R.L. Integration and interdisciplinarity: concepts, frameworks, and education. *Policy Sci* 48, 233–255 (2015).

Hsieh, H.-F., & Shannon, S. E. (2005). Three Approaches to Qualitative Content Analysis. *Qualitative Health Research*, *15*(9), 1277-1288. https://doi.org/10.1177/1049732305276687

Johnson, R. B., Onwuegbuzie, A. J., & Turner, L. A. (2007). Toward a Definition of Mixed Methods Research. *Journal of Mixed Methods Research*, *1*(2), 112-133. https://doi.org/10.1177/1558689806298224

Lenoir, Y., & Hasni, A. (2016). Interdisciplinarity in Primary and Secondary School : Issues and Perspectives. *Creative Education*, *7*(16), 2433-2458. https://doi.org/10.4236/ce.2016.716233

Loubère, L., & Ratinaud, P. (2014). *Documentation IRaMuTeQ 0.6 alpha 3 version 0.1*. http://www.iramuteq.org/documentation/fichiers/documentation_19_02_2014.pdf

MEN. (2019). *Vade-mecum co-intervention*.

Richards, L. (1999). *Using NVIVO in Qualitative Research*. SAGE.

Theric, V., Cheneval-Armand, H., & Delserieys, A. (2019). Enseignement professionnel et démarches d'investigation : Le cas du Génie Industriel Textile. *Recherches en éducation*. https://hal.archives-ouvertes.fr/hal-02429955

Veillard, L. (2017). *La formation professionnelle initiale: Apprendre dans l'alternance entre différents contextes*. PUR.

Yin, R. K. (2003). *Case Study Research : Design and Methods*. SAGE.

IS ACADEMIC SUCCESS JUST A MATTER OF SHOWING UP? A STUDY OF THE CONTRIBUTION OF INDIVIDUAL DIFFERENCES AND ATTENDANCE TO PERFORMANCE

Maura A. E. Pilotti
Prince Mohammad bin Fahd University
College of Sciences and Human Studies, Prince Mohammad bin Fahd University, Al Khobar, 80305 KSA

ABSTRACT

The present study examined the contribution of individual differences in ordinary class attendance, self-efficacy, and decision-making styles to expected or actual performance in a course devoted to research report writing. Due to the COVID-19 epidemic, the course, which was judged by past and current students as challenging, had to be delivered online. The online transfer raised concerns about the impact of passive attendance on learning in a course that had previously relied heavily on face-to-face exchanges. Thus, an objective examination of performance data was carried out. In regression analyses, attendance was the main contributor to performance on the midterm test and individual assignments. The contribution of other individual difference variables was selective and limited in scope. To wit, self-efficacy contributed to students' confidence in grade expectations, but not to their accuracy. Hyper-vigilance had a negative influence on grade expectations before the midterm examination, whereas procrastination had a negative influence on performance in initial assignments. It was concluded that the benefits of attendance may reflect students' motivation to do well, which begins with knowing what is going on in a class, an essential ingredient of academic success.

KEYWORDS

Class Performance, Attendance, Individual Differences

1. INTRODUCTION

In academia, beliefs about the impact of some particular variables on students' success abound. One of the most popular is the belief that "good students who attend class regularly make good grades". It is often mentioned to students in classes, reiterated during office hours, and referred to in casual interactions of faculty and students. The evidence is not so enticing though. Several studies have found a link between performance (as measured by grades) and frequency of attendance, thereby supporting the implication that high attendance promotes good performance (Dey, 2018; Launius, 1997; Lukkarinen et al., 2016; Kassarnig et al., 2017; Thomas & Higbee, 2000). Other studies, however, have not found evidence of a link between the two variables (Berenson et al, 1992; St. Clair, 1999). To complicate the matter is the debate of whether mandatory attendance policies not only shape attendance but also benefit students' academic success. Such policies may penalize absenteeism through administrative withdrawal if absences are above a certain level (e.g., 15 %) or through the allocation of a relatively small portion of a class grade (e.g., 10%; Rendleman, 2017) to attendance. Evidence regarding the impact of mandatory attendance policies is mixed. For instance, Marburger (2006) and Snyder and Frank (2016) report that such policies reduce absenteeism and improve performance, whereas Golding (2011) and Rendleman (2017) report a link between attendance and performance, but fail to uncover any impact of attendance policies.

The mixed findings of the role played by attendance in the extant literature became particularly relevant in the context of the COVID-19 epidemic which had suddenly forced most academic institutions to move their courses online. At institutions across the globe, an issue that took the center stage was the extent to which the frequency and quality of online attendance would impact students' performance. It was acknowledged that any of the technical platforms used to deliver courses online could easily record the presence of individual students in a given course, but whether such a measure would be meaningful was open to debate.

Concerns arose regarding passive attendance in online classes, including students who may log into a class and then devote attention to other matters, or merely listen without taking notes and contributing to lectures or class discussions. Such concerns were particularly relevant at institutions whose student-center pedagogy is the educational model and active learning of key competencies is both a strategy and a goal. The present field research arose from discussions that faculty at one of these institutions had about the impact of online teaching on learning in students who had been suddenly catapulted into a modality upon which they had only sporadically and selectively relied in the past. The main question on everybody's mind was whether learning would be jeopardized in students who were accustomed to face-to-face classes and used learning management systems, such as Blackboard, only to retrieve class documents, submit assignments, check grades, and at times take computerized (instead of pencil-and-paper) tests in a physical classroom under the watchful eyes of an instructor.

The present field study asked whether attendance mattered in an online writing-intensive course devoted to learning research methodology and applying it to the writing of a research report. Well before moving online, the course was rumored to be a roadblock in the Core program of the selected university, a program with courses devoted to learning basic academic and professional competencies. It was one of the courses that most freshmen took with little background knowledge and with considerable trepidation that rumors simply intensified. Teaching was guided by the understanding that the success of students in this course heavily relies on frequent and robust feedback on writing assignments, expert guidance on reading assignments (mostly scholarly articles), and abundant practical examples of how research is conducted and communicated to diverse audiences.

The potential contribution of students' attendance to performance on tests and assignments was examined along that of other individual-difference variables, such as self-efficacy and decision-making styles. As students' expectations of their performance in an upcoming test are generally related to the quality and magnitude of the effort devoted to preparatory activities (Covington & Omelich, 1988; Peverly et al., 2003), and thus can determine outcomes, the present research also examined whether the same individual differences could account for students' ability to accurately predict their performance and their subjective confidence in the predictions made.

2. LITERATURE REVIEW

General self-efficacy is learners' overall confidence in their ability to perform well across diverse tasks and situations. General self-efficacy is a motivational trait (Chen et al., 2000) which tends to be positively correlated with engagement (Bandura, 1989; Bandura & Schunk, 1981), persistence (Bandura, 1977; Pajares, 1997), and task completion (Eden, 1984, 1988; Pajares, 1996). In essence, general self-efficacy is a "can do" attitude that is linked to conscientiousness (Chen et al., 2001), determines exerted effort, and enables students to adapt effectively to novel and challenging situations (Judge et al., 1998; Pulakos et al., 2000). As such, it was expected to have a positive impact on performance. It was thought that self-efficacy might also impact learners' ability to predict performance outcomes accurately, such as a test grade, and their subjective confidence in such predictions. The reason being that predictions of future outcomes, the subjective confidence attributed to them, and general self-efficacy beliefs are all related to students' self-regulatory activities during the learning process, including metacognition phenomena, such as goal-setting, self-monitoring, and self-evaluation (McMillan & Hearn 2008; Stone 2000). Yet, in the extant literature, evidence of a link between self-efficacy and performance, prediction accuracy, or subjective confidence is mixed. For instance, Al Kuhayli et al. (2019) found no evidence of a link between self-efficacy and either class performance or metacognition, whereas Pilotti et al. (2020) reported low self-efficacy to be associated with poor performance.

Decision-making habits were included in the present research since they are habitual responses produced by students to cope with difficulties, such as the challenges of a tough course. According to Janis and Mann (1977), when making important decisions, such as what, how, and how much to study for an upcoming test or how to complete an assignment, learners may be vigilant, hyper-vigilant, or defensive avoidant (Burnett et al., 1989; Mann et al., 1997; 1998). The latter may entail procrastination or buck-passing (i.e., relying on others to make one's decisions). It is reasonable to assume that the more unfamiliar and open-ended (i.e., exhibiting not rigidly defined constraints) are the instructions that define a task, the more difficult are the decisions to be made at each step, creating not only uncertainty but also stress. Consider, for instance, the uncertainty that identifying, organizing, performing, and evaluating the activities involved in the writing of a research report may engender in learners with little background knowledge in research. Yet, learners might differ in their response to uncertainties of this nature. Vigilant learners might best deal with the situation at hand by clarifying objectives, exploring alternatives, calmly processing information, and evaluating alternatives carefully before making decisions. Hyper-vigilant learners, instead, might make decisions under emotional excitement without exploring all available information and alternatives. Defensive avoidant learners might attempt to escape uncertainties by either buck-passing or procrastinating. Buck-passing involves shifting the obligation of making decisions to someone else's, whereas procrastination entails postponing decision-making activities to another day. Defensive avoidance, either in the form of buck-passing or procrastination, is characterized by hesitation in making decisions, as well as incomplete and perhaps biased evaluation of information, often leading to faulty choices.

In the extant literature, evidence of which particular decision-making coping habits are linked to academic performance is meager and unclear. Filippello et al. (2013) report that vigilance is favored by high-performing students (as measured by grades), whereas avoidance is preferred by students who perform less well. Ferrari (2001) finds that procrastination (a type of defensive avoidance) differentiates poor and good performers (see also Steel et al., 2001). However, Chu and Choi (2005) do not find procrastination as capable of differentiating students by performance levels. Since vigilance involves objective decision-making processes, one might expect vigilance, rather than hyper-vigilance or defensive avoidance habits, to be linked to not only good performance, but also prediction accuracy, and subjective confidence.

The relationship between the selected individual differences (i.e., class attendance, self-efficacy, and decision-making styles) and either predicted or actual performance was investigated through the field study methodology described below. The study took place in virtual classrooms with real students during the COVID-19 epidemic.

3. METHOD

3.1 Participants

The participants were 122 female freshmen who completed all key requirements of a course primarily devoted to research methodology and report writing. Their class grades ranged from passing to failing. Eighteen additional students who withdrew from the course (12.86%) were excluded from the current analyses as they missed key requirements. All withdrawals involved students who dropped the course in the last weeks of the semester. Students were Arabic-English bilingual speakers whose ages ranged from 18 to 25. English competencies were assessed before their formal enrollment via standardized tests. Participation complied with the guidelines of the Office for Human Research Protections of the U.S. Department of Health and Human Services and with the American Psychological Association's ethical standards in the treatment of human subjects. Due to gender segregation rules, a comparable sample of male students was unavailable to the researcher.

3.2 Procedure

The selected course (3 credit hours) is part of the Core program of a University located in the Eastern Province of the Kingdom of Saudi Arabia. The University offers a curriculum of U.S. import, which is imparted through a student-centered model. English is the primary mode of instruction. The Core curriculum contains a series of courses on basic academic and professional competencies to be taken by all students irrespective of their major. The curriculum of such courses relies on syllabi approved by the Texas International Education Consortium (TIEC) and textbooks published in the U.S.

The selected course required students to write an APA-style research report in a series of steps: assignment 1 (introduction), assignment 2 (literature review), assignment 3 (method and result sections), and assignment 4. The latter asked that students complete the report by adding the discussion section and the abstract, and that they proofread, review, and revise their work before final submission. Assignment 5 entailed an open Q&A session during which students were asked questions about the rationale, methodology, results, and APA format of their research report. The aim of assignment 5 was for students to develop a working model of their research that could be communicated to a hypothetical audience ostensibly unfamiliar with their work as if they were at the poster session of a conference.

The report that students were expected to complete involved a correlational study in the behavioral sciences collectively carried out by the class during the second week of the semester. The course also required students to complete a midterm and a final test on research methods. Immediately before and after either test, students were asked to predict their test grade on a scale from 0 to 100, as well as to express their confidence in the prediction made on a scale from 0 (not at all confident) to 4 (extremely confident). They were reminded to make realistic rather than aspirational predictions. Test questions comprised five of the six types of information processing highlighted by Bloom's taxonomy (Anderson & Krathwohl, 2001; Bloom, 1956, 1976; Krathwohl, 2002). Namely, students' assessment required remembering, understanding, application, analysis, and evaluation, but excluded synthesis/creation of work due to the introductory nature of the Core curriculum. Four sections were selected of 35-37 students each, all taught by the same instructor. Because of the COVID-19 epidemic, classes were offered online through the synchronous (real-time) mode. Pedagogically, the synchronous virtual environment replicated many aspects of the face-to-face environment. Blackboard gave learners access to study materials and resources, such as study guides, textbooks, rubrics, and videos, as well as announcements about class activities and deadlines for submission. Blackboard Collaborate, which is a real-time video conferencing tool equipped with audio, video, and application-sharing tools, a text-chat box, and a whiteboard, allowed students to interact with the instructor and other students during lectures and class discussions. Comments in course evaluations indicated that students judged the course, even before its being moved to the online modality, as much more difficult than other courses in the Core program due to its coverage of unfamiliar material (i.e., research methodologies) and heavy writing workload. The course was usually taken by freshmen after a communication course on general writing principles.

After the first week of the semester, when students had the opportunity to get accustomed to the class in which they were enrolled and understand its requirements as described by the instructor, they completed two surveys as part of a self-assessment protocol: the Melbourne Decision-Making questionnaire (DM; Mann et al., 1997), and the New General Self-Efficacy (NGSE) questionnaire (Chen et al., 2001; Chen et al., 2000). The DM, which is a revised version of the Flinders Decision Making instrument (Mann, 1982), measured a variety of decision-making styles through statements that students were asked to evaluate on a 3-point Likert-type scale, including "true for me" (2), "sometimes true" (1) and "not true for me" (0). Included styles were vigilance (6 statements), hyper-vigilance (5 statements), procrastination (5 statements), and buck-passing (6 statements). Instead, the NGSE measured students' general confidence in their ability to deal with a broad range of life challenges (Bandura, 1989). Students reported the extent to which they agreed with each of eight statements of general confidence on a 5-point Likert-type scale from strongly disagree (-2) to strongly agree (+2) with 0 serving as the neutral point.

At the end of the semester, a file was created with all performance and individual difference data. In the file, codes were given to students to eliminate identifying information. Attendance records, treated as an index of motivation, merely referred to the number of credit hours attended (50 minutes each) across a 15-week semester divided by the number of hours offered by the course. The quotient was then multiplied by 100 to obtain the percentage of hours attended by each student (see Table 1).

Important to note is that a mandatory attendance policy applied to all online classes offered by the selected university, according to which students whose attendance rates were less than 85% could be administratively withdrawn from a course. However, because of the ongoing COVID-19 epidemic, and the possibility for students who were absent to hear recorded sessions of the class they missed, the policy was relaxed. Thus, although attendance was mandatory, thereby boosting rates well above the rates of courses without this obligation (see Lukkarinen et al., 2016), sufficient variability existed in students' attendance to allow its use as a variable indexing overall motivation to do well. In the present study, all absences were counted without regard to the presence or absence of a justification.

Even though attendance was automatically recorded by Blackboard Collaborate, concerns existed that a course that had relied on face-to-face interactions for collaborative revisions of written work would be damaged by passive attendance. Thus, administrative guidelines were issued in advance of this course being moved to the online modality, which required the instructor to query the entire class often during each session and to offer abundant feedback on students' writing products during class as well as during scheduled or unscheduled office hours. The insistence on feedback given publicly was intended to convey the message that "what is useful to one student may also be useful to others", thereby overcoming the potential obstacles that the online medium might present to students' collaborative work. The number of questions posed by the instructor to the entire class to ensure engagement varied from 5 to 13 per session, depending on the nature of the instruction, whose format combined class discussion and lecture. A record of the number of comments made by students per class session divided by the number of students who attended was collected by the instructor after each class without reference to specific students. The sessions devoted to the midterm and final tests were not included. The participation quotient included comments, mostly prompted by the instructor's queries and written in the chatbox of Blackboard Collaborate rather than being spoken through the microphone. It ranged from .38 to 4.37 comments per student during a class session ($M = 1.89$; $SEM = .062$). Notwithstanding efforts to prompt responses from all attending students, the instructor reported that some students participated more frequently than others did, but individualized records were not provided.

4. RESULTS

The results presented below are organized in two sections differentiated by the aims of either describing selected characteristics of the participants or using inferential statistics to predict the contribution of particular characteristics to either predicted or actual performance. All results are considered significant at the .05 level.

4.1 Description of the Sample

Table 1 illustrates the means and standard errors of the mean for individual difference variables as well as indices of performance and estimated performance of students who completed the course. Students' performance was averaged across assignments 1-3 because these writing products, which were parts of a paper finalized in assignment 4, displayed the same pattern of influences. It is reasonable to conceptualize assignments 1-3 as entailing the development of the research report, assignment 4 as requiring the completion of the report, and assignment 5 as forcing self-reflection and critical analysis of the work accomplished.

The midterm was administered in week 8 of the semester, preceded and followed by questions requiring students to predict the likely grades as well as to express their degree of confidence in the predictions made. Accuracy was measured as the difference between estimated grade and actual grade. Thus, a positive value indicated overestimation, a negative value implied underestimation, and a value of 0 reflected an accurate prediction. As students' midterm grades increased, the accuracy of their predictions, both before and after the test, increased too, $r = -.83$, $n = 122$, $p < .001$, and $r = -.63$, $n = 122$, $p < .001$, respectively. These rather robust correlations suggest that students' estimates largely relied on information and processes that shaped test performance. As illustrated by coefficients of determination, before the exam estimates captured 69.06% of the variance in students' performance, whereas, after the test, estimates captured 39.31% of that variance, suggesting that direct knowledge of the test made students less likely to judge their competence objectively and more likely to be conservative in their estimates. Subjective confidence in such predictions was not correlated with students' test performance when predictions were made before the test, $r = -.05$, *ns*. After the test, as grades increased, students'confidence increased too, $r = +.21$, $n = 122$, $p = .019$. As expected, students were more accurate at predicting their performance after than before the test, $F(1, 121) = 25.19$, $p < .001$, $MSE = 124.56$, *Partial Eta Squared* = .172, whereas, their confidence remained unchanged, $F(1, 121) = 1.65$, *ns*. Equivalent analyses on final test grades were not performed due to institutional restrictions that made final scores unavailable.

Table 1. Descriptive Statistics

Variables	*Mean*	*Standard Error of the Mean*
Individual Differences		
Self-Efficacy	1.08	.048
Vigilance	1.19	.022
Hyper-Vigilance	1.39	.035
Buck-Passing	.83	.046
Procrastination	.80	.056
Attendance (%)	90.96	1.063

Performance		
Assignments 1-3 (%)	88.09	1.258
Midterm Test (%)	70.96	1.797
Assignment 4 (%)	91.18	1.349
Assignment 5 (%)	92.66	2.112
Prediction of Test Performance		
Accuracy Before Midterm Test (%)	14.37	1.902
Confidence before Midterm Test (%)	1.75	.085
Accuracy After Midterm Test (%)	7.19	1.521
Confidence After Midterm Test (%)	1.63	.096

4.2 Factors Accounting for Performance

Linear regression analyses were conducted with individual difference variables as predictors (self-efficacy, decision-making styles, and attendance records) and performance, predicted performance, or subjective confidence as the outcome variable.

The evidence illustrated in Tables 2-3 can be summarized in three main points: (a) Attendance made a positive contribution to class performance as measured by all assignments and midterm test. The higher was the attendance, the greater was students' subjective confidence after the midterm. (b) Procrastination impaired performance in assignments 1-3, whereas buck-passing, improved performance in assignment 5. (c) The greater was students' self-efficacy, the greater was the confidence with which grade predictions were made both before and after the test. Students' hyper-vigilance, however, reduced confidence before the test. No evidence was found that any of the individual difference variables significantly contributed to the accuracy of grade predictions.

Table 2. The contribution of individual differences to performance

Variables	*B*	*SE*	*Beta*	*t*	*Sign.*
Assignments 1-3	48.424	12.532			
Self-Efficacy	1.429	2.434	.054	.587	*ns*
Vigilance	1.899	5.194	.033	.366	*ns*
Hyper-Vigilance	-.590	3.036	-.016	-.194	*ns*
Buck-Passing	3.350	2.466	.122	1.358	*ns*
Procrastination	-5.131	2.191	-.230	-2.342	.021
Attendance	.418	.102	.353	4.086	.000
Assignment 4	54.493	13.668			
Self-Efficacy	1.471	2.654	.052	.554	*ns*
Vigilance	.095	5.665	.002	.017	*ns*
Hyper-Vigilance	-2.322	3.311	-.060	-.701	. *ns*
Buck-Passing	4.543	2.690	.154	1.689	*ns*
Procrastination	-4.604	2.390	-.193	-1.926	*ns*
Attendance	.419	.111	.330	3.757	.000
Assignment 5	7.771	21.393			
Self-Efficacy	.598	4.154	.014	.144	*ns*
Vigilance	2.612	8.866	.027	.295	*ns*
Hyper-Vigilance	3.455	5.182	.057	.667	*ns*
Buck-Passing	9.598	4.210	.208	2.280	.024
Procrastination	-.859	3.741	-.023	-.230	*ns*
Attendance	.759	.174	.382	4.350	.000
Midterm	29.803	18.528			

Self-Efficacy	3.261	3.598	.087	.906	*ns*
Vigilance	-8.396	7.679	-.102	-1.093	*ns*
Hyper-Vigilance	6.159	4.488	.119	1.372	*ns*
Buck-Passing	3.055	3.646	.078	.838	*ns*
Procrastination	-4.961	3.240	-.156	-1.531	*ns*
Attendance	.445	.151	.263	2.942	.004

Assignments 1-3: $R = .474$. Assignment 4: $R = .445$. Assignments 5: $R = .445$. Midterm Test: $R = .411$.

Table 3. The contribution of individual differences to performance predictions

Variables	*B*	*SE*	*Beta*	*t*	*Sign.*
Accuracy Before Test	35.106	20.780			
Self-Efficacy	.062	4.035	.002	.015	*ns*
Vigilance	7.809	8.612	.089	.907	*ns*
Hyper-Vigilance	-8.529	5.034	-.155	-1.694	*ns*
Buck-Passing	-2.989	4.089	-.072	-.731	*ns*
Procrastination	3.690	3.634	.109	1.016	*ns*
Attendance	-.205	.169	-.115	-1.211	*ns*
Conf. Before Test	1.290	.877			
Self-Efficacy	.436	.170	.245	2.560	.012
Vigilance	-.309	.363	-.079	-.849	*ns*
Hyper-Vigilance	-.549	.212	-.223	-2.583	.011
Buck-Passing	.139	.173	.075	.805	*ns*
Procrastination	-.103	.153	-.068	-.670	*ns*
Attendance	.012	.007	.149	1.671	*ns*
Accuracy After Test	11.112	16.599			
Self-Efficacy	-1.030	3.224	-.032	-.320	*ns*
Vigilance	12.299	6.880	.176	1.788	*ns*
Hyper-Vigilance	-6.394	4.021	-.145	-1.590	*ns*
Buck-Passing	-5.194	3.266	-.156	-1.590	*ns*
Procrastination	-1.041	2.903	-.039	-.359	*ns*
Attendance	-.037	.135	-.026	-.272	*ns*
Conf. After Test	.451	.980			
Self-Efficacy	.517	.190	.257	2.717	.008
Vigilance	-.567	.406	-.129	-1.397	*ns*
Hyper-Vigilance	-.413	.237	-.149	-1.742	*ns*
Buck-Passing	.228	.193	.108	1.182	*ns*
Procrastination	-.101	.171	-.059	-.590	*ns*
Attendance	.019	.008	.214	2.420	.017

Accuracy before the test: $R = .259$. Confidence before the test: $R = .410$. Accuracy after the test: $R = .263$. Confidence after the test: $R = .434$.

5. DISCUSSION

The findings of the present investigation suggest that attendance is a critically important ingredient of good performance even in courses for which it is mandatory. It can be argued that attendance stands for the overall motivation that students have to do well. Yet, it may simply represent students' knowledge of what is going on in the class, including awareness of the content and timing of various requirements. This finding fits popular anecdotes regarding the importance of class attendance, as well as evidence reported by earlier studies attesting that good grades are linked to high attendance (Launius, 1997; Thomas & Higbee, 2000; Moore, 2003).

It is important to note that although attendance in the online courses offered by the selected university was mandatory and automatically recorded by Blackboard Collaborate, considerable concern had existed about online passive attendance in synchronous classes. Namely, fears existed that students would simply log in, but their attention would be tuned to other matters. In all the sections of the selected course, these fears were not supported by the behavioral evidence collected. The instructor documented consistent actions of active participation by students, mostly in the form of answers to the instructor's questions, and much less as requests for clarification of concepts and procedures or as independent contributions to the content of lectures and discussions. Students' preferred mode of participation was through text written in the chatbox of Blackboard Collaborate, whereas spoken communication was rarely relied upon. Although communication in the online class was mostly written and in response to queries, the instructor noted that some students participated more often than others did. Since participation records were holistic and could not be linked to specific students, whether greater participation was reflected in higher attendance is difficult to determine.

Although the findings of the present investigation support the truism that "good students who attend class regularly make good grades", they do not negate the existence of students who diligently and independently complete the required classwork even though their attendance records are poor (see Lukkarinen et al., 2016). The evidence collected merely suggests that in the online environment of a writing-intensive, demanding course, where collaborative exchanges between the students and the instructor are a key aspect of the learning experience, at the minimum, attendance affords awareness of class activities, deadlines, and requirements, which is helpful for success in the course. The present findings are inconsistent with those that claim that it does not matter whether students attend synchronous virtual classes or inspect the recordings of such classes (Nieuwoudt, 2020). Indeed, although some students might have believed that they could make up their absences by reviewing classmates' notes, listening to the recordings of missed classes, studying the assigned readings, and figuring out independently the required steps of a given assignment, these beliefs appeared to represent more unrealized intentions than overt actions (as per students' informal comments made during office hours). When overt action was initiated to catch up, it was reported to be less effective than the experience of attending class. This students' sentiment is not surprising. The curriculum included scholarly articles that are generally difficult to read without the expert guidance of an instructor who, in real-time, can explain novel terms, concepts, theories, etc., thereby helping students to overcome particular difficulties, and undoubtedly making class attendance relevant.

In comparison to attendance, individual difference measures made a limited contribution to performance, either negatively, such as procrastination, or positively, such as buck-passing. The negative impact of procrastination on assignments 1-3, but not on later performance measures, may reflect students' growing realization that postponing writing assignments until the last moment or cramming for the midterm test may not be feasible given the amount and quality of the information to be learned and applied, a realization that some students casually communicated during class and office hours. The positive impact of buck-passing on performance in the Q&A session (assignment 5) appears at first perplexing. Yet, in the context of a Q&A task, buck-passing, as a strategy to cope with a challenging novel situation, may merely reflect learners' attempt to escape the uncertainty of the task by giving up on attempts at forecasting potential questions, thereby diminishing the anxiety generated by multiple predictions whose likelihood may be equally uncertain. Not surprisingly, however, as general self-efficacy increased, students' confidence in their predictions of midterm performance also increased, suggesting that a "can do" attitude, albeit general, can shape how students approach specific tasks and envision their outcomes. Yet, hyper-vigilance was linked to a reduction of such confidence. To wit, making decisions under emotional excitement without exploring all alternatives and available information, generally because of perceived or misperceived time pressure, does not engender confidence in the decisions made. Surprisingly, no impact of individual difference factors, including attendance, was detected on the accuracy of the grade predictions made by students, even though a considerable portion of the variance in performance was captured by the students' estimates (as per coefficients of determination). One possibility is that these estimates reflect a host of emotionally laden thoughts that can overshadow the impact of personal dispositions.

6. CONCLUSION

The findings of the present field study suggest that the association between performance and attendance does not exclude college courses in which attendance is mandatory, as it is implicitly or explicitly suggested in some of the extant literature (Dey, 2018; Hyde & Flournoy, 1986; Kassarnig et al., 2017). They are consistent with those of Rendleman (2017) who reported a link between attendance rates and grades in a topical Core curriculum course (i.e., introductory agricultural economics), irrespective of whether attendance was treated as mandatory or optional.

Students, educators, and advisors alike, who have been engaged in online classes because of the COVID-19 pandemic, may find the findings of the present research useful. They can be used not only to give all students a good reason to attend but also to advise those for whom frequent attendance is not a matter of great importance. College students are adults who judge the benefits of attending a class against the costs of not attending. The message that the present findings deliver to them is clear: for a writing-intensive course that covers unfamiliar material and that heavily relies on targeted feedback by the instructor, independent study, albeit possible, is unlikely to lead to optimal outcomes. Of course, educators are responsible for making their classes valuable to students. Yet, students' awareness of the role that attendance may play in their academic success, particularly in challenging courses, may entice them to attend more frequently, thereby rendering punitive policies about mandatory attendance irrelevant.

The current field study has limitations to be addressed in future research. First, the generalizability of its findings is to be assessed in other courses that vary in content, difficulty, and instructional modes. Second, the withdrawal rates of the selected course need to be analyzed to determine whether the characteristics of the students who withdraw differ from those who persist, albeit all may exhibit less than optimal performance. Regretfully, Blackboard, which served as the platform that preserved students' performance records, automatically deleted the records of students who withdrew from the course before the instructor had the time to log them into a different record-keeping system. Missing or incomplete records could not be used for analysis. Third, due to gender-segregation rules, participation was limited to female students. Cortright et al. (2011) report a link between attendance and test performance in female, but not male students. The examination of gender differences is to be pursued in future research.

ACKNOWLEDGEMENT

A special note of appreciation goes to the members of the Cognitive Science Research Cluster for their contribution to the present study.

REFERENCES

Al Kuhayli, H. A., Pilotti, M. A. E., El Alaoui, K., Cavazos, S. E., Hassan, S. A. M., & Al Ghazo, R. (2019). An exploratory non-experimental design of self-assessment practice. *The International Journal of Assessment and Evaluation, 26*(1), 49–65. https://doi.org/10.18848/2327-7920/CGP/v26i01/49-65

Anderson, L. W., & Krathwohl, D. (Eds.). (2001). *A Taxonomy for learning, teaching and assessing: A revision of Bloom's taxonomy of educational objectives*. Longman.

Bandura, A. (1977). Self-efficacy: Toward a unifying theory of behavioral change. *Psychological Review, 84*(2), 191–215. https://doi.org/10.1037/0033-295X.84.2.191

Bandura, A. (1989). Human agency in social cognitive theory. *American Psychologist, 44*(9), 1175–1184. https://doi.org/10.1037/0003-066X.44.9.1175

Bandura, A., & Schunk, D. H. (1981). Cultivating competence, self-efficacy, and intrinsic interest through proximal self-motivation. *Journal of Personality and Social Psychology, 41*(3), 586–598. https://doi.org/10.1037/0022-3514.41.3.586

Berenson, S. B., Carter, G., & Norwood, K. S. (1992). The at-risk student in college developmental algebra. *School Science and Mathematics, 92*(2), 55–58. https://doi.org/10.1111/j.1949-8594.1992.tb12141.x

Bloom, B. S. (Ed.). (1956). *Taxonomy of educational objectives. Cognitive domain*. McKay.

Bloom, B. S. (1976). *Human characteristics and school learning*. McGraw Hill.

Burnett, P. C., Mann, L., & Beswick, G. (1989). Validation of the Flinders Decision Making Questionnaire on course decision making by students. *Australian Psychologist, 24*(2), 285–292. https://doi.org/10.1080/00050068908259567

Chen, G., Casper, W. J., & Cortina, J. M. (2001). The roles of self-efficacy and task complexity in the relationships among cognitive ability, conscientiousness, and work-related performance: A meta-analytic examination. *Human Performance, 14*(3), 209-230. https://doi.org/10.1207/S15327043HUP1403_1

Chen, G., Gully, S. M., & Eden, D. (2001). Validation of a new general self-efficacy scale. *Organizational Research Methods, 4*(1), 62–83. https://doi.org/10.1177/109442810141004

Chen, G., Gully, S. M., Whiteman, J.-A., & Kilcullen, R. N. (2000). Examination of relationships among trait-like individual differences, state-like individual differences, and learning performance. *Journal of Applied Psychology, 85*(6), 835–847. https://doi.org/10.1037/0021-9010.85.6.835

Chu, A. H. C., & Choi, J. N. (2005). Rethinking procrastination: Positive effects of "active" procrastination behavior on attitudes and performance. *Journal of Social Psychology, 145*(3), 245–264. https://doi.org/10.3200/SOCP.145.3.245-264

Cortright, R. N., Lujan, H. L., Cox, J. H., & DiCarlo, S. E. (2011). Does sex (female versus male) influence the impact of class attendance on examination performance? *Advances in Physiology Education, 35*(4), 416–420. https://doi.org/10.1152/advan.00021.2011

Covington, M. V., & Omelich, C. L. (1988). Achievement dynamics: The interaction of motives, cognitions, and emotions over time. *Anxiety Research, 1*(3), 165–183. https://doi.org/10.1080/08917778808248717

Dey, I. (2018). Class attendance and academic performance: A subgroup analysis. *International Review of Economics Education, 28*, 29–40. https://doi.org/10.1016/j.iree.2018.03.003

Eden, D. (1984). Self-fulfilling prophecy as a management tool: Harnessing Pygmalion. *Academy of Management Review, 9*(1), 64–73. https://doi.org/10.5465/amr.1984.4277938

Eden, D. (1988). Pygmalion, goal setting, and expectancy: Compatible ways to boost productivity. *Academy of Management Review, 13*(4),639–652. https://doi.org/10.5465/amr.1988.4307530

Golding, J.M. (2011). The role of attendance in lecture classes: You can lead a horse to water… *Teaching of Psychology 38*(1), 40–42. https://doi.org/10.1177/0098628310390915.

Ferrari, J. R. (2001). Procrastination as self-regulation failure of performance: Effects of cognitive load, self-awareness, and time limits on "working best under pressure." *European Journal of Personality, 15*(5), 391–406. https://doi.org/10.1002/per.413

Filippello, P., Sorrenti, L., Larcan, R., & Rizzo, A. (2013). Academic underachievement, self-esteem and self-efficacy in decision making. *Mediterranean Journal of Clinical Psychology, 1*(3), 1–11. https://doi.org/10.6092/2282-1619/2013.1.934

Hyde, R. M., & Flournoy, D. J. (1986). A case against mandatory lecture attendance. *Journal of Medical Education, 61*(3), 175–176. https://doi.org/10.1097/00001888-198603000-00005

Janis, I. L., & Mann, L. (1977). *Decision making: A psychological analysis of conflict, choice, and commitment*. Free press.

Judge, T. A., Erez, A., & Bono, J. A. (1998). The power of being positive: The relation between positive self-concept and job performance. *Human Performance, 11*, 167–187. https://doi.org/10.1207/s15327043hup1102&3_4

Kassarnig, V., Bjerre-Nielsen, A., Mones, E., Lehmann, S., & Lassen, D. D. (2017). Class attendance, peer similarity, and academic performance in a large field study. *PloS one, 12*(11), e0187078. https://doi.org/10.1371/journal.pone.0187078

Krathwohl, D. R. (2002). A revision of Bloom's taxonomy: An overview. *Theory into Practice, 41*(4), 212–218. https://doi.org/10.1207/s15430421tip4104_2

Launius, M. H. (1997). College student attendance: Attitudes and academic performance. *College Student Journal, 31*(1), 86.

Lukkarinen, A., Koivukangas, P., & Seppälä, T. (2016). Relationship between class attendance and student performance. *Procedia-Social and Behavioral Sciences, 228*(16), 341–47. https://doi.org/10.1016/j.sbspro.2016.07.051

Mann, L. (1982). *Flinders Decision Making Questionnaire II* [Unpublished Questionnaire]. Department of Psychology, The Flinders University of South Australia.

Mann, L., Burnett, P., Radford, M., & Ford, S. (1997). The Melbourne Decision Making Questionnaire: An instrument for measuring patterns for coping with decisional conflict. *Journal of Behavioral Decision Making, 10*(1), 1–19. https://doi.org/10.1002/(SICI)1099-0771(199703)10:1<1::AID-BDM242>3.0.CO;2-X

Mann, L., Radford, M., Burnett, P., Ford, S., Bond, M., Leung, K., Nakamura, H., Vaughan, G., & Yang, K. S. (1998). Cross-cultural differences in self-reported decision-making style and confidence. *International Journal of Psychology, 33*(5), 325–335. https://doi.org/10.1080/00050068908259567

Marburger, D. R. (2006). Does mandatory attendance improve student performance? *The Journal of Economic Education, 37*(2), 148–155. https://doi.org/10.3200/JECE.37.2.148-155

McMillan, J. H., and Hearn, J. (2008). Student self-assessment: The key to stronger student motivation and higher achievement. *Educational Horizons, 87*(1), 40–49.

Moore, R. (2003). Attendance and performance. *Journal of College Science Teaching, 32*(6), 367–371.

Nieuwoudt, J. E. (2020). Investigating synchronous and asynchronous class attendance as predictors of academic success in online education. *Australasian Journal of Educational Technology,* 36(3), 15-25. https://doi.org/10.14742/ajet.5137

Pajares, F. (1996). Self-efficacy beliefs in academic settings. *Review of Educational Research, 66*(4), 543–578. https://doi.org/10.3102/00346543066004543

Pajares, F. (1997). Current directions in self-efficacy research. In M. L. Maehr & P. R. Pintrich (Eds.), *Advances in motivation and achievement* (pp. 1–49). JAI Press.

Pilotti, M. A. E., El Alaoui, K., Mulhem, H., & Salameh M. H. (2020). A close-up on a predictive moment: Illusion of knowing or lack of confidence in self-assessment? *Journal of Education.* Advance online publication. https://doi.org/10.1177/0022057420944843

Peverly, S. T., Brobst, K. E., Graham, M., & Shaw, R. (2003). College adults are not good at self-regulation: A study on the relationship of self-regulation, note taking, and test taking. *Journal of Educational Psychology, 95*(2), 335–346. https://doi.org/10.1037/0022-0663.95.2.335

Pulakos, E. D., Arad, S., Donovan, M. A., & Plamondon, K. E. (2000). Adaptability in the workplace: Development of a taxonomy of adaptive performance. *Journal of Applied Psychology, 85*(4), 612–624. https://doi.org/10.1037/0021-9010.85.4.612

Rendleman, C. M. (2017). Do attendance policies improve student performance? The relationship among attendance, class policies, and grades 1. *NACTA Journal, 61*(4), 347–349.

Snyder, J., & Frank, L. A. (2016). Attendance policies, instructor communication, student attendance, and learning. *Journal of Education for Business, 91*(2), 108–116. https://doi.org/10.1080/08832323.2015.1128383

St. Clair, K. L. S. (1999). A case against compulsory class attendance policies in higher education. *Innovative Higher Education, 23*(3), 171–180. https://doi.org/10.1023/A:1022942400812

Steel, P., Brothen, T., & Wambach, C. (2001). Procrastination and personality, performance, and mood. *Personality and Individual Differences, 30*(1), 95–106. https://doi.org/10.1016/S0191-8869(00)00013-1

Stone, N. J. (2000). Exploring the relationship between calibration and self-regulated learning. *Educational Psychology Review, 12*(4), 437–475. https://doi.org/10.1023/A:1009084430926

Thomas, P. V., & Higbee, J. L. (2000). The Relationship between Involvement and Success in Developmental Algebra. *Journal of College Reading and Learning, 30*(2), 222–232. https://doi.org/10.1080/10790195.2000.10850097

OPTIMIZING VIDEO TUTORIALS FOR SOFTWARE TRAINING THROUGH CUEING

Vasiliki Ragazou[1] and Ilias Karasavvidis[2]
[1]*PhD Student, Department of Early Childhood Education, Ilias Karasavvidis University of Thessaly, Volos, Greece*
[2]*Assistant Professor, Department of Early Childhood Education, University of Thessaly, Volos, Greece*

ABSTRACT

Video tutorials substantially support demonstration-based training where the main goal is to enhance procedural knowledge by observing various understandable examples of performing a task. Although video tutorials are broadly popular nowadays, little attention is given to the design features of an instructional tutorial. The aim of this study is to investigate the use of cueing on video tutorials for software training. Task performance, mental effort, and self-efficacy were included as dependent variables to explain possible effects mechanisms. The experiment included 118 undergraduate students with ICT experience from a Computer Science department in Greece. All subjects viewed three video tutorials on video editing software followed by practice. The participants achieved significant learning gains, reaching moderate to high levels of success on task performance. No cueing effect was found. The discussion proposes several alternatives for improving the effectiveness of video tutorials.

KEYWORDS

Video Tutorials, Software Training, Cueing, Task Performance, Mental Effort, Self-Efficacy

1. INTRODUCTION

Over the past thirty years, the new advances of technology have introduced the term “digital media literacy” that refers to the individual’s ability to identify the significance of media, understand, create, and share multimedia content (Buckingham, 2005). For instance, creating a poster on Photoshop, editing a video on YouTube, designing a multimedia app are examples of actions that are enabled by a subset of software which called media software or cultural software (Manovich, 2013). Therefore, many users are seeking tutorials to gain more information and consequently acquire more experience in media software.

Video tutorials are a popular learning tool that presents how-to information about software tasks (van der Meij and van der Meij, 2013). They are portrayed through a screen capture with synchronized narration. Today, popular video-sharing websites, such as YouTube and Vimeo, host thousands of informal video tutorials for performing numerous complex software-related tasks such as video editing. A question that arises is what type of software applications can be characterized as complex? According to HCI studies (Leutner, 2000), complex software applications involve a lot of related entities to accomplish complex workflows. As the number of entities rises, the degree of complexity would grow and therefore users should put more mental effort to know and understand all of them.

Since the popularity of video tutorials has been exponentially increasing, there have been many approaches for designing instructional videos. The Cognitive Theory of Multimedia Learning (CTML; Mayer, 2001) and the Cognitive Load Theory (CLT; Sweller, 2005) (1) take into consideration the limitations of human working memory capacity while processing information simultaneously, and (2) interpret how the features of the working memory influence cognitive processes. The CLT and CTML have proposed a set of guidelines for effective dynamic representations (i.e., videos). For example, learners benefit more from words and pictures than only words (multimedia principle) or learners learn better when words are presented as speech rather than on-screen text (modality principle). Several multimedia studies have explored the contribution of multimedia principles in learning with low prior knowledge users (Kalyuga, 2014). Also, Mayer (2001) argues that multimedia design principles may be more beneficial for learners with low prior knowledge than for high prior knowledge learners. Therefore, research on the effectiveness of these principles for high prior knowledge learners has received little attention. This study contributes to literature by exploring cueing with domain experts -Informatics students who had attended several courses on media but novices in the specific sub-field -video editing software.

2. THEORITICAL BACKGROUND

2.1 Cueing

The cueing (or signaling) principle (Mayer, 2001) posits that people learn better when non-content information (e.g., cues) guide user attention to the critical points of the material or emphasize the organization of the material. Cueing is operationalized in many ways, i.e., colour, shapes, zoom, luminance. The question that arises is how cueing improves task performance and, therefore, facilitates learning. A recent meta-analysis of 29 experimental studies (Alpizar et al., 2020) on cueing indicated the following. Firstly, cues may be beneficial for learners in terms of guiding the user's attention to the critical points of a multimedia presentation. Secondly, the use of cueing allows learners to organize and integrate relevant information with prior knowledge. Third, cueing can reduce the visual-search time, thereby releasing working memory resources.

Some researchers have reported that cueing can lead to improved task performance (Amadieu et al., 2011; De Koning et al. 2010) while others have found no effects on learning (Kriz and Hegarty, 2007). Previous research on cueing has some limitations. First, the studies have used self-paced animation or videos with static images and not on videos with a constant flow. Second, the video tutorials used in these studies targeted software with simple interfaces (i.e., word editing, web-based forms) rather than more complex ones (e.g., image or video editing). To the best of our knowledge, there was only one cueing study that has been conducted in the field of software training. Jamet and Fernandez (2016) integrated cueing in self-paced interactive multimedia tutorials that demonstrated how to fill out a web-based form. Cueing was empirically regulated and was implemented through green arrows pointing to elements of the interface. The participants in both conditions (cueing vs no cueing) had the opportunity to tackle each procedure in a step-by-step manner with the step names serving as labels. The results indicated that students in the cueing condition selected the relevant information more quickly compared to students in the no cueing condition. While this finding is clearly in line with MLT, cueing did not influence task performance.

2.2 Mediators of Learning

Another issue that invites further exploration is how individual characteristics such as prior knowledge, mental effort, and self-efficacy affect learning through multimedia. Not all users have the same expertise; some of them are novices while others are experts. Multimedia research considering users' expertise discrepancies has revealed that prior knowledge or prior experience is a crucial variable that influences various cognitive and affective measures. The expertise reversal effect postulates that effective strategies for novices can be redundant or even detrimental for knowledgeable users (Kalyuga, 2014). Most empirical studies have shown that users with low expertise focus on salient elements of information, while users with high expertise can ignore the irrelevant information and focus on the essential elements of the material (Jarodzka et al., 2010).

Multimedia learning materials usually have an inherent level of difficulty, and learners often have no idea of how to select the relevant information in a limited time frame. In this context, the total cognitive load that learners experience can easily surpass the limited capacity of cognitive resources. According to CLT, cueing can avoid cognitive load; however, individuals thoroughly diverge in their processing capacity (Arslan- Ari et al., 2020). Experts have a high level of experience regarding a specific task which reduces the cognitive load associated with the task. Contrarywise, novices lack experience or knowledge and thus face higher cognitive load. In multimedia research, different methods have been used to measure cognitive load with mixed results. Mental effort reflects the amount of cognitive processing a person is engaged. This conceptualization of mental effort by Paas (1992) has been widely accepted in the field of learning and instruction because it has good reliability and validity.

Self-efficacy is an important motivational factor that influences performance (Eccles and Wigfield, 2002). This construct refers to learners' belief that they feel confident to succeed in each task (Bandura, 1997). More specifically, it comprises a user's evaluation of what he or she can do in future task performance. In the last few years, self-efficacy beliefs have been targeted by several software training studies (see van der Meij, 2018). Previous studies have examined an ensemble of design features related to the Demonstration Based Training approach (Brar and van der Meij, 2017) and reported positive effects on self-efficacy. Nevertheless, to this date, no study has thoroughly investigated the unique contribution of cueing on self-efficacy.

2.3 Rationale of the Study and Research Questions

The previous literature review implies that, as a design principle for video tutorials, cueing could potentially improve task performance. This technique appears to be advantageous for learning though it has been explored in combination with other design features. Thus, its possible unique contribution to learning from videotutorials has not been verified. The present study aims to fill this gap by exploring the educational effectiveness of videotutorials that was designed with cueing. Also, it measures task performance, mental effort, and self-efficacy considering one demographics population with high ICT experience in the context of complex media software.

More specifically, the following research questions were investigated:

RQ1: Does the use of cueing on videotutorials for software training enhance task performance? Regarding previous multimedia research, it was hypothesized that cueing would lead to high scores on task performance (Amadieu et al., 2011).

RQ2: How does the use of cueing on videotutorials influence the resulting mental effort and self-efficacy? According to the Expectancy Theory (Eccles and Wigfield, 2002), self-efficacy is a crucial factor in developing a positive attitude towards task performance (Bandura, 1997). Hence, we hypothesized that cueing would boost students' self-efficacy on performing tasks. For mental effort, we hypothesized that cueing would decrease users' mental effort during training.

3. METHOD

3.1 Participants and Design

Participants in this study were 118 (90 male, 28 females) volunteer undergraduate students (mean age:21 years) at a Computer Science in mainland Greece. The students were in their fourth year of Computer Science study and had high expertise in ICT knowledge and software skills. None of the participants reported any familiarization with the video editing software application used in this study.

The research was implemented with the use of an experimental 2x2 mixed factorial repeated measures design. The research plan included two factors of two levels each: (a) cueing (plain, enriched) and (b) practice (practice after the video tutorial, stepwise viewing-based practice). Due to space limitations, we limit ourselves to the examination of one of the factors, cueing. The students were randomly assigned to four groups. The participants in each group watched three different, short video tutorials on video editing.

3.2 Materials

3.2.1 Videotutorials

Three videotutorials were used. The video tutorials were made in vitro and covered aspects of video editing using Video Sequence Editor (VSE) which is bundled with Blender 3D. The first video tutorial presented the VSE interface in Blender with an introduction to basic operations (selecting a clip, changing the position of a clip in time and space (channel). The second videotutorial presented how to apply a transformation effect to achieve a complex action (e.g., zoom, rotation). Finally, the third videotutorial presented an even more complex topic like the simultaneous projection of two pictures in a frame. As the native language of all participants was Greek, all videotutorials were in Greek.

3.2.2 Operationalization

Cueing was operationalized through shapes and high brightness frames that emerged in key points, in the enriched video tutorials for software. Figure 1 shows an example of cues used in the video tutorials of the present study.

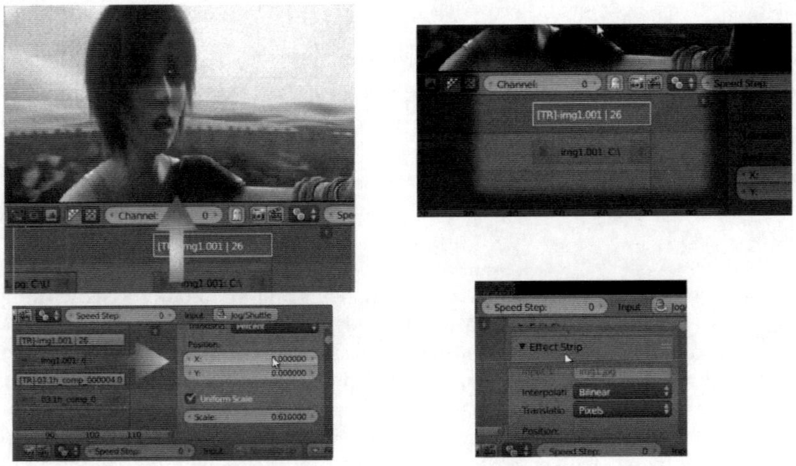

Figure 1. Examples of cueing used in video tutorials

3.3 Measures

3.3.1 Task Performance

Three tasks were used for the purposes of the study. Every task included five questions: two declarative knowledge questions, two procedural knowledge questions, and one transfer knowledge question. The declarative knowledge test comprises of two closed-type questions (e.g., multiple-choice items with three response options, True/False). This measure assessed the amount of information the participants remembered from the videotutorial (Examples: Which of the following colours denotes a transformation effect clip? a) Cyan b) Green c) Purple). The procedural knowledge test consisted of two items that asked students to complete tasks related to those presented on the videotutorial, i.e., adding a transformation effect, adjusting scale for an object (Examples: The top screenshot features two strips from images in the VSE. Add the corresponding transform strips and rearrange them to create the stack featured in the screenshot below). The transfer knowledge test asked students to apply the knowledge gained from the last two video tutorials on a given Blender file to complete the task. Binary coding was used to score all the tasks (1: correct, 0: wrong). A sample transfer question was "The screenshot to the left depicts a composite picture. Use the image strips on VSE to create this picture effect". The declarative items were administered in paper, while the procedural and transfer knowledge items were administered electronically via the LMS platform. For the statistical analysis, the task performance scores were converted to ratios. The reliability analysis indicated high scores for all three tasks (task 1: $\alpha = 0.80$; task 2: $\alpha = 0.81$; task 3: $\alpha = 0.81$).

3.3.2 ICT Experience

A subjective self-report measure of previous ICT experience was used to assess the participants' previous knowledge of multimedia software and the use of the Internet and Computers on a 6-point scale, ranging from very little (1) to very much (6). A sample ICT item was "Please rate your degree of familiarity with Word Processing Applications (e.g., MS-Word, Open Office Writer), Image Editing Software Applications (e.g. Adobe Photoshop, GIMP)". Cronbach's alpha value was approximately 0.7.

3.3.3 Mental Effort

A subjective self-report of mental effort scale was used to assess the measure of cognitive resources that participants invested during the instruction. This item was adapted from Paas (1992) and translated in Greek. The scale asked learners to assess the mental effort they invested while studying the instructional material on a 7-point scale ranging from extremely low (1) to extremely high (7). The overall Cronbach's alpha value across the three tasks was high (0.88).

3.3.4 Self-Efficacy

The participants were asked to rate their knowledge on how well they could perform the actions on a scale from 0 to 100% (Bandura, 2006). There were three questions on Video #1, five questions on Video #2 and six questions on Video #3. (Examples: Image strip selection; Moving image strip to horizontal axis x frames; Moving image strip to vertical y-axis channel". Reliability was perfect for all three tasks 0.99, 0.96, and 0.98, respectively.

3.4 Procedure

The experimental session lasted about 2 hours. The participants were randomly assigned to four conditions. In the beginning, the students were briefed about the study. Next, they logged in the course's LMS, and, depending on their condition, they accessed a specific learning path. After introductory information was given, the students completed the demographic data and previous ICT knowledge questionnaire. Then the participants watched the first videotutorial. Next, they filled out (a) an assessment of the mental effort and (b) an assessment of their self-efficacy. The following step involved the administration of the task performance measure. The same step-sequence was followed for the second and the third videotutorial. It is worth noting here that the students watched each video tutorial once only. All students were instructed to work independently and to call for help only when they faced technical problems.

4. RESULTS

A mixed factorial repeated measures ANOVA was carried out with the cueing as the between-subjects factor and the time after the video tutorial as a within-subjects factor. An alpha value of 0.05 was used throughout the analysis. The Bonferroni correction was applied whenever multiple tests were conducted, thereby reducing the probability level as needed. Finally, because the assumption of sphericity was violated in some cases (i.e., Mauchly's test of sphericity was statistically significant), the corresponding Greenhouse-Geisser F value and degrees of freedom were used.

4.1 Task Performance

Table 1 shows the descriptive statistics for the mean success rates for the tasks in the two conditions. As the inspection of the mean scores shows, the average performance of the participants across the conditions was relatively high, ranging between 70 to 80%. Consequently, the tasks were not particularly challenging for the participants. The above issue should come as no surprise considering that they were studying applied Computer Science; this should also suggest that the students were by no means novices in ICT in general.

A two-way mixed ANOVA failed to show a significant effect of cueing on task performance, $F(1,114) = 0.574$, $p = .450$. As far as the within-subjects factor is concerned (i.e. time), the repeated measures ANOVA did not indicate any significant time by cueing interaction ($F(2,228)=0.137$, $p= .872$). Therefore, performance is not dependent upon cueing. This finding is not in line with our initial hypothesis that cueing would yield higher learning gains compared to the respective reference condition, e.g., plain videotutorials.

Table 1. Mean scores and standard deviations on task performance, mental effort, and self-efficacy rates

Condition	Task performance M (SD)	Mental effort M (SD)	Self-efficacy M (SD)
Plain (n=60)	72.56 (33.58)	3.99 (0.89)	77.82 (19.80)
Cueing (n=58)	76.67 (30.76)	3.91 (1.00)	79.47 (20.70)

4.2 Mental Effort

Interestingly enough, there was no significant effect of cueing on mental effort, $F(1,114)=0.311$, $p= .578$. Subsequent examination of differences of practice with form indicated no significant differences between the two conditions. The average perceived difficulty was 2.92 for the first video, 3.80 for the second video and 5.12 for the last one. This finding agrees with the general trend of learning scores reported in the previous section, lending support to the idea that the difficulty of the videos (and hence the tasks that followed them) increased. The pairwise comparisons of the means indicated that the mean perceived difficulty of the second video was significantly higher than the first and that the mean perceived difficulty of the last video was significantly higher than that of the second.

4.3 Self-Efficacy

The two-way mixed ANOVA failed to show a significant effect of cueing on self-efficacy, $F(1,114)=0.232$, $p= .631$. However, there was a time simple main effect, $F(1.341, 152.867)=20.758$, $p= .000$, $\eta^2=.154$. In the case of cueing, the findings indicate an increase in self-efficacy after watching each software screencast for both factor levels, plain and cueing.

5. DISCUSSION

The study reported in this paper systematically investigated whether the use of cueing in video-based software training affects task performance, mental effort, and self-efficacy.

The results showed that the participants in the cueing condition performed slightly better ($M = 76.67$, $SD = 33.58$) compared to the participants in the plain (i.e., no cueing) condition ($M = 72.56$, $SD = 30.76$). However, this difference was not systematic. One plausible explanation, which is supported by multimedia research, is that cueing favours low prior knowledge users in the stages of the selection, organization, and integration of new information with existing knowledge (van Gog, 2014). This finding also resonates in multimedia research meta-analyses (Alpizar et al., 2020; Richter et al., 2016). Compared to low experienced learners, high prior knowledgeable learners have already constructed mental models in long-term memory (Kalyuga, 2014). Hence, it might be concluded that the presence of cueing hindered high experienced users from understanding the most important information. For this reason, future research should consider the amount of cueing for high experienced users when learning a new software application.

A second possible explanation lies in the modality of cueing used. The present study has used only one type of modalities, such as arrows, geometric shapes, and high-brightness frames. The monotonous appearance of these signals may have been attenuated during software training. According to Xie's et al. (2019) meta-analysis, combining two types of modality simultaneously (visual and verbal) can help learners integrate words and images to focus more time on the essential element of learning material. Thus, future studies should investigate a dual modality of cueing in videotutorials to enhance task performance.

Regarding mental effort, the findings indicated that cueing had no influence on mental effort. This finding is in line with many empirical studies (Lowe and Boucheix, 2011). One possible explanation is that users with experience in the subject have already created a mental representation in their long-term memory. Any external information received through a teaching tool, such as dynamic representations (e.g., videotutorials), may conflict with pre-existing knowledge, and this may result in the appearance of a cognitive burden. Therefore, experienced users may need to watch the video several times to cover up their misunderstandings.

Students' self-references to the cognitive effort reinforce the above claim, stating that they used high cognitive resources. According to Kriz and Hegarty (2007), the iterative learning process benefits users with a high level of expertise to resolve the conflict that arises between new knowledge and the existing mental schemas.

Regarding self-efficacy, no cueing effect was detected. One plausible explanation lies in the participants' academic background. Yokoyama's (2019) review has shown that academic self-efficacy plays an essential role in academic task performance. For example, if a student's self-efficacy is enhanced, the student may be able to achieve higher educational scores. Several studies have assumed that self-efficacy is the most significant factor for students to achieve high scores on task execution (Honicke and Broadbent, 2016). In this study, cueing did not affect self-efficacy and hence task performance, creating a domino effect.

Taking all into consideration, the presence of cueing did not improve learning from video tutorials on software training. Empirical studies in multimedia learning have revealed positive outcomes of cueing when learning from static materials. In the case of dynamic representations, cueing may not work for video tutorials. Due to the transient nature of the video, the effect of cueing might fade. For this reason, future studies need to investigate the amount of cueing and the modality of cueing during software training. Also, future research will need to replicate the current findings with other complex software applications and different user demographics. To date, most studies have used relatively simple applications rather than complex ones.

Additionally, while former studies have examined cueing, the present study is the first one to experimentally examine it in the case of complex software training with participants who were complete novices in the software tool used but domain experts. Thus, we have attempted to systematically extend former research by investigating the effect of cueing in novel contexts, with complex software applications, and different user expertise levels. While this is, obviously, an essential step in a new direction, more systematic research is required.

5.1 Limitations

A limitation of the study is gender bias in the sample used. Since the research was conducted in a Computer Science department, the sample was dominated by males. In the future, it would be advisable to replicate the findings with a similar user population that is more balanced in terms of gender.

A second limitation is that we used a specific measure for mental effort. Even though it is a reliable and valid scale, it might not provide an overall accurate representation of the students' total cognitive load. Future studies should adopt new cognitive load strategies, i.e., electroencephalography (Antonenko et al., 2010) to provide more sufficient data for more in-depth learning.

6. CONCLUSION

All in all, the findings of the present study indicate that cueing does not improve task performance in the case of complex software as far as experts in the domain but novices in the specific sub-field are concerned. Since there is scarce empirical evidence on the role of software screencasts on learning complex software applications, it can be argued that the picture that emerges warrants further systematic exploration. Future studies need to investigate how specific design guidelines in various combinations affect complex software training. Finally, in the case of software training, the relative expertise of learners needs to be taken into consideration as high ICT knowledge users might respond differently to cueing and practice.

ACKNOWLEDGEMENT

The authors would like to thank the students of Computer Science of Central Greece for their participation in the study.

REFERENCES

Alpizar, D. et al, 2020. A meta-analysis of signaling principle in multimedia learning environments. *Educational Technology Research and Development*, pp. 1–25.

Amadieu, F. et al, 2011. The attention-guiding effect and cognitive load in the comprehension of animations. *Computers in Human Behavior*, 27(1), pp. 36-40.

Antonenko, P. et al, 2010. Using electroencephalography to measure cognitive load. Educational Psychology *Review*, 22(4), pp. 425-438.

Arslan-Ari, I. et al, 2020. How Much Cueing Is Needed in Instructional Animations? The Role of Prior Knowledge. *Journal of Science Education and Technology*, 29(5), pp. 666-676.

Bandura, A., 1997. *Self-efficacy: The exercise of control*. New York: Freeman and Company.

Bandura, A., 2006. *Guide for constructing self-efficacy scales*. Self-efficacy beliefs of adolescents, 5(1), pp. 307-337.

Brar, J. and van der Meij, H., 2017. Complex software training: Harnessing and optimizing video instruction. *Computers in human behavior*, 70, pp. 475-485.

Buckingham, D., 2005, Media Literacy of Children and Young People Literature Review: A Review of the Research *Literature on Behalf of OFCOM*, OFCOM, London.

De Koning, B. et al, 2010. Attention guidance in learning from a complex animation: Seeing is understanding?. *Learning and instruction*, 20(2), pp. 111-122.

Eccles, J. S. and Wigfield, A., 2002. Motivation beliefs, values, and goals. *Annual Review of Psychology*, 53(1), pp. 109–132.

Honicke, T. and Broadbent, J., 2016. The influence of academic self-efficacy on academic performance: a systematic review. *Educational Research Review*. 17, pp. 63–84.

Jamet, E. and Fernandez, J., 2016. Enhancing interactive tutorial effectiveness through visual cueing. *Educational Technology Research and Development*, 64(4), pp. 631-641.

Jarodzka, H. et al, 2010. In the eyes of the beholder: how experts and novices interpret dynamic stimuli. *Learning and Instruction*, 20(2), pp. 146–154.

Kalyuga, S., 2014. Prior knowledge principle in multimedia learning. In R. E. Mayer (Ed.), *The Cambridge handbook of multimedia learning*, New York: Cambridge University Press, pp. 576–597.

Kriz, S. and Hegarty, M., 2007. Top-down and bottom-up influences on learning from animations. *International Journal of Human Computer Studies*, 65(11), pp. 911–930.

Leutner, D., 2000. Double-fading support—a training approach to complex software systems. *Journal of computer assisted learning*, 16(4), pp. 347-357.

Lowe, R. and Boucheix, J. M., 2011. Cueing complex animations: Does direction of attention foster learning processes?. *Learning and Instruction*, 21(5), pp. 650-663.

Manovich, L., 2013. *Software takes command* (Vol. 5). A&C Black.

Mayer, R. E., 2001. *Multimedia learning*. New York: Cambridge University Press.

Paas, F., 1992. Training strategies for attaining transfer of problem solving skill in statistics: a cognitive load approach. *Journal of educational psychology*, 84(4), pp. 429–434.

Paas, F. et al, 2003. Cognitive load measurement as a means to advance cognitive load theory. *Educational Psychologist*, 38(1), 63–71. https://doi.org/10.1207/S15326985EP3801_8.

Richter, J. et al, 2016. Signaling text-picture relations in multimedia learning: A comprehensive meta-analysis. *Educational Research Review*, 17, pp. 19-36.

Sweller, J., 2005. Implications of cognitive load theory for multimedia learning. In R. E. Mayer (Ed.), *The Cambridge handbook of multimedia learning*. New York: Cambridge University Press, pp. 19–30.

van Der Meij, H., 2018. Cognitive and motivational effects of practice with videos for software training. *Technical communication*, 65(3), pp. 265-279.

van der Meij, H. and van der Meij, J., 2013. Eight guidelines for the design of instructional videos for software training. *Technical communication*, 60(3), pp. 205-228.

Van Gog, T., 2014. 11 The Signaling (or Cueing) Principle in Multimedia Learning. *The Cambridge handbook of multimedia learning*, 263.

Yokoyama, S., 2019. Academic self-efficacy and academic performance in online learning: A mini review. *Frontiers in psychology*, 9, 2794.

Xie, H. et al, 2019. Coordinating visual and auditory cueing in multimedia learning. *Journal of Educational Psychology*, 111(2), pp. 235–255.

A MIXED METHODS STUDY OF ENGINEERING UNDERGRADUATES' ADAPTIVE LEARNING EXPERIENCES

Seok Joo Kwak[1] and Joi-Lynn Mondisa[2]
[1]*Prior Affiliation: University of Michigan*
Current Affiliation: Independent
Seoul, South Korea
[2]*University of Michigan, Ann Arbor, MI 48109*

ABSTRACT

Open-access online courses, called massive open online courses (MOOCs), have received much attention from higher education institutions and course designers for their potential to reshape learning opportunities. Among the challenges in learning from MOOCs or in an online setting is that students may have insufficient prerequisite knowledge about the topic being presented. If so, students may have a limited understanding of the material and they cannot ask questions in person to clarify their understanding. To address this problem, researchers have been developing adaptive learning technologies. Adaptive learning is a form of learning in which a computer changes the lecture content to best fit a given student based on the student's interactions with the interface. However, current literature suggests that behavioral patterns such as boredom or frustration in adaptive online learning tasks should be explored in order to improve students' learning experiences. This study investigated engineering undergraduate students' perceptions of an adaptive learning environment using MOOCs materials. In this exploratory mixed-methods study, we collected and analyzed survey and interview data and post-test scores for 18 students in our experiment. The results of the evaluation suggest a negative correlation in the relationship between students' learning gains and their perceptions of their enjoyment of the videos.

KEYWORDS

Adaptive Learning, MOOCs, Personalized E-Learning

1. INTRODUCTION

Over the past decade, massive open online courses (MOOCs) have received a great deal of attention in the education field (Gaebel, 2013). MOOCs provide high-quality learning resources for millions of students to access at their convenience, at little or no cost. However, MOOCs come with many challenges. One challenge is that although many students enroll in MOOCs, the retention rates for these courses are very low and only a very small proportion of students complete the courses (Khalil & Ebner, 2014). According to Belanger and Thornton (2013), another challenge is that students who participate in MOOCs may have insufficient prior knowledge about the course topic. This may lead to their becoming frustrated while watching a MOOC, and being unable to process the material they are learning. As a result, they may be unable to go on to the next steps. Furthermore, while using MOOC content, students may have no one to turn to for help (Belanger & Thornton, 2013). Therefore, the second main problem with MOOCs is that personalized support is unavailable to students and there is a lack of interaction between instructors and students (Zhang, Zhu, Wang, & Chen, 2018).

According to Brame (2016), there are three elements that must be considered in educational video design and implementation in order to keep students engaged and for the video to serve as a productive part of a learning experience. They are: (1) cognitive load (channels relate to where the processing of the incoming information takes place); (2) non-cognitive elements that impact engagement (e.g., shortness of content-delivery segments and a conversational style of delivery); and (3) features that promote active learning (e.g., interactive activities, homework).

Also, Guo, Kim, and Rubin (2014) state that in order to optimize the cognitive load and keep students engaged during an e-learning experience, it is recommended that videos be kept short, preferably under 6 minutes. Furthermore, appropriately using both auditory and visual channels in videos has been shown to maximize students' retention of the material and increase student engagement (Guo et al., 2014). Guo et al. (2014) also reported that student engagement was dependent on the narrator's speaking rate, such that student engagement increased as the speaking rate increased.

One way to help students and to enhance their online learning experiences would be to develop intelligent tutoring systems that provide additional explanations of materials to learners (Aleven & Koedinger, 2002). Building on decades of research in intelligent tutoring systems, psychometrics, cognitive learning theory, and data science, researchers have developed adaptive learning technologies (Rosen et al., 2018). The defining feature of adaptive learning is that a computer algorithm analyzes the student's interactions with the interface and changes the lecture content to best fit that student. However, Rosen et al. (2018) suggested that behavioral patterns in learners in performing adaptive tasks should be explored in order to identify ways to improve adaptive tasks (Rosen et al., 2018). Our research study explores the effects of adaptive interactive tasks from students' perspectives and potential factors that might improve adaptive learning environments.

It is clear that MOOCs providers want students to learn as much as possible. But currently, the dropout rate is really high due to learners' frustration with online learning. However, minimal data exists in regard to what factors may contribute to online learners' frustration in an adaptive learning environment (e.g., too many adaptive quizzes, monotony of the lecturer's voice, etc.). As a result, these factors may lead learners to dropout or quit. The purpose of this experimental pilot study is to explore how students' adaptive learning experiences influence their levels of frustration and enjoyment using online learning modules.

2. DESCRIPTION OF EXPERIMENT

The primary purpose of the research study was to explore how students' perceptions of adaptive learning environments are related to frustration with and enjoyment of the modules. To this end, we developed and executed an exploratory mixed methods research design (Creswell, 2002), which involved surveying and interviewing participants to investigate their adaptive learning experiences. The experiment was conducted to address the following hypothesis: As students are exposed to an adaptive learning environment, they may experience frustration, but also an increased sense of enjoyment.

We analyzed the survey and interview data to elicit the most emergent themes. Ultimately, we hope to: (1) understand whether students become frustrated in engaging in adaptive learning environments and, if they do, why and (2) determine whether students' enjoyment increases due to engaging in an adaptive activity. In the following paragraphs, we detail the procedures used to conduct the research study.

2.1 Participants

In order to have a population with the same amount of knowledge, it was essential to recruit students with little exposure to the lecture topic featured in the online learning material. This allowed us to measure learning gains across students with the same knowledge level of the topic. Thus, we initially attempted to recruit University of Michigan (UM) engineering undergraduate students who had not taken any industrial and operations engineering (IOE) courses. If they had not taken any IOE courses, then it was more likely possible to measure their learning gains related to the topic material. In a previous study, Pomales-Garcia and Liu (2006) recruited 18 participants to effectively analyze learners' perceptions and the impact of web modules on their learning experiences. For this pilot study, after receiving approval from the UM Institutional Review Board, we requested that department program coordinators distribute the recruitment email through their undergraduate email listservs. We recruited 18 UM engineering undergraduate students for our sample population.

The average age of the sample was 20.38 years, and the average GPA was 3.48 on a 4.00 scale. Among the participants, 10 students were male and 8 students were female. Participants self-identified their racial backgrounds as: Asian (9), White/Non-Hispanic (5), Hispanic or Latinx (2), American Indian or Alaska Native (1), and Black or African American (1). The participants' demographics by academic major were: Mechanical Engineering (9), Industrial Engineering (5), Chemical Engineering (1), Biomedical Engineering (1), Civil Engineering (1) and Not yet declared (1).

2.2 Instruments and Data Collection Procedures

A survey and interview protocol were developed to collect information about participants' experiences in performing adaptive learning tasks in an adaptive learning environment. Demographic information (i.e., academic major, race, gender, etc.) about participants was also collected.

2.2.1 Learning Modules Materials

To examine the effects of the adaptive learning environment, the experiment consisted of participants watching a 20 to 30 minute lecture that included adaptive tasks (for each concept that was covered), intermittent assessment (approximately 3 to 10 minutes) of the participants' content knowledge via survey, and then interviewing the participants about their experiences. Specifically, we created an adaptive learning task experience for participants using online learning videos from YouTube and electronic survey software. The chosen topic for the video lecture was basic Economic Order Quantity (EOQ), which focuses on optimizing order quantity to minimize total costs. This concept requires that a student be knowledgeable about economic concepts, calculus, and inventory management. We first created the video module by splicing together content from existing YouTube videos that had the most views about EOQ topics. Then, we created a survey of content knowledge questions using Qualtrics software that asked participants questions after each topic was taught.

2.2.2 Survey Protocol Development

The study's survey consisted of nine questions. Six questions requested demographic information (e.g., race/ethnicity, sex/gender, academic status, age, major, and citizenship status). In addition, three survey items were modified and adapted from Pomales-Garcia and Liu (2006). These questions asked participants to rate their own perceptions of knowledge (i.e., understanding of the material presented in the video) gained using a five-point Likert scale (1 = strongly disagree to 5 = strongly agree). This was done to collect information about their perceived adaptive learning experiences as quantifiable data. These questions were:

a) Before watching the video modules, how much did you know about the topic discussed in the module using a scale of 1-5, where 1 = completely new material and 5 = expert?
b) After watching the video modules, how much did you know about the topic discussed in the module using a scale of 1-5, where 1 = completely new material and 5 = expert?
c) If the rating for the level of difficulty of a children's story for a four-year-old represents a rating of 1, what is the level of difficulty of the content that this module presented?

2.2.3 Interview Protocol Development

We created an interview protocol composed of 17 questions. The interview protocol was developed in collaboration with mixed methods study experts in Dr. John W. Creswell's mixed-method workshop in 2018. The interview questions required the participants to offer more details about their adaptive learning experiences in the pilot study. The first question asked participants about their overall adaptive learning experience. The interview questions focused on three sets of themes: frustration, attention level, and enjoyment of the material. Rosen et al. (2018) suggest that behavioral patterns in adaptive tasks should be explored. Thus, we created interview questions that examined three topics: (1) enjoyment: the enjoyment students experience in an adaptive online learning environment; (2) frustration: the frustration students experience in an adaptive online learning environment; and (3) online video usage: students' use of online videos as an educational supplement. For each topic element, there were corresponding interview questions. For enjoyment, there were six questions (e.g., "What did you like about your experience in completing the module?"). There were six items that measured frustration (e.g., "Describe a time in this process in which you felt frustrated"). For the topic of online video usage, there were two questions (e.g., "Do you use online videos or MOOCs as a supplement in your studying?"). The two final questions inquired if participants wanted to provide any additional thoughts about the overall experience, and, finally, if there were any final thoughts they would like to add in general.

2.2.4 Administering the Survey and Interviews

Survey response data was collected using an online Qualtrics survey. To maintain participants' privacy, the names of the participants were changed to pseudonyms and any identifiable information has been removed from the reported data. The interview voice recordings were transcribed verbatim by the first author. Voice recordings were deleted immediately after the transcription. Prior to conducting this research, this study was approved by the UM Institutional Review Board.

2.2.5 Experimental Procedure

The experimental procedure consisted of several steps. First, the researcher discussed the outline of the procedure with the participant, and then the participant signed an informed consent form. Next, the participant watched the adaptive video lecture lesson, and then took a post-test. The post-test consisted of questions about EOQ topics to assess students' knowledge of what they had learned in the video. Next, the participant completed a survey that collected demographic information and examined their learning experience and, finally, participated in an interview with me in which data was collected using the Samsung Galaxy s6 voice recording program. These procedural steps are discussed in detail in the following sections.

2.2.6 Lecture Procedure

After consenting, the participants went through a lecture procedure that involved watching a video lecture and taking content quizzes at specific places in the video. Specifically, the participants performed the following steps:

(1) Video: Participants watched a video about an EOQ topic.

(2) Content Quiz: After each topic was explained, the system displayed a short multiple-choice quiz about the topic. There were three questions asked per adaptive task. The adaptive tasks were administered two times. There was one content quiz administered at the end of the lecture procedure.

(3) Remediation Videos: After the participants completed the content quiz, they were administered one of two types of remediation videos (i.e., short and long). Remediation videos are additional videos that provide a more detailed explanation of the video that they watched. Shorter remediation videos (3 minutes) were shown to the first nine participants who participated in the experiment, and longer remediation videos (8 minutes) were shown to the remaining nine participants. This was done to initially examine how the length of the remediation video affects students. However, we did not find any significant effect on students.

(4) Post-Test: Following the lecture procedure, all participants took a post-test about what they had learned. The post-test consisted of eight questions about EOQ topics to assess students' knowledge of what they had learned during the whole learning process. An example of a post-test question is: "What would happen to economic orders quantity if other items remained the same in the EOQ model, with double annual demand and double the unit cost of purchased materials?"

2.2.7 Administering the Survey and Interview

After participants completed the post-test, the researcher administered a survey to collect information about participants' demographic characteristics and their experiences. After the participants completed the survey, we conducted interviews with them. The interviews were conducted in an enclosed room. The interviewer asked questions and the interviewee answered in a conversational style. This allowed us to see in detail what the students were experiencing during the learning process.

3. DATA ANALYSIS

After the data collection procedure, we used quantitative (e.g., descriptive statistics) and qualitative (e.g., thematic analysis) methods to analyze the survey and interview data, respectively. Three themes (i.e., Enjoyment, Frustration, Use of Online Learning) were explored qualitatively. First, we performed descriptive statistics analysis and organized students' responses according to the corresponding theme. Then, we transcribed the 18 interviews. Finally, we thematically analyzed the interview data to identify major emergent themes (Creswell, 2002). Details about steps performed in analyzing the data quantitatively and qualitatively are explained in the following sections.

3.1 Quantitative Phase

We wanted to explore the differences in frustration between students who did extremely well on the post-test (scored 100%) and students who did not. Therefore, we divided students into two groups: those with perfect scores and those with non-perfect scores. Then we looked at each score group's transcribed data. From the transcribed data, we divided the data into groups of students who expressed that they were frustrated and those who did not express that they were frustrated about the adaptive learning environment. Next, we tallied how many students were in each category. The findings are displayed in Section 4. Within the group of students who expressed frustration, we qualitatively explored why they were frustrated, which will be explained in the next section.

To investigate whether and why students use online videos as educational supplements, we coded the transcribed data into themes. We tallied how many students used online videos to supplement their college study and learning experiences. Then we organized these results.

To assess the correlation between students' post-test scores and their perceptions about the enjoyment gained from the adaptive learning activity, we assessed Pass/Fail scores. First, we collected test score data. Then, a Pass was assigned to scores greater than 70 out of 100 points. Under the enjoyment data, we filtered data corresponding to students who passed and those who failed. Next, we tallied how many students were in each group.

3.2 Qualitative Phase

Interview transcripts (n = 18) were thematically coded and used in conjunction with the descriptive statistics information to explore and understand how learners' perceptions of learning environments were affected by the adaptive tasks and the explanation videos. Specifically, thematic analysis (Boyatzis, 1998) was performed using the following method. First, using the interview data, we assessed and categorized participants' most frequent and common responses that arose about frustration, enjoyment, and the use of online educational videos. Answers that commonly arose were grouped into the same category theme. For example, six students expressed that they were frustrated with the professor's tone and energy. Their specific responses were grouped into one qualitative category (i.e., frustration) to assist with further interpreting the quantitative data. Specifically, the interview data allowed us to examine similarities or differences in the interviews of participants and their descriptive statistical data in frustration and enjoyment and the use of videos. The data analysis findings and a discussion of the implications of this research are presented in the next section.

4. RESULTS AND DISCUSSION

From the data, three main themes emerged about engineering undergraduates' adaptive learning experiences in regard to enjoyment, frustration, and online video usage. Those themes are: (1) Adaptive Learning Environments are Enjoyable, (2) Frustration Linked to Teacher Energy and Lack of Student Knowledge, and (3) High Rates of Online Video Usage as Educational Supplements.

4.1 Adaptive Learning is Enjoyable

Findings seem to suggest that students found the adaptive learning experience enjoyable. Among all students who expressed that the overall adaptive learning process was helpful and enjoyable (n = 15), approximately half (n = 8) earned a passing quiz score (i.e., more than 70 out of 100 points).

It is clear that MOOCs providers want students to learn as much as possible. But currently, the dropout rate is really high due to frustration. However, there is minimal data that exists in regard to what factors may contribute to online learners' frustration (e.g., too many adaptive quizzes, monotony of lecturer's voice, etc.). As a result, these factors may lead learners to dropout or quit. The purpose of this experimental pilot study is to explore how students' adaptive learning experiences influence their levels of frustration and enjoyment in using online learning modules.

Some of the reasons about enjoyment given by students who did not earn a passing score were:

> *"It (the learning experience) was interesting. It (if I already knew the material) would save me a lot of time because if I already learned most of it or just the little things here, then I can move on to different videos."*

> *"It (the learning experience) was good. I liked (that) the quiz asked about content that's included in (the process). That's great because I have that question in mind so the next video, I could expect the video to talk about it."*

> *"I thought it (the learning experience) was great. I feel like this can be used to bridge the gap instead of watching the whole lecture."*

From the data, it seems that students perform more poorly in retaining online content knowledge if they do not enjoy the online video. Specifically, findings seem to suggest that there is a negative relationship between students' final post-test scores and their perceptions of enjoying the video. This might occur because the videos automatically display information for students and reduce students' motivation to search for examples. This relationship suggests that the adaptive learning environment may play an important role in facilitating help, but it also reduces students' germane load (i.e., a cognitive activity that deals with interpreting, exemplifying, classifying, inferring, differentiating, and organizing).

4.2 Frustration Linked to Teacher Energy and Lack of Student Knowledge

Results seem to indicate that students' frustration with the adaptive learning tasks may be linked to the monotony of the video instructor or the students' own lack of content knowledge. In regard to the theme of frustration, among the 12 students (n = 12) who did not achieve a perfect score on the final test, 50% of those students found the adaptive learning session frustrating.

When asked in the interview, 50% of students said that they felt frustrated. We found two different reasons why students were frustrated: (1) they did not like the energy (i.e., monotone and low enthusiasm) of the teacher in the video; and (2) they lacked knowledge about the adaptive tasks they were tested on. Some of the quotes about frustration given by students were:

> *"I was frustrated when he (the video instructor) took a while to explain things."*

> *"This video (...) was like boring, it was like slow sort of, but not really due to the content."*

> *"When the quizzes were talking about something else (I had not learned yet), it was kind of confusing at first."*

Similarly, among the six students who performed perfectly on the final test, 50% (n = 3) found the adaptive learning session frustrating because it tested them on the knowledge that they did not yet possess. Both groups (frustrated and not frustrated) stated that, after they watched the remediation videos that explained the missing concept thoroughly, they felt more confident about the process.

From the findings, it seems that students got frustrated engaging in the adaptive learning activity when they did not know the answers to questions they had not learned about. In particular, the adaptive task questions were designed in such a way that if students had strong backgrounds in mathematics and/or economics, they would be able to solve the mini-adaptive tasks. However, the adaptive learning process may have created students' frustration because the initial instructions were not clear. The tasks tested them on the knowledge that they did not yet possess.

According to one study, researchers found that engaged concentration and frustration are correlated with positive learning outcomes (Pardos, Baker, San Pedro, Gowda, & Gowda, 2013). Therefore, it is worthwhile to examine ways to reduce students' enjoyment of a video while increasing the frustration necessary to evoke a student's positive learning gains. Furthermore, it is valuable to explore what factors in adaptive learning environments create frustrations that add value to students' learning gains, as well as what factors do not add value. According to Guo et al. (2014), using a conversational, enthusiastic teaching style enhances students' engagement. The current study results seem to support their conclusion in that some students found the adaptive learning session frustrating because the energy of the teacher was low. Thus, to reduce students' frustration, videos with a conversational and enthusiastic style should be selected for use in adaptive learning environments.

4.3 High Rates of Online Video Usage as Educational Supplements

The data seems to suggest that students use online videos to help supplement their understanding. From the interview data, in regard to online education, 94.4% of the participants (n = 17) indicated that they use MOOCs or YouTube Education videos outside of school courses to help them with concepts. Some students explained how they used online educational materials:

> *"I watch Khan and YouTube videos. I take like bits and pieces (of) knowledge that I need help (with) for school."*

> *"If I am looking for a specific topic that I don't understand, I just search on YouTube instead of having to browse through an entire (set of) notes."*

> *"If a professor doesn't really explain it (a specific topic) all the way, I prefer using online videos because I can pause (the videos and watch) it over (again)."*

Students seem to regularly use online videos as supplemental learning tools. In Jaffar (2012) descriptive and experimental study on college students (n = 91), he illustrates that 98% of respondents were using online learning videos as a source of information. Even though our study is based on a smaller sample size (n = 18), our result is consistent with Jaffar's result by indicating that more than 90% of engineering undergraduate students are using MOOCs or YouTube Education videos outside of school courses.

Results from this study may reinforce the claim that online video education has become essential for new millennial learners in their undergraduate learning. Therefore, teachers and online course designers should also increase their efforts to continuously improve online teaching quality in order to help students.

4.4 Limitations

This study has some limitations. First, the sample size was very small. However, as a pilot study, this study assists in determining an experimental research design for future research on frustration, enjoyment, and the use of online educational videos. Second, this study is limited in its analysis of the behavior of learners who participated in an adaptive learning activity featuring MOOC material from a single lecture. Learners viewing or posting comments were not considered. Future research should examine how MOOCs' forums and posted comments may also play roles in affecting students' adaptive learning experiences. Third, this study focused on using thematic analysis of the qualitative data. Future research studies could employ more advanced statistical analyses to analyze the frustration and engagement of learners in adaptive learning environments.

5. CONCLUSIONS AND FUTURE WORK

Prior research suggested that behavioral patterns in adaptive tasks should be explored in order to improve students' learning experiences (Rosen et al., 2018). Using collected survey data, interview data, and post-test scores from the 18 students in our experiment, this study investigated engineering undergraduate students' perceptions of an adaptive learning environment. After the data collection, an analysis of the descriptive statistics and interview data were used to identify emergent themes. In this experiment, the results suggest that there may be a negative correlation between students' learning gains and their perceptions of enjoying an adaptive task.

There were several insights gained from this pilot study that may help to inform the design of future research studies of adaptive learning experiences. First, we learned that for future research studies, we will administer a pre-test to all students before they engage in the adaptive lecture lesson. This will allow us to compare learning gains across students who perform various adaptive tasks. Also, future research designs should use a machine learning model to better predict the learners' path. In addition, detailed qualitative data collected through open-ended interview questions should be used to better understand the quantitative data and the survey results.

REFERENCES

Aleven, V. A., & Koedinger, K. R. (2002). An effective metacognitive strategy: Learning by doing and explaining with a computer-based Cognitive Tutor. *Cognitive science, 26*(2), 147-179.

Belanger, Y., & Thornton, J. (2013). Bioelectricity: A quantitative approach Duke University's first MOOC.

Boyatzis, R. E. (1998). *Transforming qualitative information: Thematic analysis and code development*: sage.

Brame, C. J. (2016). Effective educational videos: Principles and guidelines for maximizing student learning from video content. *CBE—Life Sciences Education, 15*(4), es6.

Creswell, J. W. (2002). *Educational research: Planning, conducting, and evaluating quantitative*: Prentice Hall Upper Saddle River, NJ.

Gaebel, M. (2013). MOOCs Massive open online courses. *EUA Occasional papers*.

Guo, P. J., Kim, J., & Rubin, R. (2014). *How video production affects student engagement: an empirical study of MOOC videos.* Paper presented at the Proceedings of the first ACM conference on Learning@ scale conference.

Jaffar, A. A. (2012). YouTube: An emerging tool in anatomy education. *Anatomical sciences education, 5*(3), 158-164.

Khalil, H., & Ebner, M. (2014). MOOCs Completion Rates and Possible Methods to Improve Retention-A Literature Review.

Pardos, Z. A., Baker, R. S., San Pedro, M. O., Gowda, S. M., & Gowda, S. M. (2013). *Affective states and state tests: Investigating how affect throughout the school year predicts end of year learning outcomes.* Paper presented at the Proceedings of the Third International Conference on Learning Analytics and Knowledge.

Pomales-Garcia, C., & Liu, Y. (2006). Web-based distance learning technology: The impacts of web module length and format. *The American journal of distance education, 20*(3), 163-179.

Rosen, Y., Rushkin, I., Rubin, R., Munson, L., Ang, A., Weber, G., . . . Tingley, D. (2018). *The effects of adaptive learning in a massive open online course on learners' skill development.* Paper presented at the Proceedings of the Fifth Annual ACM Conference on Learning at Scale.

Zhang, M., Zhu, J., Wang, Z., & Chen, Y. (2018). Providing personalized learning guidance in MOOCs by multi-source data analysis. *World Wide Web*, 1-31.

USING MOBILE TECHNOLOGY TO PROMOTE HIGHER-ORDER THINKING SKILLS IN ELEMENTARY MATHEMATICS

Debbie Marie B. Verzosa[1], Ma. Louise Antonette N. De Las Peñas[2], Jumela F. Sarmiento[2], Maria Alva Q. Aberin[2], Mark Anthony C. Tolentino[2] and Mark L. Loyola[2]
[1]Department of Mathematics and Statistics, University of Southern Mindanao, Philippines
[2]Department of Mathematics, Ateneo de Manila University, Philippines

ABSTRACT

The problem of rote-based learning in mathematics is well documented. Mobile technology can provide a potential solution, especially when application (app) design is based on sound pedagogical principles and gamification elements. However, an inventory of available mobile apps for mathematics reveals that many of the available apps are guided by a behaviorist perspective that favors repetition over meaningful learning. This paper reports on the design of mobile mathematics apps that harness gamification techniques to promote higher-order thinking skills (HOTS) even in basic elementary school concepts such as number comparison, and addition and subtraction. The integration of these apps in the classroom is also discussed.

KEYWORDS

Mobile Technology in Teaching Mathematics, Mobile Learning, Numeracy Apps, Higher-Order Thinking Skills, HOTS

1. INTRODUCTION

Despite the long history of reform education in mathematics, rote learning and low-level thinking are still prevalent in mathematics classrooms in many countries (Cox, 2015; Nag et al., 2014). Teachers struggle to teach mathematical concepts meaningfully and instead resort to explicating procedures disconnected from important elementary school concepts such as place value or number magnitude (Verzosa, 2020). Traditional instruction focuses on teaching rules rather than on promoting critical thinking or problem solving, which are the twin goals of Philippine mathematics education (Department of Education, 2016).

Mobile technology offers a potential solution for mathematical learning, particularly if it is designed well (Calder, 2015). It can provide an additional medium for helping students visualize abstract mathematical concepts and can promote confidence and enjoyment in doing mathematics (Fabian, Topping, & Barron, 2018). A meta-analysis of research on the use of mobile technology demonstrates its potential for developing higher-order thinking skills (HOTS), independent learning, and reflective thinking (Ahmad et al., 2020). Unfortunately, a large proportion of the available apps perform the same function as practice worksheets; and are guided by a behaviorist perspective favoring repetition over meaningful learning (Highfield & Goodwin, 2013; Papadakis, Kalogiannakis, & Zaranis, 2018). This is despite the plethora of research that promotes sense-making and higher-order thinking in mathematics (Burns, 2007; Van de Walle, Karp, & Bay-Williams, 2015).

This paper reports on three numeracy apps that target a wide range of competencies in elementary school mathematics. The design of these apps was guided by the literature on mathematics education and are intended to promote higher-order thinking. The apps are designed in a game like environment. The use of games in mobile devices within lessons in primary mathematics has resulted in improved student engagement and made mathematics more enjoyable (Attard, 2018). Game-based learning is said to provide good exposure and experience in helping the learning process (El-Nasr & Smith, 2006).

These apps are a product of an ongoing government-funded project entitled "Technology Innovations for Mathematical Reasoning, Statistical Thinking and Assessment". In this project, mathematical apps also help teachers address the shift in modalities in education brought about by the pandemic. The apps serve as rich resources for both synchronous and asynchronous lessons in blended learning. Because the apps can be installed on mobile devices, these can be used by more school children and teachers who have access to cellphones and tablets, rather than computers and laptops.

2. HIGHER-ORDER THINKING SKILLS

A classic framework for analyzing student tasks is provided by Bloom's Revised Taxonomy (Anderson & Krathwohl, 2001). Remembering and understanding comprise the lowest level of thinking. These consist of tasks that require students to copy, listen, memorize, or compute. By contrast, verbs associated with the higher levels of mathematics require students to investigate, represent, predict, construct or create (Van de Walle et al., 2015). Students who demonstrate higher-order thinking do not just know how to manipulate numeric symbols. They can form their own strategies and apply their knowledge to solve non-routine tasks, or tasks that cannot be solved by a specific algorithm.

2.1 Foundational Ideas in Elementary Mathematics

Higher-order thinking requires knowledge of foundational mathematics concepts. In the elementary grades, some of the most important ideas involve number sense (Yang, Li, & Lin, 2008), which includes various components such as number magnitude (Siegler & Lortie-Forgues, 2014), the effect of operations, and conceptual place value (Ellemor-Collins & Wright, 2011). These concepts provided the pedagogical basis for the apps designed through our project.

3. NUMERACY APPS

3.1 Ordering Game

The *Ordering Game* is based on a game described by a recognized expert in mathematics education, Marilyn Burns (cited by Silva, n.d.). Burns' game involves whole numbers, but our team's mobile app extends the game to include fractions and integers (Figure 1). In this game, one or two numbers are generated at random (Figure 1a). The user must choose one number and drag it to a row. As the process repeats, the user places more and more numbers on the row with the condition that the numbers appear in ascending order. The goal of the game is to fill-up the entire row within the allowed number of chances, indicated at the bottom part of the screen. The game becomes more difficult as it progresses because it becomes more likely that a randomly selected number cannot be correctly placed in any of the remaining slots.

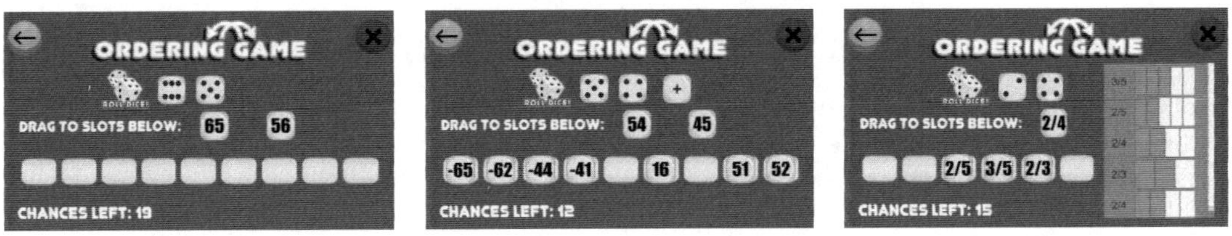

(a) (b) (c)

Figure 1. Screenshots from the *Ordering Game* for (a) Whole Numbers, (b) Integers, and (c) Fractions

The game offers opportunities to develop higher-order thinking skills. First, it pushes the user to reason with numerical magnitude, which is one of the key learning competencies in elementary mathematics (Siegler & Lortie-Forgues, 2014). Numerical magnitude understanding is necessary for estimating and comparing the sizes of numbers. Second, the game provides a natural environment to learn probability concepts. For example, if the randomly generated numbers are within the range 11 to 66 and the randomly generated number is 60, then the user must consider the likelihood that the next generated numbers will be higher or less than 60. Since there is a relatively low probability that a succeeding number will be greater than 60, then it is wise to place 60 somewhere near the right end of the row.

The app also presents appropriate representational media that enable users to reason mathematically. The game presents a variant of a number line estimation task, which is one of the tasks often used to measure symbolic numerical magnitude understanding (Fazio et al., 2014). In the case of fractions (Figure 1c), a regional model of each fraction is also shown, to support the visualization and comparison of fraction magnitudes.

Additional options are also available for each number type. For whole numbers (Figure 1a), users may choose among varying number range choices from 0 to 99,999. For integers (Figure 1b), users may choose to play within a number range between from -99,999 to 99,999. In the case of fractions (Figure 1c), users may choose to work with fractions with denominators from 1 to 6 or denominators from 1 to 9. In addition, users may also choose among Easy, Medium, or Challenging levels, which determine the number of chances available in each game.

3.2 Target Number Game

In the *Target Number Game,* users can choose one of the following targets: Greatest Sum, Least Sum, Greatest Difference or Least Difference (Figure 2a). Two sets of three-digit numbers are given and the goal is to rearrange the six digits, by swapping two at a time, so that the answer, either the sum or difference, shows the target. The game provides feedback on whether the user is able to get the target answer. It also gives hints so that the user can eventually reach the optimal solution.

To reach the target, users must have the knowledge of numerical magnitudes and the effect of operations. Higher-order thinking emerges from the number of considerations required to solve the problem. How do you form two three-digit numbers, from the given six digits, to form the largest or smallest possible sum? For example, to get the greatest sum in Figure 2b, the user should place the two largest digits in the hundreds place of each of the three-digit numbers. Then the next two largest digits should be in the tens places. The user can also discover that although the maximum sum is unique the two sets of three-digit numbers are not unique. In Figure 2c, another possible choice for the addends are 621 and 851. To get the least sum, the user should use the opposite strategy, that is, to place the two largest digits in the ones place, and so on.

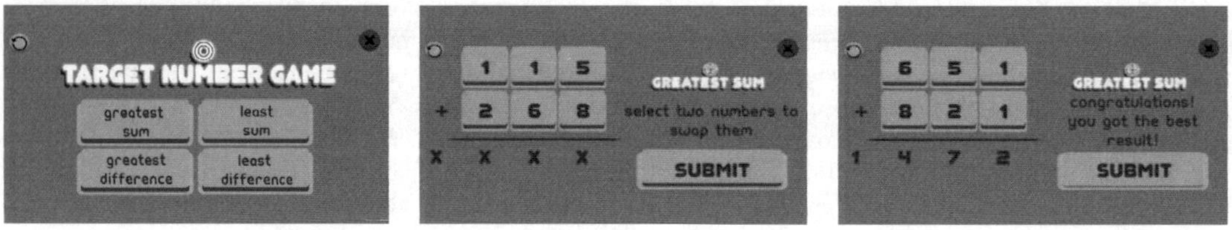

(a) (b) (c)

Figure 2. Screenshots from the *Target Number Game* (a) Main Menu, (b) Example of Greatest Sum, and (c) An Optimal Solution to an Example of Greatest Sum

Finding the greatest or least difference requires even more thinking. To find the greatest difference of two three-digit numbers formed using six digits, the user should realize that the first three-digit number must be as large as possible and the second three-digit number as small as possible. The most challenging target is finding the least difference. Unlike the other problems, there is no simple strategy such as placing the largest digits in the hundreds place or the ones place. The reason for the difficulty is that the difference must be a positive number. Thus, it is not only a matter of making the first three-digit number as small as possible and making the second three-digit number as large as possible. For example, in Figure 3a, the user must rearrange the digits to get the least difference. The user will try out different possibilities such as in Figure 3b, which will not give the target answer. Thus, the user will try out other arrangements until the target is achieved (Figure 3c). By playing the game a number of times, the user will be able to find a strategy to find the least difference.

Pilot testing revealed that even adults need to think to solve problems presented by the *Target Number Game*. But since the app involves only basic addition and subtraction, it can present the same thinking opportunities for elementary school children.

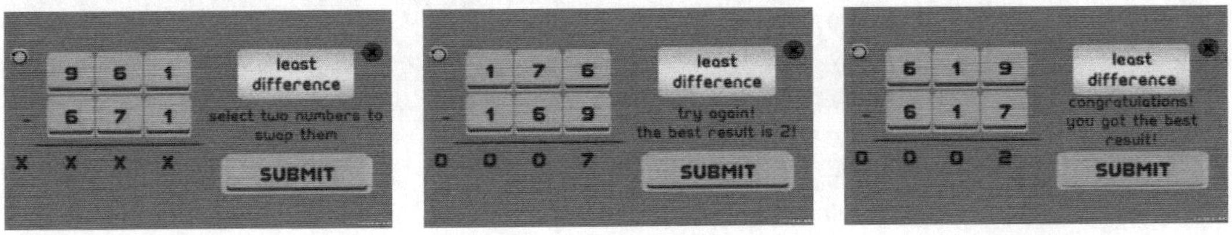

(a) (b) (c)

Figure 3. Screenshots of finding the least difference from the *Target Number Game*

3.3 Grid Game

In *Grid Game,* a 10 by 10 grid is shown on the screen, together with a beginning number and a target number. The user has to click the buttons (e.g., +1, -1, +10, -10) in order to reach the target number. For example, if the beginning number is 35 and the target is 49 (Figure 4a), then a possible solution is to click +10 once and +1 four times. The learning objective is to support children's structuring of multi-digit numbers by training them to increment and decrement by tens starting any number, such as knowing that 56 and 10 more is 66 (Ellemor-Collins & Wright, 2011).

There are several levels available. In the *Explore* level, any solution is accepted, as long as the target number is reached. At the more advanced levels, the user has to complete the task in the shortest or most efficient way possible, as indicated by the number of allowed moves ("Moves Left" in Figures 4b and 4c). These levels promote higher-order thinking skills by forcing the user to move from counting by ones or just pressing +1 or -1 multiple times to reach the target. An efficient strategy requires knowledge of incrementing and decrementing by 10 and then pressing +1 or -1 a few times.

There are also variations in the type of visual support offered by the app. In the *Advanced* level, only a blank grid is shown (Figure 4b); in the *Challenging* level, no grid is shown (Figure 4c).

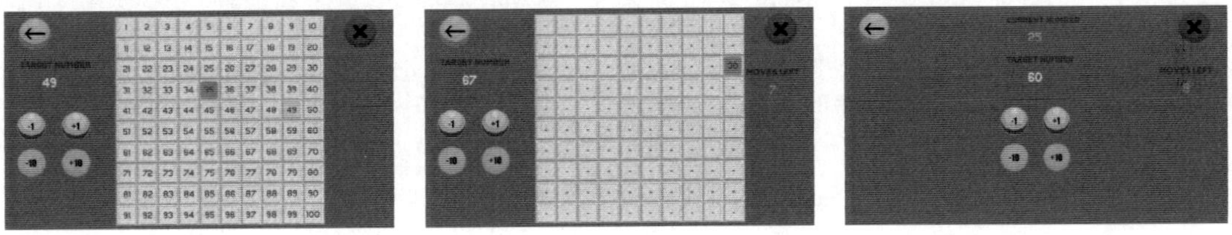

(a) (b) (c)

Figure 4. Screenshots from the *Grid Game* for Whole Numbers (a) Explore, (b) Advanced, and (c) Challenging levels

Because of the base-10 structure of the number system, the app can also be extended to larger whole numbers (in the range of 1-1000; Figure 5a), decimals (Figure 5b), and integers (Figure 5c). As in the previous app, the *Grid Game* involves only addition and subtraction and yet offers opportunities for higher-order thinking. For example, to get from 577 to the target 979 (Figure 5a) in 6 moves requires a correct combination of buttons +1, -1, +10, -10, +100, and -100. If the user fails to solve the problem, the app presents the same problem again so that the user always has chances to think of the most effective strategy.

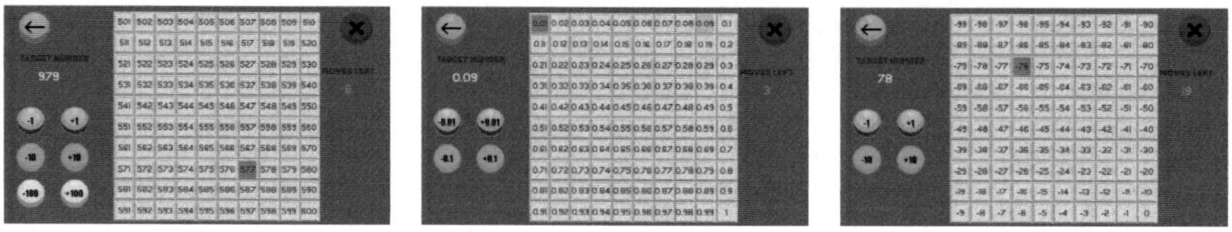

(a) (b) (c)

Figure 5. Screenshots from the *Grid Game*: (a) Whole Numbers (range 1-1000), (b) Decimals, (c) Integers

4. GAMIFICATION FEATURES

Employing gamification, or the application of game design elements, techniques, and principles, in education across different subjects and different learning activities, has been prevalent in the past years. Primarily, gamification is used to motivate and engage students better, with the hope of increasing the effectiveness of learning materials, as well as to hone skills such as creative thinking and independent learning (Caponetto et al., 2014). Moreover, video and mobile games enjoy widespread popularity among the youth; for instance, in the Philippines, it is reported that there are approximately 40 million gamers with around 75% of them playing games on mobile devices (Elliot, 2020). Thus, it is opportune to use gamified environments in education to take advantage of students' familiarity with and disposition towards games.

The design of the *Ordering Game*, *Target Number Game*, and *Grid Game*, as described in the previous section, was guided by gamification principles and took advantage of game-like elements and settings to maximize their effectiveness and encourage student participation. More specifically, these three apps adhere to the Educational Games Design Model (Ibrahim & Jaafar, 2009), which consists of Game Design, Pedagogy, and Learning Content Modelling. Table 1 provides the details of the apps' Game Design.

Table 1. Game Design of *Ordering Game*, *Target Number Game*, and *Grid Game*

	Element	Implementation
Usability	Satisfaction	The vibrant color theme, large font styles, and visual designs in the three apps are catered to its target users, who are primarily grade school students. The apps feature different modes and difficulty levels for more diverse experiences.
	Efficiency	The three apps feature simple menus and interfaces. Users can immediately go into a game level after a few menu selections. Transitions between levels are quick and the controls are simple and responsive.
	Effectiveness	The three apps simulate learning activities that can help students develop their numeracy skills. Each app allows the users, with the guidance of an adult, to customize the app's topic and level to match the students' level.
Multimodal	Multimedia	The apps make use of texts, icons, figures, simple animations, and sound prompts.
	Interaction	The apps are interactive with users being able to tap, click, or drag objects on the screen directly using touch gestures, or indirectly using an input device.
Fun	Challenge	The difficulty level of the games can be adjusted so that users can start with easy levels and progress to more challenging levels on their own or as instructed by their teachers. The topics covered as well as game elements can be adjusted.
	Clear goals	Each app has a single clear goal. The user is prompted once the game is done or the goal is achieved.
	Uncertain outcome	The problem in each game is randomly generated but strategically planned. Moreover, solving each problem requires higher-order thinking. For example, in *Ordering Game*, there is some uncertainty in the sequence of numbers that will be generated, so users are potentially confronted with a new set of challenges each time.
	Self-esteem	The customization of the difficulty levels allows the user to build their self-esteem as they successfully win more difficult levels.

On Pedagogy, the previous section details how the strategy for each game requires knowledge and skills on numeracy. To summarize, the strategy for *Ordering Game* requires estimation skills and knowledge of number magnitude; for *Target Number Game*, the strategy requires knowledge of number magnitude and the effect of operations; and for *Grid Game*, the strategy requires knowledge of incrementing/decrementing by ones and tens. With the tiered difficulty levels implemented in the apps, users can develop knowledge and skills as they encounter the need to formulate new strategies for the increasingly difficult levels. Moreover, the three apps can be used independently, requiring little guidance from adults or teachers.

On Learning Content Modelling, the three apps were designed so that the math topics involved therein are aligned with some of the most essential learning competencies for Grades 1 to 6 (Department of Education, 2020) prescribed by the Philippine Department of Education. These apps can also be used as remediation or enrichment activities for students in higher grade levels. As previously described, the contents and game structure of each app were designed to promote higher-order thinking skills so that even older children or adults can be challenged by the apps.

5. INTEGRATION OF THE APPS INTO THE CLASSROOM

The nature and gamification features of the apps described in the previous sections ensure opportunities for students to engage in non-routine problems which require analysis, estimation, making predictions and conclusions, and reasoning. Such engagement promotes active learning and the prospect of developing higher-order thinking skills. There are several approaches in which the app can be integrated in the classroom to support student learning and develop higher-order thinking skills among students.

All the three apps (*Ordering Game*, *Target Game* and *Grid Game*) can be used to provide input for meaningful mathematical activities. When these are utilized, it should be directed towards (1) reasoning; (2) inference making; (3) creation of a strategy and (4) collaborative interaction with classmates. To illustrate, in the instance of *Ordering Game* shown in Figure 1a, the teacher can ask questions such as: *Which of the numbers 56 and 65 should be used? In which position should it be placed? Why?* These questions engage students and can develop reasoning skills, form inferences and eventually devise a winning strategy.

Similarly, in the *Target Game,* the teacher can pose questions as a scaffolding technique towards stronger understanding and reasoning. In the problem shown in Figure 2b, teachers can ask: *Which two numbers can be placed in the hundreds place to get a four-digit sum? What numbers should be placed in the tens digit to get the greatest sum? How many possible answers are there?* After several examples, the teacher can lead the students to make a generalization on how to create the greatest sum from the given digits.

In the Grid game task shown in Figure 5a, teachers can ask: *Which of the buttons should be used to go from 577 to 979 within 6 moves? Is it possible to do it if the +1 button is used? Why? How about if the +10 button is used? How many solutions are possible to get the target number?*

The team has also conducted a series of webinars and training for teachers to introduce them to the apps and highlight its potential for developing higher-order thinking skills. Initial feedback is promising. Some comments indicate that the apps are "very enjoyable and motivating" and "will help students ignite their interest" through "its game like features", and that learners "will be able to enjoy, think and [be] challenged a lot". A more robust implementation will form the next phase of this ongoing project (although initial implementation has started for the apps in October 2020 in selected Department of Education School Divisions). It is anticipated that the apps, which are designed on the basis of research in mathematics education (Ellemor-Collins & Wright, 2011; Siegler & Lortie-Forgues, 2014; Van de Walle et al., 2015) and mobile technologies (Fabian, 2018; Ibrahim & Jaafar, 2009) can facilitate mathematical thinking.

6. CONCLUSION

The numeracy apps presented here address an urgent need, especially because many of the available apps focus on rote learning rather than on developing deep conceptual understanding and higher-order thinking (Papadakis, Kalogiannakis, & Zaranis, 2018). The three apps described in this paper were designed on the basis of mathematical and pedagogical frameworks, and on gamification strategies. Further, the apps are aligned with official learning competencies, while also promoting higher-order thinking skills. The apps were designed to run on mobile technologies to encourage and enhance the student learning experience. Another intention was to maximize the benefits of mobile technologies such as mobility and portability, to overcome time and space constraints in the learning environment. Beyond pedagogical and gamification designs, the role of the teacher and the educational context are crucial elements in the success of integrating the mathematical apps in learning.

The development of the mathematical apps described in this paper is funded by a government agency, and partnerships with various school divisions had been forged. The next step in the project is to study the effectiveness of the apps for student learning, and possibly how these affect the students' attitude toward mathematics, which will be conducted with partner Department of Education School divisions.

ACKNOWLEDGEMENT

The authors would like to thank the Department of Science and Technology-Philippine Council for Industry, Energy, and Emerging Technology Research and Development (DOST-PCIEERD) and the University Research Council (URC), Ateneo de Manila University for the support of the development of the interactive resources discussed in this paper. Acknowledgement also goes to Dr. Ma. Mercedes T. Rodrigo and the Ateneo Laboratory for the Learning Sciences (ALLS) for providing technical assistance. Deep gratitude is extended to our app developers: Mr. Victor Antonio M. Ortega and Mr. Nigel Cargo; and app designer Mr. Amiel Damian F. Justiniani.

REFERENCES

Ahmad, M. et al., 2020. Mobile Technology in Enhancing Students' Higher Order Thinking Skill. *Journal of Physics: Conference Series*, Vol. 1529, 042057.

Anderson, L.W. & Krathwohl, D. R. (Eds.), 2001. *A Taxonomy for Learning, Teaching, and Assessing: A Revision of Bloom's Taxonomy of Educational Objectives: Complete Edition*. Addison Wesley Longman, New York, USA.

Attard, C., 2018. Mobile Technologies in the Primary Mathematics Classroom: Engaging or Not? In N. Calder, K. Larkin, & N. Sinclair (Eds.), *Using Mobile Technologies in the Teaching and Learning of Mathematics,* Springer, pp. 51-65.

Burns, M., 2007. *About Teaching Mathematics: A K-8 resource* (3rd ed.). Math Solutions Publications, Sausalito, CA.

Calder, N., 2015. Apps: Appropriate, Applicable, and Appealing? In T. Lowrie, R. Jorgensen (Zevenbergen) (Eds.), *Digital Games and Mathematics Learning*. Springer, Dordrecht, the Netherlands, pp. 233-250.

Caponetto, I. et al., 2014. Gamification and Education: a Literature Review. *Proceedings of the 8th European Conference on Games-Based Learning - ECGBL 2014*, pp 50-57.

Cox, R. D., 2015. "You've Got to Learn the Rules:" A Classroom-level Look at Low Pass Rates in Developmental Math. *Community College Review*, Vol. 43, No. 3, pp. 264-286.

Department of Education (DepEd), 2016. K to 12 Curriculum Guide: Mathematics. [Online]. Available: https://www.deped.gov.ph/wp-content/uploads/2019/01/Math-CG_with-tagged-math-equipment.pdf

Department of Education (DepEd), 2020. K to 12 Most Essential Learning Competencies with Corresponding CG Codes. [Online]. Available: https://commons.deped.gov.ph/K-to-12-MELCS-with-CG-Codes.pdf

El-Nasr, M. S. & Smith, B. K., 2006. Learning through Game Modding. *Computer Entertainment*, Vol. 4, No. 1, Art. 3B, pp. 1-20.

Ellemor-Collins, D. & Wright, R., 2011. Developing Conceptual Place Value: Instructional Design for Intensive Intervention. *Australian Journal of Learning Difficulties*, Vol. 16, No. 1, pp. 41-63.

Elliott, R., 2020. The Philippines' Games Market: Data and Insights. [Online]. Available: https://newzoo.com/insights/articles/data-and-insights-on-the-philippines-games-market/#:~:text=Share%3A,Southeast%20Asia's%20overall%20games%20market.

Fabian, K., Topping, K.J, & Barron, I.G, 2018. Using Mobile Technologies for Mathematics: Effects on Student Attitudes and Achievement. *Education Tech Research Dev*, Vol. 66, pp.1119-1139.

Fazio, L.K. et al., 2014. Relations of Different Types of Numerical Magnitude Representations to Each Other and to Mathematics Achievement. *Journal of Experimental Child Psychology,* Vol. 123, pp. 53-72.

Highfield, K. & Goodwin, K., 2013. Apps for Mathematics Learning: A Review of 'Educational' Apps from the iTunes App Store. In V. Steinle, L. Ball & C. Bardini (Eds.), *Mathematics Education: Yesterday, Today and Tomorrow (Proceedings of the 36th Annual Conference of the Mathematics Education Research Group of Australasia).* Melbourne, Australia, pp. 378-385.

Ibrahim, R. & Jaafar, A, 2009. Educational Games (EG) Design Framework: Combination of Game Design, Pedagogy and Content Modeling. *Proceedings of the 2009 International Conference on Electrical Engineering and Informatics, ICEEI 2009*, pp. 293-298.

Nag, S. et al., 2014. Literacy, Foundation Learning and Assessment in Developing Countries: Final Report. *Education Rigorous Literature Review*. Department for International Development, United Kingdom.

Papadakis, S., Kalogiannakis, M., & Zaranis, N., 2018. Educational Apps from the Android Google Play for Greek Preschoolers: A Systematic Review. *Computers and Education*, Vol. 116, pp. 139-160.

Siegler, R. S. & Lortie-Forgues, H., 2014. An Integrative Theory of Numerical Development. *Child Development Perspectives*, Vol. 8 No. 3, pp. 144-150.

Silva, M. (n.d.) Place Value Activity Package. [Online]. Available: http://www.mathematicshed.com/uploads /1/2/5/7/12572836/place-value-activity-pack.pdf

Van de Walle, J.A., Karp, K S., & Bay-Williams, J. M., 2015. *Elementary and Middle School Mathematics: Teaching Developmentally* (9th ed.). Pearson, Essex, UK.

Verzosa, D. M. B., 2020. Pre-service Elementary Teachers' Reasoning in Introducing Multidigit Subtraction. *International Journal of Mathematical Education in Science and Technology,* Vol. 51, pp. 876-892.

Yang, D. C., Li, M. N., & Lin, C. I., 2008. A Study of the Performance of 5th Graders in Number Sense and its Relationship to Achievement in Mathematics. *International Journal of Science and Mathematics Education,* Vol. 6, pp. 789-807.

TRACING THE VIEWS OF GREEK SECONDARY SCHOOL TEACHERS ON MOBILE LEARNING

Manolis Kousloglou[1], Kleopatra Nikolopoulou[2] and Euripides Hatzikraniotis[1]
[1]*Aristotle University of Thessaloniki, Greece*
[2]*National and Kapodistrian University of Athens, Greece*

ABSTRACT

Teachers' attitudes and views towards mobile learning are essential since they affect their actual use of mobile technology in the classrooms. This study investigated secondary school teachers' mobile learning perceptions, by using the Mobile Learning Perception Scale. An online questionnaire was administered to 208 teachers in Greece and three factors were revealed, *mTech Fit for teaching and learning*, *Specialization*, and *Communication*. Teachers' views were, in general, positive, with female teachers expressing more positive views for the *Specialization* factor. No significant differences were revealed with regard to age, years of teaching experience, and specialization/discipline.

KEYWORDS

Mobile Learning, Teacher Views, MLPS Questionnaire, Greece, Secondary Education

1. INTRODUCTION

Research indicates the increasing use of digital mobile devices in primary and secondary education (e.g., Leem & Sung, 2019). Mobile technology has the potential to support mobile learning in classrooms and teachers' attitudes are important since they affect the actual use of mobile technology in the classroom (Kim & Kim, 2017) and consequently students' learning. Teachers' mobile learning views were explored in different countries. Montrieux et al. (2014), in Belgium, found that secondary school teachers' acceptance of tablet computers was, in general, positive. Teachers were intrinsically motivated, while their acceptance seemed related to attaining a positive attitude, social influence and the sense to master the new mobile technology. Black-Fuller et al. (2016), in the USA, found that secondary school teachers had positive attitude towards mobile learning. Al-Furaih and Al-Awidi (2018), in Kuwait, investigated secondary school teachers' readiness to adopt smartphones as instructional tools, with respect to their personal concerns, technological competency and personal characteristics; teachers' perceptions of the adoption of smartphone technology were associated with their stages of concern and smartphone competency level. In Korea, Leem and Sung (2019) investigated primary and secondary school teachers' technology acceptance of smart mobile devices in their lessons. Their results indicated that teachers' beliefs consistently revealed the factors of immediacy, interest, interactivity, instability and inconvenience. Kim and Kim (2017) explored the perceptions of teachers in Korean rural schools regarding teaching and learning, including technology preparedness, performance, difficulties, and continuing integration in tablet-based interactive classrooms; teachers reported that their continuing integration of lessons with tablets was correlated with their beliefs about the applicability of tablets for lessons, their personal interests, as well as students' satisfaction with previous lessons and expectations. Uzunboylu and Ozdamli (2011), in N. Cyprus, found that teachers exhibited above medium levels of perception towards m-learning, while later, Ozdamli and Uzunboylu (2015) reported positive perceptions towards mobile learning among secondary school teachers; teachers wanted to use m-learning in education, but their adequacy levels were not sufficient. Teachers were better users of devices that they use in their daily routines such as mobile phones, while they wanted to make use of m-learning applications with the aim of supporting classroom teaching.

In parallel, some studies indicated the impact of variables on teachers' mobile learning perceptions; e.g., age (O'Bannon & Thomas, 2014), years of teaching experience (Baek et al., 2017), teacher training in ICT (Kousloglou & Syrpi, 2018; Nikolopoulou et al., 2020) impact on teachers' views.

Within the Greek context, although the integration of mobile devices/phones in schools is negatively affected by the current regulations (June 2018), some teachers make their own decisions about the extent of mobile technology use in classrooms (Nikolopoulou & Kousloglou, 2019). In Greek context there is insufficient empirical evidence regarding teachers' mobile learning views. Kousloglou and Syrpi (2018) investigated secondary school teachers' perceptions on the use of mobile phones for educational purposes; around 38% of the sample said they often use mobile phones/tablets for educational purposes, while 75% of respondents expressed willingness to integrate mobile devices in the learning process (they said, it is likely to increase students' interest/motivation), if the law allows it. Nikolopoulou et al. (2020) found that primary and secondary school teachers expressed positive perceptions on mobile learning readiness. The highest percentage of agreement regarded the possibilities of mobile learning (over 60%), while ICT training and attendance of ICT conferences, both affected positively teachers' perceptions on mobile learning benefits and preferences. A study with high school teachers (Nikolopoulou & Kousloglou, 2020) indicated teachers' perceived advantages (interactive/enjoyable lesson, students' motivation and engagement/participation and their familiarity with the technology), obstacles (lack of equipment, official legislation) and concerns related to tablet and mobile phone usage in the classrooms.

The purpose of this study was to investigate secondary school teachers' views towards m-learning. The research questions were as follows:

1. What are teachers' views toward m-learning?
2. Do teachers' views differ significantly according to gender, age, years of teaching experience, and specialization?

Tracing teachers' views on mobile learning is significant because their views are linked to their classroom practices. Although similar research has been conducted internationally, earlier results show that the cultural context of each country influences teachers' views. Additionally, mobile learning is an underexplored field in Greece. Thus, the present research, which was conducted in Greece, provides an added value in international research, and the findings are expected to have implications for researchers, school policy and educational policy makers. In particular, in the era of COVID-19 pandemic that secondary school education transitioned to online teaching and learning, and the use of mobile devices is encouraged (official framework became more favorable).

2. METHOD

2.1 Research Hypothesis

The null research hypothesis is that teachers' views do not differ significantly according to gender, age, years of teaching experience, and specialization.

2.2 Sample

The sample of this study consisted of 208 secondary school teachers (students' ages 12-18). It was obtained through convenience sampling, a method which is very common, especially for the pandemic situation. The teachers, 82 males and 126 females, ranged in age from 25 to 65+ years, and in years of teaching experience from 1 to 30+ years. Half of them (119) declared to have an extensive experience in using ICT in their classroom; however, most of the participants (136) state that they rarely use m-Learning technology in their teaching, despite that the majority of the participants (194) use mobile/tablet on daily basis. With regard to their specialization/discipline, 63 were teachers of science and 60 of Greek language and the rest taught other disciplines (math, computer science, foreign languages, etc.).

2.3 Procedure

An online questionnaire was administered during the school year 2020-2021. Ethical issues were considered (according to the new General Data Protection Regulation), and the participation in the survey was voluntary. The teachers were informed that the questionnaire is anonymous and the data collected will be used solely for research purposes.

2.4 The Research Instrument

Data were collected via an online questionnaire (MLPS), which included the statements and demographic characteristics. The Mobile Learning Perception Scale (MLPS) consists of 26 items and three subscales/factors, and was developed by Uzunboylu and Ozdamli (2011). The first factor/sub-dimension (Aim-Mobile Technologies Fit) regards teachers' perceptions on the aim-purpose and appropriateness of mobile technology in teaching and learning. The second factor (Appropriateness of Branch) regards the appropriateness of mobile technology for the teachers' specialization/discipline. The third factor (Forms of M-learning Application and Tools' Sufficient Adequacy of Communication) regards teachers' views on the forms-types of mobile learning applications (e.g., email), as well as the adequacy of these apps/tools for communication (mainly between teacher-student, student-student).

The original questionnaire was checked for internal consistency coefficient and reliability of the scale. The questionnaire was translated into the Greek language, adapted and validated by Boufidou (2018) for content and construct validity. The translated questionnaire was administered to Greek teachers and was checked for the internal reliability by Cronbach-α. Teachers were asked to rate their views on a 5-point Likert-type scale (strongly disagree to strongly agree). A significance of $p=0.05$ was accepted as a conventional level. To identify whether a significant gender, age, discipline or years of experience difference occurred, one-way ANOVA analysis was applied. The correlation coefficient was interpreted in terms of its statistical significance, in order to indicate whether the results are unlikely to have occurred by chance.

3. RESULTS AND DISCUSSION

For the first research question "What are teachers' views toward m-learning?" a descriptive analysis was done. The three factors in this study were "*mTech Fit for teaching and learning*" (F1), "*Specialization*" (F2) and "*Communication*" (F3). Table 1 shows the 3 factors in the original study (Uzunboylu and Ozdamli, 2011), the questions involved and compares the values of Cronbach-α for each factor, between the original study and ours. As can be seen, the Cronbach-α in our study is lower than in the original. In order to improve the internal consistency in our study, we have performed exploratory factor analysis which resulted in a redistribution of the questions in three factors, as shown in Table 2, with a higher Cronbach-α per factor. The redistribution of the questions may be attributed to the different perceived meaning of the same question in the two populations, due to the difference in cultural background and/or to the difference and the ICT experience. As shown in Table 2, the mean values per factor are high, taking into account that teachers rarely use m-Learning in their teaching. Unpublished results in Boufidou's Master's Thesis (2018), indicate similar views of Greek teachers in primary education, thus, we may conclude that the views of Greek teachers on mobile learning are similar regardless the level of education.

The second research question investigated whether teachers' views toward mobile learning differ significantly according to their gender (Table 3), age (Table 4), teaching experience (Table 5) and specialization (Table 6). The findings shown in Table 3, indicate that significant differences existed only for *Specialization* (F2) ($p<0.05$) where female teachers expressed more positive perceptions. No significant differences were revealed with regard to age, years of teaching experience, and specialization/discipline (Tables 4, 5 and 6, respectively); and thus the null research hypothesis was confirmed. Table 4 shows that factor F2 (*Specialization*) had higher values, in comparison to the other two factors, for all teachers; for age group 25-50 (mean=3.94) and for age group 51-65+ (mean=3.98). Table 5 shows that factor F2 (*Specialization*) had higher values, in comparison to the other two factors, for all teachers; i.e., mean values 3.96 and 3.95 for 1-20 and 21-30+ years of teaching experience, respectively. Table 6 shows that factor F2 (Specialization) had higher values, in comparison to the other two factors, for all teachers; i.e., mean values 3.99 and 3.94 for language and science specialization, respectively. The data presented in the last three tables show that, although no significant differences were revealed with regard to age, years of teaching experience, and specialization, teachers' views were slightly more positive with regard to the factor *Specialization.*

Table 1. Comparison of the values of Cronbach-α for each factor, between the original study and ours

Factor	Question	Cronbach-α Original[(*)]	Cronbach-α ours
mTech Fit	Q1, Q2, Q5, Q8, Q11, Q13, Q20, Q23	0.894	0.777
Specialization	Q4, Q9, Q10, Q14, Q15, Q17, Q18, Q21, Q24	0.940	0.760
Communication	Q3, Q6, Q7, Q12, Q16, Q19, Q22, Q25, Q26	0.944	0.814

(*)after Uzunboylu & Ozdamli, 2011

Table 2. Redistribution of the questions in three factors

Factor	Question	Mean	Std Deviation	Cronbach-α
mTech Fit	Q2, Q3, Q4, Q6, Q9, Q10, Q11, Q13, Q21, Q20, Q23	3.86	0.72	0.901
Specialization	Q5, Q14, Q15, Q16, Q18, Q25	3.96	0.67	0.820
Communication	Q7, Q8, Q12, Q17, Q19, Q22, Q24, Q26	3.72	0.78	0.818

F1: mTech Fit for teaching and learning, F2: Specialization, F3: Communication

Table 3. Views toward mobile learning according to gender

	Male (N=82)		*Female (N=126)*		*F*	*P*	*Partial eta squared*
	M	*SD*	*M*	*SD*			
F1	3.83	0.71	3.88	0.73	0.547	0.460	0.030
F2	3.84	0.66	4.10	0.67	10.362	0.010	0.048
F3	3.64	0.81	3.72	0.80	2.246	0.136	0.011

Table 4. Views toward mobile learning according to age

	25-50 (N=99)		*51-65+ (N=109)*		*F*	*P*	*Partial eta squared*
	M	*SD*	*M*	*SD*			
F1	3.86	0.77	3.87	0.71	0.000	0.994	0.000
F2	3.94	0.7	3.98	0.65	0.625	0.430	0.003
F3	3.68	0.83	3.72	0.76	0.615	0.434	0.003

Table 5. Views toward mobile learning according to years of teaching experience

	1 – 20 years (N=101)		*21 - 30+ years (N=107)*		*F*	*P*	*Partial eta squared*
	M	*SD*	*M*	*SD*			
F1	3.90	0.75	3.88	0.68	0.128	0.721	0.001
F2	3.96	0.69	3.95	0.65	0.033	0.855	0.000
F3	3.68	0.84	3.72	0.74	0.599	0.440	0.003

Table 6. Views toward mobile learning according to teaching discipline

	Language (N=60)		*Science (N=66)*		*F*	*P*	*Partial eta squared*
	M	*SD*	*M*	*SD*			
F1	3.81	0.81	3.93	0.64	1.852	0.176	0.015
F2	3.99	0.74	3.94	0.65	0.789	0.376	0.006
F3	3.71	0.81	3.67	0.76	0.004	0.952	0.000

4. CONCLUSIONS

The aim of this study was to explore Greek secondary school teachers' mobile learning perceptions, by using the MLPS survey. Teachers' perceptions were, in general, positive. This indicates an agreement with earlier studies conducted in Greece (Boufidou, 2018) as well as in other countries (e.g., Uzunboylu & Ozdamli, 2011; Montrieux et al., 2014; Black-Fuller et al., 2016; Leem & Sung, 2019). In particular, Greek secondary school teachers' views towards mobile learning were more positive than their colleagues' views who participated in the original study; where the same questionnaire (MLPS) was used. As mentioned before, this may be due to the ICT experience of the two populations and/or the differences in cultural context

The positive views in all factors mean that teachers perceive mobile learning as appropriate for the educational process, for teaching their subject, and for communication purposes. Teachers' views on F2 (Specialization) were more positive in comparison to their views on the other two factors.

The findings of this study reflect a situation in a micro-level and can contribute to the enrichment of the literature in the field of mobile learning; a field that has not been systematically integrated into the curriculum. This is a work/study in progress. Future plans include investigating teachers' views with regard to other characteristics such as ICT experience, technology use in classroom etc. Currently, empirical evidence on how mobile phones or tablets are used in secondary schools in Greece shows that it is in embryonic stage (e.g., for science, Nikolopoulou & Kousloglou, 2019), however, since things are changing as most of the classes were given on-line during the COVID pandemic, it is planned to investigate whether the teachers' willingness in using m-Learning in class is changed, what type of mobile devices will be adopted as well as the learning activities in different subjects.

REFERENCES

Al-Furaih, S.A.A., & Al-Awidi, H.M. 2018. Teachers' change readiness for the adoption of smartphone technology: Personal concerns and technological competency. *Technology, Knowledge and Learning*, 1-24.

Baek, Y., Zhang, H., & Yun, S. 2017. Teachers' attitudes toward mobile learning in Korea. *TOJET: The Turkish Online Journal of Educational Technology*, 16(1), 154-163.

Black-Fuller, L., Taube, S., Koptelov, A., & Sullivan, S. 2016. Smartphones and pedagogy: Digital divide between high school teachers and secondary students. *US-China Education Review A*, 6(2), 124-131.

Boufidou, D. 2018. An investigation of the perceptions of primary school teachers about mobile learning. Postgraduate Dissertation, Thessaloniki, University of Macedonia (in Greek)

Kim, H.J., & Kim, H. 2017. Investigating Teachers' Pedagogical Experiences with Tablet Integration in Korean Rural Schools. *Asia-Pacific Education Researcher, 26(1–2),* 107–116.

Kousloglou, M., & Syrpi, M. 2018. Perceptions of secondary school teachers on the use of handheld devices in schools as learning tools. *5th Pan-Hellenic Educational Conference of Central Macedonia "ICT use and integration in educational practice*", April 27-29, 2018, Thessaloniki (in Greek)

Leem, J., & Sung, E. 2019. Teachers' beliefs and technology acceptance concerning smart mobile devices for SMART education in South Korea. *British Journal of Educational Technology*, 50(2), 601-613.

Montrieux, H., Courtois, C., Raes, A., Schellens, T., & De Marez, L. 2014. Mobile learning in secondary education: teachers' and students' perceptions and acceptance of tablet computers. *International Journal of Mobile and Blended Learning, 6*(2), 26-40.

Nikolopoulou, K. Gialamas, V., Lavidas, K., & Komis, V. 2020. Teachers' readiness to adopt mobile learning in classrooms: A study in Greece. *Technology, Knowledge and Learning*. DOI 10.1007/s10758-020-09453-7.

Nikolopoulou, K., & Kousloglou, M. 2019. Mobile learning in science: A study in secondary education in Greece. *Creative Education*, 10(6), 1271-1284.

Nikolopoulou, K., & Kousloglou, M. 2020. What are the views of high school teachers' on mobile technology use in classrooms? *Open Education – The Journal for Open and Distance Education and Educational Technology*, 16(1), 176-190 (in Greek)

O'Bannon, B., & Thomas, K. 2014. Teacher perceptions of using mobile phones in the classroom: Age matters! *Computers & Education*, 74, 15-25.

Ozdamli, F., & Uzunboylu, H. 2015. M-learning adequacy and perceptions of students and teachers in secondary schools. *British Journal of Educational Technology*, 46(1), 159-172.

Uzunboylu, H., & Ozdamli, F. 2011. Teacher perception for m-learning: scale development and teachers' perceptions. *Journal of Computer Assisted Learning*, 27, 544–556.

ANALYZING MOBILE LEARNING KEY SUCCESS FACTORS IN CATALONIA

Sofia Moya and Mar Camacho
Dr.
Universitat Rovira i Virgili, Spain

ABSTRACT

This study investigates the factors affecting mobile learning adoption in Catalonia. The main methodology is an expert judgement where 7 Catalan experts participated, including three school leaders, two university experts and two education inspectors. The findings reveal that the factors that affect mobile learning can be grouped into five categories ordered from the highest to lowest impact as follows: leadership, personal character, attitudes and ethics, pedagogical, digital literacy, and technological resources. The findings of these insights are expected to be useful to improve the efficiency of mobile learning adoption.

KEYWORDS

Mobile Learning, Technology Integration, Success Factors

1. INTRODUCTION

1.1 Theoretical Framework

There are numerous mobile learning definitions, most of them highlight the amin affordances such as mobility, ubiquity, interaction, learner-centred approach, formative assessment, collaborative sharing, and personalization (Ada, 2018; Alrasheedi & Capretz, 2015; Crompton & Burke, 2018; Hwang & Wu, 2014; McDonald et al., 2018; Peng et al., 2009; Teoh, 2011).
Literature has proven mobile learning positive benefits both cognitive and affective (Crompton & Burke, 2018; Krull & Duart, 2017; Moya & Camacho, 2020; Pimmer, 2016; Zheng et al., 2018).

Multiple studies have studied the factors that influence the adoption of mobile learning. Moya and Camacho (2019) carried out a study identifying 361 critical factors that affect the adoption of mobile learning that they classified into 5 categories: digital literacy, leadership, pedagogy, personal character, attitudes and ethics, technological resources.

1.2 Purpose of the Study

The objective of this study is to validate and evaluate the categories of critical factors that affect the adoption of mobile learning in Catalonia. The specific research question guiding this study is: What categories of success factors are given more importance in Catalonia?

2. METHODOLOGY

Expert Judgement: has been the methodology that has guided this research. Expert judgement process consist of experts given their opinions in a context of decision-making (Benini et al., 2017). This study brought together 7 experts to evaluate the dimensions that most affected the adoption of mobile learning. The process that was followed was that suggested by Benini et al. (2017): (1) background and preparation, (2) recruitment of experts, (3) elicitation and recording, (4) Aggregation and synthesis, (5) Communication of findings. The seven experts contributed different envoys: three were school leaders:. The seven experts contributed different envoys: three were school leaders, two educational inspectors and two university experts. The participants were provided with a dossier containing information about the research, a description of the five categories of factors that affect mobile learning, and a detail of 50 factors and their descriptions. The data collected manually during the expert judgement meeting, was manually uploaded and analyzed using the SPSS statistical package. Appendix A, Table A.1 summarizes the Expert Judgement protocol.

3. RESULTS

Informants validated the initial categories of factors. The experts subsequently classified the five categories using a Likert-type scale. Figure 1 represents the priorities of the experts. Table 1 shows the mean and standard deviation grouped by type of experts..

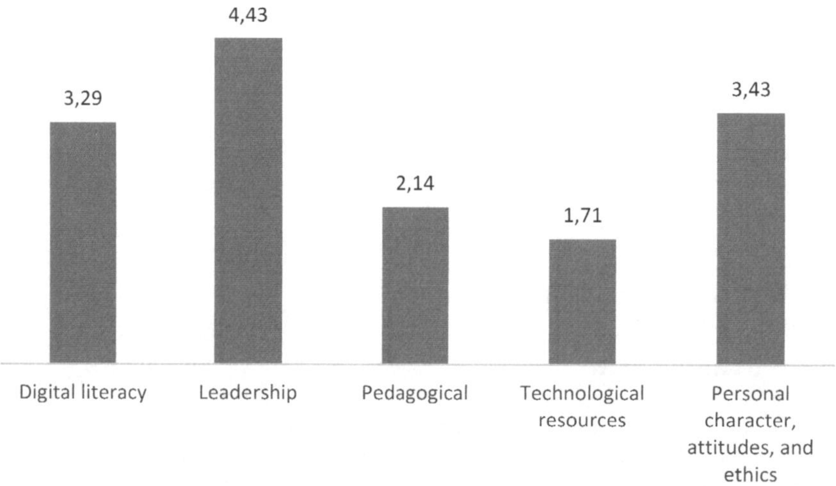

Figure 1. Categories of factors affecting mobile learning relevance assessment

One of the factors that stood out the most within the leadership category was collaboration. The least influential category was technological resources. Between groups, the differences were not significant, except in relation to pedagogical aspects highly valued by university experts and less by inspectors.

Table 1. Prioritization of categories affecting mobile learning perceived by experts

Category of factors	**Inspectors' mean (*SD*)**	**School leaders' mean (*SD*)**	**University expert's mean (*SD*)**	**Mean (*SD*)**
Personal character, attitudes, and ethics	3.00 (1.41)	3.50 (0.71)	3.67 (1.15)	3.43 (0.98)
Leadership	5.00 (0.00)	5.00 (0.00)	3.67 (1.53)	4.43 (1.13)
Technological Resources	1.50 (0.71)	2.50 (2.12)	1.33 (0.58)	1.71 (1.11)
Pedagogical	3.00 (0.00)	1.50 (0.71)	2.00 (1.00)	2.14 (0.90)
Digital Literacy	2.50 (2.12)	2.50 (0.71)	4.33 (0.58)	3.29 (1.38)

Correlation coefficients are all positive and significantly high in the case of university expert and inspectors. Table 2 depicts the Pearson correlation coefficient among groups of participants.

Table 2. Pearson correlation coefficient among groups of participants

	University Expert	**Inspector**	**School leader**
University Expert	1		
Inspector	0.741249317	1	
School leader	0.489274892	0.496291667	1

The experts were then asked to evaluate and classify the list of 50 factors into the five categories. The results were consistent with the ordering of the categories that they had done previously. The two most prominent factors were teacher's open minds (Khan, 2005) and Type and quality of student assessment (Volery & Lord, 2000). Two of the participants included "teacher's open minds" factor in the category of leadership and personal character, attitudes, and ethics. Assessment factor was classified in pedagogical category, except two participants who included it in the category of digital literacy. Table 3 Shows the key factors affecting mobile learning ordered by the number of times the participants selected them. For all the factors classified in more than one category, the category that best fit was debated and agreed upon, in this particular case, it was pedagogical. A general comment was related to the difficulty of analyzing isolating factors due to the high correlation between them.

Table 3. Key factors affecting mobile learning ordered by the number of times the different categories of participants selected them

Category	**Main factor**	**Times selected**
Leadership	Lack of clear vision and mission (Ekberg & Gao, 2018)	10
	Clear guidelines and framework (Khan, 2005)	10
	Resources plan (Fresen & Lesley, 2006)	10
	Credibility (Hackman & Johnson, 2013)	10
	Culture (Asiimwe Moses, 2017)	9
Personal character, attitudes, and ethics	Teacher's open minds (Khan, 2005)	12
	Enthusiastic teachers (Fresen & Lesley, 2006)	9
	Resistance to change (Orcutt & Alkadri, 2009)	9
Pedagogical	Type and quality of student assessment (Volery & Lord, 2000)	12
	Organizational capacity (Orcutt & Alkadri, 2009)	10
Digital literacy	Knowledge construction(Hao, Dennen & Mei, 2017)	9
	Group learning (Fresen & Lesley, 2006)	9
Technological resources	Trust in technology (Ekberg & Gao, 2018)	9

4. CONCLUSIONS

The purpose of this study is to validate and evaluate the categories of critical factors that affect the adoption of mobile learning in Catalonia. The results validate the classification and reveal that soft categories are more influential in the adoption of mobile learning. Leadership has been identified as the most influential category, follow by personal character, attitudes, and ethics. Pedagogical factors and digital literacy are the are the categories valued in the centre of the ranking, and the category considered less influential has been related to technological resources Among the different groups of participants: inspectors, school leaders and university experts; there have been no significant discrepancies in relation to the most and least relevant category.

One of the limitations is the lack of approaches from other members of the educational community, mainly teachers and learners. At the methodological level, the selection of the panel of experts has not followed a validated process

REFERENCES

Ada, M. (2018). Using design-based research to develop a Mobile Learning Framework for Assessment Feedback. *Research and Practice in Technology Enhanced Learning*, *13*(1), 3. https://doi.org/10.1186/s41039-018-0070-3

Alrasheedi, M., & Capretz, L. F. (2015). Determination of critical success factors affecting mobile learning: A meta-analysis approach. *The Turkish Online Journal of Educational Tec*, *14*(2). https://doi.org/10.1109/tale.2013.6654443

Benini, A., Chataigner, P., Noumri, N., Parham, N., Sweeney, J., & Tax, L. (2017). The Use of Expert Judgment in Humanitarian Analysis: Theory, Methods, Applications. In *Assessment Capacities Project ACAPS.*

Crompton, H., & Burke, D. (2018). The use of mobile learning in higher education: A systematic review. *Computers & Education*, *123*, 53–64. https://doi.org/10.1016/j.compedu.2018.04.007

Hwang, G.-J., & Wu, P.-H. (2014). Applications, impacts and trends of mobile technology-enhanced learning: a review of 2008–2012 publications in selected SSCI journals. *International Journal of Mobile Learning and Organisation*, *8*(2), 83–95. https://doi.org/10.1504/ijmlo.2014.062346

Khan, B. H. (2005). *E-learning quick checklist*. IGI Global.

Krull, G., & Duart, J. M. (2017). Research trends in mobile learning in higher education: A systematic review of articles (2011 - 2015). *International Review of Research in Open and Distance Learning*, *18*(7), 1–23. https://doi.org/10.19173/irrodl.v18i7.2893

McDonald, E. W., Boulton, J. L., & Davis, J. L. (2018). E-learning and nursing assessment skills and knowledge – An integrative review. *Nurse Education Today*, *66*, 166–174. https://doi.org/10.1016/j.nedt.2018.03.011

Moya, S., & Camacho, M. (2020). A taxonomy of Mobile Learning based on Systematic Review. *International Journal of Mobile Learning and Organization*, *14*(4), 425–455. https://doi.org/10.1504/IJMLO.2020.10030686

Moya, S., & Camacho, M. (2019). What factors matter most for mobile learning adoption? *Proceedings of the 15th International Conference on Mobile Learning 2019, ML 2019*, 27–34. https://doi.org/10.33965/ml2019_201903l004

Peng, H., Su, Y., Chou, C., & Tsai, C.-C. (2009). Ubiquitous knowledge construction: Mobile learning re-defined and a conceptual framework. *Innovations in Education and Teaching International*, *46*(2), 171–183. https://doi.org/10.1080/14703290902843828

Pimmer, C. (2016). Mobile Learning as Boundary Crossing: An Alternative Route to Technology-Enhanced Learning? In *Interactive Learning Environments* (Vol. 24, Issue 5, pp. 979–990).

Teoh, K. (2011). An examination of critical success factors in the implementation of ePortfolios in universities. *Journal of Academic Language & Learning*, *5*(2), A60–A72.

Volery, T., & Lord, D. (2000). Critical success factors in online education. *International Journal of Educational Management*, *14*(5), 216–223. https://doi.org/10.1108/09513540010344731

Zheng, L., Li, X., Tian, L., & Cui, P. (2018). The effectiveness of integrating mobile devices with inquiry-based learning on students' learning achievements: a meta-analysis. *International Journal of Mobile Learning and Organisation*, *12*(1), 77. https://doi.org/10.1504/IJMLO.2018.10009960

APPENDIX A

Table A.1. Expert judgement protocol

Issue	Detail
Research Topic	Adoption and sustained use of mobile learning
Research Question	What categories of success factors are given more importance in Catalonia?
Research objective	To collect evidence regarding the importance of the most common barriers and enablers of mobile learning in Catalonia. To explain and validate findings from previous research
Participants	7 experts in the context of Spanish secondary schools, participated in the expert judgement. Three participants were three school leaders: two educational inspectors and two University experts. Participants included two males and five females
Day and location	20th of February 2018, Universitat Rovira I Virgili, Tarragona, Spain
Facilitator	Researcher

Time required	90 minutes
Transcript	The whole meeting was recorded in video. Transcript was developed from digital recording and notes taken by the researcher
Documents	Participants were formally invited. Research Participant's a dossier working document was handed during the expert's judgment meeting, a thank you note was e mailed to all participants
Analysis	Coding, conceptual mapping and cross tabulation were used for the analysis.
Data collection	Different sources of evidence were gathered such as documents: video, photographs, and observation notes. Informants completed and handed their dossiers

THE CRUX OF MOBILE LEARNING: KEY ASPECTS IN TEACHING WITH MOBILE DEVICES

Judith Balanyà Rebollo and Janaina Minelli de Oliveira
Universitat Rovira i Virgili, Tarragona, Spain

ABSTRACT

This work aims to analyze and validate the didactic elements to implement mobile learning in education and to provide teachers with specific actions to consider in the process of designing, implementing and evaluating mobile devices in their classroom. The research was designed according to Design-Based Research in which has allowed us to sequence the process from phases: this article presents the first phase of the validation process of the didactic elements of mobile learning selected from the literature review, systematic review and based on expert judgement evaluation. The findings derive a seven-category cluster: academic knowledge of the content; methodological strategies; activities; evaluation; mobile resources; technological learning spaces and teachers. The main results could be useful so they can later be applied by the teachers on didactic mobile learning design in their classrooms.

KEYWORDS

Mobile Learning, Educational Innovation, Technology Integration, Educational Strategies

1. INTRODUCTION

1.1 Theoretical Framework

It is currently an undeniable fact that a large part of the population has mobile devices that are used daily. One of the challenges that governments, educational institutions and educators, in general, must face today is related to the use of such devices as tools at the service of learning. Mobile devices can offer the possibility of actively searching, selecting, and producing information, through multiple languages and opening up possibilities for collaboration and socialization relevant to a real transformation of education.

The European Union has stated the importance of promoting 21st -century skills to be digital citizens competent. Citizens must be able to develop autonomously in the new digital scenarios opened by the digital world (Domingo-Coscollola *et al.*, 2020; Jahoor, Botha and Herselman, 2020; Gaebel *et al.*, 2021) Education must contribute to social inclusion and equip students with tools and capacities to face the challenges of the "global economy". The success in consolidating these competencies does not pass only through the students but also involves the teachers, who are also learners of this competency learning. Today's digital skills are closely related to the use of mobile devices (UNESCO, 2018). The OECD (OECD, 2019) highlights and propose various actions to accelerate the incorporation of information and knowledge technologies, from now on, ICT in classrooms that lead to an optimal result: redesign the functioning of the schools and their project, taking into account the new learning models, the students as co-creators or creators and not mere recipients.

Mobile learning is associated with the use of mobile technology in education and is located at the intersection of mobile computing and e-learning to produce an educational experience anywhere and at any time Jahoor and Herselman (2020) state that to establish a definition of mobile learning, three key concepts cannot be ignored: mobile technologies; ubiquity linked to mobility and educational uses in variable contexts.

The introduction of ICT in the school has a profoundly transformative potential of the methodology, because of the new creative and interactive possibilities of the new technologies. Thus, ICT can become a facilitator of learning and a motivator for the student to become an active learner comments that with different media not only does one learn differently but also different learning occurs, which decisively influences how knowledge is constructed and represents a reconceptualization and a fundamental reorganization in teaching dynamics: at the level of development, discipline and resources (Moore, 2019)

In any case, is evident mobile devices are being strategic tools that have the potential to facilitate the creation of teaching materials and improve educational quality. Also, the role of teachers has changed compared to a traditional model of lectures. From this perspective, the dynamism of learning is one of the most important premises and, at the same time, a requirement to carry out this type of educational methodology. To all this, educational didactics plays an important role in mobile learning since it involves scientifically posing the ideal guidelines for developing learning based on specifics in the methodological, content, teacher and student aspects, construction and theoretical justification. All these important characteristics should be considered before carrying out this type of activity since the importance of educational reflection falls within the design itself (Camacho and Esteve, 2016; Camacho *et al.*, 2017; Castañeda and Selwyn, 2018; Bautista *et al.*, 2019; Ifinedo and Rikala, 2019; Oliveira and Esteve-González, 2020; Jahoor, Botha and Herselman, 2020)

1.2 Purpose of the Study

The present research aims to analyze the conditions in which the use of technology can support learning among students. Specifically, it seeks to i) identify key elements that support the design of educational activities with the use of mobile devices and ii) validate the relevance of elements identified to help teachers reflects on how knowledgeable they are of the crux of mobile learning.

The research question to be answered in this paper is: What are the central aspects and pedagogically sound characteristics that can support the didactics of educational mobile learning? Thus, the two specific research questions driving this study are.

1) What is the appropriate theoretical framework for the design activities of mobile learning?

2) How crux factors affecting mobile learning can be grouped into a communal taxonomy?

2. METHOD

This research follows the approaches of "Design-based research" which is developed in a series of iterative phases (Herrington et al., 2010; Pool and Laubscher, 2016; Biase, 2020). These phases allow the observation of the practice of teachers and students in a cyclical way to determine problems and principles of solutions applicable in reality from the implementation and evaluation of the educational proposal.

This article presents the initial phase of the broader research process consisting of three phases, namely, a) the identification of key elements of pedagogical interventions that rely on the use of mobile devices; b) the creation of a formative self-assessment tool for the analysis of pedagogical designs based on the elements identified in the first phase; c) the analysis of the system of pedagogical, social and cultural transformations that take place when pedagogical designs are implemented using the tool developed in the second phase.

As for the data collection techniques used different methods and mixed collection data tools in the phase that is the object of this study, it is used, initially a literature review and a systematic review (Bedenlier et al.,2020; Newman et al., 2020; Zawacki-Richter et al., 2020). Has been used to review the Rayyan software that is a free web-based systematic review platform (Ouzzani et al. 2016) which has been specifically designed to carry out systematic reviews, its design accelerated the synthesis process and trend identification. The literature review leads to the identification of the previously mentioned seven-category cluster: the elements of pedagogical interventions that rely on the use of mobile devices. These elements will allow the design of a self-assessment tool to help teachers reflect on how knowledgeable they are of the crux of mobile learning. On the other hand, once the categories were determined, an evaluation of the expert judgment has been used a digital questionnaire to triangulate and validate research and prove evidence.

2.1 Instruments

With objective to identify the main factors first has been systematic review search string on differents database like Web of Science, ERIC, Scopus. A systematic review search string was carried out from different topics and clusters.

1. Academic knowledge "the content": "TPACK" OR "TPK "OR "TCK" OR "PCK" OR "computer-based learning" OR "technology-enchanced learning" OR "Technology-mediated learning".

2. Methodological strategies: "educational technology" OR "Learning technology" OR "digital technology" OR "learning managment system" OR "mobile learning" OR "m-learning"

3. Activities: "eActivities" OR "collaborative learning" OR "game-based learning" OR "flipped classroom" OR "mobile activities"

4. Evaluation: "eAssessment" OR "assessment" OR "mobile learning assessment" OR "mobile learning evaluation"

5. Mobiles resources: "open resources" OR "app" OR "accessibility" OR "tablet" OR "mobile devices"

6. Technological learning spaces: "clever classrooms" OR "educational environment" OR "school environment" OR "smart classrooms"OR "accessibility" OR "accessible technology".

7. Teachers: "digital competence" OR "teacher's digital competence" OR "methodological digital competence" OR "future teachers' training"

The research process initially yielded 289 publications must have been published between 1961 and 2020. A total of 50 studies were excluded based on inclusions decisions. The vast majority of the studies come from scientific journals, some 168 studies, some 39 RPRT, 27 books, 14 chapters, and others.

For the validation of the elements, a questionnaire was designed that was administered digitally. The objective of the questionnaire is to validate the elements identified in the literature review by teachers and researchers in educational technology.

The questionnaire presents different statements regarding the degree of agreement or disagreement following the Likert (Fabila et al., 2013) assessment scale; 1) Totally disagree; 2) In disagreement; 3) Undecided; 4) In agreement and 5) Totally in agreement. Each section also includes a non-mandatory open question at the end, in which comments are requested on aspects to be taken into account about each element.

The participating subjects were 16 in total; 8 education teachers (5 men, 3 women, with considerable experience in the use of mobile devices in the classroom; and 8 university researchers, 4 women, 4 men, with extensive participation in projects at the national and international level in the field of educational technology. These two groups were selected because they have in common the concern for the integration of technology in education, either because of the use that primary education teachers make of it in the classroom or because of the lines of research developed by university researchers.

3. FIGURES AND OUTCOMES

Table 1 shows the median of the scores for each item in relation to the usability and applicability of the instrument. Following the degrees of assessment of the Likert scale: (1) totally disagree, (2) in disagreement; (3) undecided; (4) in agreement; (5) totally agree.

Table 1. Scores of participants on the assessment tool of the elements of the Mobile Learning

General evaluation of the questionnaire		
Issues assessment instrument	**Score (median)**	
	Reserchers	**Teachers**
The number of elements and characteristics that make up the self-assessment tool are adequate.	4	4,2
The 7 elements that make up the self-assessment tool represent the concepts of the Mobile Learning didactic.	4	4,4
The self-assessment tool shows conceptual concretion in its elements and characteristics.	3,5	4,4
The structure of the self-assessment tool promotes teacher reflection to design, implement and evaluate educational activities with mobile devices.	4	4,6
The characteristics that make up the self-assessment tool addresses the design, development, and implementation.	4	4,4
The elements of the self-assessment tool address the teaching and learning processes of the students.	4	4,4
Total median	3,9	4,4

Table 2 shows the mode of the scores of the elements that have been repeatedly valued the most, with (4) being in agreement and (5) totally in agreement. On the other hand, the adjoining column shows the median of the total obtained from the elements by the participants, from which the scores are higher than 4, with 5 being the maximum score. Therefore, the elements have received positive ratings.

Table 2. Percentage of the total score of the categories (1) totally disagree; (2) In disagreement; (3) undecided; (4) in agreement; (5) totally agree

Elements	*1*	*2*	*3*	*4*	*5*
1.Academic knowledge: the content	0%	0%	8,55%	41,03%	50,43%
2.Methodological strategies	0%	0%	9,23%	44,62%	46,15%
3.Activities	1,54%	6,15%	10,77%	40,00%	41,54%
4. Evaluation	0%	1,28%	7,69%	43,59%	47,44%
5. Mobiles resources	0%	0,77%	9,23%	43,08%	46,92%
6. Technological learning spaces	0%	0%	10,58%	36,54%	52,88%
7. Teachers	0%	0%	13,46%	46,15%	40,38%

Finally, and once all the information has been triangulated, we can establish the seven-category that didactics encompass in the mobile learning application.

The first category is related to **academic knowledge of the content:** What are they going to learn and what educational resources about the content exist to give it scientific value? The second category is **methodological strategies:** What are the educational methodological strategies that most favor work and meaningful learning of the selected content from the use of mobile devices? A third category refers to **activities:** What types of activities are the most appropriate to work the content in a meaningful way from the use of mobile devices? The fourth category integrates **evaluation:** What type of evaluation best fits and respects the student's learning process based on the acquisition of content from the use of mobile devices? Regarding the pedagogical evaluation, answers are sought to the questions: 1. When? 2. What?, 3. For what?, 4. How?, 5. With what? and 6. Who? The fifth category refers to **Mobile resources:** What type of technology and resources are optimal in terms of pedagogical usability to develop and enhance content acquisition? The sixth category integrates **technological learning spaces:** What are these spaces and what characteristics must be considered so that they develop the educational maximum both for students and in the teaching practice in the use of mobile devices? The seventh category includes **teachers:** What is the level of digital competence and knowledge of the content, as well as what should be the role of the teacher to enhance the learning of students from the use of mobile devices?

4. CONCLUSION

The contribution of this document lies in the identification of the crux elements that teachers must take into account in the design of their activities with mobile devices. This research should help to consider what conditions are necessary for the use of technology to support the teaching and learning processes.

The elements will influence design processes, and educational approach to the use of mobile devices and must also lead to a pedagogical reflection of educational action by the teacher. The next phase of this research is planned to be carried out in educational organizations within the framework of the educational mobile plan project of the Department of Education of the Government of Catalonia (Spain).

Therefore, the results presented, and which support the proposal of the pedagogical elements necessary to take into account in the design, implementation and evaluation process, may be implemented in the second phase of the research: b) the implementation of the identified elements to the pedagogical proposals of the educational organizations. For this implementation will participate teachers who will develop educational activities in the framework of the project of use of mobile devices in the classroom promoted by the government of Catalonia (Spain).

REFERENCES

Bedenlier, S. et al. (2020). Learning by Doing? Reflections on Conducting a Systematic Review in the Field of Educational Technology. *Systematic Reviews in Educational Research. Springer Fachmedien Wiesbaden*, pp. 111–127. doi: 10.1007/978-3-658-27602-7_7.

Bautista, G. et al. (2019). Diseño y validación de un instrumento para medir las dimensiones ambiental, pedagógica y digital del aula. Revista Mexicana de Investigación Educativa RMIE, 24.

Camacho, M. et al. (2017). Tablets en educación: hacia un aprendizaje basado en competencias. Madrid: Samsung Electronics Iberia.

Castañeda, L. and Selwyn, N. (2018). More than tools? Making sense of the ongoing digitizations of higher education. International Journal of Educational Technology in Higher Education. Springer Netherlands. doi: 10.1186/s41239-018-0109-y.

Gaebel, M. et al. (2021) Digitally enhanced learning and teaching in european higher education institutions. Available at: www.eua.eu.

Ifinedo, E. and Rikala, J. (2019). TPACK and Educational Interactions–Pillars of Successful Technology Integration. New Orleans, Louisiana, United States.

Jahoor, F., Botha, A. and Herselman, M. (2020) Conceptualizing mobile digital literacy skills for educators.

Moore, R. (2019). Evaluation of Mobile Teaching and Learning Projects, an Introduction. Handbook of Mobile Teaching and Learning. Springer Berlin Heidelberg, pp. 1–5. doi: 10.1007/978-3-642-41981-2_23-3.

Newman, M. and Gough, D. (2020). Systematic Reviews in Educational Research: Methodology, Perspectives and Application. Systematic Reviews in Educational Research. Springer Fachmedien Wiesbaden, pp. 3–22. doi: 10.1007/978-3-658-27602-7_1.

OECD (2019). Digital Innovation: Seizing Policy Opportunities, Digital Innovation. Paris: OECD Publishing. doi: 10.1787/a298dc87-en.

de Oliveira, J. M. and Esteve-González, V. (2020). Navigating choppy discourses: A conceptual framework for understanding synchronous text-based computer-mediated communication. Text and Talk, 40(2), pp. 171–193. doi: 10.1515/text-2020-2056.

Ouzzani, M. et al. (2016). Rayyan-a web and mobile app for systematic reviews. Systematic Reviews, 5(1). doi: 10.1186/s13643-016-0384-4.

Rikala, J., Kankaanranta, M., & Vesisenaho, M., 2015. *Teachers' attitudes, competencies, and readiness to adopt mobile learning approaches.* Frontiers in Education Conference, FIE. San Jose: Institute of Electrical and Electronics Engineers Inc.

UNESCO, 2018. Skills for a connected world. Report of the UNESCO Mobile Learning Week 2018. Paris, France.

Zawacki-Richter, O. et al. (2020). Systematic Reviews in Educational Research. doi: https://doi.org/10.1007/978-3-658-27602-7.

M-LEARNING IMPACT ON SELF-DIRECTED LEARNING IN ZIMBABWE HIGHER EDUCATION

Lydia Maketo, Tomayess Issa, Theodora Issa and S. Zaung Nau
Curtin University
Bentley Campus, Perth, Australia

ABSTRACT

Higher education is being influenced by mobile technology use for education purposes. This paper draws opinions from Zimbabwean lecturers on how self-directed learning (SDL) affects m-learning. The study takes a qualitative approach, in which 30 lecturers were interviewed. Semi-structured email interviews were conducted as lecturers were not available for face-to-face interviews. Thematic analysis was applied to the data collected and NVivo (Version 12 Pro software) was used for coding the data This paper explains what SDL is, the link with m-learning and what affects SDL. The paper also discusses how students can be prepared for SDL, which subsequently prepares students for m-learning. Consequently, this will allay concerns by lecturers that students are not ready for m-learning because students are not self-directed. This paper sheds light on how students who are not self-directed learners can be assisted to become more self-directed and better prepared for m-learning. Limitations of this paper are that this study was limited to only 30 lecturers.

KEYWORDS

M-Learning, Self-Directed Learning, University, Lecturers

1. INTRODUCTION

The use of mobile technologies has affected various service sectors. Higher education is being influenced by the use of mobile technologies for education purposes. Mobile devices have become more sophisticated with more capabilities making them educational tools. Although there have been improvements in educational indicators in Zimbabwe, such as increased enrolment across the different levels of education, the quality of education still faces noteworthy challenges. Higher education institutions in Zimbabwe are currently in a series of crises due to a decline in economic growth resulting in under-funding coupled with high student enrolment (Kariwo, 2007). Technology adoption in Zimbabwe is under-researched with organisations in education apprehensive about technology adoption (Chiome, 2013).

Mobile learning(m-learning) can be defined as any learning that happens when a student is not at a fixed predetermined location, or learning that occurs when a student takes advantage of learning opportunities offered by mobile technologies (Crompton, 2013). Initially, m-learning definitions were device-driven (Hwang & Tsai, 2011). However, this has shifted to personal and social-driven definitions which take into consideration the technological affordances of the mobile technologies (Baran, 2014).

This paper is part of a PhD research to develop a model for m-learning for higher education in Zimbabwe. In developing a model for Zimbabwe higher education, the study sought opinions from different stakeholders. This paper addresses the following research question:

RQ: What are the stakeholders' perceptions of the mobile learning model in Zimbabwe higher education?

This paper draws on opinions from lecturers when asked to comment on the following statement: Using mobile devices for teaching and learning will allow students to be capable of self-study or self-learning without much intervention from lecturers.

2. BACKGROUND ON SDL AND M-LEARNING

2.1 Self-Directed Learning & M-Learning

SDL is the ability to take an initiative to diagnose one's learning needs with or without the help of others, identifying the resources required to help in the individual's learning and selecting the appropriate learning strategies (Knowles, 1975). Self-directed learners are more willing to achieve learning goals (Geng et al., 2019). For successful SDL it is important to ensure that learners have access to many information resources to meet their learning needs (Gokcearslan, 2017). SDL with technology refers to the use of information communication technologies (ICT) for learning experiences that enable learners to take control of planning, implementing and evaluation their own learning (Lee et al., 2014). M-learning facilitates SDL (Taylor et al., 2006).

M-learning is largely self-directed as learners have to "find their own way to make a learning situation personalised and sensitised to them" (Park et al., 2010, p. 57). Learning that is aided with mobile technologies implies the learner can take charge of their learning. Fahnoe and Mishra (2013) argue that technology-rich learning environments promote opportunities for SDL as learners have to manage and appropriately use information. Yet, Bartholomew et al. (2017) in their study showed that SDL correlated more closely with student and classroom characteristics than it did with technology tools. Liu et al. (2010) assert that adoption of mobile technologies does not guarantee adoption of m-learning, yet promoting a learner's self-management capabilities will ensure effective use of m-learning. Equipping students to become self-directed learners may help learners to autonomously utilise mobile technologies to fulfil their learning goals. It may be concluded that access to technology may not translate to SDL however; mobile technologies increase access to learning resources that can also encourage self-directed learning.

2.2 What Affects SDL?

It has been noted that individual differences of learners affect SDL (Kreber, 1998) since, individual characteristics will in turn determine how learners embrace m-learning platforms on a formal or informal level (Karimi, 2016). According to Spear and Mocker (1984) readiness for SDL can be identified by eight important factors: (1) Openness to the learning opportunities, (2) The concept of self as an effective learner, (3) learning initiative and independence, (4) Accepting informed responsibility, (5) learning love, (6) creativity, (7) future orientation and (8) ability to use basic working and problem solving skills. Yilmaz et al. (2017) argue that to increase SDL with technology there is a need to first develop self-management and intentional learning competences for the students. Lalitha and Sreeja (2020) assert that learners face challenges in making choices on what to choose from given the variety of online resources when adopting SDL. SDL can be achieved by equipping students with skills in planning, monitoring and evaluating their learning processes (Yilmaz et al., 2017). While lecturers may encourage SDL and create environments conducive for SDL, success in SDL seems to depend on how learners are ready for SDL.

3. RESEARCH METHODS

A qualitative approach was adopted in this study to gather perceptions of SDL and m-learning from 30 lecturers. Semi-structured email interviews were conducted, as most lecturers could not attend to other forms of interviews due to other time-competing activities. Analysis started during data collection, with notes made from that stage. Thematic analysis was applied to the data, following the six-step process suggested by (Braun & Clarke, 2006). While the steps are presented as a linear step-by-step procedure, the actual analysis is not linear but iterative. The steps for the thematic analysis are explained in table 1.

Table 1. Thematic analysis steps and description of steps

Step	What is involved in the step
1. Become familiar with the data	Transcribing data, reading and re-reading data, noting down initial ideas.
2. Generate initial codes	This involves generating concise labels for important features of the data of relevance to the research question(s) guiding the analysis.
3. Search for themes	A theme is a coherent and meaningful pattern in the data relevant to the research question(s). Searching for themes involves looking into the codes to identify similarities and differences and coming up with new codes in some cases. Themes are constructed based on different codes. All the coded data relevant to each theme are collated.
4. Review themes	Checking if themes work in relation to the coded extracts and the entire data set.
5. Define themes	Defining and naming themes involved a detailed analysis of each theme. This involved: ➤ Exploring what story each theme told. ➤ Examining how the theme fits into the overall story about the data ➤ Identifying the "essence" of each theme and coming up with a concise and informative name of the theme.
6. Producing report	Final opportunity of analysis. Selection of compelling extract examples and relating back to research question(s) and literature.

3.1 Research Outcomes

A diagram extracted from NVivo shows some of the nodes used in coding the data gathered from lecturers are shown in Figure 1.

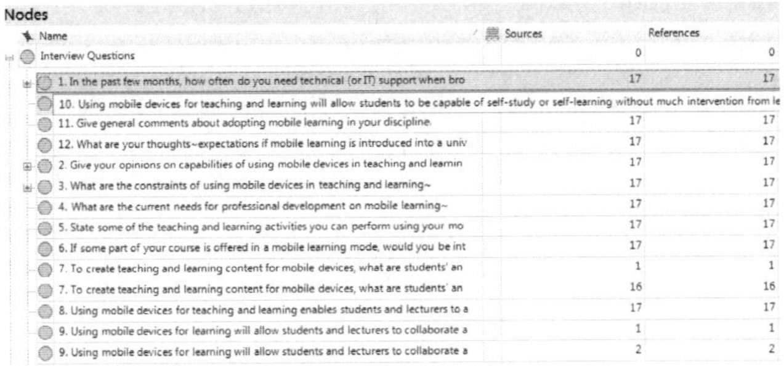

Figure 1. A diagram on coding extracted from NVivo 12

Opinions differed as to whether m-learning improved self-learning. While some lecturers argue that m-learning encouraged SDL, others felt SDL would only benefit certain students and others felt that m-learning would not necessarily translate to SDL. Some lecturers argued that self-learning would benefit certain students who did not require constant monitoring or supervision. One lecturer highlighted that there is a need to train learners to avoid distractions or activities that hinder their learning when using mobile technologies so that they can study independently.

Some comments from lecturers regarding m-learning and SDL are given below:

Lecturer_2: *"It [m-learning] works fairly well with self-actualised students, those who depend on supervision it might not work."*

Lecturer_4: *It [SDL] is possible where students are self-starters. Where they are used to being provided with everything the students may initially struggle."*

Lecturer_20: *"On-self-learning and self-study am not sure students will have that discipline to do so completely without some oversight from the lecturer."*

Lecturer_23: "*Develops an independent learner who is equipped for problem solving."*

Some lecturers' concur with previous research that mobile technologies disrupt conventional approaches to knowledge transfer from teacher to student, thereby leading to self-learning (Wang et al., 2009). Some of the findings in this study align with those of Wang et al. (2009) who claim that self-learning plays a critical role in m-learning acceptance. Amongst the lecturers in Zimbabwe universities there are different opinions on how m-learning is impacted or impacts SDL. The findings from this study indicate that some lecturers are of the impression that most students are not self-directed learners.

There are suggestions from this study that learning in some Zimbabwe tertiary institutions is teacher-centred as indicated by comments from the lectures below:

Lecturer_5: *"This is more applicable in andragogy where the lecturer is there to provide guidance and not to drill as it were in pedagogy."*

Lecturer_8: *"M-learning is a good concept but it requires a firm reading culture which lacks in our students who are only driven by the need to earn marks rather than learning."*

It is encouraging that some lecturers believe there is potential in increasing SDL through mobile technologies. These lecturers appreciate that m-learning will place them in a facilitator role in which the learning is more student-centred. While there is a huge concern that some students are not self-directed learners' comments from some of the lecturers below indicate that lecturers would like the learners to be more involved in SDL. M-learning may be the vehicle to promote SDL with lecturers still playing a significant role in facilitating the learning.

Lecturer_6:" *That is true, the lecturer is placed in the background thereby fostering greater interaction between students and learning material and amongst students themselves. The lecturer plays the role of moderator, supervisor and guide."*

Lecturer_7: *"Students are more attached to their mobile devices, having learning material with them on those devices may help them take an initiative to learn."*

Lecturer_11: *"We cannot invalidate the role of the teacher in the learning process. Whilst students can enhance how they learn, the teacher still needs to be able to supervise all self-studies that occur."*

Lecturer_23: *"It gives students independence to study on their own and in their own time."*

Lecturer_24: "With calls for student-centred learning, this empowers the learner and gives the learner control over his/her learning."

Although lecturers have differing opinions on whether m-learning would improve SDL there are suggestions from lecturers that m-learning could help develop self-directed learners. It may be concluded that learners and lecturers need to cooperate in using m-learning to develop SDL.

3.2 Findings

Lecturers in Zimbabwe have different opinions on how m-learning impacts self-directed learning (SDL). Some lecturers are of the opinion that their students are not capable of self-directed learning yet, with other lecturers expressing that m-learning could lead to SDL. With students not ready for SDL, some lecturers are concerned that such students would not benefit from m-learning. Herrador-Alcaide et al. (2020) conclude that SDL is positively related to use of technology for learning however, the findings from this research do not confirm this.

3.3 Future Research

Future research could involve a study with the students in Zimbabwe higher education, to gather their perspectives on M-learning and SDL to get a more holistic understanding.

3.4 Limitations

The study was limited to only 30 lecturers, this study could be extended to more lecturers, and a survey could be conducted for generalisations of findings.

4. CONCLUSION

Opinions on how mobile technologies impact SDL are different among lecturers in Zimbabwe. The differing opinions suggest that it may be important to ready students for SDL in preparation for m-learning. There are suggestions that students' take ownership of their learning by planning, monitoring and evaluating their learning process. Ownership of learning by students could include a variety of activities. Students should be able to set their own learning objectives as part of planning. In the monitoring process students should check if they can move on the right path and decide on the point they are in and the process they are following. To evaluate the learning process, students should evaluate their performance by considering whether they have achieved or not achieved their goals. M-learning is likely to benefit students who can independently undertake learning activities. It is encouraging that even if students are not yet ready for SDL all students can be trained to become more autonomous in terms of their learning. M-learning can be a vehicle to promote SDL in contexts similar to Zimbabwe, in which learning has been more teacher-centred.

ACKNOWLEDGEMENT

Lydia Maketo extends her gratitude to her academic supervisors Tomayess Issa, S Zaung Nau and Theodora Issa, for their advice and guidance during preparation of her PhD thesis that inspired this paper and subsequent co-authoring of this paper.

REFERENCES

Baran, E. (2014). A review of research on mobile learning in teacher education. *Journal of Educational Technology & Society, 17*(4), 17.

Bartholomew, S. R., Reeve, E. M., Veon, R., Goodridge, W., Lee, V. R., & Nadelson, L. (2017). Relationships between access to mobile devices, student self-directed learning, and achievement. *Journal of Technology Education, 29*(1), 2.

Braun, V., & Clarke, V. (2006). Using thematic analysis in psychology. *Qualitative research in psychology, 3*(2), 77-101.

Chiome, C. (2013). e-infrastructure acceptance in e-health, e-learning and e-agriculture in zimbabwe: the quest for the user acceptance variable.

Crompton, H. (2013). A historical overview of m-learning. In *Handbook of mobile learning* (pp. 41-52). Routledge.

Fahnoe, C., & Mishra, P. (2013). Do 21st century learning environments support self-directed learning? Middle school students' response to an intentionally designed learning environment.Society for information technology & teacher education international conference,

Geng, S., Law, K. M., & Niu, B. (2019). Investigating self-directed learning and technology readiness in blending learning environment. *International Journal of Educational Technology in Higher Education, 16*(1), 17.

Gokcearslan, S. (2017). Perspectives of Students on Acceptance of Tablets and Self-Directed Learning with Technology. *Contemporary educational technology, 8*(1), 40-55.

Herrador-Alcaide, T. C., Hernández-Solís, M., & Hontoria, J. F. (2020). Online Learning Tools in the Era of m-Learning: Utility and Attitudes in Accounting College Students. *Sustainability, 12*(12), 5171.

Hwang, G. J., & Tsai, C. C. (2011). Research trends in mobile and ubiquitous learning: A review of publications in selected journals from 2001 to 2010. *British Journal of Educational Technology, 42*(4), E65-E70.

Karimi, S. (2016). Do learners' characteristics matter? An exploration of mobile-learning adoption in self-directed learning [Article]. *Computers in Human Behavior, 63*, 769-776. https://doi.org/10.1016/j.chb.2016.06.014

Kariwo, T. M. (2007). Widening Access in Higher Education in Zimbabwe. *Higher Education Policy, 20*(1), 45-59. https://doi.org/10.1057/palgrave.hep.8300142

Knowles, M. S. (1975). Self-directed learning: A guide for learners and teachers.

Kreber, C. (1998). The relationships between self-directed learning, critical thinking, and psychological type, and some implications for teaching in higher education. *Studies in Higher Education, 23*(1), 71-86.

Lalitha, T., & Sreeja, P. (2020). Personalised Self-Directed Learning Recommendation System. *Procedia Computer Science, 171*, 583-592.

Lee, K., Tsai, P. S., Chai, C. S., & Koh, J. H. L. (2014). Students' perceptions of self-directed learning and collaborative learning with and without technology. *Journal of Computer Assisted Learning, 30*(5), 425-437.

Park, J., Parsons, D., & Ryu, H. (2010). To flow and not to freeze: Applying flow experience to mobile learning. *IEEE transactions on Learning Technologies, 3*(1), 56-67.

Spear, G. E., & Mocker, D. W. (1984). The organizing circumstance: Environmental determinants in self-directed learning. *Adult education quarterly, 35*(1), 1-10.

Taylor, J., Sharples, M., O'Malley, C., Vavoula, G., & Waycott, J. (2006). Towards a task model for mobile learning: A dialectical approach. *International Journal of Learning Technology, 2*(2-3), 138-158.

Wang, Y. S., Wu, M. C., & Wang, H. Y. (2009). Investigating the determinants and age and gender differences in the acceptance of mobile learning. *British Journal of Educational Technology, 40*(1), 92-118.

Yilmaz, R., Yilmaz, F. G. K., & Ezin, C. C. (2017). Self-Directed Learning With Technology and Academic Motivation as Predictors of Tablet PC Acceptance. *Handbook of Research on Mobile Devices and Smart Gadgets in K-12 Education*, 87.